ADVERTISING WORKS 7

ADVERTISING WORKS 7

Papers from the IPA Advertising Effectiveness Awards

Institute of Practitioners in Advertising, 1992

Edited and introduced by

Chris Baker

NTC PUBLICATIONS LIMITED

First published 1993 by **NTC Publications Limited**
Farm Road, Henley-on-Thames, Oxfordshire, RG9 1EJ, United Kingdom
Telephone: 0491 574671

British Library Cataloguing in Publication Data
Advertising Works 7: papers from the IPA Advertising Effectiveness Awards 1992.
  1. Great Britain. Advertising
  I. Baker, Chris   II. Institute of Practitioners in Advertising
  659.111

ISBN 1–870562–08–9

Typeset by NTC Publications Ltd
Printed and bound in Great Britain
by BPCC Wheatons, Exeter

Contents

CONTENTS

IPA
Advertising Effectiveness Awards
1992

This book is the 'volume of record' of the seventh biennial IPA Advertising Effectiveness Awards Scheme. *Advertising Works 7* follows its six predecessors by documenting the winning entries to the latest competition. The 21 case histories from 1992 published here add to the bank of over 120 made available via previous *Advertising Works* volumes.

The aims of the IPA Advertising Effectiveness Awards remain the same as when they were first set up in 1980:

1. To generate a collection of case histories which demonstrate that, properly used, advertising can make a measurable contribution to business success.
2. To encourage advertising agencies (and their clients) to develop ever-improving standards of advertising evaluation (and, in the process, a better understanding of the ways in which advertising works).

The format and judging criteria remain fundamentally the same, but there has been significant evolution as well, most notably via the introduction of the Longer and Broader 'brand effects' category in 1990, and a European category in 1992.

The driving force behind the Awards also remains unchanged: the need for an industry with a turnover of nearly £6 billion pa to provide *convincing proof* of the commercial value of its product (to its customers). Collectively the assembled case histories do indeed make a strong general case that advertising can make large, measurable and cost-effective contributions to business success. Thus the chosen title of this series of books, *Advertising Works*.

However, they could just as truthfully be entitled '*How* to produce advertising that works'. Each case history provides a wealth of very practical 'how to' insights and information about how to get the most out of your advertising expenditure:

— how to identify the optimum role for advertising (it can't do everything);
— how to plan a winning strategy (coherent, challenging and competitive);
— how to evaluate the effects of your advertising in the marketplace (it's not easy);
— how to learn from the thinking behind successful advertising in similar markets or analogous situations;
— how some of the best, most successful advertisers and agencies do it.

In short, overall 'best practice' on how to approach an advertising task in almost every respect.

The case histories which follow are full and detailed. With minor editing changes (eg some technical appendices have been omitted), what is published is the same as that originally submitted to a group of very sceptical judges. All provide a full background to the business context and strategic thinking behind the advertising concerned, a description of the advertising itself, as well a necessarily detailed analysis isolating the specific contribution made by advertising to overall business success. As a result, this is not the kind of book to be read 'cover to cover'. Rather it is a reference book to be dipped into, to be informed and stimulated by those case histories which are of relevance and interest at a given point of time. To help in this respect, there is a short guide to the 21 case histories at the end of this introductory section.

Before this there is a fuller background on 'the competition', plus some broader observations about the state of the advertising art that can be drawn from the 'class of '92'.

THE COMPETITION

Prior to 1980 there was virtually no case history material demonstrating advertising effectiveness, anywhere in the world, which was both *published* and sufficiently *rigorous* in its analysis and presentation of data to be convincing. This was a major barrier to both justifying the industry's services to its customers, and the promotion of best practice and an increasingly accountable culture within advertising.

These Awards were designed to help fill this vacuum and have done so very successfully since 1980, producing a fresh tranche of effectiveness cases every two years. The demands for proof are considerably more rigorous than those made by effectiveness awards in the USA and in continental Europe. Elsewhere, the Advertising Federation of Australia (from 1990) and Canadian Congress of Advertising (this year) have based their awards on the UK IPA format.

Entries for the Awards are required to be in the form of written papers, up to 4,000 words in length (6,000 for the new European category), not counting appendices and charts. Each entry form must be countersigned by the agency's chief executive and by a competent representative of the client, by which act copyright is passed to the IPA: all papers, successful or not, are kept on file at the IPA in Belgrave Square, and may be inspected on request by a member of any IPA agency.

The criteria on which entries are judged are perhaps best explained by quoting from the actual instructions given to the judges. These are substantially the same as those formalised by Paul Feldwick, my predecessor as Convenor of Judges, and Editor of *Advertising Works 5* and *6*.

Notes for Judges

1.   The main criterion for judging is simple: *how convincing is the case put for the specific contribution of advertising to business success?* The onus is on the author to anticipate questions and counter-arguments. Many papers fail because they do not consider all the relevant facts, or present data in an

obfuscatory way (on purpose or through carelessness). If you – as a sceptical but not necessarily 'expert' reader – feel reasonably convinced that it was indeed the advertising that produced the results claimed for it, then the paper is a contender.

2. However, when you read the papers you will find it is not quite so simple. In some cases it is almost absurdly easy to demonstrate the advertising effect (eg for a 'partwork' magazine or direct response-based cases). In other cases, the task of isolating the effect is fiendishly difficult. Car campaigns are a good example. In some instances it is, perhaps, literally impossible. Clearly it would be absurd and contrary to the spirit of the awards only to reward simple and obvious entries. We therefore find in practice we have to judge the arguments relative to the difficulties they have faced, both in terms of the advertising task and the evaluation of its effects.

3. Effectiveness in these awards is defined as contribution to the business. This does not mean that measures such as awareness or brand image are irrelevant – far from it, they are often vital – but there needs to be some sort of argument which links these to business objectives, ultimately in terms of sales or profitability. We also need to be careful that we do not only reward short-term paybacks – the long-term competitiveness, resilience and leverage of the brand can be at least as important. (This is especially true, of course, in the Longer and Broader category.)

4. Papers will obviously be less likely to convince if they are poorly written or presented. Good clear English, clarity of argument, and good presentation of data all help. You should expect to see a clear exposition of the background to the campaign, the development of the strategy, and a clear statement of what was actually done and when (creative work and media plans), as well as the review of performance.

5. You are not expected to be an expert in statistical modelling. Papers which use such techniques still have a duty to be intelligible to the general reader. If you feel the argument does depend heavily on modelling, arrangements can be made for independent technical advice to be taken. Authors who have vague claims about models without presenting sufficient detail and technical evidence do not help their case.

6. You should not be influenced by whether you personally liked or hated the advertising, or whether it was 'creative' or not; you should judge the argument objectively. An author may as part of the case show that 'creativity' contributed to the effectiveness: that is a different matter.

7. 'Bonus points' should certainly be added for papers which add something new to our knowledge, or make an original point. They must of course conform to the basic criteria as well.

These criteria clearly establish the difference between these awards and other advertising industry awards (which generally focus on the recognition of original thinking and craft skills), ie a single-minded focus on the rigorous proof of effectiveness. This difference is reinforced by the fact that, as in previous years, the majority of the judging panel is drawn from *outside* the advertising agencies.

The Entry – By Category

The 1992 entry of 80 was excellent both in terms of quantity and quality. Encouragingly too, these entries come from 39 different agencies, large and small, an all-time record for the Awards. The six categories in which entries were judged were as follows:

1. Longer and Broader Effects.
2. Established Consumer Goods and Services.
3. New Consumer Goods and Services.
4. Small Budgets (any campaign which has been supported by an annual advertising budget of less than £500,000).
5. European (campaigns running in the UK and at least two other European countries).
6. Special (any campaign not covered in the other categories, eg financial, recruitment, corporate, public information).

As in previous years, there was strong competition and a good level of entry in all categories, excepting the European category:

Category:	1	2	3	4	5	6	Total
1984	n/a	27	11	12	n/a	9	59
1986	n/a	24	11	11	n/a	13	59
1988	n/a	29	15	8	n/a	19	71
1990	16	18	10	27	n/a	16	87
1992	14	17	11	18	1	19	80

Overall the level of entry per category has been very stable, the most notable changes being largely the result of rule changes: the 'Longer and Broader' category introduced in 1990 attracted some entries which would have otherwise gone to 'Established Goods and Services' (as well as generating additional entries); the raising of the 'Small Budget' limit from £250,000 to £500,000 in 1990 also attracted more entries to this category.

The Charles Channon Award

The run-up to the 1992 Awards was marred by the death of Charles Channon, latterly Director of Studies at the IPA. Charles had been a judge in the past four Awards, and was Convenor of Judges – and Editor of *Advertising Works 3* and *4* – in 1984 and 1986. The 'Longer and Broader' category relates to the type of advertising effects he regarded as most valuable. He was there at its birth, and indeed coined the new category's name. His contribution to the Awards was second only to his personal and intellectual contribution to the UK advertising industry generally. To commemorate this, it was decided that the First Prize in the 'Longer and Broader' category would be named The Charles Channon Award.

BROADER OBSERVATIONS AND LESSONS FROM 1992

A number of hurdles stand between an effective piece of advertising and a successful entry to the Awards: adequate data have to be available, a well-argued case needs to be assembled, and the client must give permission for the agency to enter (regrettably not always granted). As such, the 21 case histories in this book are unlikely to be *wholly* representative of 'effective' advertising over the past two or three years. However, they do comprise a widely drawn sample from which we can learn a lot about the ingredients of success and what works in current market conditions.

Advertising in a Recession

The 1992 Awards presented perhaps the most exacting test to date. As previously, entrants faced the often daunting task of isolating advertising's contribution to business success, and providing convincing evidence of the value of the money spent. To compound the problem, the evidence required relates mainly to a period (1990–1992) when the economy, and most markets, were in decline.

In many ways the value of advertising itself was on the line. Never mind the technical challenge of measuring advertising effects, would there be effects worth measuring? Can advertising be a cost-effective commercial tool in a recession?

On the evidence of the 1992 Awards entry, the answer to this question must be a resounding 'yes'. As already noted, the near record entry of 80 case histories was of high overall quality. The 31 entries shortlisted – and the 21 subsequently published here – represent excellence both in terms of the advertising effects achieved and, necessarily, the evaluation of these effects. These were the entries which, in the Judges' collective view made the best case, but other non-shortlisted cases should not be discounted; most also made a good case that the advertiser's money had been well spent.

Despite this evidence – that for many companies advertising *still* works in a period of recession – advertising expenditure in the past three years is well down on the levels which prevailed during the second half of the 1980s. Advertising's share of GDP rose by over 40% between 1979 and 1989 (from 1.26% to 1.79%) – by 1991 it had fallen back to close to 1984 levels in these terms (1.50%). It has been estimated that recession has been four times worse in advertising than in the overall economy.

The fact remains that advertising is something that most companies do more of when overall corporate profits are increasing, but is amongst the first things to go when profits are under pressure. There is a degree of inevitability about this – advertising is treated as a current cost on the balance sheet, and is one of the easiest and quickest elements of corporate expenditure to cut. Less inevitable is the readiness of senior management to cut advertising budgets in the belief that, because its effects are less tangible and harder to evaluate than the effects of other areas of expenditure, advertising is of dubious commercial value.

There is considerable general evidence that cutting advertising expenditure in a recession does in fact carry a serious opportunity cost. Some of this is available in an IPA information pack 'Advertising in a Recession'[1]. To quote from the James Capel report included in this pack 'In the 1974–75 recession, those companies which maintained or increased their advertising had 27% higher sales (versus those who did not) over 2 years, and 30% higher sales over 5 years. In 1981–82, the results were even more pronounced with those companies maintaining or increasing their advertising experiencing 81% higher sales over 2 years and 215% higher sales over 5 years.' This difference between 'maintainers' and 'cutters' may not be totally due to advertising. The maintenance of advertising investment will relate to overall corporate strength, market orientation and a company's commitment to developing its brands and markets; ie companies more likely to prosper anyway. Nevertheless, advertising is clearly one of those areas where companies have not learnt from previous recessions, or where 'corporate memory' has simply failed after a prolonged period of growth.

Difficult times make it harder for the advertising industry to argue for the value of its product to its clients. The 'Mandy Rice-Davies' response – 'They would say that wouldn't they' – is inevitable, closely followed by the injunction to 'prove it'. General evidence of the nature referred to above invites the criticism that it may not be relevant 'to my specific situation' or, that being the result of 'macro' analysis provides little opportunity for the reader to inspect it to make up their own mind about its validity and relevance ('lies, damn lies, and statistics').

The case histories in this book are of great value in this respect. They provide a detailed and transparent analysis of the specific ways in which specific advertisers have benefited from advertising in a period of recession, including full supporting data. In addition to specific evidence, they provide broader insights about what it takes to succeed via advertising. Two main ingredients emerge over and above basic strategic competence: *confidence* and *creativity*. Neither are strangers when it comes to effective advertising in any economic climate, but when the going gets tough both become doubly important.

Confidence

In a recession there are two types of company: those who (at least implicity) use the economy as an excuse and wait for overall consumer confidence to return, and those who take their destiny in their own hands and go out actively to instil consumer confidence in their products or services. If a manufacturer does not show confidence in his own brands, why should consumers or the retail trade? David Robey (then of Tesco) recently made the distinction between 'real' brands and 'pseudo' brands, which due to neglect and a lack of investment are effectively 'manufacturer's label' products rather than desirable brands[2].

In many ways, this year's Award winners are a 'roll of honour' of confident companies. They include established goods and services with the confidence to build their consumer franchise and actively go after business when market trends and general economic factors were against them. The dairy industry's Milkman campaign, Kellogg's All-Bran, *The Economist* and Whipsnade are all examples of this. There are companies with the confidence to launch new brands with creativity and panache – Häagen-Dazs, Gini, the Renault Clio, K Shoes and Cussons Limelite – or to develop an underdeveloped consumer franchise, such as Scottish Amicable and Direct Line. Others demonstrate how long-term commitment to building confidence in their brands (mainly via advertising) has allowed them to prosper even in the face of competitive pressures and sometimes difficult market conditions; Andrex, Oxo, Volkswagen Golf, Stella Artois and Alliance & Leicester are examples of this. In the new European category we find Levi Strauss, a company with the confidence to use a strong creative idea developed in the UK to develop their business across diverse European markets. And finally, in the Save the Children Fund, the winner of the *Marketing* Award for Innovation, an organisation with the confidence to recognise, and concentrate its efforts behind, a powerful fund-raising idea.

Creativity

The relationship between 'creativity' and effectiveness is a time-old debate which these Awards are particularly well-placed to inform. This debate was well-delineated by Paul Feldwick in his introduction to *Advertising Works 6*.

Of course it all depends upon what one means by 'creativity' in an advertising context. To propose a commonsense working definition: 'creativity' is that quantity which helps draw attention and open minds to a selling or brand message, and to add value to that message by capturing the imagination and helping it live on in people's minds. 'Creativity' in these terms becomes more important when the basic selling message is not in itself unique or intrinsically highly motivating, and at a time when differentiation at a product level is harder to achieve in most markets.

One common assumption is that 'creative advertising' is something to indulge in when the going is easy, but does not really 'do the numbers' when the going gets tough. The type of 'effective advertising' that leads from this assumption tends to be characterised as 'hard sell', product fact and USP-driven, often with a strong immediate 'promotional' offer. It comes from the propositional 'advertising as a salesman' school of advertising expounded by such gurus as Rosser Reeves and James Webb Young in the 1950s and 1960s.

Despite recessionary times, there appears to be an absence of this type of advertising amongst the 1992 Effectiveness Award winners. Some of the advertising may be said to be 'propositional' in nature – Kellogg's All-Bran, K Washable Leather Trainers, International Fund for Animal Welfare, Save the Children, Limelite – but none (with the possible exception of Limelite which employs a strong problem/solution approach) could really be characterised as 'hard sell'.

The alternative assumption, that 'effective advertising' is generally speaking 'creative advertising' especially when the going gets tough, is lent considerable support by the 1992 Award winners. Despite being judged solely on the criterion of commercial effectiveness, they represent a very credible selection of the 'Best of British advertising' from a creative point of view.

Most fall within the added value, brand image, more humanistic school of advertising pioneered by, amongst others, David Ogilvy, who aimed to 'give a brand a first class ticket through life'. The 1992 IPA Advertising Effectiveness Awards winners include multiple Creative Award winners in Häagen-Dazs, *The Economist*, Levi Strauss, VW Golf and Oxo. Interestingly they also include several campaigns which score very highly with consumers in terms of likeability. In a recent Adwatch survey in *Marketing* magazine[3] IPA Award winners took three of the top four places in terms of consumers' 'favourite ads': Andrex came first (for the second successive year), PG Tips was second (IPA Grand Prix winner in 1990), and the 'Milkman' campaign (Grand Prix winner in 1992) came fourth. The 1992 winners included other campaigns which receive very high favourability ratings within their sectors, such as Scottish Amicable and Alliance & Leicester.

The pattern we see amongst 1992 Award winners is entirely consistent with work reported on by Biel[4], and later corroborated by the Advertising Research Foundation in New York, which suggests that 'likeability' is the factor which correlates most strongly with commercial effectiveness (which is not to say that *all* effective ads need to be likeable). The role for creativity, and the 'softer' aspects of advertising generally, is further developed in a recent paper by Biel and Lannon[5], who conclude that an effective 'visual metaphor' tends to be much more powerful than the pursuit of 'sales point playback'.

'New News' versus 'Consistent Theme Advertising'

The growing debate in this area is not unrelated to the creativity debate. For 'new news' people tend to read 'effective', rational and product-driven (not always rightly); for 'consistent theme' read 'creative', emotional and brand-driven.

'New news' has recently come more to the fore due to a number of factors. With most consumer markets, mature or in decline, companies have become more fixated on short-term sales uplifts. The availability of continuous consumer tracking data and more recently weekly, even daily, sales data from EPOS scanning and consumer panels further tends to focus attention on short-term advertising effects. These data show consistently and unambiguously that advertising influences both core attitudes and sales *most immediately* when it gives *new information* in some sense. Moreover this is plainly common sense: why should anything change unless you do something different?

On face value an analysis of IPA Effectiveness Awards winners provides strong support for the 'new news' approach. The papers from a recent seminar held by Millward Brown International[6] include an analysis of IPA Award winning papers (TV cases only) and an average week's TV advertising. The advertising was classified in terms of five categories: a new product or variant; a brand that had not previously been advertised or at least not advertised for a very long time; a new strategic approach, ie new information or a clear new angle on the brand; a continuation of existing strategy; and, for completeness, public information ads. The outcome of this showed an apparent strong bias towards 'new news' amongst Effectiveness Award winners.

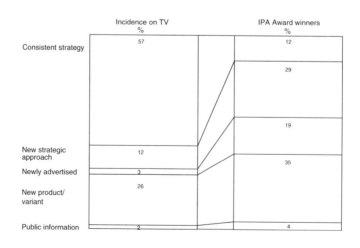

Applying this classification to the nineteen 1992 Effectiveness Award winners reveals a similar pattern:

— only four cases relate their effects *predominantly* to consistent (longer term) strategy (Andrex, Oxo, Stella Artois and Alliance & Leicester);
— six were centred on a new strategic approach/campaign (All-Bran, VW Golf, Levi Strauss, Scottish Amicable, *The Economist*);
— two were newly advertised, at least in recent times (Milkman, Whipsnade);
— five related to new products (Gini, Renault Clio, Limelite, Häagen-Dazs, K Washable Leather Trainers);
— two were for charities (Save the Children, IFAW), both with 'new news'.

Of course, there may be an in-built bias in the IPA Advertising Effectiveness Awards process. The need to produce case histories every two years and the mix of categories inevitably focuses entrants on the new and the recent. More insidious is a bias towards those cases where the advertising effect is easiest to isolate and so prove: when dynamic short-term shifts have occurred coincident with advertising, it is generally easier to discount other potential influences on sales. Indeed the 'Longer and Broader' category was introduced in 1990 to help counteract this bias and encourage a greater focus on harder to prove, longer term advertising effects.

We need to beware favouring the 'easy to measure' at the expense of the truly valuable. Sir John Banham put it well when talking about how the City puts a value on companies: 'We are in danger of valuing most highly those things which we can measure most accurately, which means that we are often precisely wrong rather than approximately right.' The Millward Brown papers[6] also make a strong case for the existence and value of inevitably harder to measure longer term effects of advertising.

So where does this leave the 'new news' versus 'consistent theme' debate? The problems really emerge when people start treating these approaches as alternative world views to apply to all cases, all of the time, of which one is right – *the* way to do it – and the other wrong. The growing number of companies selling 'persuasion shift' dominated advertising pre-testing systems fall into this trap; their techniques are essentially designed to test the power of 'new news' to motivate, but their marketing carries the strong presumption that this is the *only* way to advertise.

The truth is that both approaches work, but tend to apply in different situations and at different times within the marketing cycle. It must also be recognised that 'new news' can come from a new creative approach not only from a new product message (eg VW Golf, Levi Strauss, Scottish Amicable, *The Economist*), and that 'consistent theme advertising' can often incorporate changing 'product news' very effectively (eg Oxo, Alliance & Leicester).

One definition of a brand is 'an entity with which consumers (and all other relevant parties) have a relationship based upon factors over and above its functional performance'[7]. 'Consistent theme advertising' is often the main means by which the strong relationships (or 'added values') which make strong brands are built. There is clearly a place for it, at least where brands are involved (and they usually are). Equally it would be perverse to ignore the fact that 'doing something different' is generally at the root of advertising (and indeed business) success.

A deeper analysis of the 1992 Award winners helps 'square the circle' by suggesting a temporal relationship between the two types of advertising. Tracking each of the case histories back in time shows that virtually all did something 'new and different' at some time in the past; or, to put it another way, did something which disrupted the (then) conventions of their marketplace to create a new generic of their own. The Andrex Puppy, the PG Chimps and the Oxo Family may now seem part of the furniture, but they were very definitely 'new creative news' when they first appeared. Having successfully staked out a strong and unique territory for the brand via a new, unique and totally ownable creative theme, this theme has been consistently developed to further strengthen and protect this brand territory.

Most of the more recently commenced effectiveness cases, essentially based on a new approach, have since focused upon developing this new theme rather than embarking on a continuous programme of 'new news'. The success of advertising campaigns for such as *The Economist*, Levi Strauss, Milkman, Scottish Amicable, Direct Line, Renault Clio and Häagen-Dazs was initially due to a new approach, but has been maintained by turning their new approach into a consistent theme.

Future Development of the Awards

Everything considered, the IPA Advertising Effectiveness Awards are in good shape despite a difficult period for advertising. But just as the advertising industry has had to change to adapt in a different business environment, ways of further improving the effectiveness of the Awards are being considered.

There seems little need for fundamental change to the basic format (which works) or eligibility for entry (which already embraces virtually anything an IPA agency does), although this is a need to clarify what qualifies as advertising and what does not. The encouragement of pan-European cases should continue; despite logistical difficulties in putting together a multi-country case history, advertising across borders is increasingly a fact of life in UK advertising. The Levi case history is proof it can be done, and provides guidance on how to do it.

The main change which is under consideration relates to the design of the categories and the allocation of cases between them. Some anomalies currently exist in terms of financial campaigns: why should they be treated separately from other goods and services? And the 'Small Budget' category can be difficult to judge: there is a large difference for instance between a small brand with limited resources, a strong regional brand, and a regional test market designed to be rolled out at a later stage.

One approach under active discussion is to structure the categories single-mindedly in terms of the role of the advertising concerned: eg whether it is primarily to introduce a new (or previously little known) product or service, to change the market position of an established product, or to sustain a brand position over the longer term.

This would help draw a distinction between cases which are driven by 'new news' (whether new product, new claim or new creative) and cases driven by developing a consistent brand theme. As such it would help more clearly to recognise *all* the ways advertising can contribute to business success, and hopefully make *Advertising Works 8* an even more useful guide for how to produce effective advertising.

REFERENCES

1. 'Advertising in a recession' – information pack available from the IPA including:
    — The Global Advertising Marketplace, James Capel, Dec 1988 pp 23–26;
    — The Deadly Cutbacks Trap, Simon Broadbent, *Campaign*, 3 Oct 1980, p15;
    — Advertising in Recession Periods, American Business Press/Meldrum and Fewsmith Inc 1979;
    — The 1979 ITV Strike: Its Effects on Sales, Andrew Roberts, Masius, 1980;
    — Coping with Recession: Why budget-cutting may not be the answer, Alex Biel, ARF, 1991;
    — Keeping Spend Up in a Downturn, Alex Biel, 1991.
2. Robey D, IPA 75th Anniversary Conference, 2 October 1992.
3. Adwatch Sector Survey, 'Favourite Ads', *Marketing*, 11 February 1993.
4. Biel, A. 'Love the ad. Buy the product?', *Admap*, September 1990.
5. Biel, A and Lannon J, 'Steel bullet in a velvet glove?', *Admap*, April 1993.
6. Millward Brown International 'People, Brands and Advertising', Papers from a seminar held in September 1992 (available direct from Millward Brown).
7. Feldwick, P and Baker, C. 'The Longer and Broader Effects of Advertising: Some Observations and Recent Evidence', ESOMAR Seminar on 'How advertising works and how promotions work', April 1991.

A SHORT GUIDE TO THE CASE HISTORIES

Established Consumer Goods and Services

National Dairy Council – the Milkman Relaunch (pp3–22)

Coverage:	How advertising very cost-effectively helped mitigate a serious long-term decline in purchase of milk from the milkman in the face of strong competition from supermarkets (who are able to charge lower prices).
Period:	1991–92
Medium:	TV
The Judges' View:	Despite a strong field, the judges quickly agreed that this was the case that most deserved the Grand Prix this year. It had strength in all key areas: strategic thinking, creative and media execution, and thoroughness of evaluation. However, the factor that singled it out above all others was the magnitude of the problem that advertising had to overcome. Powerful social, industrial and economic factors are stacked against the home delivery of milk, and at the time of the campaign's inception there was considerable scepticism about its chances of success. The advertising developed was not only highly popular and successful in engaging consumers' emotions, but also it was orchestrated to produce a strong behaviourial effect. The achievement in holding up volume is exceptional and, whatever the future of home delivery, the advertising monies spent to date by the industry have been paid back handsomely.

The Rejuvenation of Kellogg's All-Bran (pp23–37)

Coverage:	Though a strong brand, All-Bran sales were declining due to broader market trends. A change in advertising strategy turned a 10% pa sales decline into strong volume growth.
Period:	1990–92
Medium:	TV
The Judges' View:	A change of creative strategy successfully represented the brand's core benefits in a relevant and contemporary way. This is a very straightforward case but, in a situation where no other factor materially affected the brand's performance, it shows the power of advertising (when you get it right) to make a major impact on sales.

'I Never Read *The Economist*' (pp38–49)

Coverage:	Faced with recession and increasing competition for its readers' scarce time from other media (especially newspapers), the confident use of advertising was both profitable in the short-term and strengthened the publication in the longer term. It made *The Economist* an essential read for more business people and an essential part of more advertisers' schedules.

Period: 1988–1991

Medium: Posters and national press

The Judges' View: The basic commercial case here is very strong: coincident with a very bold new approach to advertising, readership, cover-price revenue and advertising revenue have all grown and held at levels much higher than could otherwise have been expected. The case could perhaps have been more fully supported by evidence of how the attitudes of potential and actual readers, advertisers and agencies had been affected. However, this is mitigated by the fact that *The Economist*'s success took place in a period when much of its 'specialist' competition fell by the wayside.

Longer and Broader Effects

Andrex – Sold on a Pup (pp53–74)

Coverage: How advertising has built and maintained the brand strength which has been central to the maintenance of Andrex's sales, price premium and profitability. Over 20 years the 'emotional power' of Andrex – fed by advertising – has helped the brand resist competitive pressures on all fronts.

Period: 1972–1992

Medium: TV

The Judges' View: It is easy to accept the pre-eminence of Andrex as a just fact of life rather than a tremendous success story. Going back over 20 years, an overwhelming case is made for how advertising helped to build and maintain a dominant brand position. Part of Andrex's brand strength is excellent consumer value offered by the product, but this case shows how the emotional power of Andrex, built mainly by advertising, has survived periods when it has been exposed at the product level by competitive launches and green/recycled papers. Comparisons with related UK markets, and toilet-tissue markets overseas, add further conviction to an already convincing case for the value of advertising in building long-term brand strength.

The Volkswagen Golf 1984–1990 (pp75–99)

Coverage: How advertising helped give the Volkswagen Golf Mark II the real brand values which helped sustain high sales levels over several years (to defy the usual car model life cycle).

Period: 1984–1990

Medium: Primarily TV

The Judges' View: This was a highly successful and mould-breaking advertising approach, with what (for cars) was a relatively modest budget. The VW Golf succeeded by encouraging potential buyers to identify with the types of people who drive the car, rather than just showcasing the product. A telling feature of the case is an innovative approach to evaluation – namely, a comparison with the sales curves of other new-model launches through the 1980s.

Oxo Cubes and Gravy Granules (pp100–121)

Coverage: The role of advertising in ensuring the profitable survival of Oxo over the past 30 years, despite massive changes in the nation's eating habits, and competitive pressure. This was achieved by maintaining a strong emotional bond, keeping the core product relevant to changing lifestyles and eating habits, and by aiding brand extension.

Period: 1955–1992

Medium: Primarily TV

The Judges' View: Although the quality of evidence produced falls behind Andrex's, Oxo is a strong contender to be the advertising success story of the past 30 years. Brands such as Persil have persisted with considerable assistance from advertising, but also due to product and packaging innovation. The core Oxo product – the beef cube – has not in any way moved with the times, but its advertising has continuously 'reframed' the product against contemporary lifestyles and food trends. Competitive activity has been resisted and the case is strengthened by the way the brand has made successful and very cost-effective extensions into vegetable cubes and gravy granules, without undermining the core product.

'Reassuringly Expensive' – **A Case History of the Stella Artois Press Campaign** (pp122–138)

Coverage: How advertising helped Stella Artois remain the pre-eminent brand in the fast-growing premium lager market in a highly cost-efficient way. In particular this case shows how the 'broader' influence of a platform established by advertising in the trade impacted on the brand's performance and profitability.

Period: 1981–1990

Medium: Primarily Press

The Judges' View: Stella Artois' case was based on advertising's role in building brand strength. This case was singled out by the way the strong advertising platform was established – 'reassuringly expensive' – to underpin a bold marketing strategy (premium pricing in an already premium sector). An excellent example of how diverging from established advertising and marketing conventions can pay off. Stella's franchise was built on a lower spend, and in a different medium (press rather than television), than lager market advertising conventions might suggest.

An Eye to the Future – **The Role of Advertising in Raising Optrex's Defences** (pp139–159)

Coverage: How a continued commitment to advertising has paid off for a brand with an already dominant share of the not particularly large (but high margin) eye-care market.

Period: 1983–1991

Medium: TV

The Judges' View: This case is commended as being an almost 'textbook' answer to the question 'why advertise when we already own the market and major growth seems unlikely?' Optrex advertising has prevented incursions by strong competitors from elsewhere in the world, and grown the market to their advantage in the process.

European

Jeans San Frontières – How Advertising Generates and Protects Levi Strauss Jeans Sales Across Europe (pp163–187)

Coverage: How advertising contributed to the highly successful development of the Levi Strauss jeans brand across Europe using a single campaign vehicle. Covering five European markets – France, Germany, Italy, Spain and the UK – it builds upon a 1988 case history with a predominantly UK focus (see *Advertising Works 5*).

Period: 1988–1991

Medium: TV

The Judges' View: Whilst currently most multi-country campaigns appear to be driven by issues of efficiency rather than effectiveness, this case very clearly shows how advertising can very effectively cross borders. Levi rose to the daunting challenge of demonstrating a commercial effect in three or more European markets. A simple structure is adopted and inter-country differences dealt with thoroughly and intelligently. Essentially the same campaign has run everywhere, but the overall mix of executions has been orchestrated to tap into the different cultural values found across Europe. A convincing case is presented that the advertising has helped make a lot of money in Europe where, largely thanks to advertising, Levi command a higher price than in the US.

New Consumer Goods and Services

Häagen-Dazs: Dedicated to Pleasure – Dedicated to Advertising (pp191–216)

Coverage: The role of advertising in the highly successful launch of what was effectively a new 'super premium' category of ice cream. In particular how it accelerated trial by encouraging rapid trade adoption, press coverage and word of mouth, in addition to its direct effect on consumers.

Period: 1991–1992

Medium: National Press/Magazines

The Judges' View: New brand launches often present problems in providing a neat evaluation of the specific contribution of advertising. Because of its explosive growth, Häagen-Dazs presented a bigger challenge than most. It was a supremely confident piece of marketing – including a very bold stance on price – surrounded by a lot of hype and word of mouth, but justified by excellent product delivery. The ad campaign was clearly not the sole determinant of the brand's success. However, sufficient evidence is produced to convince that advertising has added value to an already premium product, driving sales to higher levels more quickly than would have been achieved by a more conventional approach.

The Launch of Gini (pp217–233)

Coverage: How advertising helped orchestrate a successful launch in a crowded marketplace via the development of a distinctive and (for the carbonated soft drinks market) sophisticated positioning.

Period: 1991

Medium: TV

The Judges' View: Schweppes Gini is a simple, but admirable, case which shows how advertising can be used to develop a distinctive positioning in a relatively undifferentiated marketplace. This is not a mould-breaking case, but the initial strategic thinking is particularly worthy of note and everything else through execution to evaluation was got absolutely right. The end result was a profitable niche positioning in a market characterised by mega-brands, without spending the earth.

Renault Clio: Adding Value During a Recession (pp234–253)

Coverage: The contribution of advertising to the successful launch of an important new model for Renault, which aimed to reach a rather different market from that of its predecessor, the Renault 5.

Period: 1991–92

Medium: TV, supported by National Press and Posters

The Judges' View: Isolating the effect of advertising in new-model car launches is inevitably difficult, particularly in the early stages – as in the case of the Renault Clio. Given these difficulties a convincing case is made. Sales were higher than the Renault 5 had achieved since 1981, a premium price was realised and a much broader buyer profile achieved (in line with strategy) – all in difficult market conditions.

Call Waiting – A New Service From BT (pp254–268)

Coverage: How advertising helped support the launch of a new added value service to BT's residential customers. In particular this case shows how advertising can add an important emotional benefit to what could otherwise be seen as a purely functional service, and how it greatly improved the productivity of direct mail activity.

Period: 1991–92

Medium: Press and Radio

The Judges' View: This paper was commended for its overall clarity and, in particular, the way that it very clearly demonstrated that advertising and direct marketing are not necessarily alternatives. Advertising was used to generate awareness, interest and emotional benefits which made concurrent direct mail activity very much more productive than solus direct mail in a control area.

Small Budgets

Whipsnade Wild Animal Park – How TV Advertising Helped Reverse a 30 Year Decline (pp271–284)

Coverage: As competition for the 'day-out' market proliferated, Whipsnade was gradually eclipsed and by the late 1980s attendance figures were at an all-time low. The well-targeted use of a small budget has re-awakened the public's interest and stimulated large increases in numbers of visitors.

Period: 1990–91

Medium: TV

The Judges' View: This case stood out due to a mixture of confidence and competence – everything was well done from strategy to evaluation. A small budget was used confidently, creatively and flexibly to reverse a long-term decline in visitors, increasing revenue and profit.

The Launch of K Shoes Washable Leather Trainers (pp285–299)

Coverage: How advertising helped to launch a new type of shoe aimed particularly at the 'K Woman' and cost-effectively generate sales above what could otherwise have been expected from a normal (ie non-advertised) launch in this market.

Period: 1991

Medium: Women's magazines (supported by 4-sheet posters)

The Judges' View: This was a clever, well-planned piece of advertising, complemented by a difficult evaluation task, approached in a terrier-like way. It is a good example of how much can be achieved with a relatively small amount of money in a non-traditional area for advertising.

The International Fund for Animal Welfare – How a Single Advertisement Saved 500,000 Lives (pp300–311)

Coverage: How a timely advertisement marked the turning point in a campaign to change the Canadian Government's policy on seal culling.

Period: 1992

Medium: Press

The Judges' View: The International Fund for Animal Welfare (IFAW) campaign shows how a small amount of advertising pressure applied in the right place at the right time can achieve what might otherwise have taken months of lobbying (and quite possibly failed). This case is notable for an innovative creative approach for an animal rights charity: a mixture of humour and ridicule backed by solid fact, rather than the usual shock-horror approach. And, of course, it worked.

Marketing 'Desperation': The Launch of Limelite (pp312–330)

Coverage: How a relatively small advertising budget helped launch a successful new brand of domestic limescale remover. In doing so it also helped transform what was previously a small and stagnant specialist sector.

Period: 1991–92

Medium: TV

The Judges' View: The launch of Limelite was a straightforward, but well-planned and evaluated piece of advertising. By a pragmatic approach to media buying, Cussons began building a profitable sector with very limited expenditure to date.

Special

Scottish Amicable – How it Paid to be Amicable (pp333–358)

Coverage: How advertising helped to break through the high levels of consumer disinterest which characterise the life assurance market to effect major improvements in Scottish Amicable's 'sellability' – consumers more willing to accept and brokers, consequently, more willing to recommend.

Period: 1990–1992

Medium: TV

The Judges' View: Relatively few advertisers in the financial area have succeeded in both identifying a clear strategic role for advertising and striking the right creative note to engage consumers. Scottish Amicable got it absolutely right – from a sure strategic grasp through a confident creative execution to excellent results, convincingly and thoroughly evaluated. Two additional factors particularly recommended this case. First, how a bold creative approach greatly improved the productivity of Scottish Amicable's advertising. Second, the analysis of how advertising directly and indirectly impacted on intermediaries (the trade), greatly to the benefit of Scottish Amicable's premium income.

Alliance & Leicester Building Society – Advertising Effectiveness 1987–91 pp(359–382)

Coverage: How the ongoing 'Fry and Laurie' campaign has contributed to the Alliance & Leicester's consumer standing, market share and profitability since it commenced in 1987. This paper takes a broader view than previous case histories relating to specific aspects of the campaign – its impact on savings (published in

Advertising Works 5) and mortgage business (*Advertising Works 6*).

Period: 1987–1991

Medium: Primarily TV (supported by press)

The Judges' View: This case shows the value (and cost-effectiveness) of a strong consistent overall campaign vehicle in what is a multi-faceted and often rapidly changing market. Perhaps its most telling aspect is a comparison with the performance of the Nationwide (Anglia), which went through a similar merger and identity change in the mid-80s. Advertising with consistency and personality has helped the Alliance & Leicester develop its business and consumer franchise much more effectively than the Nationwide (which has chopped and changed both creatively and in terms of strategic focus), despite a much smaller advertising spend.

Direct Line Insurance – Direct Response and Brand Building is Possible! (pp383–396)

Coverage: As a 'direct' operation, Direct Line depends heavily on advertising to generate new customers. This case shows how a shift from press to TV advertising helped Direct Line not only improve its response rates, but also stand out from its competition and accelerate the development of a strong brand franchise.

Period: 1990

Medium: TV

The Judges' View: The Direct Line campaign demonstrated a confident approach to direct response advertising which has paid off in several respects and accelerated the development of a highly successful business. This case shows the benefits of challenging some of the accepted conventions of the marketplace, proving TV can be an excellent direct response medium, and that direct response and brand-building are not necessarily inconsistent objectives.

Marketing *Award for Innovation*

Skip Lunch. Save a Life – Advertising Success on a Plate (pp399–415)

Coverage: How a powerful marketing idea – 'Skip Lunch, Save a Life' – helped overcome 'compassion fatigue' to raise £5.5 million for Save the Children.

Period: 1991

Medium: 'Through the line'

The Judges' View: The advertising component paid for itself many times over, but this case is singled out for a big marketing idea, implemented strongly through the line by agency and client. It clearly demonstrates how 'ideas' really make the difference: 'Skip Lunch, Save a Life' delivered ten times the income generated in similar circumstances in previous years.

IPA ADVERTISING EFFECTIVENESS COMMITTEE

Michael Hockney, Managing Director, Butterfield Day Devito Hockney

Chris Baker, Planning Director, Bainsfair Sharkey Trott

Rita Clifton, Head of Planning, Saatchi & Saatchi

Martin Durham, Publishing Director for *PR World*, *Marketing* and *Moves Magazine*, Haymarket Publishing

Paul Feldwick, Executive Planning Director, BMP DDB Needham

Jerry Fielder, Chairman, Leagas Delaney

Tessa Gooding, Communications Officer, IPA

Chris Jones, Managing Director, J Walter Thompson

Tim Lefroy, Chairman and Chief Executive, Alliance Advertising London

Sue Pedley, Joint Planning Director, Euro RSCG

Nick Phillips, Director General, IPA

Hamish Pringle, New Business Director, CME.KHBB

Charlie Robertson, Head of Planning, The Leith Agency

Mark Robinson, Business Development Director, GGK London

Clare Rossi, Planning Director, GGT Advertising

Mike Walsh, Chairman, Ogilvy & Mather UK

1992 JUDGES

Sir John Banham, Former Director-General CBI; Chairman, Local Government Commission for England; Chairman, Westcountry Television Ltd

Chris Baker, Planning Director, Bainsfair Sharkey Trott

Patrick Barwise, Professor of Management and Marketing, London Business School

John Brady, Principal, McKinsey and Company

Jeremy Bullmore, Non-Executive Director, WPP Group

Paul Feldwick, Executive Planning Director, BMP DDB Needham

Peter Mitchell, Strategic Affairs Director, Guinness

Dan O'Donoghue, Chief Executive and Joint Managing Director, Publicis

Christine Restall, Deputy Managing Director, The Research Business International

Mike Sommers, Marketing and Premises Director, TSB Group

ACKNOWLEDGEMENTS

The success of the 1992 IPA Advertising Effectiveness Awards owed a great deal to *Campaign*, *Marketing* and *Admap* who gave free space to advertise the Awards.

The IPA thanks *Marketing*, the principal sponsor of the Awards presentation and the following companies whose support helped make the presentation possible:

BRAD
BMP DDB Needham
Channel 4 Television
IPC Women's Weeklies
ITV Association
J Walter Thompson
KPMG Peat Marwick
Mirror Group Newspapers
The National Magazine Company
Ogilvy & Mather
RSL – Research Services Ltd

Many people worked hard to make the awards a success, especially Michael Hockney, Chairman of the Advertising Effectiveness Committee. Mark Robinson's successful advertising contributed much to the high profile of these awards. For the Institute of Practitioners in Advertising thanks are due in particular to Tessa Gooding, Secretary to the IPA Advertising Effectiveness Committee and to Janet Mayhew for organising the judging and certificates for prize winners.

Prizes

ESTABLISHED CONSUMER GOODS AND SERVICES

FIRST PRIZE AND GRAND PRIX

National Dairy Council – the Milkman Relaunch
John Grant
  BMP DDB Needham for *National Dairy Council*

SECOND PRIZE

The Rejuvenation of Kellogg's All-Bran
Carole Lee
  Leo Burnett for *Kellogg Co of GB*

THIRD PRIZE

'*I Never Read* The Economist'
Laura Marks
  Abbott Mead Vickers.SMS for The Economist *newspaper*

CERTIFICATE OF COMMENDATION

Findus Lasagne – Beating the Recession
Paul Hackett
  J Walter Thompson for *Findus*

*Irn Bru – How a Change of Creative Strategy Gave a Long Established Brand
New Life*
Cathy Clift
  Lowe Howard-Spink for *Irn Bru*

Trebor Bassett – The Day the World Turned Bertie
John Bunyard
  Ayer for *Trebor Bassett Ltd*

LONGER AND BROADER EFFECTS

FIRST PRIZE

Andrex – Sold on a Pup
Mary Stow
  J Walter Thompson for *Scott Ltd*

SECOND PRIZE

The Volkswagen Golf 1984–1990
Gavin Macdonald and Antony Buck
  BMP DDB Needham for *VAG UK Ltd*

Oxo Cubes and Gravy Granules
Giles Lury and Paul Hackett
  J Walter Thompson for *Brooke Bond Foods*

THIRD PRIZE

'Reassuringly Expensive' – A Case History of the Stella Artois Press Campaign
Robert Heath
  Lowe Howard-Spink for *Whitbread Beer Co Plc*

CERTIFICATE OF COMMENDATION

Green Giant – a Jolly Good Advertising Success
Lucy Edge and Paul Harris
  Leo Burnett for Green Giant UK

An Eye to the Future – The Role of Advertising in Raising Optrex's Defences
Louise Cook, Anna Hutson and Diana Redhouse
  BMP DDB Needham for *Crookes Healthcare*

EUROPEAN

*Jeans Sans Frontières – How Advertising Generates and Protects Levi Strauss
Jeans Sales Across Europe*
Stephen Walker
  Bartle Bogle Hegarty for *Levi Strauss Europe*

NEW CONSUMER GOODS AND SERVICES

FIRST PRIZE

Häagen-Dazs. Dedicated to Pleasure – Dedicated to Advertising
Nick Kendall
  Bartle Bogle Hegarty for *Häagen-Dazs*

SECOND PRIZE

The Launch of Gini
Anneke Elwes
  BMP DDB Needham for *Schweppes GB*

THIRD PRIZE

Renault Clio: Adding Value During a Recession
Caroline Chandy and Douglas Thursby-Pelham
  Publicis for *Renault UK*

CERTIFICATE OF COMMENDATION

Hats Off to Mercury
Sarah Ablett
  Hoare Wilkins for *Mercury Communications*

Call Waiting – A New Service From BT
Stephen Pickthall
  Cousins Advertising for *BT*

SMALL BUDGETS

NO FIRST PRIZE

SECOND PRIZE

Whipsnade Wild Animal Park – How TV Advertising Helped Reverse a 30 Year Decline
Cathy Clift
  Lowe Howard-Spink for *Whipsnade Wild Animal Park*

THIRD PRIZES

The Launch of K Shoes Washable Leather Trainers
Liz Watts
  Bartle Bogle Hegarty for *K Shoes*

The International Fund for Animal Welfare – How a Single Advertisement Saved 500,000 Lives
Patrick Barnes
  Bartle Bogle Hegarty for *IFAW*

Marketing 'Desperation': The Launch of Limelite
Ged Parton and Paul Jeffrey
  Bowden Dyble Hayes for *Cussons*

CERTIFICATE OF COMMENDATION

Flowers and Plants Association – Never Underestimate the Power of Advertising
Katrina Michel and David Furnish
  Ogilvy & Mather for *Flowers & Plants Association*

Smiths Crisps – Climbing a Mountain – the Launch of Tudor Specials
Jem Keen and John Robson
  Abbott Mead Vickers for *Smiths Crisps*

Neutrogena Reveals its Core Values
Crawford Hollingworth
  Chiat Day for *Neutrogena*

Skip Lunch. Save a Life – Advertising Success on a Plate
Julie Davey
  Ogilvy & Mather for *Save the Children*

SPECIAL

FIRST PRIZE

Scottish Amicable – How it Paid to be Amicable
Richard Storey
  BMP DDB Needham for *Scottish Amicable*

SECOND PRIZE

Alliance and Leicester Building Society – Advertising Effectiveness 1987–1991
Will Collin
  BMP DDB Needham for *Alliance & Leicester*

THIRD PRIZE

Direct Line Insurance – Direct Response and Brand Building is Possible!
Andrew Ingram
  Hoare Wilkins for *Direct Line Insurance*

CERTIFICATE OF COMMENDATION

Health Education Authority – How Advertising Helped to Protect More Children from Childhood Diseases
Craig Kleber
  Laing Henry for *Health Education Authority*

Barclaycard – How a Bungling Secret Agent Did More Than You'd Credit
Sarah Carter
  BMP DDB Needham for *Barclaycard*

MARKETING AWARD FOR INNOVATION

Skip Lunch. Save a Life – Advertising Success on a Plate
Julie Davey
  Ogilvy & Mather for *Save the Children*

Section One

Established Consumer Goods and Services

1

National Dairy Council – the Milkman Relaunch

INTRODUCTION

Your client is the brand leader in a £3.2 billion food market. Because his competitors are far cheaper, he is losing more than a million customers a year. What could advertising do to help?

In this case the product was the milkman and the competitor the supermarkets.

The obvious answer was to target customers who were about to cancel their milkman. But we discovered that advertising could do little to dissuade them. It would be too little, too late.

Then we examined the move from milkman to supermarkets in more detail. We discovered that there was a *crucial first step* towards cancelling. This was when milkman customers started to buy some of their milk from the supermarkets on a regular basis. Here, it seemed, advertising could have an effect. By targeting these people advertising could not only return a very considerable short-term profit; it could also reduce the rate of cancelling in the future. In fact, we will show that advertising in this way actually halted the decline in the milkman's share during 1991.

What we learned was that you cannot assume the answer to a problem is always to confront that problem directly. In this case prevention proved far more effective than cure.

A HISTORY OF THE MILKMAN

— Door-to-door delivery of milk is a very old British tradition. It dates back to the last century, when handcarts were used to deliver the milk.
— After the Second World War the doorstep service was expanded to its current scale. War-time agriculture had created a huge milk surplus. The Milk Marketing Board (correctly) assumed that if milk was delivered daily, households would use more milk.
— As recently as 1980, almost 90% of households had a milkman.
— Since 1980 the milkman has been in steady decline, partly due to demographic and lifestyle trends but mostly due to competition from supermarkets, whose milk is cheaper.
— In the late 1980s the price gap between the milkman and the supermarkets became larger.
— As a result the milkman's decline accelerated (Figure 1).

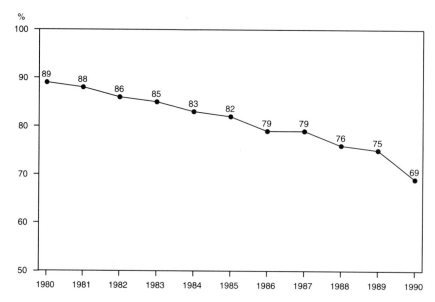

Figure 1. *Percentage of households who have a milkman nowadays*
Source: NOP

WHO CARES IF THE MILKMAN DECLINES?

The Milk Marketing Board (MMB)

— The MMB buys all the milk from the dairy farmers and sells it to dairies.
— The MMB operates, on behalf of farmers, to maximise consumption of milk products.
— Households which have a milkman use more milk. An econometric model in the late 1980s showed that, 'for every 1% fall in doorstep deliveries, milk sales will fall nearly 0.2%.' (MMD Ltd.)
— The reason for this is that daily milk delivery puts milk 'on tap'. Once bought it tends to get used up. Milkman customers are also less prone to running low and restricting consumption. (BMP Qualitative.)

The Dairies/Delivery Companies

— The dairies process, package and distribute milk. This is then sold through the dairies' own milkmen, or to independent delivery companies, or to retailers and wholesalers.
— The dairies and delivery companies make more profit if milk is sold through the milkman:

NDC estimates of dairy profits:

19.5p	Profit per pint sold through a milkman
7.5p	Profit per pint sold through shops
12.0p	Incremental profit per pint, if that pint is sold by the milkman rather than the shops

Source: NDC

— In addition the dairies have made a massive historical investment in doorstep delivery. Thousands of milkmen and dairy employees depend on it for a living.

In short, the whole milk industry (excluding the retailers) had a strong interest in stemming the decline of the milkman. All these groups contribute a levy for advertising to the National Dairy Council (NDC) which is our client. The NDC co-ordinates advertising, promotions, PR, sponsorship and education for the milk industry in England and Wales. (Separate Dairy Councils cover Scotland and Northern Ireland.)

WHY WERE MILKMAN SALES DECLINING?

It was clear that the milkman was losing both volume share and customers to its competitors; the supermarkets and small shops.

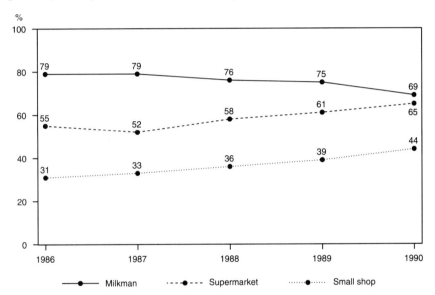

Figure 2. *Sources from which milk ever bought*
Source: NOP

The recent increase in small shop penetration is misleading – they only account for 10% of volume. The main problem was the supermarkets.

The question was, why was the milkman losing share to the supermarkets?

Price

Supermarket milk is much cheaper than milk from the milkman. Supermarkets sell milk at virtually cost price because they want to gain share of a £3.2 billion market. Milk is the biggest household staple and is bought frequently. Retailers could use milk to generate store traffic. Cheap milk could also add to their reputation for good value.

An econometric analysis (MMD Ltd) concluded that the price difference between doorstep and shop milk was responsible for two-thirds of the milkman's decline in 1989. Since then this price gap has widened further.

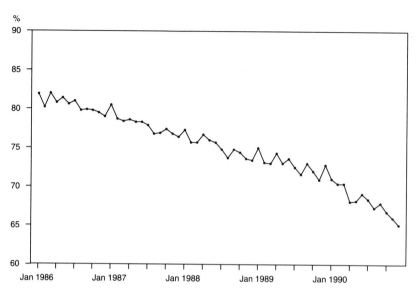

Figure 3. *Milkman volume share – doorstep proportion of household milk*
Source: MMB/Nielsen

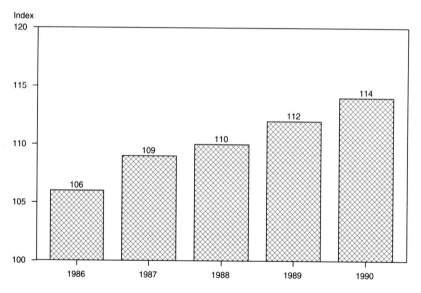

Figure 4. *Relative price of doorstep to supermarket milk*
Source: Nielsen/DTF

Supermarketing

As well as cut-throat pricing and promotions, the supermarkets have also invested in product quality (eg freshness); packaging (eg 4 pint containers); merchandising (eg prominent displays of low fat milks); advertising and leafleting to publicise their cheap prices. The growth of supermarkets, their improving image and the move to out of town shopping have also contributed to their increasing share.

Service

The quality of milkmen and service factors (eg frequency of delivery) affect the value of the milkman service and hence his share. For instance, with fewer customers, the milkman cannot afford to deliver as often. There is therefore a vicious spiral of falling share and reductions in quality of service.

WHAT DID WE THINK WAS GOING TO HAPPEN IN THE FUTURE?

Share had been steadily declining from 82% in 1986 to 65% by the end of 1990. The price gap between milkman and supermarkets was continuing to widen. The decline therefore was expected to continue and, probably, to get even steeper. It was reaching a level such that it became a priority issue for the NDC. Something had to be done to stem the decline.

WHAT COULD BE DONE?

Some of the factors affecting the milkman are out of the milk industry's control (eg supermarket price). There are only three important factors which the milk industry could control:

1. *Price*
   A substantial price reduction would be needed to influence people who were about to cancel their milkman. Unfortunately this reduction in price would obviously have to be offered to all customers, not just those about to cancel. Profitability would be decimated.

2. *Service*
   Improvements might increase loyalty. Various initiatives are now being tested (eg guaranteed early delivery). However, these changes take time (at least two years) to implement.

3. *Advertising*
   Given these stark choices, the milk industry agreed that if an advertising campaign could be developed which would help to stem the decline (at least until longer term solutions could be found) it would receive their full support.

DEVELOPING A MARKETING AND ADVERTISING STRATEGY

Marketing Objective

To slow down the decline in the milkman's share of total milk sales.

Interestingly, we found that with a sizeable advertising budget of £5 million we would only have to stem the decline by ½% share point for the advertising to pay back.

For advertising to repay a budget of £5 million:

   ½%   x   12p (incremental milkman profit – NDC estimate)
         x   8.9 billion pints (household milk volume – MMB)
         =   £5m extra profit

This equates to 45 million extra pints sold by the milkman.

Target Audience and Desired Change in Behaviour

The decline in the milkman's volume share was accompanied by a decline in the proportion of households having a milkman, from 82% in 1985 to 69% in 1990. Once these customers had been lost, the dairies knew (from experience of door-to-door canvassing) they would be very hard to get back. If the decline continued at its present rate then there would be no milkman customers left within 12 years. It seemed clear that there were two possible strategies:

1. Stop people from cancelling.
2. Recruit new milkman customers.

We were able to reject the second option because it was too small. The NDC estimated that at most only 2% of households are potential new milkman customers every year, whereas 6% of households had cancelled their milkman in the last year (Source: NOP). We decided that new customers were not a large enough audience to be the main focus of our advertising. (We have not completely dismissed this option. Later in 1992 advertising carrying a phoneline number was used to recruit new customers. This coincided with a major canvassing drive by the dairies.)

We were left with the first option, which was to stop customers cancelling. We needed to find out who they were and why they were cancelling. Equally we needed to find out why other customers weren't cancelling.

We therefore conducted some qualitative research among past and present milkman customers. What we found was that it was unrealistic to expect advertising to affect cancelling. But in the process we discovered another unexpected way to stem the decline.

What We Found

Research amongst those who had actually cancelled told us that:

— Consumers do not simply buy all their milk from the milkman, then suddenly decide to cancel.
— Those who cancelled had first gone through a phase when they had regularly bought extra milk from the supermarkets. Typically, they would 'stock up' with extra milk for the weekends – often buying 4 pint containers.
— Only when they had regularly bought from the supermarket for some time were they confident in this source of supply; its constant availability, its freshness, the convenience of picking it up 'when you're there anyway'.
— Because they bought regularly from both sources, these people became more aware of the price difference. Some then felt 'irresponsible' spending so much extra to have milk delivered.
— Even so, cancelling the milkman was a big decision. Many 'agonised' over it, weighing up their experience of each source. Some were also anxious about upsetting their milkman.
— They were often therefore prompted to cancel by an 'event'; eg a row with their milkman over the bill.

Source: BMP Qualitative

How could advertising influence people who had regular experience of both sources, who were fully aware of how much extra the milkman cost, who were virtually looking for an excuse to cancel anyway? Advertising had nothing new to tell these people. It was unrealistic to expect advertising to persuade them not to cancel. It would be too little, too late.

What Could We Do Then?

Past research had told us that most milkman customers buy from the shops occasionally, when they run out of milk. This latest research had told us that before cancelling, customers had first gone through a phase of buying quite a lot of milk from the supermarkets much more *regularly* (eg with their weekly shopping). In retrospect this was obvious. In fmcg purchasing people very rarely go from being 100% loyal to one brand to being 100% loyal to another brand. There is nearly always a period of trial and conversion.

This is the crucial finding that influenced our advertising strategy. It seemed that customers moving from the milkman to the shops followed a series of steps.

Milkman customers
(occasionally buy from the
shops as distress purchases)

↓   **'Drifting'**

Customers who still buy
most of their milk from the
milkman, but regularly stock up
from the shops

↓   **Cancelling**

Shop only customers

The key step we were interested in was when milkman customers moved from occasional distress purchasing to regular purchasing from the shops. We will call this step 'drifting' from now on, for the sake of brevity.

Before reaching the 'regular supermarket stage', milkman customers:

— were often unsure of the price difference (and often underestimated it);

— were not at all confident that the supermarkets could supply all their milk,
(eg without shopping much more regularly).

Source: BMP Qualitative

Because they were 'drifting' into supermarket purchasing and were not yet strongly affected by price they seemed far more likely to respond to advertising.

The research told us that consumers tended to take their milkman for granted. They seldom saw their milkman apart from on pay day. They came to expect pints of milk just to 'turn up on the doorstep'. However, on probing they did recognise that there were strong rational and emotional benefits to having a milkman:

— The main benefit of the milkman service is the *considerable convenience* he provides; you don't have to carry all that heavy milk, you don't have to go out and get it, you don't have to worry about it, it's there in time for breakfast, etc.
— The milkman service also has warm *emotional values*; friendly, helpful, traditional, a family ritual, part of the local community ('like a village bobby').

Source: BMP Qualitative

If we could make these benefits more salient it could provide a strong counter argument against drifting into supermarket purchasing.

In addition, we had a number of new things to say in our advertising, which might lead to them buying more of their milk from the milkman instead of the shops.

— *Green*
The green bandwagon was in full swing. Yet, because returnable glass milk bottles are so familiar, few had 'realised' they were better for the environment.
— *Low fat milks*
Some weren't sure if the milkman sold these.
— *Weekend milk*
They often didn't think about extra milk for the weekend until they reached the shops – but did find it heavy and bulky to get home. It would make more sense to leave a note for the milkman.

It seemed likely therefore that advertising *might work*, in deterring some of these consumers from 'drifting' into regular shop purchasing. We then needed to check if this was a worthwhile target.

Is This a Worthwhile Opportunity?

From an annual source of purchase data we were able to calculate that between June 1989 and June 1990:

— 9% of housewives 'drifted' into regular supermarket buying, while keeping their milkman.
— 6% of housewives cancelled their milkman.

(Source: NOP Annual Survey)

NOP also told us that on average the milkman customers who regularly purchased from the shops bought; eight pints a week from the milkman and four pints a week from the shops. We could therefore estimate how much volume per week was lost by the milkman, from the two migrations:

Drifting: 9% of 20 million households x 4 pints/week = 7.2 million pints/week
Cancelling: 6% of 20 million households x 8 pints/week = 9.6 million pints/week

Drifting was therefore responsible for nearly half the volume lost by the milkman.

Our research had told us that only those who had gone through a phase of regular shop purchasing tended to cancel their milkman. Our strategy aimed to reduce the number of milkman customers who entered this phase. It was therefore possible that any success would have an *additional long-term effect*, by reducing future cancelling.

In fact, there was evidence for just such a long-term process. MMD econometric modelling in the past had picked up a relationship between the amount of volume share lost in one year and further longer term losses. They call this the 'feedthrough effect'.

Summary of Creative Brief

Target audience	Housewives with a milkman who occasionally buy extra milk from the shops.
Who are they?	25–45 year old housewives, with children, heavier purchasers of milk.
Objective	Persuade them to continue buying from the milkman (or buy more from him) rather than drifting into the habit of regularly stocking up at the supermarket.
Proposition	Don't forget how helpful and convenient your milkman is.
Support	(i) The lovable, friendly, archetypal milkman – they've forgotten how wonderful he is.
	(ii) He delivers low fat milks.
	(iii) His returnable glass bottles are friendlier to the environment.
	(iv) He's more convenient for weekend extras than carrying heavy, bulky milk home.

Guidelines

A blockbusting relaunch was needed. One extra task, which was added to the brief at the suggestion of the client was targeting milkmen themselves (as a secondary audience) in order to improve morale.

Media Planning

TV was chosen as the only medium sufficiently impactful and involving to stage a major relaunch. The media target audience was housewives with children. The media plan is shown below.

Media timing/weights

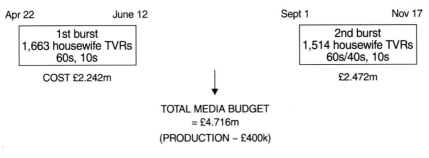

'DAYBREAK' ADVERTISING (60 SECONDS)

  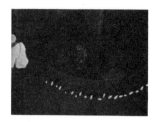

'DAYBREAK' ADVERTISING (10 SECONDS)

MVO: It's a lot easier to get all your weekend milk from your milkman.

VO: Whole milk, semi-skimmed, skimmed, your milkman can deliver them all.

VO: What's all this fuss about being green?

You've been returning our bottles for years.

Creative Development

The 'Daybreak' advertising was written to this brief. Most TV viewers now know this as 'the one with the dancing bottles'. The creative team had worked out roughly how many bottles of milk a milkman delivers a day (about 900). This impressive scale, plus the almost 'magical' way in which milk 'appears' on your doorstep inspired the main (60 second) commercial.

To keep the main ad as magical as possible, the rational support messages were relegated to 10 second ads. These were shown 'top and tail' with the 60 second (ie first and last ads in the commercial break).

This advertising became one of the most liked and noticed campaigns on TV. It also received recognition of the advertising industry, by winning Gold awards from the Creative Circle and British Television Awards. We believe that much of the credit for the advertising effectiveness must go to the creative team, for producing such a famous and distinctive, yet relevant campaign.

TABLE 1: THE TOP 10: SPONTANEOUS RECALL
Q: Thinking back over the past week, which commercials can you remember seeing or hearing?

	Account	Agency
1	Milk	BMP DDB Needham
2	Persil	JWT
3	Coke/Coca-Cola	McCanns
4	Radion	Ogilvy & Mather
5	Carling Black Label	WCRS
6	Fairy Liquid	Grey
7	Guinness	Ogilvy & Mather
8	British Telecom/BT	JWT
9	PG Tips	BMP DDB Needham
10	TV Quick	Lowe Howard-Spink

Source: *Marketing*, 27th June 1991

EVALUATION OF THE CAMPAIGN

Sales Results (MMB/Nielsen Data)

— Figure 3 showed that the milkman's share of household milk was in long-term decline. This decline continued up until April 1991.
— From January 1990–April 1991 the milkman's share declined at an average of 0.43% share points per month.
— However, from May–December 1991, when we advertised, this stabilised, resulting in a decline of only 0.01% share points per month, ie the decline had been almost completely halted in the advertising period.

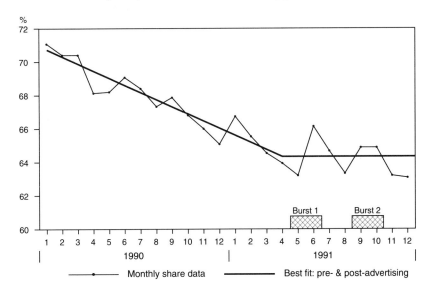

Figure 5. *Milkman volume share – doorstep proportion of household milk*

TABLE 2: AVERAGE MONTHLY RATES OF DECLINE
(Share points per month)

	Jan '90–Apr '91	May '91–Dec '91
Average monthly decline	−0.43 (Pre-advertising)	−0.01 (Advertising)

Source: MMB/Nielsen

— Not only did we see the milkman's decline nearly halted during the advertising period. We also saw two significant *increases* in milkman share, coinciding exactly with the advertising bursts.

Advertising burst	Milkman share
Apr–May	+ 2.9% pts
Aug–Sep/Oct	+ 1.5% pts

We do not have sales figures since December 1991, due to the time needed by the MMB to collect total milk market data. However, in only eight months, we have seen a very pronounced effect.

Effect on Drifting

TABLE 3: RATE OF DRIFTING

	June '89-June '90	Feb '91-Jan '92
% of households drifting (Sample)	9% (1,600)	−2% (800)

Sources: NOP, Millward Brown

As we have seen from annual purchasing data, between June 1989 and June 1990, 9% of households (who had a milkman) drifted into regular shop purchasing. The advertising was designed specifically to combat this. We therefore set up a continuous measure (from February) of source of purchase using Millward Brown. In 1991, after the advertising began we actually saw 'negative drifting'. No volume was lost, therefore, in 1991 due to drifting.

The advertising seemed to be working very effectively in the way it was designed to.

Effect on Cancelling

We did not expect to affect cancelling (in the first year) and we were right. Cancelling continued in 1991; 7% of housewives cancelled their milkman in 1991, compared with 6% in 1990 (Source: NOP).

We predicted that if we reduced drifting in the short-term, cancelling would be reduced in the longer term (the 'feedthrough effect'). The latest data we have, from 1992, shows the reduction in cancelling that we predicted actually happened early in 1992. The advertising seems to have had the longer term effect we had hoped for.

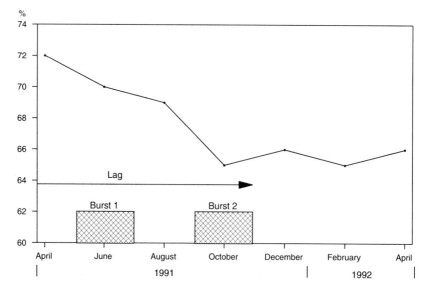

Figure 6. *Percentage of housewives who have a milkman*
Source: Millward Brown

The Unexpected Effect

— We assumed that, if we stopped drifting altogether, the best we could hope for would be to slow down share decline by nearly 50% (because in 1990 nearly half the volume lost by the milkman was through drifting). In fact it appears that we had underestimated the power of our advertising.

— Cancelling continued, yet share was flat rather than declining at half the previous rate.

— The only explanation is an effect we hadn't expected. We had thought of drifting in the absolute sense of changing source of purchase; rather than 'drifting' in the true sense of a continuum from occasional to regular shop purchasing.

— What appears to have happened is that those who still had a milkman but had not 'drifted' during 1991 (in the absolute sense) bought more milk from the milkman and less milk from the shops.

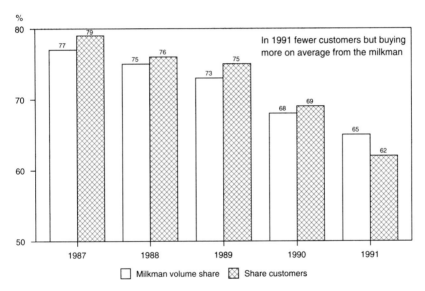

Figure 7. *Milkman volume share vs share of customers*
Sources: NOP, MMB/Nielsen

— This could explain why there were such immediate sales peaks during our advertising bursts (eg milkman customers remembering to order extra from their milkman). In retrospect, this is how we should have expected the advertising to work – particularly the 10 second tactical ads.

— We can estimate the size of this effect from the fact that volume share only declined by 3% in 1991. From the rate of cancelling, we would have expected a decline of 7 or 8%:

Extra volume = 4% x 20 million households @ 8 pints
= remaining 62% x 20 million milkman customers @ ½ pint.

That is, every remaining milkman customer bought on average an extra pint every two weeks from the milkman instead of the shops.

Consumer Evidence of the Advertising Effect
Performance on the Advertising Tracking Study

The NDC has used Millward Brown for over ten years to monitor the performance of its advertising. In its first year, our milkman advertising achieved higher levels of spontaneous awareness and proven recall than any previous milk campaign.

TABLE 4: MILLWARD BROWN – AWARENESS LEVELS (end of 1st year)

(Housewives)	Spontaneous awareness	Proven recall
'Daybreak' campaign	60%	67%
Previous highest scores	48%	62%
Average (last 3 campaigns)	42%	48%

The communication objectives of the campaign were monitored by the following prompted statements. These showed an unprecedented strength and depth of communication.

TABLE 5: PROMPTED COMMUNICATION (MILLWARD BROWN)

(Housewives)	(Pre) Jan/Feb '91	(Post) Oct/Nov '91
'The milkman is the best way to buy fresh milk'	29%	56%
'The milkman delivers semi-skimmed milk'	9%	39%
'Milk delivery is environmentally friendly'	7%	40%
'The milkman can handle difficult orders'	4%	33%

A separate survey was carried out among 70 milkman at the end of the first advertising burst by Gordon Simmonds Ltd. This found that:

— Awareness and communication were strong.
— Milkmen believed they could and should live up to the image portrayed; in being cheerful, friendly and helpful.
— One-third of them reported sales increases recently, very few reported a decline.

Qualitative research was also conducted among housewives who had a milkman after the first burst, to check how the campaign was working;

— It was most repondents' favourite advertising on TV – 'straight away you have a smile on your face when it comes on, even if you're down.'
— The Disney-like imagery and music transported the viewer into childlike feelings of security and pleasure; these feelings were linked to having a milkman – a magical figure who has everything under control.
— Overall, the advertising made them feel good about having *their* milkman. It made them appreciate him and inclined to use him more. The 10 second ads (eg 'Green') provided extra (rational) reasons to do so.

Source: BMP Qualitative

ISOLATING THE ADVERTISING EFFECT

As we have seen in Figure 5 there were two significant increases in the milkman's share coinciding with our two advertising bursts. As a result the decline in milkman's share was halted.

We can eliminate all other factors which could possibly have caused this change in the rate of decline in the middle of 1991.

Price

The price difference between milkman and shops increased during the second half of 1991, when the ads were on air. If anything, therefore, the milkman share should have declined faster in the second half of the year.

TABLE 6:   RELATIVE PRICE OF DOORSTEP TO SUPERMARKET MILK

	Jan/Apr '91	May/Dec '91
Index	112	115

Sources: DTF, Nielsen

Distribution

Nothing untoward happened (eg a strike at supermarkets or an increase in the number of milkmen) during 1991 to affect either source. If anything supermarkets should have gained share due to store openings and Sunday trading in the second half of the year.

Service

Presumably, those who thought their milkman service had improved might be responsible for a slowing down in the decline of milkman sales.

There has been a general drive within the milk industry to improve service, in response to falling sales. As a result there have been slight improvements in the perceptions of the service. However, there was no significant change in these improvements between the first and second half of 1991.

TABLE 7:   BMRB TELEPHONE AD HOC 'SERVICE' SURVEY – SAMPLE 1000
('Over the past three months, would you say that the service your milkman has given you has:')

	Pre-advertising (Mar 91)	Post-advertising (Nov 91)
Improved	7%	8%
Stayed the same	91%	90%
Got worse	2%	2%

There is no evidence, therefore, that service changes had an increased effect on the milkman's share, after our advertising began.

Other Activity

There was no other national marketing activity supporting the milkman in 1991.

Any local activity which existing customers responded to favourably would have been seen by them as a service improvement.

But we know that service improvements did not have an increased effect after our advertising began.

Conclusion – Isolating the Advertising Effect

There were clear increases in the milkman's share of milk coinciding exactly with our two advertising bursts. As a result the decline in the milkman's share was halted in the advertising period.

No other factors which influence the milkman's share of milk changed in a way which could have caused this. In fact, the major factor which influences the milkman's share (ie price) changed in a way which should have increased the decline during the advertising period.

ESTIMATING THE OVERALL EFFECT OF ADVERTISING

Short-term Effect

— As we have seen the average monthly rate of decline in the milkman's share of volume from January 1990 to April 1991 was 0.43 share points.

— There is nothing to suggest that this rate of decline would not have continued through the rest of 1991. Indeed, the price increase suggests it might have got worse.

— In fact, share declined by 0.01 share points per month from May 1991 to December 1991.

— If we assume share would have continued to decline at 0.43 share points per month without the advertising then we can calculate the additional volume due to the advertising.

Average share May–December 1991

With advertising	Without advertising
64.2%	61.7%

Additional share points	=	2.5%
In 8 months, total household volume	=	5.95 billion pints
Additional milkman volume	=	2.5% x 5.95 billion
	=	150 million pints
Additional profit	=	150 million x 12p
		(NDC estimate of extra profit from milkman per pint)
	=	£18 million

As well as extra profit, we know that milkman sales bring extra volume because milkman customers use more milk; an extra 0.2% in milk volume for every 1% of extra milkman share (Source: MMD).

The milkman's share was on average 2.5% higher when we advertised, than expected from previous declines. We can therefore estimate the amount of extra milk consumption due to the advertising:

Additional volume	=	5.9 billion pints x 2.5 x 0.2%
	=	30 million pints
Extra profit	=	30 m x 15p (NDC estimate
		of average profit for milk)
	=	£4.5 million

The total extra profit was therefore £22.5 million. The total advertising spend was only £5.1 million. The advertising paid for itself more than four times over in 1991.

It had exceeded not only our objectives but our wildest dreams of what we could achieve.

Longer Term Effect

We had a theory that slowing 'drifting' in the short-term, would lead to a reduced rate of cancelling in the future ('feedthrough effect'). We have seen some earlier evidence that this was happening. This adds even more volume saved (and profit generated) by the advertising, in the longer term. And it contributes to the industry's longer term objective of turning around the decline.

SUMMARY

— The milkman was rapidly losing share to the supermarkets, which were cheaper. This had very big implications for the volume of milk used and the profit made by the dairy industry.

— We were briefed to develop advertising to stem this decline. Even ½% less share lost in 1991 would pay for our advertising.

— The obvious solution was to stop customers from cancelling. However, on further investigation it did not appear realistic that advertising could do this.

— We discovered that there was a crucial first step towards cancelling – when milkman customers started regularly purchasing extra milk from the supermarkets.

— This migration accounted for nearly half the volume lost in the short-term. It also gave us a way to nip future decline in the bud.

— This focused and innovative strategy was translated into advertising of the highest creative standards.

— The advertising slowed down the decline by 150 million pints. We can see this from the change in the rate of decline which occurred after the advertising started.

— Penetration data showed that the advertising worked as intended – in stopping consumers drifting more into regular shop purchasing. There also was an unexpected effect in increasing the amount of milk bought from the milkman by those customers who did not 'drift'.

— The advertising performed outstandingly on awareness and communication measures.
— We can demonstrate that the advertising was responsible for the sales effect, because nothing else changed in a way which could have caused it.
— The advertising paid for itself more than four times over, in extra profit saved by the milkman in 1991.
— There is some evidence that this effect led to reduced cancelling in the longer term which would mean further profit generated by the advertising.

CONCLUSIONS

We were given a very big task – to tackle what seemed a terminal decline within a £3.2 billion market. In only eight months we virtually halted this decline. Hopefully, with our advertising continuing, the milk industry may find a lasting solution to this problem.

There was no guarantee of success. A previous attempt to stem this decline (in 1984) targeted those who were about to cancel, with an exhortation not to 'let the milkman become a thing of the past'. There is no evidence that this had any effect. Only through the innovative strategy of targeting prevention rather than cure and through outstanding creative advertising, do we believe it was possible to achieve such remarkable results.

POSTSCRIPT

This case is based on 1991 data. In 1992 we continued to run the 'Daybreak' campaign. All the data so far indicate that the advertising has continued to be just as successful and profitable in its second year as it was in its first.

2

The Rejuvenation of Kellogg's All-Bran

INTRODUCTION

This is a classic study of advertising copy effectiveness. After several years of rapid sales decline, a new campaign which completely re-positioned the brand was developed. Sales responded immediately, with an equally rapid increase, whilst all other factors, such as price and distribution, remained essentially the same.

BACKGROUND

Kellogg's All-Bran was launched in the UK in 1922. In its early years the brand was supported by press advertising, positioning it as an aid to regularity and a cure for constipation. Whilst this has given the brand a tremendous heritage, it also explains some of the negative imagery associated with All-Bran. Words such as 'old-fashioned', 'geriatric' and 'medicinal' come to mind, whilst a typical comment from projective techniques would be: 'an elderly librarian with a stringy bun'.

From the early 1970s, sales of the brand took off in line with healthier eating habits, finally peaking in 1983, after the launch of the F-Plan diet, which specifically mentioned All-Bran in its recipes.

For the next three years (1984–1986), sales were slightly down, but still remained buoyant. However, in 1987, sales declined by 11% and then continued to fall, by 7% in 1988 and by 10% in 1989.

It was clear that the brand was in serious trouble and a major analysis and strategic development programme was put in hand, in order to stem the decline in sales.

THE PROBLEM

Kellogg's All-Bran is a type of cereal known as a 'shredded bran'. Whilst there are no branded direct competitors, most of the multiples have an own label copy of the product.

However, from a consumer point of view, All-Bran competes with all the bran/fibre cereals in the market of which there are many including Kellogg's Bran Flakes, Bran Buds, Sultana Bran and Fruit 'n' Fibre (launched 1984) as well as Weetabix Farmhouse Bran (now replaced by Oat and Bran flakes) and the own label variants of these cereals.

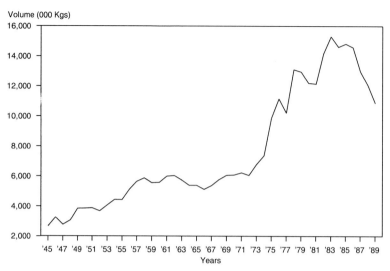

Figure 1. *All-Bran volume 1945–89*
Source: Kellogg

In addition, other cereals such as muesli, Weetabix and especially Shredded Wheat (because of its fibrous texture) are seen by consumers as good sources of fibre.

Additionally, outside the breakfast category, as healthy eating continued to increase in importance, the number of foods within supermarkets labelled as 'high fibre' or 'higher fibre' continued to grow.

On the one hand, therefore, All-Bran had been helped by the drive towards healthier foods, but, on the other, this trend had also led to increasing competition both from the development of additional competitive brands and from existing fibre foods, upweighting their support behind a stronger 'health/fibre' positioning.

This is seen very clearly by looking at the bran/fibre cereal market, as a whole.

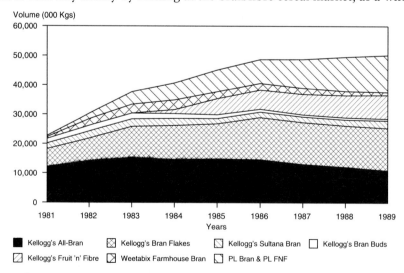

Figure 2. *Bran/fibre sector 1981–89*
Source: Kellogg

Whilst the total bran/fibre cereal market grew from 1981-1989, All-Bran's share declined steadily from 1986 onwards. This was partly due to an increase in sales of own label shredded brans, but the biggest effect came from the increase in sales of Kellogg's Bran Flakes and Fruit 'n' Fibre.

This also coincided with an increasing consumption of other foods which people perceived as being high in fibre such as brown/wholemeal bread.

TABLE 1: CONSUMPTION OF WHITE/BROWN BREAD
(Oz per Person per Week)

	1981	%	1989	%
White	21.85	(80)	15.32	(66)
Brown/wholemeal	5.56	(20)	7.77	(34)
	27.41	(100)	23.09	(100)

Source: NFS

It appeared that the problem was not one of declining interest in fibre. Consumers were eating more bran/fibre cereals than ever, as well as more of the foods that are seen to be high in fibre such as brown and wholemeal bread.

So why were our increasingly fibre-conscious consumers not choosing Kellogg's All-Bran to satisfy their requirements? To answer this question we needed to look in detail at our consumers.

THE CONSUMER

The data bore out our image of the typical All-Bran eater. Approximately two-thirds of the volume was eaten by women and half the volume was eaten by those over 60. Additionally All-Bran is relatively more important in AB and E households.

TABLE 2: PROFILE OF KELLOGG'S ALL-BRAN VOLUME
BASED ON HELPINGS

	1986 %	1989 %
Male	30	37
Female	70	63
Under 21	6	5
21–34	13	11
35–44	10	10
45–59	23	24
60+	48	49
Total	100	100

Source: RBL Consumption Study

TABLE 3: VOLUME OF KELLOGG'S ALL-BRAN INDEXED TO
VOLUME OF ALL RTEC PURCHASED BY HOUSEHOLDS

	1986	1989
AB	107	111
C1	112	100
C2	82	79
D	92	91
E	122	137

Source: AGB (TCA)

Our hypothesis was that during and after the F-Plan period (1983–1986), a different type of user was attracted to All-Bran. This user was younger, female and C1C2.

The comparison of 1989 with 1986 in Tables 2 and 3 does support this hypothesis. It appears that, as the excitement associated with the F-Plan diet calmed down, the brand reverted back to its older (E) profile, and the ratio of female to male eaters declined slightly.

As Table 4 shows, the decline in sales between 1986 and 1989 coincided with a decrease in penetration and a worrying decline in the number of 'heavy' and 'medium' buying homes.

This pattern is either explained by a general trading down to fewer packets, with some of the light users dropping out of the brand and/or heavy and medium users switching away completely from All-Bran to other brands.

The decline in heavy users (either because of trading down or because they had switched completely to other brands) suggests that even committed users of the brand were switching to other fibre foods to supply their fibre needs.

TABLE 4:   PENETRATION AND WEIGHT OF PURCHASE

	1986	1989
Cumulative penetration (%)	18.9	13.6
Average number of purchases per buying home	4.9	4.3
Profile of buying homes by purchase level		
Heavy (16+)	6.2	4.6
Medium (7–15)	18.0	16.5
Light (1–6)	75.8	78.9
Total	100.0	100.0
Profile of volume in buying homes		
Heavy (16+)	30.5	24.1
Medium (7–15)	37.7	41.9
Light (1–6)	31.7	34.0
Total	100.0	100.0

Source: AGB (TCA)

Finally, in 1989, a programme of group discussions with consumers and potential consumers of all ages, helped to throw light on how All-Bran was viewed. It was clear that the majority of people, who are interested in healthy eating believe they are personally eating enough fibre. Respondents were very satisfied – even complacent – that their habitual cereal, plus fresh fruit and vegetables and some other 'whole' food in the day (eg bread or jacket potatoes) gave them ample fibre.

Not only were consumers, typically, well-satisfied with the level of fibre in their diet; they also believed that all bran cereals and indeed, all 'healthy' cereals including muesli, Weetabix and Shredded Wheat were equally good sources of fibre.

'For all their knowledge about the ground rules of diet, specific information was far shakier or absent, and only the few All-Bran loyalists, were aware of differing fibre ratios between "bran" cereals.' (Nidus Research)

This meant of course, that, since consumers felt that all bran cereals gave more or less the same level of fibre (and, in any case, the fibre level in their diet was already high thanks to their switch to brown bread and inclusion of more fruit and vegetables in the diet), they were turning to the tastier cereal options.

'Consequently, products which disguised or dressed up the bran were very much preferred, accounting for the relative popularity of Bran Flakes and Fruit 'n' Fibre.' (Nidus Research)

There was no question of consumers no longer wanting fibre or seeing it as important. This was also confirmed quantitatively by the National Health Survey (Q3, 1989) where fibre, as an important component of healthy food, was rated 4.65 (on a 5 point scale) second only to vitamins at 4.69. This meant that there was no need to educate consumers as to the benefits of fibre, since they already appreciated its role in regularity and general health/well-being. (In fact, when we pushed more benefit-orientated roles in research, such as disease prevention, these were rejected as over-claims for a breakfast cereal.)

THE ADVERTISING

All-Bran advertising in the 1980s associated All-Bran with fibre, rather than differentiating it from other 'fibre' foods.

This worked during the early 1980s when the fibre craze was at its height, but, after 1986, when people were choosing tastier fibre alternatives, the benefits such as 'keeping you fit on the inside', 'making up the one-third of fibre missing from the average persons diet' and the attempt to associate the fibre in All-Bran with a general positive outlook on life (eg the 'Granny' commercial in 1988) were too generic to give consumers reasons to choose All-Bran vs other fibre foods.

SUMMARY OF THE PROBLEM

From the mid-1980s, although consumers still wanted the benefits of fibre, they were switching from All-Bran to other foods which they felt contained as much fibre as All-Bran, but were a lot tastier.

THE NEW STRATEGY FOR ALL-BRAN

When Leo Burnett began working on the brand in 1989 the planning process that was set in motion quickly established one key fact about All-Bran, which had not been used strategically before in television advertising:

All-Bran contains a lot more fibre than most of the other foods which people perceive as being high in fibre.

Tables of comparison were drawn up giving examples, such as the fact that to get as much fibre as in a single bowl of All-Bran, you would have to eat:

—   9 slices of brown bread
—   21 new potatoes
—   8 bananas etc.

When tested in research this strategy generated tremendous interest. The new information that it contained explained All-Bran's superiority and gave respondents a rational reason to choose the brand instead of other perceived 'high fibre' foods, even if they actually preferred the taste of these foods.

The rational reason was, importantly, complemented by a tone of voice, which normalised All-Bran, by positioning it in the context of other everyday foods:

'It was flattering to its loyalists, as not being freaky, sick or old.' 'It makes it seem familiar.' 'Nothing peculiar in that lot.' (Nidus Research)

The new strategy made people re-think their view of the brand. In this case, we communicated that All-Bran contains a lot more fibre than most other perceived high fibre foods.

Firstly, whatever they personally believed was the benefit of fibre, All-Bran could deliver that benefit.

Secondly, this route highlighted the extreme convenience of All-Bran as a fibre provider.

Thirdly, it threw into relief their lack of real knowledge about fibre intake, the comparative lack of fibre in many foods and, consequently, their own mistaken complacency regarding the amount of fibre that they obtained from their diet.

'I thought I knew everything about diet – it's shaken me.' (Nidus Research)

The results for this route from the strategic research (which also examined a number of other possible strategic options) were so positive that we proceeded to a creative brief.

CREATIVE BRIEF

Role of Advertising

Principally to attract new and lapsed users to the brand, by positioning All-Bran as the 'Gold Standard' in fibre provision.

Target Market

All adults who believe that fibre is important in the diet, but who currently obtain their fibre from other sources than All-Bran, such as brown bread and fresh fruit and vegetables. These people over-estimate the amount of fibre in these foods and are therefore complacent about the amount of fibre in their diet.

Desired Consumer Response

I didn't realise that All-Bran could give me so much more fibre than the other so-called high fibre foods that I have been eating. I need to eat All-Bran to make sure I am getting enough fibre.

Consumer Proposition

Kellogg's All-Bran contains a lot more fibre than most of the other foods which people perceive as being high in fibre.

Support

There is as much fibre in a bowl of All-Bran as in nine slices of brown bread.

Executional Guidelines

Appeal to a broad target audience, all adults 25+.

Initially three executions were developed comparing All-Bran to nine slices of brown bread, eight bananas and 21 new potatoes. Later in 1990, two further ads were made comparing All-Bran with eight bowls of brown rice and five portions of cabbage. In 1991, there were two new executions, comparing All-Bran with eight carrots and six brown bread rolls.

MEDIA

Television was chosen for its impact and its ability to reach a broad target market (in this case, all adults 25+).

All executions are 20 seconds in lengths and each burst generally rotates three commercials, in order to help show that All-Bran is a superior source of fibre compared to many everyday 'high fibre' foods.

Comparing 1990/1991 with 1989 (Table 5) we see:

—   A different campaign/copy strategy
—   20 second instead of 30 second commercials
—   Rotation of commercials instead of one per burst
—   A change of buying strategy (all adults 25+ vs women over 45)
—   Absolute TVRs up 30 to 40%

However, 30 second TVR equivalents were up only about 5–11%, so the success of the new campaign cannot be explained simply by an increased media weight argument.

KELLOGG'S ALL-BRAN BROWN BREAD
TV SCRIPT

VISION   **SOUND**

OPEN ON A CLOSE UP OF TOASTER WITH A SINGLE SLICE OF BREAD IN IT. WE THEN SEE A FEMALE HAND PLACE A SECOND SLICE OF BROWN BREAD INTO THE GRILL.

½ second silence.

MVO: It's a fact that nine out of ten people still aren't eating enough fibre.

WE THEN START TO PULL BACK TO REVEAL NINE SLICES OF BREAD AS THE HAND DEPRESSES THE LEVER THAT LOWERS THE BREAD INTO THE TOASTER.

So it's worth knowing that in every bowl of Kellogg's All-Bran there's about as much fibre as you'd find in nine nutritious slices of brown bread.

THIS IS NO ORDINARY TOASTER. IT HAS BEEN EXTENDED SO THAT IT CAN CONTAIN NINE SLICES OF BREAD IN A LONG LINE.

SUDDENLY THE TOASTER POPS AND ALL NINE SLICES LEAP INTO THE AIR.

OUR CAMERA FOLLOWS THEM AND THEN CUTS TO A SHOT OF AN EMPTY CEREAL BOWL BESIDE A PACKET OF KELLOGG'S ALL-BRAN.

THE NINE SLICES THEN LAND NEATLY IN THE BOWL AND WE FREEZE THE FRAME.

Kellogg's All-Bran.

A great fibre provider.

TABLE 5: KELLOGG'S ALL-BRAN MEDIA

	Women over 45 TVRs	30 second equivalent women over 45 TVRs	TV spend £000	Press spend £000
1989	2,313	2,313	2,519	415
	Adults 25+ TVRs	30 second equivalent adult 25+ TVRs		
1990	3,223	2,578	3,520	—
1991	2,972	2,437	3,483	—

The campaign is planned nationally on equal impacts by region. Our evaluation of its effectiveness·is therefore based on its overall national performance.

EVALUATING THE EFFECTIVENESS OF THE ADVERTISING

At the time of writing (April 1992), the campaign has been running for two years and three months.

SALES

In simple terms, the oil tanker has been made to perform a U-turn. Volume which was declining at the rate of around 10% pa, increased by 8% in 1990 and by 14% in 1991. (Source: Kellogg ex-factory sales.)

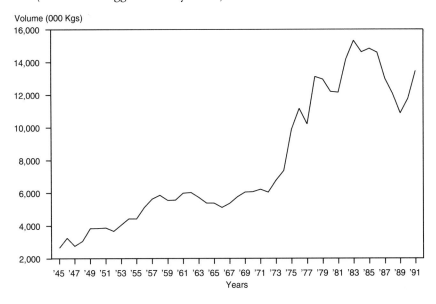

Figure 3. *All-Bran volume 1945–91*
Source: Kellogg

The success continues into 1992, with sales for Q1 holding at similar levels to those for Q1 1991.

In share terms, All-Bran's volume share has increased from 3.2% of all ready-to-eat cereal at the end of 1989 to 3.8% at the end of 1991, indicating that it is growing well ahead of the market.

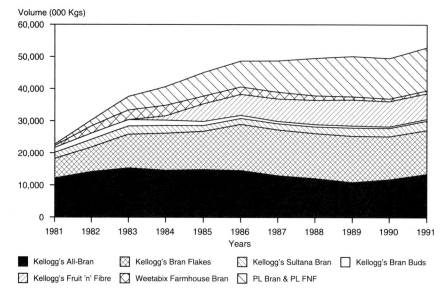

Figure 4. *Bran/fibre sector 1981–91*
Source: Kellogg

All-Bran has gained volume, firstly at the expense of own label bran shreds.

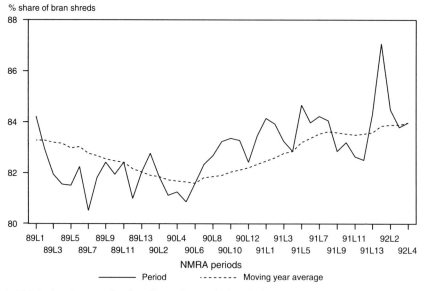

Figure 5. *NMRA volume share – total market Kellogg's All-Bran within bran shreds sector*
Note: NMRA designates 13 four-weekly periods L1 to L14 each year.

Secondly, All-Bran's extra volume has come from the tastier bran cereals such as Bran Flakes.

THE CONSUMER

In developing our new strategy, we were keen to attract younger people (under 60) to the brand.

The data that we have from our consumption study suggest that overall penetration has increased.

TABLE 6

	Oct 87– Sept 88	Oct 88– Sept 89	Oct 89– Sept 90	Oct 90– Sept 91
% of households with brand in-stock during week	13	12	12	13
% of total who are All-Bran eaters during week	2.5	3.0	2.7	3.3
% of 21–34s who are All-Bran eaters	1.1	1.7	1.8	2.8
% of 35–59s who are All-Bran eaters	2.9	3.8	2.8	3.6
% of 60+s who are All-Bran eaters	5.2	6.0	5.6	6.2

Source: Kellogg RI Consumption Study

The period Oct 90–Sept 91 on the Consumption Study, was the first period on the study where the campaign was running for a full year. This shows in Table 6 that the proportion eating All-Bran in an average week, has increased significantly since the campaign began. This increase is particularly marked for 21–34s. The data in Figure 6 also show marked increases in per capita consumption amongst the 21–54 age groups.

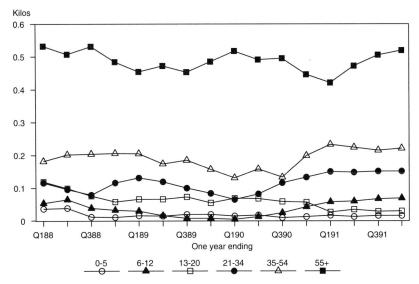

Figure 6. *Per capita consumption by age (All-Bran)*
Source: Kellogg

The campaign had attracted younger consumers to the brand and encouraged those who were eating to eat more All-Bran.

Our regular All-Bran users were not the principal focus of the advertising, but they obviously constitute an important secondary target. It is clear from the data that although the increase in sales has come mainly from new users, the campaign has maintained usage amongst our previous loyalists. This we would expect, as these people already appreciate the benefits of the brand and its superior fibre provision. Comparing the volume consumed in 1991 vs that in 1989, it is up 54% amongst 21–34s, 45% amongst 35–54s and 10% amongst those over 55 (Source: RI Consumption Study and Kellogg estimates).

In order to find out exactly how the campaign was working, a number of research studies were conducted.

A quantitative tracking study showed that the calibration was clearly being communicated. On average, across the total sample, people believe that more of the alternative 'high fibre' food is now required to equal the equivalent fibre to that found in a bowl of All-Bran.

TABLE 7

	Pre-advertising Jan 1990	Post-advertising Mar 1991
Amount with equivalent fibre to a bowl of All-Bran:		
Slices of brown bread	3.1	5.4
New potatoes	4.1	7.2
Bananas	2.9	4.3

Source: NOP Omnibus

Group discussions carried out by Linda Jones in May 1991 concluded that the campaign potentially worked in a number of ways:

1. Awareness: The campaign acted as a reminder about fibre generally, and All-Bran in particular.
2. Positions All-Bran as the gold standard for fibre: it dramatises All-Bran's superiority as a fibre provider, differentiating it from other fibre foods. In this way, it can challenge consumers' complacency regarding the fibre spectrum and the foods that they are eating.
3. Suggests other benefits for All-Bran: these are notably, convenience and the possibility of it having a role in slimming.
4. Imagery: consumers recognise that this advertising is not directed at the old, nor does it have an old-fashioned feel.

Importantly, it is seen to be an essential adjunct to health generally rather than simply an aid to regular bowel function. It also positions All-Bran alongside other foods, as a brand for sensible eating, rather than a medical solution.

There is thus plenty of feedback from our data on consumers and the research that we have conducted with them to believe our campaign is working. This is supported by the remarkable turn around in sales coinciding with the start of the campaign. However, we now need to look at all other possible factors which could have influenced the result.

The Marketplace

Throughout the period in question (1986–1991), sales of all ready-to-eat cereals grew consistently at an average 3% pa. All-Bran's sales pattern of sharp decline, followed by sharp upturn, was clearly out of line with this. Its sales pattern is not in line with the market.

Similarly, if we focus on the bran/fibre sector of the market (as in Figures 2 and 4) there has been a steady increase in sales, whilst All-Bran's share has rapidly declined and then increased.

Finally, amongst the direct own label competitive 'bran shreds' there has been no withdrawal of brands which would help to account for All-Bran's sales bouncing back.

The Product

Kellogg are always striving to improve the quality of their brands and small changes are constantly made to upgrade their products. However, it is fair to say that All-Bran as a product has remained essentially unchanged.

Packaging

Again, Kellogg constantly review the packaging for each brand, and the All-Bran pack front did undergo minor revisions in 1990. (Back and side panels are always changing, depending on which promotions are on offer.)

However, again it is difficult to believe that this has significantly affected sales.

Price and Distribution

Kellogg's All-Bran is a relatively cheap cereal. Its price indexed to the price of all ready-to-eat-cereals (RTEC) stands at about 80.

During the campaign, All-Bran's price relative to both all RTEC and specifically to own label Bran shreds has increased. This indicates that the sales effect has not been achieved by dropping the price. The campaign appears to be adding value to All-Bran so that sales are increasing despite the relative price rising.

All-Bran has always had high distribution, with little variation.

On commonsense grounds, therefore, price and distribution changes cannot explain the recovery of the brand.

Consumer Brand Equity

Consumer brand equity was explained by Simon Broadbent in 'Using data better' in *Admap*, January 1992.

It is the sales share the brand would have had if its price and distribution had been average (and its elasticities were also average). In other words, it shows how consumers value the brand over and above price and distribution effects:

Equity = Share/(Price effect and distribution effect)

The plot of equity in Figure 7 is very like that of All-Bran volume share. It confirms that an upturn started in the first quarter of 1990, with our first burst, and the trend is now upwards.

It is concluded that the recovery of All-Bran can be attributed only to the new advertising, which resulted in extra value being added to brand.

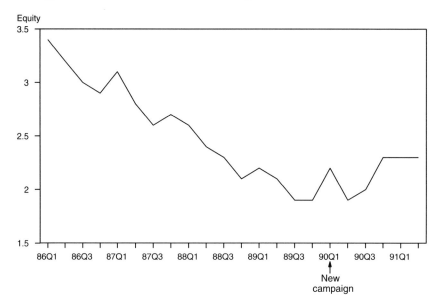

Figure 7. *All-Bran consumer brand equity*

Trade Promotions

Kellogg regularly organise focus periods for their brands with the trade, in which extra in-store display and prominence is achieved.

For All-Bran there was in fact no focus period in 1990. Thus focus periods do not explain the sales improvement that we have seen.

Consumer Promotions

A consideration of the sales promotions run in 1988 and 1989, with those run in 1990 and 1991, suggests no significant effects due to consumer promotions, as they were of a similar level and quality before and after.

In any case, the main effect of non-advertised promotions is to encourage regular eating amongst users and to help protect the brand from own label shredded brans. It is unlikely that promotions could generate the increased penetration, amongst younger consumers, that we have seen for the brand.

Regionality and Seasonality

As a national brand, eaten (and advertised) all year round, there are no significant regional or seasonal effects which can be related back to advertising activity.

CONCLUSION

This case history demonstrates that it is not advertising per se which is effective, but specific strategic, creative and media solutions.

In summary, we can show that a change of All-Bran campaign, has led to a radical up-turn in sales for a brand that was in long-term decline.

No other significant changes took place at this time, either within the marketplace or within the marketing of the brand itself.

In developing the new campaign, our strategy required us to attract younger consumers to the brand, who were either non-users or lapsed users. The increase in penetration of All-Bran amongst younger age groups confirms our success in adopting this strategy. At the same time, in research, the consumers themselves tell us that the advertising works as we wanted it to. Rationally, it presents All-Bran as the superior fibre provider, challenging their complacency about the level of fibre provided by other foods in their diet. Emotionally, it positions All-Bran as younger, and an everyday food (rather than an old-fashioned medical problem-solver).

The campaign not only attracted younger consumers; regular All-Bran users also remained with the brand.

Finally, in terms of profit for The Kellogg Company, All-Bran was able to contribute a greater percentage in 1991 than in 1989, confirming the value of the new campaign in supporting the brand.

3

'I Never Read *The Economist*'

INTRODUCTION

The Economist's advertising campaign, 1988–1991, has been one of the most discussed and commended poster and press campaigns of the period. The distinctive style and the biting wit of the captions has been widely noted and, indeed, awarded. This paper will demonstrate that the campaign has not only been noticed but has actually contributed to the business at a time when, given the economic climate, quite the opposite might have been feared. This case history is quite remarkable given the discretionary nature of *The Economist*. In times of severe recession the publication has not only fought off decline but has actually shown growth. This is almost entirely attributed to a distinctive and relevant campaign which, despite a climate of fear and cutbacks, was bravely continued and which paid dividends.

There are no real competitors for *The Economist*, being one of the only UK based, serious news and analysis weekly publications. Similar weekly publications such as *Business Magazine* and *Investors Chronicle* have been forced to close or have faced huge losses during the recession. In this paper, therefore, we have used the quality press as 'the competition'. This is actually quite tough competition as daily or Sunday papers are generally considered a necessity, whilst *The Economist* has always been an additional or discretionary read. In tough times, one might expect *The Economist* to suffer more than other newspapers and to follow the demise of other weekly reads. As we shall show, this is not the case at all.

The case is built on evidence to show that income from additional circulation along with that from additional advertising revenue more than paid for the advertising. In both cases, the performance of *The Economist* has been compared with the trend in the rest of the quality papers' market* in order for figures to be calculated. It is important to note that no other factors changed during the campaign period which might account for the success, and possible variables, other than advertising, are discussed later on in this section.

* The papers included in the 'quality press' are: *The Times, The Independent, The Guardian, The Daily Telegraph, Financial Times, The Sunday Times, The Sunday Telegraph, The Observer*. The *Independent on Sunday* has been excluded as it was launched half way through the campaign period.

"I never read
The Economist."

Management trainee. Aged 42.

It's lonely at the
top, but at least there's
something to read.

The Economist

The Economist

The Campaign Strategy

The campaign strategy came, quite simply, from the consumer. We knew that *The Economist* was becoming inessential in the new era of instant information and electronic data sources. We also realised that in rational terms, reading a huge range of publications can yield similar information to *The Economist*. What we also found, however, in extensive qualitative research, was that there is a belief amongst businessmen that *The Economist* actually provides something different and extra – a cachet and a sense of knowing. There is a feeling that readers of *The Economist* do actually have a lead over non-readers and this emotional response formed the basis for the advertising strategy.

'It's the sort of thing you can get caught out on at dinner parties when your boss said "did you read so and so in *The Economist*" and you didn't.' (Banker, 1988)

We identified AB businessmen, particularly those with an international interest, as our target audience. The advertising objective was to increase readership by suggesting that the benefits of *The Economist* can give the businessman the edge in his business. The role of advertising was to increase readership and, in turn, to generate additional revenue through circulation and ad revenue increases. Even at the time this seemed ambitious as the recession was starting and ad revenues were in danger of falling. *The Economist* was becoming more and more marginalised not only as a read but also on advertisers' media schedules.

The intention was always to make the campaign highly impactful and clearly branded given the relatively low media spend vs the major newspapers. The campaign which emerged, based on the distinctive red logo, had wit and bite. It played heavily on emotional reasons to read the publication so developing a highly competitive positioning.

Media Strategy

Given our target audience, the campaign was to run posters on cross tracks, and in the national quality press from the autumn of 1988. In 1989 the campaign, which had included small tactical press ads and long copy cross tracks was refined, and the distinctive advertising style emerged supreme. Cross tracks were replaced with 48 and 96 sheet outdoor sites and tactical small space ads in the press were discontinued. The media laydown, in brief, is shown below.

Media Plans

The Economist campaign ran on posters and in the press.

1. Posters:
    48 and 96 sheet high quality sites in London and in the major regional towns.
2. Quality national press:
    Colour pages in the *Financial Times*, *The Times* and *The Independent*
    DPS mono in colour supplements in 1988 only
    Small, tactical ads in the *Financial Times* and *The Times* from 1988–90.

For the sake of consistency, we have used Advertising Association (AA) adjusted MEAL expenditure figures throughout this paper for press spend. Poster spend figures are provided by Concord-Posterlink, so should be accurate. The figures in Table 1 are the entire laydown of monies for *The Economist* campaign from 1988–1991.

TABLE 1: CAMPAIGN SPEND (£000)

	Posters	Press (adjusted MEAL/AA)	Total spend
1988	85	225	310
1989	330	304	634
1990	720	863	1,583
1991	815	415	1,454
			3,981

Sources: MEAL, AA, Concord-Posterlink, AMV

Variables Other Than Advertising

This campaign did not surround a new product launch, or indeed, a relaunch. It was a new campaign for an existing product which had often been supported in the past. What we had was an existing brand where the only variable to change was the advertising campaign. Other factors have been examined and are discussed below:

— The nature of the publication, where no significant changes took place. A new editor in 1988 generated momentum and improvements but fundamentally the publication changed little.
— Cover price increased slightly in excess of inflation, but this will be allowed for in the calculations.
— Distribution, which was definitely facilitated as a result of the advertising, but was not approached in a different way. There was no change in methodology nor were new avenues opened during the campaign period.
— Ad sales methodology, which was greatly improved during the campaign period by training and re-organisation. It was facilitated by the powerful advertising.
— Trade press advertising, which may well have encouraged ad sales. At £30K it was not a significant factor in the financial equation but it did support the campaign amongst media buyers and advertising managers. Informal research amongst these people over the past three years in interviews and discussions has revealed a very high awareness of the total campaign, though it is impossible to isolate the trade press element. The trade campaign deliberately adopted the consumer style to maximise impact and fully alert the trade to the consumer campaign.

Money talks, but sometimes it needs an interpreter.

The Economist

An election promise from The Economist. We'll tax nothing but your intelligence.

Insider reading.

The Economist

MEASURES OF SUCCESS

There are several ways in which to evaluate this campaign. The main evidence for success which will be presented pertaining to circulation and ad sales revenue, comes from published and authoritative sources. Both of these grew substantially during the campaign period – generating sufficient additional revenue to pay for the campaign.

We can be confident that the additional income was due to the advertising as other factors have already been excluded. We can also look at the trends in awareness of the campaign and readership figures which both show a significant increase vs the market. These provide a clear basis for ad sales growth and circulation increases. The businessman, noticing and responding to the emotive encouragement to read *The Economist* was indeed purchasing and reading the publication. In turn, advertisers recognised this trend and spent their media money in *The Economist*.

In this section we will look briefly at awareness of the campaign and readership and then study, in closer detail, the ad sales and circulation figures which account for the financial success of the campaign.

Awareness of the Campaign

The impact of this campaign is so powerful that to deny its effect is impossible. In 1991, 37% of AB businessmen claimed to have seen the campaign on an *Economist* BMRB Survey. No other newspaper scored over 13% with the vast majority below 10% on the unprompted measure despite huge advertising spends. When prompted, ie when people were asked if they recognised the campaign when shown, the figure rose to an incredible 57%. The campaign has only run in quality newspapers with high visibility positions and the very best poster sites, both 48 sheet and, increasingly the more impactful 96 sheets.

The campaign has been noticed and digested due, presumably, to its relevant message, its distinctive style and its media placement.

Although we have no hard data, we know from qualitative work amongst media planners and indeed by discussion with the marketing fraternity that this campaign was highly visible. A small trade campaign along very similar lines ran in *Campaign* and *Marketing* magazines to reinforce the campaign. We have no doubt that decision makers, spending advertising money, noticed the campaign and registered both the message and the target audience.

Readership

Figure 1 demonstrates that *The Economist* significantly increased readership over the campaign period whilst almost all the other quality newspapers lost readers. We have plotted a few major competitors' performance against that of *The Economist* to demonstrate this clear trend. *The Economist* was the only quality paper to show a consistent upward trend over the campaign period.

These figures are echoed in the BMRC figures for 1988 to 1990 (the most recent available). Despite a huge increase in the BMRC universe, readership increased by 9.8% during the two year period, almost the only quality newspaper to show an increase. The next BMRC figures will not be available until 1993.

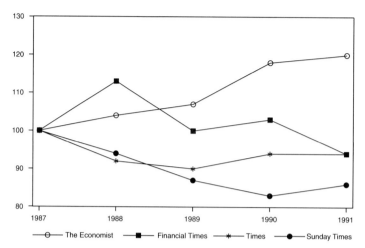

Figure 1. *Readership trends (index vs 1987)*
Source: AB TGI

The Economist also conducted a tracking study through BMRB, using a pre- and post-advertising methodology. Unfortunately we did not start the research until the second year of the campaign. However, we did find that not only did awareness of the campaign jump up but so did claimed readership. These figures were not significant but they showed a clear trend in the right direction.

In qualitative research we found a hugely positive reaction to the campaign. It clearly struck a chord with young ambitious businessmen who were anxious to achieve success. It was also enjoyed by current regular readers who felt part of the club of *Economist* readers and chuckled at the executions.

Circulation

During the campaign period, circulation of *The Economist* increased significantly faster than that of the market. Most of the quality papers actually decreased circulation whilst *The Economist* increased overall from 86,000 in 1987 (pre-campaign) to 98,000 in 1991, an increase of 14%. The only exception to the trend, as can be seen in Table 2, was *The Independent*, the newest publication in the group, and even this suffered a fall from 1990 to 1991.

TABLE 2: CIRCULATION TRENDS 1987–91

	1987	1988	1989	1990	1991
Economist	100	102	106	114	114
Independent	100	105	114	114	103
Sunday Times	100	105	100	93	92
Daily Telegraph	100	96	94	92	91
Guardian	100	95	94	92	89
Times	100	97	96	94	86
Financial Times	100	87	87	83	79
Sunday Telegraph	100	94	86	80	77
Observer	100	87	84	72	72

Source: ABC July to Dec figures (indexed on 1987)

In a market which contracted, *The Economist* actually gained circulation. In order to calculate the real levels of growth we need to compare the trend in the market with that of *The Economist*. The relevant figures are shown in Table 3.

TABLE 3:   CIRCULATION TRENDS

	1987	1988	1989	1990	1991
Market size (000)	5,550	5,404	5,182	5,280	4,928
Economist circulation	85,666	87,971	91,483	97,766	97,903
Economist share of market (index vs 1987)	100	104.5	113.3	118.9	127.5

Source: ABC

By indexing the figures we can easily compare the market with *The Economist*. The huge growth in *The Economist*'s share of the declining market can be seen.

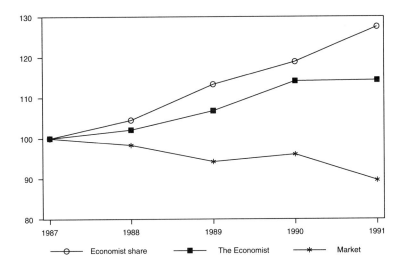

Figure 2. *Circulation trends (index vs 1987)*
Sources: ABC, AMV

By using the predicted circulation for *The Economist*, based on maintaining 1987 share in the market, we can calculate circulation gains each year for *The Economist* stripping out the effects of growth/decline in the market. These are shown in Table 4.

TABLE 4:   REAL ADDITIONAL CIRCULATION

	1988	1989	1990	1991
Circulation gains stripping out effect of market growth/decline	3,761	7,126	4,553	6,655
Annual gains	195,600	370,500	236,800	346,000

Sources: ABC, AMV

In order to calculate the financial gain from this additional circulation we need to make some estimates. We can assume that the majority of costs for production of *The Economist* are fixed. About 40% of the cover price goes to the trade and, we can assume, another 30% is used in variable costs such as postage. This leaves 30% of the cover price from these extra copies as pure income. As such, we can calculate the annual income from these additional copies during the campaign period (see Table 5).

TABLE 5: ADDITIONAL REVENUE FROM CIRCULATION

	1988	1989	1990	1991
Cover price	£1.30	£1.40	£1.50	£1.60
Assumed profit per additional copy	40p	42p	45p	48p
Annual additional copies	195,600	370,500	236,800	346,000
Additional income	£72,240	£155,610	£106,560	£166,080

During the campaign period we can assume that additional circulation generated £506,490 of additional income.

Advertising Revenue

Over the campaign period advertising sales increased dramatically from £14m in 1988 to £19m in 1991 (MEAL figures UK only). This achievement is quite exceptional given the depth of the recession particularly on advertising expenditure. It makes this case study all the more remarkable. The advertising played a major role in supporting the sales effort and so generating additional advertising revenue. It is acknowledged, by *The Economist* management team, to have created the right environment for the sales team to operate effectively.

> 'The campaign has proved a great success. Not only has it built awareness and usage but, importantly, it has played a major role within the marketing world. Our sales force has really benefited from this effect which has helped generate healthy advertising revenue in a difficult climate.' (Hugh McCahey, Director of Marketing Advertising)

In order to evaluate the real success of the campaign we need to look at trends in the quality papers' market in ad revenue and compare them with income at *The Economist*. This allows us to calculate the additional income for *The Economist* within the context of this market. To define 'the market' we have used the AA figures for revenue in quality newspapers and colour supplements. These are adjusted MEAL figures which have been reduced by an AA calculated factor in line with the 'true' ad revenue figures each year. They are the same figures that we used to calculate the campaign spend earlier on in the paper. These adjustment factors vary by year and are shown in Table 6.

Clearly, *The Economist* like any other publication, will not reveal the levels of discounting in their ad sales department. Industry sources, however, assure us that discounting at *The Economist* is almost non-existent and to use the same adjustment factors would be unrealistic. So we have made an estimate of 5% for

The Economist adjustment factors to produce 'real' income levels. These are in no way official levels but they reflect the strong feeling that discounting hardly takes place at *The Economist*.

TABLE 6:   ADJUSTMENT FACTORS FOR CALCULATING REALISTIC ADVERTISING REVENUE

	1988	1989	1990	1991
Adjustment factor for all quality press (used to calculate ad revenue for this sector by AA) %	26.6	28.8	31.1	35.0
Estimated adjustment for The Economist (used to calculate adjusted Economist ad revenue) %	5.0	5.0	5.0	5.0

Sources: AA, AMV

Using these figures we can now make a fair comparison between the market (quality press) revenue and that of *The Economist*.

We have assumed that the effect of the advertising could not be felt until 1989, three months after the campaign. Therefore we have looked at ad revenue from 1989 onwards.

TABLE 7:   AD REVENUE TRENDS

	1988	1989	1990	1991
Quality papers ad revenue (adjusted) £m	386.9	423.4	404.2	375.7
The Economist revenue (adjusted) £000	13,348	13,969	16,794	18,390
Economist share of market (indexed)	100	90.9	111.4	129.8

Sources: MEAL(adjusted), AMV

From these figures we can calculate the 'real' advertising revenue gains once the effect of the market growth/decline has been removed. What we see is that in 1989, the first full year of the campaign, the advertising seemed to be having little effect. *The Economist* remained loyal to the campaign and continued the slow build poster and press approach and in 1990 and 1991 it yielded results. The effect had not been immediate but it was strong and robust once initiated.

	1989	1990	1991
'Real' Economist ad revenue (removing effect of the market) £000	–£638	+£3,458	+£2,780

Ad revenue grew over the campaign period by £5,600,000

In calculating the effect of our campaign on advertising sales for *The Economist,* we have discounted MEAL figures by 5% which, we believe, is a realistic figure over the campaign period. It is further testimony to the power of the campaign that this was achieved at a time when recession forced competitors to increase their discount levels from 26.6% to 35.0%.

It is worth exploring what the effect on revenue might have been had *The Economist* been forced to increase its discount over the period. In the worst possible hypothetical scenario, that is, had *The Economist* been forced to match its competitors' price cuts year by year, pound for pound, the campaign would have only marginally fallen short of break even. The loss would have been £400,000 over a four year period. These calculations are included in the appendix. We reiterate that these levels of discounting were not experienced by *The Economist.* Indeed, few media buyers would find such a theory credible. *The Economist* does not discount in line with the market.

CALCULATING EFFECTIVENESS

In terms of payback, we can calculate the effectiveness of the campaign quite easily. The additional revenue from circulation and from ad revenue constitute the effect of the advertising and these must be balanced against the cost of the campaign.

Income (£)

Circulation revenue	506,490
Ad sales revenue	5,600,000
	6,106,490

Cost of Campaign (£)

Media	3,981,000
Production (est)	350,000
	4,331,000

The total surplus from the campaign was £1,775,490.

This case study has actually been extremely hard on *The Economist.* A different approach, and some might say a fairer one, would have been to compare the performance of *The Economist* with other quality UK based periodicals. Table 8 shows changes in ad revenue of some of these publications over the same period of time. If we had used these publications as 'the market' instead of the more robust quality press, the case study would have been even more 'impressive'. In a market that was collapsing in recession *The Economist* showed remarkable gains.

TABLE 8:   AD REVENUE FOR QUALITY PERIODICALS (£000)

	1988	1991	Change (%)
The Economist	14,051	19,358	+38
The Director	2,709	2,275	−16
Management Today	4,721	4,405	−7
Investors Chronicle	3,072	1,785	− 42
Business Magazine	2,993	—	—
Quality press (£m)	386.9	375.7	−3

Source: MEAL unadjusted figures, quality press adjusted figures

CONCLUSIONS

The case of *The Economist* is quite remarkable. In difficult times the circulation and ad revenue of *The Economist* grew enough to pay for the whole advertising campaign with nearly £2m of additional profit. This was achieved, not by product change or relaunch, but by a relevant, highly visible campaign that actually worked. It drove readership up when the product could have become less essential, drove circulation up when other papers saw falls and, most remarkably, grew ad revenue when media budgets were being cut especially at the margins.

APPENDIX

Hypothetical worst case scenario assuming *The Economist* was forced to match competitors' price cutting

	1988	1989	1990	1991
Market discount adjustment factor (AA) %	26.6	28.8	31.1	35.0
Achieved prices vs ratecard (indexed)	100.0	97.0	93.9	88.6
Hypothetical Economist discount levels (to match competitors' achieved prices) %	5.0	7.8	10.8	15.8
Adjusted Economist ad revenue £m	13.3	13.6	15.8	16.3
Gain/loss vs market £m	−	−1.1	+2.8	+1.6

Net gain over campaign period = £3.4m

Section Two

Longer and Broader Effects

4

Andrex – Sold on a Pup

INTRODUCTION

If a league table of Great British brands were to be compiled, Andrex would be there in the premier division, richly deserving its status as a 'Superbrand'. However, it must be said that intuitively it is strange that a brand of toilet paper should be in a position to achieve this accolade. The esteem in which this brand is held by consumers does not seem to fit with the esteem of the product and its function!

Our assertion in this paper is that this effect is due in a major part to a labrador puppy, who has appeared consistently in Andrex' TV advertising since 1972.

ANDREX' SUCCESS

Unchallenged Brand Leadership

Andrex is by far the biggest brand in its market, and has been since the early 1960s when soft toilet tissue became the norm.

No other brand has since then ever held a share in this market of over 12%.

In the period since the Puppy Advertising began in 1972, Andrex has increased its Nielsen volume share by just under 5% to over 30% (Figure 1).

The benefit of this strong share position in a market which has been growing consistently is shown in Figure 2.

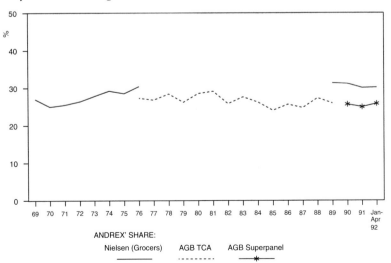

Figure 1. *Andrex' volume share, 1969-present*
Sources: AGB TCA/Superpanel, AC Nielsen

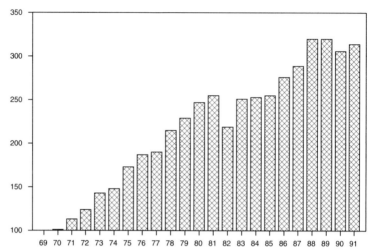

Figure 2. *Andrex' sales show strong and steady growth (1969-91 indexed on 1969)*
Source: Scott Ltd (1989 = 53 week year)

Currently Andrex is the UK's second biggest brand by value monitored on AGB Superpanel. Every day one and a half million rolls are sold in the UK.

Premium Price

Andrex is not only the biggest brand in the toilet tissue market it is also the most expensive product available. Figure 3 shows the growth in Andrex premium versus the market average since the beginning of the 1970s. It has on several occasions reached a premium of over 40% above the market average. This is even more remarkable when you consider that, perhaps following Andrex' lead, the premium sector of the market is growing. It now accounts for around 60% of the market – raising the average market price. This accounts for the apparent reduction in Andrex' premium in the most recent years.

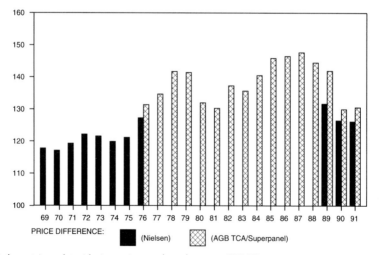

Figure 3. *Andrex sustains a substantial price premium over the market average (1969-91)*
Sources: AGB TCA/Superpanel, AC Nielsen (market average price = 100)

Rate of Sale

Andrex is the fastest selling brand in the market, selling considerably 'faster' than its competitors, as can be seen from the table below.

TABLE 1: WEIGHTED RATE OF SALE INDEXED ON ANDREX (1991 GB)

Andrex	100
Kleenex Velvet	39
Premium own label	56
Standard own label	49
Economy own label	46

Source: AC Nielsen

An important real life indication of the importance of this rate of sale is given by a recent incident involving a major multiple grocer.

Retailer intelligence tells us that brand leaders in all markets usually give the retailer the lowest margin per unit sold. Toilet tissue is no exception to this. However, when supply difficulties due to a fire at a depot forced Scott to allocate stock to retailers, one major multiple refused to accept reduced supplies of Andrex, and threatened to delist every other Scott brand it carried unless it received all the Andrex it wanted.

Loyal Buyers

Andrex buyers are particularly loyal, and increasingly so, as will be explored later. One-third of Andrex buyers *never buy any other brand of toilet tissue* (AGB Superpanel – 24 weeks ending December 1991).

Considerable Consumer Preference

Andrex is significantly preferred by consumers. Not only does the product itself perform well in blind product tests, it is markedly more preferred when branded *as Andrex* than as the unnamed product itself (Table 2).

TABLE 2: BLIND VS BRANDED PRODUCT TEST
Branded preference indexed on Blind preference

	Blind	Branded
Andrex	100	124
Kleenex Velvet	100	77

Source: Millward Brown 1992
Base: 400 (sequential monadic test)

This branded over blind preference effectively shows Andrex' 'added value' – that is the value attributed to a brand over and above its functional attributes. Bearing in mind the nature of the product, the size of this 'added value' is exceptional.

PUPPY ADVERTISING

Toilet paper is inherently a low interest, low anxiety product. For this reason it was felt at the outset that if advertising was to work effectively for Andrex it needed to create its own interest. A primary requirement for advertising on this brand would be that it should generate high awareness, and get noticed. It was also felt that it was an equally important requirement in this case that the advertising be liked. Recent evidence from the ARF in America (see A L Biel 'Love the Ad. Buy The Product?', Admap, September 1990) would seem to back up the wisdom of this stated objective.

The puppy has been central to both these requirements. Since his first appearance in 1972, he has developed into an extremely valuable brand property.

We believe there are four key ways the puppy benefits the Andrex brand in advertising. It will be seen that the performance of Andrex advertising is as exceptional as the performance of the brand itself.

Puppy Salience

Andrex advertising is exceptionally well-remembered. Andrex has a consistently strong presence in the Adwatch prompted recall chart in *Marketing* magazine, in spite of being outspent by most other brands in the top ten.

The Millward Brown 'Awareness Index' aims to discount the effect of media weight in measuring advertising awareness. Of all the brands monitored by Millward Brown, current Andrex advertising has one of the very highest Awareness Indices ever tracked (with an AI of 30). Millward Brown claim that current Andrex advertising is *eight* times more efficient than an average TV commercial in generating awareness.

Puppy Love

Andrex advertising is not only exceptionally noticed, it is also exceptionally popular. In *Marketing* magazine's Adwatch survey, an Andrex advertisement has twice been voted the public's favourite commercial of the whole year (in 1988 and 1991).

Millward Brown have also found Andrex advertising to be one of the most exceptionally liked campaigns they have ever tracked, with over 85% of respondents saying that they enjoy the advertising.

The combination of this exceptionally high likeability and the exceptionally high Awareness Index is unmatched by any other brand.

Puppy Metaphor

The puppy is central to these achievements and has come to be *inextricably* linked with Andrex. As well as demonstrating the length of the product, his softness and his strength make him a lovable and perfect metaphor for the brand and its qualities.

To illustrate how the puppy represents Andrex, Table 3 shows the rise in awareness attributable to a poster which, unusually, showed the puppy on his own – without the name Andrex or even any toilet rolls to be seen. This ran as a teaser before the launch of 'New Feel' Andrex in 1985, and we can isolate awareness levels *before* the branded posters appeared.

TABLE 3: PROMPTED RECALL OF ANDREX POSTER ADVERTISING

Pre-puppy poster 6/9/85	Post-puppy poster 30/9/85
12%	19%

Source: Millward Brown (Base: 400 per wave)
Note: No other poster advertising appeared for Andrex in this period.

Puppy Consistency

When an advertising campaign becomes tired or out of date, it ceases to be noticed and enjoyed. A continual process of revitalisation is necessary to maintain people's interest in (and thus the effectiveness of) a long-standing advertising campaign.

In Andrex' case the puppy and paper have appeared constantly now for 20 years. By continually updating the advertising whilst retaining these constants, Andrex advertising manages to achieve valuable consistency yet remains relevant to successive generations of toilet tissue buyers.

To illustrate this an abridged visual history of the Puppy Advertising is shown on the following pages, from the puppy's first appearance in 1972 to the current advertising.

PUPPY POSTER 1985 (TEASER FOR 'NEW FEEL' ANDREX LAUNCH)

PUPPY – 1972

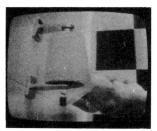 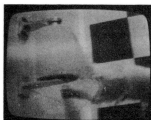 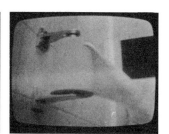

Music throughout

Male voice: JUST ABOUT
EVERYONE...

...LIKES ANDREX
BECAUSE...

 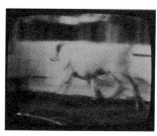 

...WELL IT'S SO...

...NICE AND SOFT...

...IT'S ALSO...

...VERY VERY STRONG...

....

...IT'S THIS SOFTNESS...

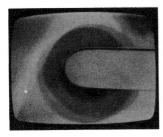

...AND STRENGTH OF
ANDREX...

...THAT MAKES IT
RATHER SPECIAL...

...BUT THERE'S
SOMETHING ELSE...

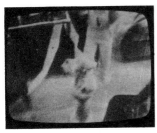

...ABOUT ANDREX...

...YOU MAY HAVE
NOTICED...

...IT APPEARS TO BE
LONGER...

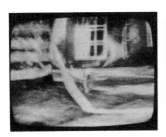

...THAN JUST ABOUT...

...EVERY OTHER...

...TOILET ROLL.

A SELECTION OF PUPPY ADVERTISEMENTS 1977–1988

Maze – 1977

Feathers – 1982

Animals – 1985

Jack – 1986

Big Basket – 1987

Re-Run – 1988

LITTLE BOY – 1991

Music throughout

boy; HELLO BOY

HEY

HA HA HA

HA HA HA HA

...

...

...

...

(shouts) MUM

fvo: SOFT AND STRONG
AND LONG ANDREX

(boy shouts) MUM!

HOW ANDREX ADVERTISING AFFECTS PEOPLE'S BEHAVIOUR

In the section above we have looked at intermediate measures of the effect of the Puppy Advertising on people. In this section we will look at two measures of the specific behavioural effects of this advertising, and thus work towards a demonstration of the way that Puppy Advertising has affected the performance of the Andrex brand.

Growing Loyalty

Figures 4 and 5 show two expressions of the growth in brand loyalty that has been achieved since the Puppy Advertising first appeared. The first of these uses data from AGB panels, and plots the growth in the proportion of Andrex buyers who buy the brand solus or give over 60% of their toilet tissue purchases to the brand. The second chart uses TGI data, which enable us to go further back in time to cover the whole period of the Puppy Advertising.

Both sources confirm the growing trend for Andrex to 'lock in' its brand users, thereby making them less vulnerable to competitive attack, as will be explored further later.

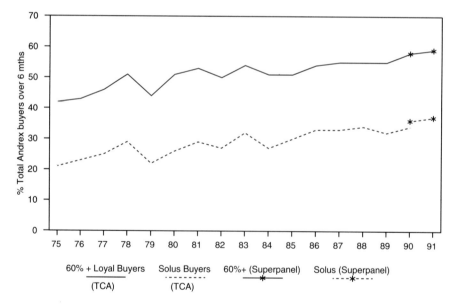

Figure 4. *Loyalty grows over time (% Andrex buyers giving over 60 % and 100% of their purchases to Andrex)*
Source: AGB TCA/Superpanel Data

The TGI data also offer us an opportunity to explore Andrex' performance on this dimension relative to other markets. There is, within marketing literature, a well-established acknowledgement of the relationship between brand loyalty and brand share. This view, that loyalty to a brand is largely a function of the 'size' of the brand, is most commonly associated with Professor Ehrenberg of The London Business School.

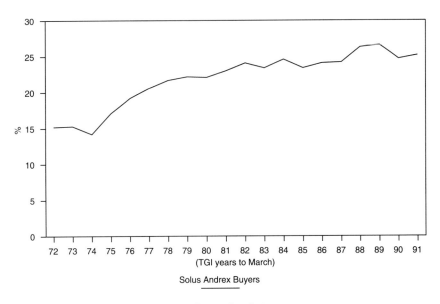

Figure 5. *Loyalty to Andrex grows over time (% housewives buying only Andrex)*
Source: BMRB TGI

Figure 6 highlights the relationship between solus usage of the manufacturer brand leader in all 104 housewife fmcg markets on current UK TGI, and overall housewife penetration. It also incorporates the equivalent toilet tissue figures from the US study produced by Simmons Market Research Bureau Inc.

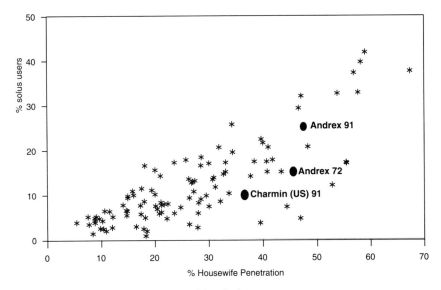

Figure 6. *The relationship between housewife penetration and claimed 'solus' use*
Sources: BMRB TGI (UK), Simmons Market Research Bureau (USA)

In 1972, before the start of the Puppy Advertising, Andrex had a relatively low level of solus usage for its overall housewife penetration.

We would suggest that this is because toilet paper is an intrinsically low interest market, so it is therefore reasonable to expect that housewives will buy from a range of brands, dependent on availability, price promotions etc. The 'exceptional' behaviour in this context is shown by the Andrex brand in 1991 (against the more expected performance of Andrex in 1972 and Charmin currently in the US).

Maintaining a Consistent Age Profile by Continually Recruiting New Users

The profile of Andrex users is very similar to that of the general population (as would be expected with nearly half the country's households buying), but the profile of its most loyal/solus users tends to be older. This is perhaps to be expected with a premium priced brand.

Table 4 shows the proportion of solus users in each demographic group as an index on the overall level of solus usership of Andrex. By removing the distraction of the growing overall percentage it is clear that there is little real change over 20 years.

TABLE 4: INDEX OF SOLUS USERS OF ANDREX

		1971	1981	1991
Age	15–24	77	80	95
	25–34	70	65	66
	35–44	75	74	81
	45–54	94	99	100
	55–64	120	127	117
	65+	138	132	132
No children		119	116	113
Children under 1 year		62	71	70
1–4 years		68	63	68
5–9 years		63	70	65
10–15 years		75	70	76

Source: BMRB TGI

The lack of change in these figures shows that a process has been continued whereby housewives grow in purchasing loyalty towards Andrex as they get older. This process shows a strong relationship with the presence (or rather the absence) of children.

Recruiting New Users

For this process to take place it is important that non-users of Andrex hold the brand in high esteem, since they must continually be recruited to usership. The following table shows the percentages of non-users (defined as 'not using Andrex nowadays') endorsing Andrex on key attributes.

TABLE 5: NON-USERS ATTITUDES TO ANDREX

Statement	% Endorsing
Best quality	57
Particularly soft	55
Really strong	60
Lasts longer than the others	47

Source: Millward Brown (Base: 386)

Whilst non-users endorse its quality they do not feel Andrex is, for them, worth buying at the moment. However it is critical for the brand long-term that these people are positively disposed to Andrex, as they are then likely to want to buy it when circumstances are more favourable.

THE PUPPY AS GUARD DOG
or How Advertising has Helped Andrex
Withstand Competitive Threats

We have seen how Puppy Advertising has increased loyalty to Andrex, by locking in an increasing number of buyers. In this section we will see how this has stood Andrex in good stead in terms of keeping at bay the various and considerable threats that have beset the brand in the past 20 years.

Own Label

As in most grocery markets, Andrex faces the considerable threat of the rise in retailers' own brands. Figure 7 shows the strong growth through the 1980s of own label toilet tissue. The chart also shows the share of own label products in the kitchen towel and facial tissue markets. Whilst own label share growth in toilet tissue has been strong, it is evident that relative to these other markets its impact has been contained. We contend that the greater containment of own label in toilet tissues is a direct effect of the high Andrex market share and the policy of continuous advertising. Neither kitchen towels nor facial tissues have a leading brand with over 15% volume share (half of Andrex' share) and advertising for these brands is, at best, sporadic.

Andrex' influence on the market is further shown, we would argue, in a more

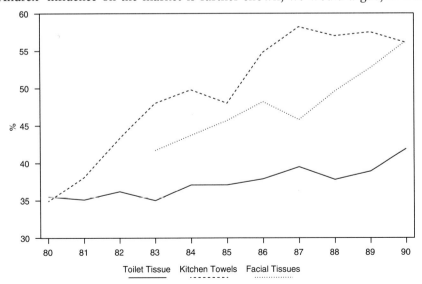

Figure 7. *The growth of own label*
Sources: AGB TCA (toilet tissue & kitchen towels), ICI Consumer Panel (facial tissues)

recent own label threat. Because of the buoyancy of the premium sector of the toilet tissue market, led by Andrex, there has in recent years been a proliferation of retailers' luxury or premium own label products. In 1988 these products accounted for 5.5% of the market by volume, in 1991 this had risen to 15.5% (AC Nielsen). These products compete more directly with Andrex than standard or economy own label toilet tissue. Andrex' share, however, remains buoyant.

Kleenex Velvet

Kleenex Velvet was launched by Kimberly-Clark in the early 1980s with the stated intention of overtaking Andrex to become the new brand leader. It has always been a high quality product, at launch it was preferred in blind product tests to the Andrex product of the time. Kleenex Velvet also looks cheaper on the shop shelf than Andrex, as it costs less per roll (however, Kleenex has only 240 sheets per roll, against Andrex' 280).

However, Andrex has more than successfully held Kleenex Velvet at bay, in spite of the fact that since launch over £23 million has been spent advertising the brand (advertising spends for both brands over the period are shown in Figure 8). Unlike the consistency of approach seen in Andrex advertising, though, this money has been spent on five very different campaigns, from animated 'fibremen' and endorsements from Frank Bruno to the current 'slice of life' campaign.

In terms of preference the difference in consumer perceptions of the brands is

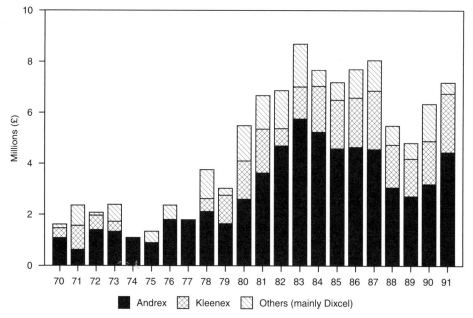

Figure 8. *Advertising spends in toilet tissue*
Source: MEAL: actual spends adjusted for media inflation (excludes moist toilet tissue)

well illustrated by the blind vs branded product test shown in Table 1. This indicates the *added* value attributed to Andrex, and the way that in consumers' minds Kleenex Velvet is significantly disadvantaged to Andrex.

The results speak for themselves. Before the launch of the Velvet product

Kimberly-Clark held 9.2% of the market (1980). By 1983, after swapping virtually all of their production into the new Velvet product, their share did rise, but only to 10.2%. This was to be the highest share the brand would achieve for the whole of the 1980s. In 1991 Velvet's share stood at 10.4% (AGB TCA/Superpanel, volume shares). Andrex' share has hardly been affected by Kleenex Velvet.

The Environment

'Green' issues made little or no impact on the toilet tissue market until 1989. However, by the end of 1991 'green' products, almost all of which are recycled products, had taken 20% of the market (Andrex is a non-recycled product) (Figure 9).

The spectacularly fast growth of this new category affected the whole market.

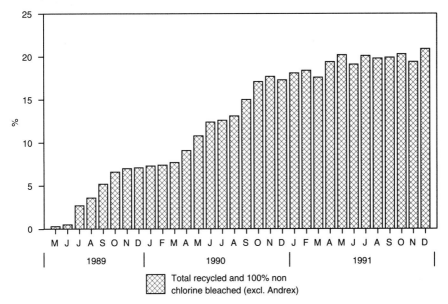

Figure 9. *The spectacular rise of 'green' products (volume share May 1989-Dec 1991)*
Source: AC Nielsen

As the biggest brand, Andrex arguably had the most to lose, but the brand's resilience has meant that this has not been the case. It could also be argued that this was the first time in the brand's history that Andrex had faced an *emotional* threat.

In spite of the fact that recycling has consistently been the biggest issue for consumers in this market, Andrex has always been seen as a more environmentally friendly brand than Kleenex (although Kleenex offers a recycled variant). Andrex ran advertising to explain that Scott are a major *planter* of trees to counter the recycling argument, but our assertion here is that the more significant advertising contribution to Andrex' defence was made by the strength of the brand's consumer franchise which effectively protected the brand.

These perceptions appear to have held sway as, in spite of early losses, Andrex has bounced back to the extent that in the most recent analysis of consumers' brand switching behaviour, Andrex was starting to take volume away from recycled products.

TABLE 6: ANDREX' GAIN/LOSS VS 'GREEN' (MAINLY RECYCLED) PRODUCTS

	%
1990	− 2.0
1991	+ 0.6

Source: AGB Gains/Loss Analyses

Successive Recessions

As a premium priced product, recession might be expected to affect Andrex adversely – when money is tight buying cheaper toilet tissue would seem an easy sacrifice to make. However, the indications are that Andrex suffers far less than one might expect.

During the recessions of the early 1970s, early 1980s and indeed in the current recession it would appear that whilst market growth slows, Andrex' share remains relatively stable and resilient, although its price premium is affected. This is shown by the slowdown during these periods in the growth of case sales (Figure 2), and similarly the relative fall in Andrex' price premium (Figure 3), although it should be noted that the absolute premium is still very strong in times of recession (falling to a low of 20% above the average market price in 1974, and 30% in 1981 and currently). (AGB TCA/Superpanel.)

ECONOMETRIC MODELLING

In 1974 Scott appointed O'Herlihy Associates (OHAL) to devise modelling for the Andrex brand. The objective was to find out more about what was influencing the brand's performance, and thus to help management make future decisions on budget allocation etc. OHAL Econometric Modelling has been running ever since, being updated and amended as new learning is acquired. The models are not therefore 'tailor-made' to help us tell our story here, but are 'live' marketing tools. It is, however, worth stating that it has always been OHAL's assertion that advertising is *the* key to the success of the brand.

The purpose of this section of the paper then is to look at how, through a greater understanding of the relationship between advertising and sales provided by the model, it has been possible to refine and enhance the effectiveness of the Puppy Campaign. To do this we will cite two specific tests which also give strong indications as to the overall sales effectiveness of the advertising.

1. *The Drip vs Burst Test*: 1976. For seven months, four TV regions (Granada, Trident (Yorks & Tyne Tees), South and Anglia) received more or less continuous schedules of 110 TVRs per month whilst four other regions (London, Midland, Harlech and Scotland) received a burst of 330 TVRs every third month.

    Three hypotheses were tested on the data. These were:

    — A convex response curve to advertising – implying drip better than burst
    — Constant return to scale
    — An S-curve – implying burst better than drip.

The convex curve was found to be best at explaining the data, and the sales difference between drip and burst was quantified at 5.0% or 6.2% of total sales depending upon which data set was analysed. Statistically the level of confidence that the convex curve hypothesis was better than the other two was in excess of 99%. This gives strong evidence that different schedules produced different sales effects, and by implication that Andrex advertising is sales effective.

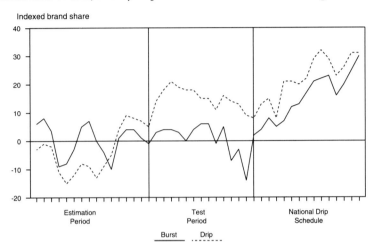

Figure 10. *The burst vs drip test 1976*

Proof of Scott's confidence in the findings is shown by the fact that drip schedules were introduced nationally from mid-1977. The annual profit benefit was calculated at that time to be in excess of £500,000 and was documented in an *Admap* article (January 1978) by the then Scott Marketing Manager, Jim Branton.

2. *The Upweight Test* – 1980/81. Three regions (Granada, Trident and Midlands) were upweighted from the average late 1970s level of 133 TVRs a month to 200 TVRs a month, as a result of an interpretation of the model which suggested that an increase in weight could increase sales profitably.

    The extra sales generated by this upweight were measured at 4% (at 85% confidence) above the sales of the control area (the rest of the country). Since the breakeven was less than 2% extra this was a very satisfactory result. Again the proof of Scott's confidence in the findings of this test is shown in the fact that as soon as money could be made available the whole country was upweighted to the new 200 TVRs a month level.

3. *The Current Model*. Modelling has of course continued since this test. The following quote, from a 1983 OHAL report, confirms the validity of these earlier findings.

    'Despite the continuous schedules being used on Andrex it is still possible to confirm the measurements on TV advertising. The measured maximum sales effect is 18% at 250 TVRs per month.'

Figure 11 shows graphically the fit achieved on the latest version of the model. The learning over 20 years is incorporated in this and reinforces the strength of advertising effect through, specifically:

1. A low exposure trigger (no more than two exposures a month are required)
2. A slow decay rate (a typical rate would be around 35% per month – the amount used by Millward Brown on their advertising model for example – Andrex' decay rate is nearer to 25%)

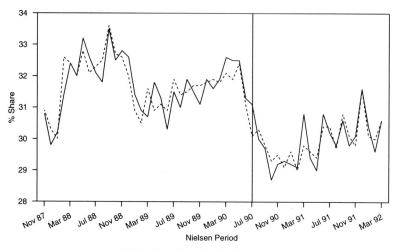

Figure 11. *Andrex market share (actual vs fitted)*
Sources: AC Nielsen (data change at July 1990 due to introduction of scanner data), OHAL

Currently it is estimated that in any one period, advertising accounts directly for between four and five share points of Andrex' 30% volume share: that is Andrex' share would drop by this amount if advertising stopped for a 12 month period (and that longer term the effects would be much greater).

ELIMINATING OTHER FACTORS

In order further to support our assertion that the Puppy Advertising has contributed so significantly to the exceptional performance of the Andrex brand it is necessary briefly to isolate and eliminate other factors which, it could be argued, could have made an equally significant or greater contribution.

Distribution

All the major brands in this market (Andrex, Kleenex, own label) enjoy near universal distribution. Rate of sale provides us with a measure of the rate at which different brands would sell were they to have equal distribution. As has been detailed earlier in Table 1, Andrex is far and away the fastest selling brand in the market on this basis.

Promotions

Promotions on Andrex can be divided into those which give extra value to the consumer (extra sheets, money off etc) and those designed to reward loyalty (collecting tokens for toy puppies etc). The former tend to produce short-term gains in share, which can be monitored, and their long-term significance discounted by econometric modelling. Since the growth in Andrex price premium over the average has been so significant since the Puppy Campaign began, it is clearly unlikely that the strong performance of the brand in this period was fuelled by value-giving promotions.

The effect of loyalty-rewarding promotions is in some respects harder to measure. However it is significant that had advertising not achieved its objectives of high awareness and popularity such promotions would not have been so successful.

The typical Andrex promotion of this type is a Puppy Calendar, Guide Dogs for the Blind Appeal, or the ever-popular soft toy. Scott estimate that they have so far despatched 450,000 toy Andrex puppies to admiring fans.

Product Quality

Product quality has clearly been fundamental to Andrex' success. In order, however, to isolate the effect of advertising for the purposes of this paper it is necessary to demonstrate that while actual quality is important, consumers' perceptions of Andrex quality exceed the reality.

With a daily production of one and a half million rolls, major innovation on Andrex is more problematical than it might be for a smaller brand, or perhaps was the case when Andrex itself was a smaller brand. However, this can be of help to us in making the case for the contribution of advertising, since we can see to what extent, if at all, perceived equality or a temporary disadvantage in product quality (inasmuch as it can be detected in blind product tests) affects consumers' *branded* preference.

At the time of its launch consumers preferred Kleenex Velvet to the Andrex product of the time in the blind product tests that Scott undertake on a regular basis. Kleenex Velvet was the result of new production techniques, and was very different from other products at the time. It was not until the launch of 'New Feel' Andrex in 1985 that statistically significant blind preference returned to favour Andrex. For these three years then it would therefore be fair to say that Kleenex Velvet was at worst equal to Andrex in product quality terms.

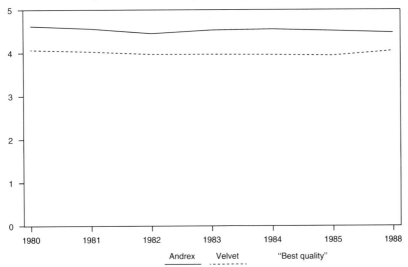

Figure 12. *Andrex seen as better quality than Kleenex Velvet (mean scores (0-5) 1980-88)*
Source: BMRB Attitude Monitor (Base: aware of each brand)

However, in spite of this, perceptions of Andrex were far more favourable than for the new Kleenex product, as can be seen from Figure 12. Throughout this period Andrex was preferred on every dimension to Kleenex Velvet, as it has been in every test that Scott have undertaken in this period. (Figures 13 and 14 provide examples of the earliest and the most recent tests on a general sample.)

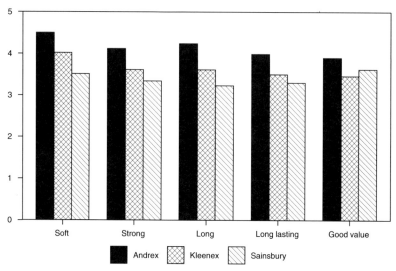

Figure 13. *Historically Andrex enjoys best image (brand images 1976 – mean score on 5 point scale)*
Source: BMRB Attitude Monitor (Base: aware of each brand)

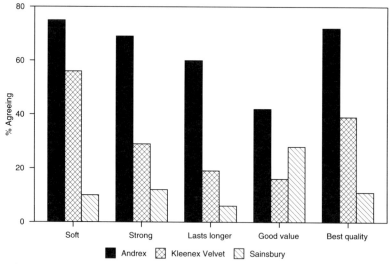

Figure 14. *Andrex enjoys the best image on all key discriminators (brand images 1990)*
Source: Millward Brown 1990 (Base: aware of each brand)

Packaging

Whilst a continual updating of Andrex' appearance on shelf is important to perceptions of the brand, we would submit that packaging preference alone could not account for the outstanding perceptions and performance of the brand since 1972.

Moreover, in a recent test when asked what in particular people liked about Andrex (unprompted), under 1% mentioned Andrex' packaging as a particular 'like' (Millward Brown 1992). Although it is notoriously difficult to get consumers to express accurately their basis for choice, we would submit that were packaging more of a factor it would be more salient than this.

Product Innovation

There have been few major innovations in the toilet tissue market since the beginning of the 1970s. Over the years pack sizes have become larger, colours have become softer, and product quality in terms of softness and strength has gradually improved.

Andrex has rarely been the first to brand to innovate (for the reasons discussed above). For example, Andrex was certainly not the first to sell a 9 roll pack, and only Kleenex Velvet and some own label currently have a larger 12 roll pack available.

Product innovation therefore does not appear to have been a significant factor in fuelling the growth of Andrex since the Puppy Advertising has been on air.

CONCLUSION

The Andrex Puppy Campaign began in 1972 and is a 'classic' example of the best of British advertising. It is exceptionally well-known and is probably the best loved campaign on a housewife target.

In evaluating its long-term effectiveness we have not had the luxury of being able to make comparisons with periods without advertising.

Throughout the last two decades the toilet paper market has grown substantially and Andrex has grown its share of it. At the same time it has always enjoyed a large, and for most of the 20 years a growing, price premium. Quantification of the total effect is not a simple matter, but the key points of our argument give an indication of the real benefits that Andrex advertising has brought to Scott:

1. As we have detailed earlier, toilet paper has not become a commodity market. This is exceptional bearing in mind:

    — the nature of the product
    — the development of related markets of facial tissues and kitchen towels where own label shares are significantly higher
    — the nature of toilet paper markets abroad.

    If we look at the development of other toilet tissue markets in Northern Europe, we can begin to see just how unusual the UK and Andrex are. In France, the biggest brand (Lotus) has a volume share of under 16%, and sells at a premium of only 19% above the market average. In Germany, the biggest brand is Bess, which has a volume share of only 11%, whilst own label has 67% of the market.

These examples highlight the benefit to Scott in being able to sustain a premium price for a premium product. Price realisation, effectively a measure of inherent profitability, is higher in the UK than in any other toilet tissue market in the world. We would contend that it is largely the influence of Andrex and its advertising that has given rise to this situation.

2. Andrex is the 'Gold Standard' toilet paper and is seen by housewives to dominate its competitors on all quality dimensions. The superiority of the brand over the product is a true indicator of added values created by advertising.

3. Whilst Andrex is not environmentally 'unfriendly', its 'green' credentials are more complex and harder to grasp than for recycled products. However, the great respect for Andrex, built through advertising, has given it the benefit of the doubt among most housewives and it has been able to retain share against the growth of recycled brands.

4. Throughout the two decades of Puppy Advertising, more and more Andrex buyers have switched to buying just this one brand. In addition, new users have joined them as they pass through the less well-off years with children.

   We have calculated, using TGI data and cross-referencing our results with Scott's ex-factory data, that if this shift in usership had not taken place, Andrex would have lost 8.6% of its sales volume or 2% points of volume share as measured by AGB Superpanel. This is on top of the short-term sales effects of advertising and ignores the fact that a greater 'solus' user profile has helped isolate the brand from the effects of new competitors (both branded and luxury own label).

5. Econometric modelling has shown advertising to have had a strong positive influence on Andrex' sales. Over the last 10 years, OHAL estimate that TV advertising has accounted for 20-25 million cases which at current prices is in excess of £300 million for a MEAL listed expenditure of £54 million.

Andrex is an exceptional brand. Andrex Puppy Advertising is, according to all available measures, equally exceptional in its performance, and this paper demonstrates what effective advertising can achieve for a product as dull as loo paper.

For Scott Worldwide, the parent company of Scott Ltd, proof of their belief in the power of the puppy is shown in the fact that he has been 'exported' to Italy and Spain to advertise their premium product in these markets (Scottex). Imitation is the sincerest, and we would argue the most 'tangible' form of flattery. There appears to be no doubt in the minds of Scott as to the value of this labrador puppy to their business.

5

The Volkswagen Golf
1984–1990

INTRODUCTION

In the IPA booklet 'How to Win – A Guide to Authors' it is stated that, 'Allowance is made for how difficult it is in each case to isolate advertising effect. In some cases eg car campaigns, it is fiendishly difficult.'

In the introduction to a number of recent 'Advertising Works' volumes, comment is made about the need for new ways of looking at how advertising works and how to *prove* advertising works: 'Over time we must expect to see a development and a broadening of what is submitted and what is rewarded and published in these Awards, otherwise the advertising business will fall into the trap of believing that it has already solved all the intractable problems of measuring effectiveness.'

In this paper, we aim to address both of these points. We hope to demonstrate that:

1. Using conventional means to isolate the advertising effect of a car campaign in any long-term sense (ie not a '0% Finance' offer), is even more than 'fiendishly difficult' – it may well be impossible.
2. That a car campaign can convincingly be shown to have been effective if a new approach is taken to proving its effectiveness.

WHY IS PROVING ADVERTISING EFFECTIVENESS IN THE CAR MARKET SO DIFFICULT?

Before demonstrating how we believe a car campaign can convincingly be shown to have been effective we must explain why, in our view, isolating advertising effect in the car market is so difficult.

Our explanation concentrates on two areas:

1. The nature of the purchase process.
2. Attitudes to a marque.

The Purchase Process

The key point here is that:

1. It is a long and complex process with many stages coming between advertising and a sale.

Because

2. A car is an infrequent high risk, expensive purchase, akin to choosing a new house. If you get it wrong, you have to live with your mistake for a long time.

The implication is that trial purchasing, in the sense used in fmcg markets, does not really exist in the car market. People won't buy a car just to give it 'a go' as they might with a newly advertised lager or toilet cleaner. Hence, the usual method of showing a clear link between a particular piece of advertising causing an immediate uplift in sales followed by repeat purchase and loyalty measures, will not work in the car market.

Attitudes to a Marque

The point we want to make here is that even if we had a complete set of data covering the so called 'soft' measures of effectiveness (which we do not), it would not be particularly helpful in demonstrating the effect of advertising.

It is our contention that there is one factor of overwhelming importance that dictates imagery and attitudes to a marque or model and that is the reality of the product itself. Our analogy involving house purchase may help to explain this view. Choosing a particular model of car – say a VW Golf – is analogous to choosing to live in a particular area – say Hampstead. (The particular variant, colour and extras you choose would then be analogous to the particular house or flat you choose.) To keep the analogy fair, let us assume we have an audience of people who are already aware of Hampstead*. Now, we would suggest that it would be entirely unreasonable to expect an advertising campaign to significantly alter the image of Hampstead and people's attitudes to it.

The reality of the architecture, the local amenities, the heritage of the area and the prices of the housing will not have changed and will be too powerful to be overshadowed by paid for communication from an interested party.

On the other hand, to make the point from the opposite direction, an example would be Docklands in the mid 1980s. In Docklands, the 'product' *was* significantly altered. Redevelopment, refurbishment, new local shopping and transport facilities were all introduced and, consequently, the imagery of Docklands and people's attitudes to it changed enormously.

Together, we hope these two analogous examples show that image and attitudinal measures are of little value in proving advertising effectiveness in the car market because they don't change unless the product changes (see later). In fact, large changes in these measures would be a much better argument for the existence of improved product 'effectiveness' ie the effect of introducing better product.

---

* Awareness of Golf is close to 100%

We can demonstrate quite clearly this point that it is *the standard of the product* that determines attitudes to a marque by using one of the few measures we have (since 1982) for most marques. Fortunately, it is an important measure being, in our view, the summation of all attitudes to any marque*. The measure is that of propensity to consider. The question asked of 1,200 nationally representative car owners who bought new in the last five years is: 'Suppose you were going to buy a new car tomorrow. Which makes would you seriously consider?'

For virtually all manufacturers (we shall come onto the one exception later), this measure does not change to any significant degree. Figure 1 shows the sort of variation that is typical. This relative stasis (which corresponds to very slowly changing market share for a marque) raises a large question that relates back to our analogous examples of Hampstead and Docklands.

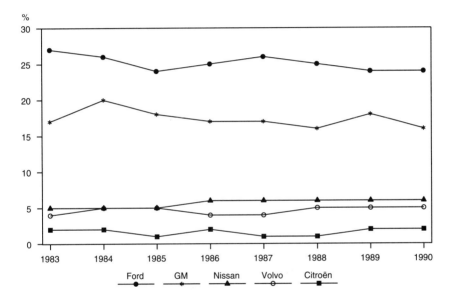

Figure 1. *Propensity to consider (Percentage share 1983–1990)*
Source: VW

After all, 'redevelopment' is a feature common to all car marques. New models costing billions of pounds in development costs are launched every year. Hundreds of millions of pounds are spent on advertising and promotions every year singing the praises of these new cars. And yet the propensity to consider or 'desirability' of a marque seems to move slowly if at all. Why should this be? The answer lies in the fact that *all* car manufacturers are continually 'redeveloping', not just the odd one or two.

Consequently, what the propensity to consider question is measuring is *relative* desirability at any given time. And, it is a fact of the marketplace that *relative* desirability doesn't change much because the *relative* strengths of different cars don't change much. It is exorbitantly expensive to design an entirely new car, and manufacturers are rightly wary of alienating the customers they already have.

* All our 'soft' data are for marques rather than models. But since Golf accounts for over half of all Volkswagens sold and is by far the best known model VW make, 'VW' is a good proxy for 'Golf'.

Hence, most new cars are simply subtle evolutions or updates of what has come before – slightly different curves reflecting changing fashion or developments in aerodynamic theory; incorporation of peripheral new technology such as ABS or lean burn engines; an improved interior. In most cases, the name is not even changed (eg Escort, Golf, Granada, Astra etc). In addition to their natural wariness, another factor is at work. All major manufacturers are working on new products using the same computers, complying with the same legislation, targeting the same audience and jealous of their competitors' previous technical advances.

The only time a given car has an advantage over its competitors is when it is new and its competitors aren't. However, this is only sustainable up to the point at which the new competitor is launched and at that point the advantage shifts to the competitor. And so it repeats itself.

THE EXCEPTION THAT PROVES THE RULE

We have said that new cars tend to resemble old cars but with the addition of today's technology. For major manufacturers, exceptions to this rule are rare and, as far as the 1980s are concerned there is, we believe, only one. The manufacturer was Peugeot, the car the 205. The 205 was not only a vast step forward for Peugeot (ie relative to its predecessor the 104), it was a vast step forward for small cars in general. From its inception onwards, the 205 was met with unconditional praise and adulation from the motoring press:

> 'In years to come 1983 may well be looked back on as something of a watershed time in the design and marketing of small cars. For with the arrival of the Peugeot 205 the small car can be seen to have come of age.' What Car?, November 1983

> 'It must be the surest winner Peugeot have ever had on their hands.' *What Car?*, November 1983

Importantly, the 205 is also an exception in terms of how long its appeal has endured:

> 'Eleven (sic) years old and the Peugeot 205 still drives rings round the opposition. Can anything beat this car?' Performance Car, June 1992

> 'The best car of the '80s and still going strong. Not many family hatches have this sort of staying power: a testimony to the design's original quality of "rightness".' Autocar and Motor, May 1992

Remembering that the propensity to consider question measures a marque's desirability *relative* to its competitors it seems clear that with the 205 we would expect Peugeot's desirability to leap up after 1983 and to continue rising as more and more people become aware of the change that had occurred. This is precisely what we do in fact see (Figure 2). The proportion of new car buyers that would consider a Peugeot increases from 3% in 1983 to 14% in 1990. Quite clearly (Figure 3), this increase in the number of people who would consider a Peugeot translates into remarkable growth through the 1980s for Peugeot.

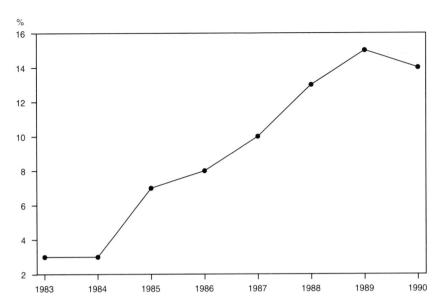

Figure 2.   *Propensity to consider Peugeot*
Source: VW

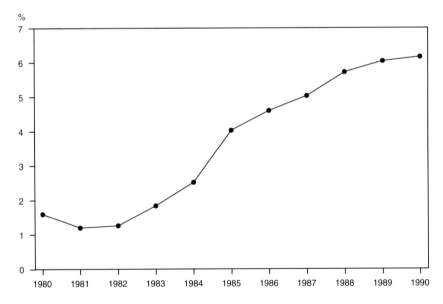

Figure 3.   *Peugeot market share (1980–1990)*
Source: SMMT

SUMMARY

Measuring advertising effectiveness in the car market is very difficult.

There is no such thing as 'trial' and hence changes in sales, repeat purchasing and loyalty are difficult to attribute to particular pieces of advertising.

The standard of the product relative both to its predecessor and the competition is the dominant factor in influencing attitudes to a marque. The nature of the marketplace tends to force a situation of status quo in both products and attitudes (Figure 4). In addition, the relative standard of product dictates the number of people who would consider a particular make in the future and hence this also tends to be static unless a quantum leap, in product terms, is made.

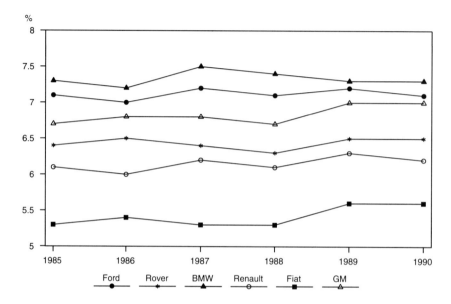

Figure 4. *Overall attitude to marque (1985–1990)*
Source: VW (average of all scores)

It seems clear that not only is measuring the effect of advertising in this market going to be difficult but that even defining what the *role for advertising* should be is by no means obvious.

THE SCOPE OF THIS PAPER

This paper deals with one decade in the history of the car market from 1980 to 1990 inclusive. The main theme is an attempt to demonstrate and quantify the part advertising played in the success of the Volkswagen Golf Mark II from launch in March 1984 onwards.

Firstly, we shall show how we developed a role for advertising that recognised the restrictions of the marketplace.

We shall go on to demonstrate the effectiveness of this advertising by developing a simple model that predicts *any* new car's behaviour in share terms. We shall show that any new car behaves (in share terms) in a well-defined way and that this behaviour is easily understood. Finally, we shall show that the Golf is the *only* car that breaks the 'laws' of the car market and that the only credible explanation for its anomalous performance is its advertising.

DEVELOPING A ROLE FOR ADVERTISING

We have written a lot about what advertising can't do or can't be seen to do. Specifically, we have shown how advertising can't overpower the reality of the product and hence significantly alter attitudes to it. We have also shown how advertising can't be seen to directly influence or cause a particular sale (because of the peculiarities of the purchase process). So what can advertising do? What could be the role for advertising?

At the time of the launch, the role for advertising is clear and simple. Namely, to build rapid awareness of the existence of the *new* car. However, assuming this role has been fulfilled, the future role for advertising is less obvious.

The answer, for VW, lies in us returning to our house buying analogy. Whilst our potential Hampstead resident may be fully *au fait* with the rational attributes of the area – the analogues to 'good performance', 'technically advanced cars', 'reliable' and 'safe' – what he or she can't know is what it *feels* like to actually live there. In other words, what does moving to Hampstead imply about him or her as a person? This is clearly a much more subjective and emotional dimension than the realities of house prices, local amenities and architecture. It was from these ideas that the advertising strategy for Golf was developed. The strategy was linked to Volkswagen's 'reliability' positioning through the idea, 'You (the driver) can rely on it (the car)'.

Role for Advertising

The role for advertising was to make our audience *like the idea* of owning a Golf more than would be expected from the reality of the car.

Target Audience

People who would consider a Golf for their next car.

Advertising Objective

To make people who would consider a Golf more likely to actually buy one, ie to provide a marginal reason for choice of a Golf rather than an Escort or Astra.

Advertising Strategy

By making the idea of being the sort of person who owns a Golf more appealing.

THE ADVERTISING

The brief for 'Casino' (see storyboard) was a copy of Rudyard Kipling's poem *If*. The task was to present the hero of the poem as the sort of person who would choose to drive a Golf. The creative team elaborated on one particular part of the poem and it was this that generated the ad:

'If you can risk all your winnings on one turn of pitch and toss. And lose and start again at your beginning and not breathe a word about your loss.'

'CASINO'

This is a man who put a
million on black

and it came up red

This is the man

who married a sex kitten
just as she turned into a cat

This is the man who moved
into gold just as the clever
money moved out

This is the man

who drives...

...a Volkswagen

Everyone must have
something in life he can
rely on.

'CHANGES'

Everyone is going through changes

and no one knows what's going on

and everybody changes places

but the world still carries on

Love must always change to sorrow

and everyone must play the game

it's here today and gone tomorrow

But the world goes on the same

Music fades

For 'Changes' (see storyboard), the brief was simply to do another 'Casino' but with a woman in it!

Both ads were solely about the drivers of the car. In the context of the product focused ads produced by competitors, they were revolutionary.

How We Thought the Advertising Would Work

Impulse purchase is not a feature of the car market. People usually end up with two or three cars that they find acceptable, each of which will have, in their minds, particular strengths and weaknesses. Anything that can add to the marginal appeal of one of their potential choices may well be enough to solve their dilemma and tip the balance in favour of that car. It seems reasonable to suppose that if someone is happy, on functional grounds, with either a Golf or an Escort, then their final decision may well rest on whether the *idea of being a Golf owner* is more or less appealing than being an Escort owner. It was this marginal factor that we hoped to influence.

THE MEDIA

The nature of the media strategy was dictated by three factors:

1. We wanted to reach the biggest, broadest possible audience, most of whom would not be replacing their car for some time.
2. We wanted to be as intrusive as possible.
3. We wanted to make our audience *feel* what it was like to be a Golf owner.

For these reasons, TV was felt to be the most appropriate medium. Golf is a mass market car, hence we went for a mass market car buying audience of ABC1 adults.

Between 1985 and 1989, 'Casino' and 'Changes' were given eight bursts of national TV airtime.

Total media spend as follows:

'Casino'	£5.2m
'Changes'	£5.7m
Total	**£10.9m**

Source: MEAL

DEMONSTRATING ADVERTISING EFFECT

Developing a Lifecycle Model

In order to demonstrate the effect of the Golf's advertising we must first develop a predictive model of the 'shape' of a new car's share performance following launch. The reason we need this model will become clear as we develop our case.

— *The General Case*
From our understanding of the market, we can state a few key facts:

(i)   A new car's main competitive advantage is, simply, that it is new.

(ii) The cyclical nature of new car launches means that this advantage will only be held for at most two or three years and will then be lost to some other manufacturer's new car.

(iii) In general, new cars are subtle evolutions of what came before and do not fundamentally upset the status quo.

(iv) Consequently, the total number of people who would consider buying one does not increase significantly, ie total potential demand is flat.

Taking these four facts it seems clear that, following launch, one would predict a couple of years of increasing share followed by gradual share decline up to the point of launch of the new car's replacement (Figure 5).

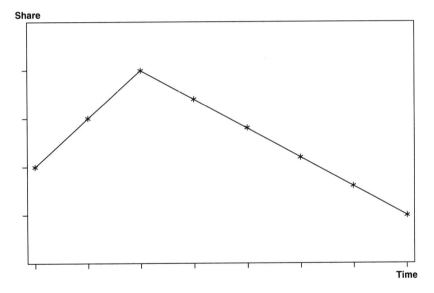

Figure 5. *The general case – predicted share pattern*

— *The Exceptional Case*
Very occasionally, facts (iii) and (iv) must be substituted for as follows:

(iii) The new car *is* a quantum leap forward relative both to what the manufacturer had produced before and to the competition. The new car fundamentally upsets the status quo.

(iv) Consequently, as awareness of this unexpected upset to the status quo grows, the number of people who would consider buying one also grows, ie total potential demand grows.

Taking these facts into consideration, it seems clear that, following launch, one would predict steadily increasing market share, perhaps beginning to tail off as the effect of the age of the car increasingly counters the effect of increasing potential demand (Figure 6).

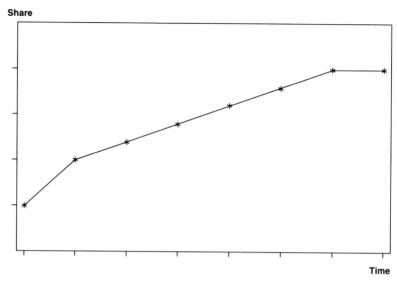

Figure 6. *Exceptional cases – predicted share pattern*

The Model

We now have a simple predictive model for the 'shape' of *any* new car's share performance from launch onwards. The model depends on only one variable, namely whether or not the new car is a dramatic leap forward both for its manufacturer and for the market.

If it is not a dramatic leap forward, as is almost always the case, then we would predict two or three years of share growth followed by gradual decline. If it is a dramatic leap forward then share should continue rising for longer with the rate of growth slowing (and maybe finally reversing) as the car's age catches up with it.

Testing the Model

To test our model, we have looked at a large sample of new car lifecycles. We confined ourselves largely to the first half of the decade for three reasons:

1. To keep the task manageable.
2. To look at the Golf's nearest contempories.
3. To provide enough time for a fully-developed lifecycle to emerge.

We tried to ensure our sample was as representative as possible by looking at:

— Both British and imported marques.
— Models launched under new names (eg Citroën Visa, Ford Sierra etc) as well as familiar ones (eg Escort, Renault 5 etc).
— Cars from every major sector of the market.

(The one major area we will ignore is Japanese manufacturers since the quota agreements mean that UK sales of Japanese cars are almost entirely supply, rather than demand, driven.)

We already know, both from our general market knowledge as well as more crucially from the potential demand data (ie propensity to consider) that only the Peugeot 205 fits into our 'exception' category. For all other cars, therefore, we would expect to see a quick rise followed by gradual decline. As can be seen (Figures 7-13) this is exactly what we find (bar the odd fluctuation probably caused by a facelift, a special edition model, or a price promotion).

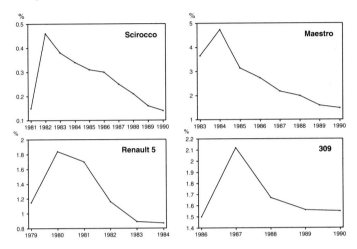

Figure 7. *Market share – Scirocco, Maestro, Renault 5, 309*
Source: SMMT

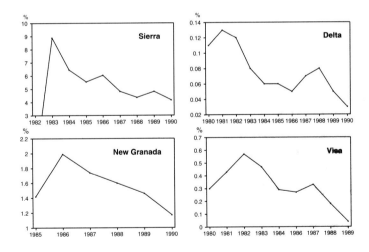

Figure 8. *Market share – Sierra, Delta, New Granada, Visa*
Source: SMMT

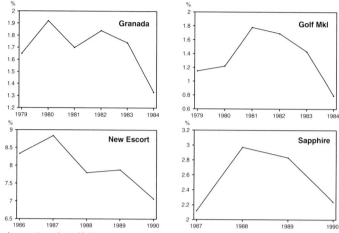

Figure 9. *Market share – Granada, Golf Mk I, New Escort, Sapphire*
Source: SMMT

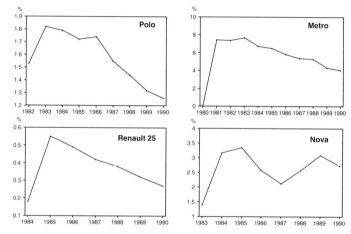

Figure 10. *Market share – Polo, Metro, Renault 25, Nova*
Source: SMMT

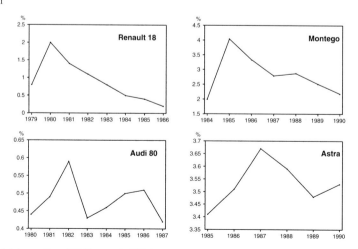

Figure 11. *Market share – Renault 18, Montego, Audi 80, Astra*
Source: SMMT

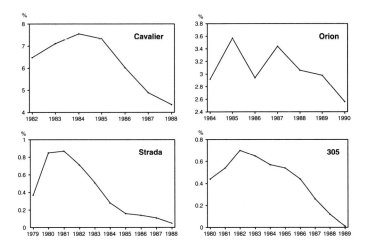

Figure 12. *Market share – Cavalier, Orion, Strada, 305*
Source: SMMT

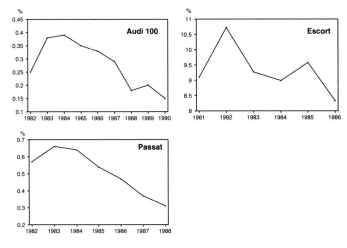

Figure 13. *Market share – Audi 100, Escort, Passat*
Source: SMMT

What is remarkable is that the model works on only one variable.

The new cars that we looked at display the same basic share performance shape:

— Regardless of manufacturer.

— Regardless of British or import origins.

— Regardless of market sector.

— Regardless of whether the new model retains the name of its predecessor (Escort) or breaks all links with the past (Metro).

Our exception, the 205, also performs as we would expect given the nature of the product and the consequent increase in potential demand (Figure 14). In fact, the 205 almost singlehandedly accounts for Peugeot's spectacular share growth as a marque.

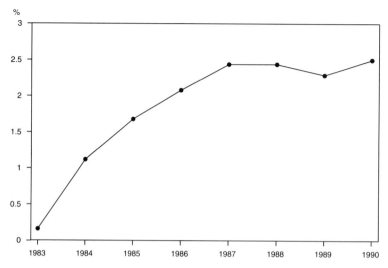

Figure 14. *Market share – Peugeot 205 1983–1990*
Source: SMMT

The Model Applied to Golf

We are now in a position to apply what we have learnt to the Volkswagen Golf Mark II, launched in March 1984. To decide what sort of future VW should have predicted for their car we need to answer only one question 'Was the new Golf a dramatic leap forward both for VW and for the market?'

The new Golf was not, unlike the 205, ever intended to be a revolutionary vehicle. It was quite deliberately a subtle evolution of the Golf Mark I. The main changes were more cabin space, reworked suspension and a larger fuel tank. Cosmetically, the lines of the car were softened for a more modern appearance. Crucially though, the car was still a 3 or 5 door hatchback, came in the same variants from the base level CL, through the GL and up to the GTi, and was still called Golf.

Contemporary reviews in the motoring press reflect how cautious VW had been:

'Then came the new Golf. The shock was the extent to which it deliberately looked like the previous model. In essence, the new Golf is little more than the old one, stretched in the wheelbase, its screen more steeply raked and its nose smoothed over for the sake of lower drag.' *Car*, March 1984

'A feeling of disappointment almost clouds our judgement on the new Golf; disappointment that the new model breaks little new ground, simply reinforcing existing strengths.' *What Car?*, April 1984

'There is no breathtaking thrill of innovative styling, no obvious new techniques of engineering, and little sign of any special new cult appeal which might develop.' *What Car?*, April 1984

In product terms, then, the Golf Mark II was no 205; like its competitors the new Escort and Astra, it fitted squarely into the 'maintaining the status quo' bracket.

From this, we would predict two things. The first is that the new Golf would have little or no effect on propensity to consider a Volkswagen. This proves to be the case (Figure 15). The second is that, in share terms, we would expect Golf to follow the common pattern of rapid growth followed by gradual decline. What actually happens (Figure 16) is completely unexpected. Share climbs steadily during the six years following launch and only dips slightly in the seventh. (As we shall see later, the drop in the seventh year was caused not by a tailing off of demand but by an extraordinary and unplanned for supply problem.)

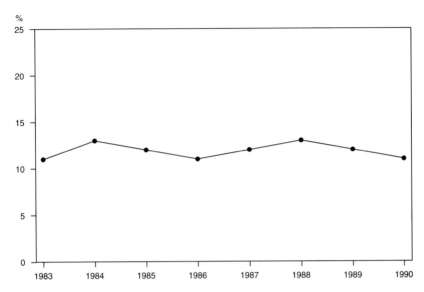

Figure 15. *Propensity to consider VW*
Source: VW

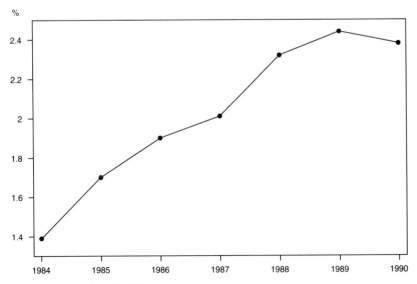

Figure 16. *Golf Mark II market share 1984–1990*
Source: SMMT

The difference between what we would expect to see and what we actually see cannot be overstated. We are not looking at a difference of degree but a fundamental change of structure. It demands an explanation. After all, in every respect Golf fits perfectly the pattern of the vast bulk of new cars:

— It is an evolutionary model.
— It has little/no effect on propensity to consider.

In fact, judging by the press comment, Golf fits in with the potentially less successful new products on the market. And yet its share performance seems to deny all the evidence. Its share performance is a total anomaly. Clearly we need to answer the question 'Why?'.

THE SEARCH FOR OTHER ANOMALIES

In fact, the search is not that difficult. We have already eliminated the main area – the product. We have seen, through three sources, that the cause cannot lie in the product itself:

— The Golf is evolutionary.
— The press response supports this fact.
— The launch has no effect on the number of people who would consider buying one.

What we are left with are the other areas of the marketing mix: price, distribution, promotion. In addition, there is one other variable pertinent to cars (especially from foreign manufacturers) which is supply (ie availability). Finally, we need to also look at competitive activity in terms of new car launches.

Price

Perhaps Golf grew share through massive price reductions as the car grew older. As is clear from Table 1, this is not the case.

TABLE 1: GOLF PRICE INDEXED ON AVERAGE OF KEY COMPETITORS*

1981	103
1982	102
1983	100
New Golf	
1984	106
1985	107
1986	109
1987	112
1988	111
1989	108
1990	104

Note: * (Escort, Astra, Maestro etc)

Distribution

Volkswagen share of distribution has remained more or less constant throughout the decade. In absolute terms, the number of VW dealerships has fallen from 354 in 1984 to 343 in 1990.

TABLE 2: VOLKSWAGEN DEALERS AS PERCENTAGE OF ALL CAR DEALERS

	%
1981	4.1
1982	4.3
1983	4.1
New Golf	
1984	4.0
1985	4.1
1986	4.2
1987	4.3
1988	4.3
1989	4.2
1990	4.3

Supply

In the first two or three months of its life, as with any new car, production problems with the new Golf had to be ironed out and supply was affected. This is expected when any new model is introduced.

Beyond this, there were no problems with supply to the UK until, ironically, towards the end of its lifecycle. When the Berlin Wall came down in November 1989, Volkswagen in Germany saw a massive new market open up. Their urgent desire to supply this new market resulted in an increase in factory time devoted to left hand drive production. Supply of (right hand drive) Golfs to the UK was significantly reduced.

Competitive Launches

As we have shown, the effect of new car launches tends to be counterbalanced by the fact that all manufacturers are continually developing new products. The period following the launch of the Golf was as rich in new car introductions as any other. Clearly, the anomaly we are searching for is not a lack of competitive product.

SOME MAJOR MODEL LAUNCHES PRE AND POST GOLF

1979	1980	1981	1982
Fiat Strada	Peugeot 305	Scirocco	GM Cavalier
Ford Granada	Audi 80	Ford Escort	Audi 100
Renault 5	Austin Metro		Passat
Renault 18	Lancia Delta		Ford Sierra
	Citroën Visa		

1983	1984	1985	1986
Peugeot 205	Austin Montego	GM Astra	Ford Escort
GM Nova	Renault 25	Renault 5	Ford Orion
Austin Maestro		Ford Granada	Fiat Croma
		Mazda 323	Nissan Sunny

1987	1988	1989
Citroën AX	Fiat Tipo	Ford Fiesta
Toyota Corolla	Colt	Renault 19
Ford Sapphire	Peugeot 405	GM Cavalier
	Seat Marbella	Proton

We now know at least what does *not* account for Golf's extraordinary performance:

—   It was NOT the product itself.
—   It was NOT its price.
—   It was NOT distribution.
—   It was NOT supply.
—   It was NOT a lack of competitive products.

We are left with a completely anomalous share performance for which we cannot find a corresponding anomaly in any of the areas we have looked at so far.

However, there remains one final area in which to search.

THE ADVERTISING

Following some fairly undistinguished launch advertising in early 1984, the Golf was supported from 1985 to 1989 with two of the most popular and unprecedented pieces of TV advertising ever made for a car. As we shall show, this is not only our view but the view of the people who saw the ads.

It is unfortunate that VW have no tracking data prior to 1990 nor any qualitative research reports from the time.

However, what we do have is the results of groups conducted amongst mixed new car buyers in early 1992. The two ads were shown once and respondents were simply asked to comment on them. The first surprise was the extent to which the advertising was universally recognised and acclaimed:

'I remember it, I think it's wonderful.'
'You could run that ad now and it would still be brilliant.'
'Was it that long ago, 1985, I can't believe it.'
'I'd describe it as timeless.'

(Casino)

'It's difficult to be objective now because it gets played on every
  review of great ads you ever see on TV.'
'That's one of my favourite ads ever.'

(Changes)

'I can't remember any other car ads.'
'They definitely stand out in my mind.'
'They're brilliant, fantastic.'
'They're streets ahead of other car advertising.'

(Both)

Both ads were felt to stand radically apart not only from other car advertising but from other advertising in general.

What was striking about the ads was the way in which they talked about the car indirectly, through the person who would drive it:

'I very strongly identify with it because I'd like to make lots of money and be very successful but I probably won't be but one of the few things that is within my control is the kind of car I buy. That says a lot about the sort of car I'd buy.'

'It's about his way of life, his style.'

'It's chin up, carry on. If at first you don't succeed and all that. It's inspiring.'

'It makes you believe the car is good. They don't even need to talk about it.'

(Casino)

'It concentrates on the buyer rather than the car. It identifies a set of values that you would identify with when you bought the car, do you see what I mean, instead of talking about 0-60 or anything like that.'

'It makes the car the woman's friend. That's very appealing.'

'It tells me everything I want to know about the car without telling me anything!'

(Changes)

'I love both of those. Especially at that time when everyone was going in the opposite direction.'

'It's streets ahead. Every other make does driving on the continent through twisty lanes. It's just on a completely different plane.'

(Both)

In addition, the ads seemed to make people emotionally closer to VW as a manufacturer. This is probably the key source of their enduring strength:

'It makes you like VW for its understanding of you.'

(Casino)

'It makes you feel really good.'

(Changes)

'They tap a real emotional vein.'

'You feel good when you watch them. A hell of a lot better than you would watching a car driving up a mountain.'

(Both)

It seems clear that the new Golf had not one, but two anomalous aspects to it:

— An extraordinary share performance.
— Extraordinary advertising.

WHAT EVIDENCE IS THERE OF DIRECT ADVERTISING EFFECT?

Despite the problems that exist in trying to directly show advertising effect, we believe there are a few clues that suggest the advertising worked in the way we had hoped.

As already stated, in general, attitudes to VW did not change and should not be expected to change. The bulk of the measures covered areas such as:

'Is very safety minded.'
'Makes mechanically reliable cars.'
'Makes cars which are reasonably priced.'
'Makes technically advanced cars.'
'Offers cars with good workmanship' etc.

These were measures of people's perception of reality and hence were most strongly influenced by reality. Taken as a whole, this battery of measures varied across the 1980s by an amount statistically equivalent to zero. Given what we know about the marketplace and the fact that respondents were inevitably scoring VW *relative* to the competition, this result is not surprising.

Fortunately, we have three measures available for VW since 1982 that are a little less rational in nature and hence may provide evidence of a change in the way people *felt* about VW.

The first two of them are included in the attitudes battery and ask respondents to mark VW out of 10 for: 'Makes cars that have personality and character' and 'Is a prestige make'.

Whilst the changes in score against these measures are undramatic, in the context of the stability of all other measures, they are significant. (Figures 17-19).

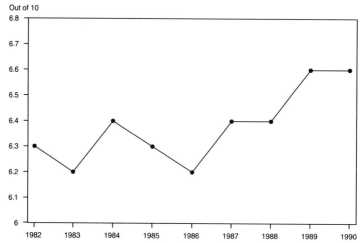

Figure 17. *Attitudes to VW – 'Cars with personality and character'*
Source: VW

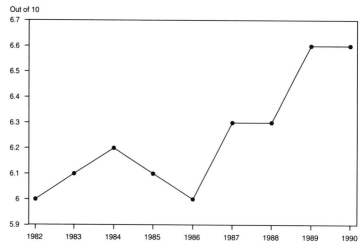

Figure 18. *Attitudes to VW – 'Is a prestige make'*
Source: VW

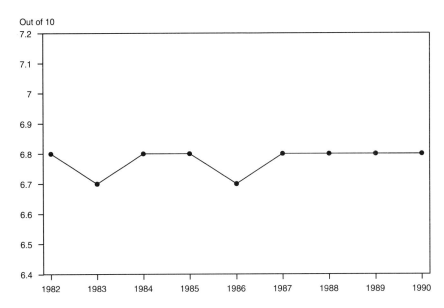

Figure 19. *Average of attitudes to VW (excl 'prestige' and 'personality')*
Source: VW

The third measure we have is also probably the closest we have to measuring the effect we wanted. This measure is 'overall liking for VW', again scored out of 10. Once again, the movements aren't spectacular but are significant (Figure 20). The increase of 'liking' for VW relative to other marques also increased (Figure 21) so this was not a market-wide effect.

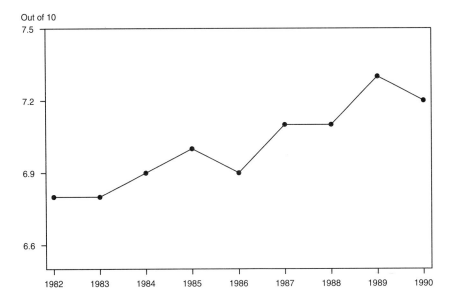

Figure 20. *VW marque 'liking' (1982–1990)*
Source: VW

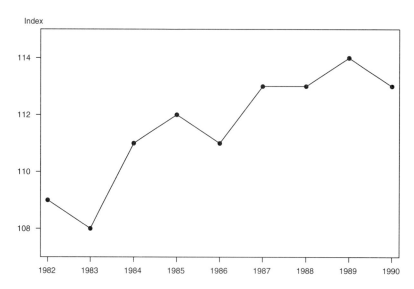

Figure 21. *VW 'liking' relative to all marques (1982–1990)*
Source: VW

We believe these three measures, together with the qualitative results, provide all the evidence we are ever likely to find that the advertising worked in the way we had hoped. We were never going to make someone who wouldn't consider buying a Golf suddenly consider it. But we could make someone who would consider a Golf more likely to ultimately choose one.

We are left with two choices. We can ignore the compelling evidence of the 'laws' of the car market and dismiss the Golf's share performance as just 'one of those things' and the advertising as an unrelated coincidence. Alternatively, we are left with the conclusion that in our search for an explanatory anomaly for the car's performance we have found only one – the advertising.

HOW MUCH DID THE ADVERTISING CONTRIBUTE TO PROFIT?

How Big was the Effect?

It is very hard to estimate what could reasonably have been expected to happen to Golf's share if it had been supported with 'ordinary' advertising.

Being as optimistic about the share performance of Golf without the ads as is reasonable, Figure 22 shows the difference between what happened and what might reasonably have been predicted to happen.

There is a difference in share only in 1988, 1989 and 1990. The difference in each case comes to:

$$
\begin{array}{lll}
1988 & : & +0.4\% \\
1989 & : & +0.6\% \\
1990 & : & +0.7\%
\end{array}
$$

In terms of number of vehicles, this equates to 36,720 extra Golfs across the period 1988–1990 or around £30m additional gross profit. With an advertising spend against Golf of only £10.9m from 1985 to 1989 this is clearly a good

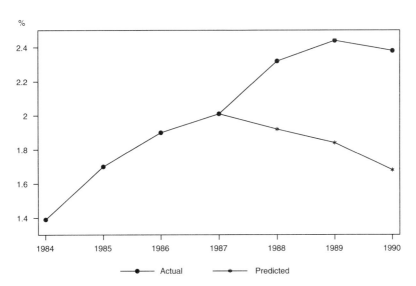

Figure 22. *Golf Mark II market share (predicted vs actual)*

investment. In addition, with loyalty averaging around 50% in the car market, any additional sale today generates at least half an extra sale in the future. This would increase the financial value of the advertising still further.

Where Did the Extra Sales Come From?

We know that the Golf's main competitors are Escort and Astra so most of the Golf's extra sales will have almost certainly come from them. Across the three years 1988–1990, a total of 821,550 Escorts and Astras were sold. The Golf's extra 36,720 sales are therefore equivalent to less than 5% of people who 'ought' to have bought an Escort or Astra buying a Golf instead. We suggested we were looking for a marginal effect and that seems to be exactly what we have got.

SUMMARY

We have shown that new cars in the car market behave in a well defined and predictable way. All the cars we looked at fit the pattern of behaviour that we described except two – the 205 because of a remarkable product and the Volkswagen Golf because of remarkable advertising. In addition, we have shown how this advertising worked by breaking the product-focused 'rules' of the market and concentrating instead on the owner of the car. Finally we have demonstrated that, even by the most conservative estimate, the advertising was a commercially successful investment.

CONCLUSION

We hope we have shown conclusively that a car campaign has been effective. However, we were lucky in that we were dealing with extraordinary advertising. Advertising that caused a change in the 'structure' of Golf sales through its lifecycle.

Proving the long-term effectiveness of more 'run of the mill' car advertising is a challenge that has yet to be answered.

6

Oxo Cubes and Gravy Granules

INTRODUCTION

On the 22nd September 1955, the opening night for ITV, 23 companies took their place in British history by being the first to advertise on TV. Gibbs SR is remembered as the first brand on air, but amongst the others was the humble Oxo cube.

Over the following 37 years, advertising has played an important part in the brand's development through three critical phases.

First, the 'Katie' campaign helped the growth of Oxo sales through the 1960s, shaking the dust from the brand's post-war image and steering it through radical changes in social and eating behaviour.

Secondly, Oxo has relied on advertising to protect profitable volumes. The 'Family' campaign of the 1980s has successfully maintained Oxo's strength and contemporary relevance, and has helped cubes increase market share.

Now we are entering a third phase as total Oxo sales are again on the increase, thanks to the highly successful launch of Oxo Gravy Granules.

THE LONG-TERM THREATS FACING OXO

Historical Perspective

Even in 1955 Oxo was an old brand. It was originally launched in 1847 as a fluid beef concentrate positioned as a diet supplement for invalids and explorers. The now famous cube was launched in 1910 through a technical process that helped broaden the brand's potential.

Cube sales built up across the next 45 years, but particularly during the two World Wars when it was used not just by the troops but on the home front where it was seen as a nutritional supplement imparting its beefy goodness to pep up the limited, often bland food available. Out of necessity a broad usage base of stews, casseroles and, of course, gravy was established.

However, as Britain began to expand in the 1950s, Oxo was faced with what was to be the first of many challenges to its central role in British cooking. Oxo had become associated with leaner times and making do, and not with the hopes and aspirations for the future.

A clear role for the newly arrived television commercial was emerging.

Powerful advertising: the Mighty Atom campaign, 1922

The Food Revolution

Over the years, the conditions of the marketplace became much tougher for Oxo, for a number of reasons:

1. *New competitors*
    Oxo's monopoly of the stock cubes market has been challenged by a number of brands. Knorr arrived in 1954, and has since introduced five new varieties – an advantage over Oxo which has helped it sustain a premium positioning. Bovril launched a cube range in 1977 which has for some time imitated the Oxo offering at lower price points.

2. *Growth of specialist products*
    In 1955, Oxo competed on a number of fronts with more specialised products; Bisto powder (gravy maker), herbs and spices (adding flavour in cooking) and Bovril as a savoury drink. This is still the case in 1992, but the specialists are far more numerous, and come in innovative and convenient forms – gravy granules, cook-in sauces and instant soups.

3. *The decline of traditional cooking and gravy making*
    Over three decades, a revolution in cooking habits has threatened the heart of
    Oxo's franchise. Convenient pre-prepared foods have reduced the universe of
    homecooked meals and the British housewife has steadily turned her face from
    her mother's family dishes and embraced all manner of foreign foods. We do
    not have figures covering the total period, but gravy making occasions (one of
    the traditional rituals) have declined by 13% in the last two years alone
    (Taylor Nelson).

4. *The move away from beef and beefy flavour*
    This has been particularly dramatic over the last decade, and affects Oxo more
    than its competitors, because the original (beef) variety accounts for over 80%
    of the brand's sales. The corresponding growth in chicken consumption has not
    helped Oxo:

TABLE 1: CONSUMPTION (OZ PER PERSON PER WEEK)

	Beef and Veal	Poultry
1954	9.23	0.52
1991	5.35	7.13

Source: National Food Survey

The trend has accompanied a change in the national palate, away from
powerful beefy flavours like Oxo which cover up an otherwise bland cuisine.

ADVERTISING STRATEGY

In the face of these fundamental changes, Oxo has depended heavily on advertising
to demonstrate its continued relevance to the foods of the day. At the same time,
the advertising has sought to preserve the emotional bond between Oxo and its
consumers, by dramatising the brand's importance to home cooking and to family
life itself. The campaigns have changed to mirror trends in family society as well as
eating behaviour. The major tool has been TV advertising, running through the
period of greatest demand, October to March. Press has also been used
sporadically.

'Katie' (1957–75)

This advertising worked primarily through the identification of British housewives
with the Katie character, and through an educational element describing how to use
Oxo. The campaign evolved through various phases: Katie as an upwardly mobile
housewife cooking intriguing new foods, to escape Oxo's postwar legacy; Katie in
America, establishing Oxo's relevance to new foods like hamburgers; Katie making
good value dishes such as leek and liver casserole in the dark days of 1973.

Katie 1957

Lynda 1975

'Family' (1983–)

The current campaign works through carefully observed points of identification with consumer's own family lives. In comparison with Katie, the greater independence of children is noticeable – both in terms of fragmented eating patterns, and friction with parents. The advertising has also sought to establish Oxo's relevance to the booming area of continental mince dishes and to new cooking methods (eg stir fry, microwaves).

Brand: OXO
Remember Preston

Sound: location effects in
background to end

Jason: What's that?

Lynda: Yes it is a surprise
No I haven't cooked it before

Yes it is foreign
No Jason it's not a hamburger

Yes Alison, Dolly will love it

No Nick no garlic

And Michael

Remember Preston?

LONGER EFFECTS: A 40 YEAR SALES PERSPECTIVE

Given the enormity of the threat posed to Oxo's volume by the changes in social and eating habits during the last 40 years it could be argued that the brand might easily have died. In fact, the successful sales drive of the 1960s and the subsequent resistance to external pressures have meant that Oxo cubes volume remains high. In fact, annual cube volume was 4% higher in 1990/91 compared with 1955/56.

LONGER EFFECTS: GROWING SHARE THROUGH THE 1980s

Market Share

Despite the arrival of competitive brands within the cubes market, Oxo remains the dominant brand, and has actually improved its share over the past decade:

TABLE 2: STOCK CUBE VOLUME SHARES

Volume shares	1983 100 %	1991 100 %
Oxo	69	72
Bovril	23	12
Knorr	6	10
Own Label	2	4

Source: AGB

The strength of the brand is most vividly demonstrated by its performance against Bovril – a very similar product which has had to sell at an increasingly competitive price.

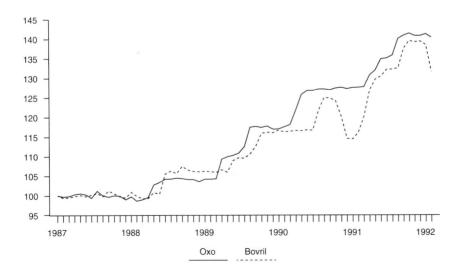

Figure 1. *Oxo vs Bovril average cube price (index 1987 = 100)*
Source: NMRA

We have developed an econometric model which isolates the effect of advertising on the market share of Oxo cubes (full details are appended). It concludes that the TV and press campaigns account for about three percentage points of Oxo's share between 1987 and 1992.

The model suggests that the advertising works in two ways. First, a short-term 'boost' in share which we ascribe to the 'reminder' or 'publicity' effect of a campaign with high salience. Second, a long-term lagged effect on share; this could reflect emotional loyalty-building or 'in-home pull-through' from greater usage in contemporary dishes.

Above and beyond the model's explanation of periodic variations, there was a residual upward trend in Oxo market share of one percentage point over the period in question. This could also be additional long-term advertising effect, but it seems more likely to derive from the launch of vegetable cubes in 1989.

It should also be noted that there is some empirical evidence of the Family campaign's effect in arresting the decline of Oxo cubes' absolute volume. The brand's sole (unplanned) advertising test took place during the 1987/88 winter season, when only a low level of activity was possible in the London TV region. The annual sales decline was 7.8% greater in London – even though the advertising was significantly reduced rather than completely withdrawn.

LONGER EFFECTS: KEEPING THE BRAND STRONG THROUGH THE 1980s

Brand Salience

We would contend that advertising has successfully maintained Oxo's salience, which is critical to the strength of a brand which could so easily have become an old-fashioned product for old-fashioned cooking.

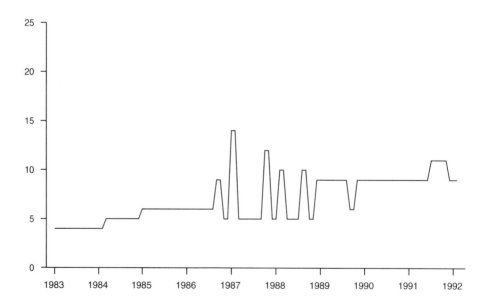

Figure 2. *Oxo advertising awareness efficiency index per TVR*
Source: Millward Brown

In recent years, salience has actually increased, as demonstrated by rising awareness of the Family advertising. Over the nine years of the campaign, advertising awareness peaks have increased from 30–40% to 50–60%. Millward Brown now rate the awareness generating efficiency of the campaign with an index of around 9, whilst previous campaigns 'scored' between 3 and 4 (the average for all commercials).

Qualitative research (especially amongst housewives) continually demonstrates the familiarity of the campaign and the empathy which people feel for it.

'The verité achieved by the Oxo campaign was not only instantly noticed by viewers, but also appreciated — indeed loved. And eight years later, despite the advent of soaps with more verité and other advertising campaigns which sought to reflect aspects of family life, it is still just as distinctive and well loved; interestingly by men as much as women. In qualitative research the Oxo campaign is frequently mentioned in the warm-up discussions, as advertising which is not only "real", but also "clever" and "amusing"'. (Source: Stephen Wells, Wells and Company)

Communication

Different cube commercials have different specific communication objectives. However, it is clear that within the context of the overall campaign certain films have shifted specific image perceptions significantly.

TABLE 3: CHANGE IN IMAGE PERCEPTIONS

Ad	Statement	Prepost period	% shift
Feed a Fever	Adds goodness to food	Nov '85–Apr '86	+7%
Turkish	Versatile	Nov '86–Jan '87	+9%
Frozen Food	Adds flavour	Nov '86–Jan '87	+11%
Just like Mama makes*			
Pulse*	Modern and up-to-date		+6%
Alone*		Oct '89–Mar '90	
Friday Night Fever*	Are getting a bit out-of-date		–6%

Note: * Run in rotation
Source: Millward Brown

Maintaining an Image of Contemporary Relevance

On the image measures which are monitored to assess Oxo's perceived relevance and benefits, only the convenience rating has dropped over the years of the Family campaign (1984–1991). Data from before 1984 are unfortunately not available. However, we would regard as a success the maintenance of Oxo's position on these dimensions over the period in question; on two measures, there has been an improvement.

The reputation of Oxo in total has now been separated from the cube specific image, to reflect the arrival of new specialist gravymakers. It is clear that new products enhance the overall brand image in a number of ways; this may have the effect of improving perceptions of the cube, and so we cannot ascribe positive shifts to advertising alone. On the other hand, the new products could have overshadowed the cube in other respects, eg convenience.

TABLE 4: OXO BRAND IMAGE

	1984	1991	
	Oxo Cubes	Oxo Cubes	Any Oxo
Base: Housewives	100	100	100
Agreeing that Oxo:	%	%	%
Is modern and up-to-date	26	33	50
Is good quality	60	62	64
Is very convenient to use	59	50	59
Is very versatile	62	62	63
Brings out the flavour of a meal	58	58	59

Source: Millward Brown

Maintaining Usage in Contemporary Cooking

As stated earlier, the advertising has consistently sought to establish Oxo's relevance to contemporary cooking and eating habits, despite the fact that what is contemporary is continually changing.

Therefore continental mince dishes like spaghetti bolognese and lasagne, and more exotic dishes like stir fries and curries, have been introduced into both the commercials and press ads rather than just showing traditional stews, gravies and casseroles.

The success of this strategy is indicated by the fact that of all the flavouring products available, Oxo is the most popular when it comes to preparing continental mince dishes:

TABLE 5: PRODUCTS USED IN CONTINENTAL MINCE DISHES

% of total meal occasions	
Red Oxo	36
Chicken Oxo	2
Other stock cubes	6
Any cook-in sauce	25
Any pour over sauce	5
Bisto Powder	5
Bisto Granules	4
Marmite Paste	5

Source: Millward Brown

As an ingredient in curry, excluding the powder itself, Oxo is second only to 'any cook-in sauce' (it is larger though than any individual type of cook-in sauce when curries are prepared at home):

TABLE 6: PRODUCTS USED IN CURRY PREPARATION

% of total meal occasions	
Red Oxo	17
Chicken Oxo	7
Vegetable Oxo	2
Other stock cubes	4
Bisto Granules	5
Marmite Paste	2
Any cook-in sauce	27
canned	14
dry	11
glass jar	2
Any pour over sauce	5

Source: Millward Brown

In addition, the proportion of Oxo used in microwave cooking has increased to around 5%, in line with usage of the microwave across all cooking occasions.

LONGER EFFECTS: ELIMINATING OTHER VARIABLES

Advertising is only one part of any marketing mix. However, in the case of Oxo it is true to say that a number of the traditional factors can be, at least partly if not fully, discounted as having had an effect on the long-term brand performance.

1. *The product*
   As mentioned earlier Oxo was launched in its cube format in 1910. Since then the product has only changed significantly once.
   In 1977 it was reformulated in response to the Bovril launch to give it a 'beefier taste'. This played a significant role at the time in the battle with Bovril. However, since then the product format and flavour profile have not been significantly changed. (One ingredient has been removed but this did not affect the format and careful research helped maintain the existing flavour profile. People like and want the taste of Oxo.)

2. *Distribution*
   Sterling distribution for Oxo cubes (excluding new varieties like Vegetable) has remained constant at nearly 100% and cannot therefore have been an agent for change.

3. *Packaging*
   Packaging has been revised over the years but the changes have been relatively minor with the retention of the famous white O–X–O out of red (yellow and now green).

4. *Seasonality*
   The stock cube market is highly seasonal with sales peaking during the winter months. However, this is an annual occurrence and as such is unlikely to affect the long-term which is the focus of this paper. The only exception to this would be long-term weather trends; a trend towards warmer winters might depress sales and vice versa.
   Data from the Met Office (see weather appendix) would suggest that if anything winters are getting warmer and therefore may be another factor which is depressing the market. We have chosen to exclude this from our modelling.

5. *Other promotional activity*
   Over the years Oxo have used below-the-line and promotional campaigns to support cubes sales. While this undoubtedly contributes to the brand we have excluded this as a variable for the following three reasons:
   — They are a consistent variable, with a number of promotional campaigns run every year.
   — Analysis of this type of promotion shows that some of the effect is to pull sales forward and so the long-term effects may be limited.
   — The sheer number and variety of these types of campaign means it is unrealistic to try and accurately incorporate them in any modelling.

Free Publicity – a broader effect of a famous campaign

BROADER EFFECTS: PUBLICITY

When the campaign started, the radical step of portraying families, warts and all, caused an outcry. Oxo received mail asking how it could do such a thing and threatening never to buy the product again. The Daily Express carried an article on it. Oxo, however, stuck to its guns and a year later was voted the most popular campaign on TV in the ITV Top Ten awards. Oxo was featured in the nationally broadcast awards ceremony that year and the following three years as winners, and in the last two years as runners up.

The Oxo campaign and Lynda Bellingham as the Oxo mum, have gone on to generate enormous amounts of free publicity. Last year Lynda appeared on *Wogan*, *Anne Diamond's TV Week* and TV-am, where in each case she was asked about her role as the Oxo mum.

She appeared on the front cover of *Chat* magazine alongside the headline 'After the Gravy Train'. In fact, Oxo's PR files for 1991 contain over 200 articles referring to the campaign, most of which come from national publications.

BROADER EFFECTS: WIDENING THE CUBE FRANCHISE

Further evidence for the contemporary strength of the Oxo brand comes from the successful launch of a new vegetable cube in late 1989. Knorr had pioneered this variety many years before, and retailers had followed. The Oxo product was a strategic move to prevent loss of brand share (eg switching from Oxo beef to Knorr vegetable) and so it was not expected to stimulate a large increase in total Oxo sales. Oxo vegetable cubes were launched through a Family commercial, and swiftly captured a dominant share of the sector:

TABLE 7: VEGETABLE STOCK CUBE VOLUME SALES (1991)

(Cases)	517,600
	%
Oxo	70
Knorr	19
Own Label	11

Source: AGB

The vegetable cube accounts for 6.2% of all Oxo sales, which is already close to matching the vegetable sector's share of the entire market (6.4%). For a brand whose values were fundamentally based around the beef variety, there seems to be considerable evidence of modern-day dynamism from its ability to make a late entry into the most contemporary sector of the market and dominate almost immediately.

BROADER EFFECTS: THE LAUNCH OF GRAVY GRANULES

Advertising, and in particular the strength of the Family campaign, played a major role in what has been the most significant brand extension to date, namely the launch of Oxo Gravy Granules.

Brand: OXO CUBES
Pulse

Sound: location effects in background to end
Jason: Oh someone's birthday is it?

Lynda: No Nick's coming remember with his flatmate

Chorus: Oh yes the vegetarian

Alison: How very sixties

Lynda: Well your brother seems to think he's ok

Alison: Sounds like a real weed to me

Michael: Yeah well I can't say I fancy a load of old lentils and beans either

Alison: Actually the correct name for them is pulses
Michael: Oh swallowed a dictionary have we?

Lynda: There we are
Nick: Hi Mum sorry we're late. This is Troy, this is my lot Mum, Dad, Alison

Troy: How do you do, pleased to meet you

Lynda: How's your pulse Alison?

Brand: OXO GRAVY GRANULES
Coffee Break

Sound: location effects in
background to end
Jason: Hi Dad What's on
tonight?

Michael: Oh some old weepy

Jason: Looks like chops to me

Michael: Very droll

There we go

Alison: Ah, Mum's chops
usually come with gravy

Michael: Do they?
Course they do

Alison: Next to the toaster in
the jar

Michael: Jar?

Gravy granules?

Mmm just as well

I wasn't making...

Jason: Coffee, can I have one?

Michael: It's true, the first 18 years are the worst

Oh you must have seen this a dozen times

Alsion: Leave her alone she's got a lump in her throat

Jason: Must be one of Dad's sprouts

Michael: More coffee, Jason?

To set the launch in historical context; the friendly rivalry of Oxo and its chief competitor in the 'meat and vegetable extracts' market, Bisto, had been shaken in 1979 with the launch of Bisto Gravy Granules.

Until then much of the gravy in the UK had been made using Oxo for flavour and Bisto to thicken. Now Bisto offered an alternative way to make complete gravy.

Having launched the product Bisto then slowly built the sector so that by 1990 Gravy Granules represented 33% of the total market and was the fastest growing sector.

However, during 1990 Oxo started work on developing their own gravy granules which would reflect the quality of the Oxo brand and hopefully create a new sector within the market. Bisto sold at around a 14% premium over own label; the Oxo granules were to be launched at a 40% premium over Bisto (85p versus 59p for 170g).

The product Oxo developed certainly met these objectives as blind product tests were to show:

TABLE 8: BLIND PRODUCT TESTS

	Oxo	Major competitor
Beefy taste	5	1
Strength of flavour	4	1.5
Consistency	4	2
Appearance	4	3.5

Note: Key: Minimum = 0, Maximum = 5
Source: Independent Research

This product was put into a Research International Microtest to help evaluate potential volume. The results were encouraging, initial volume projections were made and the project moved on to the next stages.

One of these stages was the development of advertising. A key issue however was whether to launch within the context of the Family campaign or develop something completely new.

The debate centred on whether the Oxo family was so intrinsically linked with Oxo *cubes* that the launch of this new product (which makes something that the cube is already famous for) would be lost. Against this was the known power of the Family campaign.

Oxo Gravy Granules in three varieties – Beef, Chicken and Vegetable – were launched to the trade with deliveries starting in July 1991 and a Family commercial ('Coffee Break') ran from September.

The result was both dramatic and almost instantaneous as Figure 3 shows. Ex-factory sales increased four fold within a fortnight of the campaign breaking and then continued upwards.

Sales went up to a level nearly twice that predicted by the earlier Microtest. Retailers struggled to keep product in stock and on the shelves. In face of this demand, Oxo made the decision to withdraw further marketing support till later in the year as they fought to maintain supply. Their factory at Worksop had to step up production significantly.

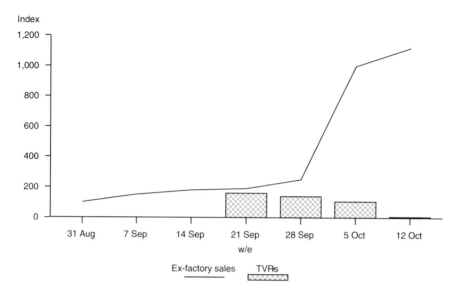

Figure 3. *Oxo Gravy Granules: immediate advertising effects*
Source: Oxo

Some of this increase in sales was attributable to increasing distribution. However, it can be seen below that the vast bulk of distribution had already been gained before the onset of advertising.

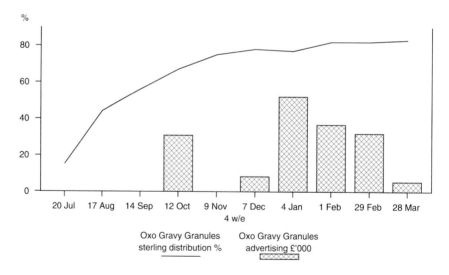

Figure 4. *Oxo Gravy Granules: distribution build*
Source: NMRA

All other variables remained constant over this period and it therefore appears that advertising must have been the catalyst for the spectacular uplift in sales. This can be further demonstrated by examining market share per point of weighted distribution.

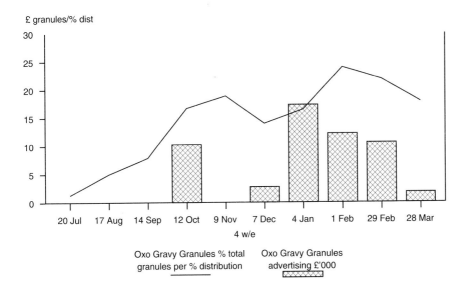

Figure 5. *Oxo Gravy Granules: share per point of distribution*
Source: NMRA

Further evidence that advertising was indeed the catalyst is provided by consumer research in the form of the Millward Brown tracking study.

The advertising awareness graph below also demonstrates the dramatic effects of this advertising; awareness went from nothing to 26% in a month as a result of only 411 TVRs.

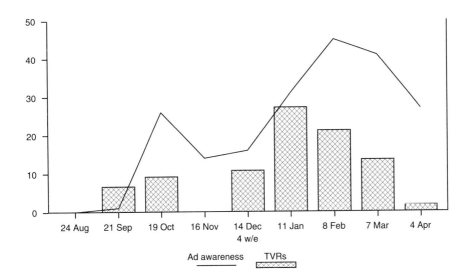

Figure 6. *Oxo Gravy Granules: TV ad awareness*
Source: Millward Brown

Advertising awareness dropped off once the initial campaign stopped but again responded immediately and strongly once the advertising restarted in December, climbing to a peak of 45%.

Of all those who recalled the advertising:
      80% recalled it as Oxo Gravy Granules
      20% recalled it as Red Oxo Cubes

Source: Millward Brown

This result further justified the decision to develop advertising within the Family campaign. The ad also clearly aroused interest in the product ('Friday Night Fever', a strong script centering on contemporary usage, is put in for comparison in the table below).

TABLE 9: PROMPTED IMPRESSIONS

	Friday Night Fever	Coffee Break
Base: all housewives	100	100
	%	%
I already like the brand and I like this ad	66	39
It made me a lot more interested in it	2 } 16	23 } 49
It made me a little more interested in it	14	26
It didn't improve my opinion of it	20	14
If anything it put me off a bit	2	–

Source: Millward Brown

Bisto responded by launching Fuller Flavour Granules as a line extension to their Original. It was in a jar, held the same volume (170g) and was the same price (85p) as Oxo. They do say 'imitation is the sincerest form of flattery'.

Because cubes and granules are competitive markets, there was concern about the level of cannibalisation from Oxo cubes. The levels which have been observed thus far are within the objective set by Oxo, but must remain confidential. However, the share gains made by Oxo Gravy Granules within its first six months make it clear that the brand has been growing within the meat and vegetable extracts market.

TABLE 10: GRAVY GRANULES VOLUME SHARES, 1991/92

4 w/e	Aug 4	Sep 1	Sep 29	Oct 27	Nov 24	Dec 22	Jan 19	Feb 16
	100	100	100	100	100	100	100	100
	%	%	%	%	%	%	%	%
Total Bisto	58	56	56	50	55	53	50	47
Total Oxo	1	3	6	11	8	9	13	19
Total Goldenfry	13	11	11	12	13	12	12	12
Total own label	28	30	27	27	24	26	24	22

Source: AGB

Oxo's share in value terms is much higher, of course. Further evidence that this launch has benefited the brand overall comes from a comparison of total Oxo sales in the first quarter 1992 compared with the equivalent period in 1991.

TABLE 11: CHANGE IN STERLING SALES

	Q1 1992 vs Q1 1991
Total meat extracts market	+7%
Total Oxo	+35%

Sources: AGB and Oxo

CONCLUSIONS

1. Advertising has played a key role in keeping Oxo strong, and central to the ever-changing eating behaviour of UK households over 37 years. Thanks to '60s growth (partly fuelled by 'Katie') and subsequent resistance to the 'food revolution' (stiffened by the 'Family'), cube sales are as high today as they were in the mid-1950s.

2. For many years, the brand has had to evolve to pull an unchanged product along with it. Now, the power of Oxo is being demonstrated by its ability to broaden its business base through new products and quickly gain significant share. The Family campaign has been successfully adapted to this purpose, most notably for the launch of Oxo Gravy Granules, with ex-factory sales quadrupling in the first fortnight.

3. It is clear that the Oxo brand and its cubes franchise has been strengthened in many ways over the years for which data have been collected, during the period of the Family campaign. Market share has grown, the brand image has been maintained or improved on nearly all dimensions and the cube is as widely used today as it was in the foods of yesteryear. How important was the Family advertising in all this? We believe that there is convincing evidence that it has made a significant contribution. A share model has isolated an advertising contribution of three share points over the 1987–92 period. The loss of media support in London had severe consequences for Oxo one winter. We have demonstrated a linkage between improvements in Oxo's measured image and specific Family commercials with related messages. Finally, the evident salience of the advertising has helped keep Oxo famous, and that surely must be important to a brand which must retain its contemporary relevance.

4. In business terms, Brooke Bond Foods own a strong brand and a profitable cubes business which has been facing very real long-term threats. It provides a platform from which successful broadening and real brand growth is clearly possible. In the first quarter of 1992, mainly thanks to Gravy Granules, total Oxo sales were 35% greater than in the comparable period a year previously.

WEATHER APPENDIX

MEAN DAILY AIR TEMPERATURE (DEGREES CELSIUS) FROM OCTOBER TO MARCH,
ENGLAND AND WALES

1960/61	7.4	1970/71	6.9	1980/81	6.6
1961/62	5.9	1971/72	7.1	1981/82	5.7
1962/63	4.3	1972/73	7.0	1982/83	6.8
1963/64	6.3	1973/74	6.8	1983/84	6.2
1964/65	6.0	1974/75	6.9	1984/85	5.9
1965/66	6.6	1975/76	6.6	1985/86	5.3
1966/67	7.0	1976/77	6.3	1986/87	6.0
1967/68	6.3	1977/78	6.7	1987/88	6.9
1968/69	6.1	1978/79	5.7	1988/89	7.7
1969/70	6.0	1979/80	6.7	1989/90	8.1
60s average	6.2	70s average	6.7	80s average	6.5

Source: Meteorological Office

TECHNICAL APPENDIX

Model of the Effects of the Family Campaign for Cubes

An econometric model was constructed to explain Oxo cubes volume share of total stock cubes over the period 4 w/e 31 January 1987 to 4 w/e 28 March 1992. The explanatory variables quantified in the model were:

— Inertia
— Seasonality
— Advertising

(Distribution and relative price were found *not* to be statistically significant.)

The model achieved an outstanding fit (the model's prediction of share of market based on the explanatory variables versus what actually happened) with a standard error of just 0.8% and an R^2 of almost 84%. The model parameters were stable over time and the model comfortably passed Henley Marketing Dynamics International's standard battery of statistical tests.

THE MODEL

	Coefficient	Standard Error	TStat
Log Oxo market share (1)	0.4608	0.0755	6.1050
Season 1	0.0251	0.0043	5.8788
Season 2	0.0126	0.0040	3.1942
Season 3	0.0095	0.0040	2.4005
Season 8	0.0107	0.0043	2.4912
Season 10	0.0147	0.0047	3.1454
Season 11	0.0150	0.0042	3.5576
Season 12	0.0186	0.0040	4.6681
Difference Log Oxo share of voice	0.0007	0.0003	2.6882
Log Oxo share of voice (1)	0.0006	0.0003	2.0435
Dummy 1	0.2993	0.0061	4.9288
Dummy 2	0.1566	0.0052	3.0297
Dummy 3	0.0249	0.0088	2.0435

R^2 = 83.6%
Adjust R^2 = 80.0%
Standard Error = 0.8%
DurbinWatson Stat = 2.0

1. *Inertia* – Broadly speaking, about half of Oxo cubes volume market share in a given time period depends on share the previous time period. This implies quite a high level of inertia in sales. This means that it takes time for the full effect of changes in advertising to fully feed through to sales.
2. *Seasonality* – Although this model is based on market *share*, there appears to be a very consistent seasonal influence. This is an effect above and beyond that of changes in share of advertising voice.
3. *Advertising* – Advertising can be expressed in terms of absolute TVR, total expenditure or as a share of voice term. The magnitude of any advertising 'carry over' effect can also be examined.

Advertising in the Oxo cube market share model takes the form of an expenditure based (TV and press) share of voice against cubes and gravies. No carry over effect was discernible above and beyond the explicit dynamics of the advertising terms and the inertia in the model.

There is a long-term effect of advertising whereby a 1% increase (percent, *not* percentage point) in Oxo share of voice will increase Oxo's market share by 0.001% (percent, *not* percentage point). This is not as small an effect as it may appear, as obviously very great changes in share of voice occur on a period to period basis.

This long-term effect of advertising appears to have a *lagged* effect of one 4 week period. Over the period examined, this long-term effect of advertising appears to have contributed consistently an average of about 2 percentage points of incremental market share each 4 week period, up to a maximum of about 5 percentage points.

There is a further short-term 'boost' effect of advertising, captured in the model by the difference in Oxo share of voice from one period to another. This suggests that *in addition* to the lagged long term effect there is an additional contemporaneous boost to sales from advertising. So, *in addition* to the long term impact, a 1% (percent, *not* percentage point) increase in advertising share of voice will boost Oxo's share of market by 0.0013% (percent, *not* percentage point). *This* effect will then tend to persist because of the effect of inertia, the share 'boost' decaying by about 50% each period. This short term effect of advertising appears to have contributed an average of about 1 percentage point in market share over the period examined. Thus, in total, advertising has contributed an average of about 3 percentage points to Oxo's market share.

This is simply a naïve quantification of the immediate impact of advertising on market share. It is interesting to note that *no* absolute, real or relative price sensitivity was discernable for Oxo cubes. This is undoubtedly the consequence of the power of the Oxo brand. No distribution effect could be quantified in the model.

Additionally, there appears to be an upward trend in Oxo market share, gaining approximately 1 percentage point (deseasonalised) over the period examined.

7

'Reassuringly Expensive'

A Case History of the
Stella Artois Press Campaign

SUMMARY

Throughout the 1980s, when lager brewers were spending millions on evermore lavish TV advertising campaigns, one brand pursued an altogether different route. It religiously eschewed the bright lights of TV in favour of a low-impact press advertising, and ran its own style of confident, at times, arrogant copy, proclaiming of all things how absurdly expensive it was. Many must have expected the brand to be consigned to a minority existence in the ever-expanding, highly competitive premium lager market; to their astonishment it not only assumed brand leadership, but holds that position even now.

During the late 1970s and early 1980s, Stella Artois had all the ingredients of a brand-leading lager, yet its sales performance was sluggish. Volume grew only in line with the market, and its share was 6% and slowly declining. In 1981, Whitbread moved the advertising account to newly-formed Lowe Howard-Spink, who realised that what the brand needed was a phrase which could unite the various aspects of the brand's appeal and act as a catalyst to drive the brand forward. This phrase was:

'Stella Artois – Reassuringly Expensive'

From this point onwards, Stella's fortunes were transformed. It outperformed every other premium lager brand, with sales increasing fivefold in just seven years; its growth outpaced the market, and as a consequence its share almost doubled. Perhaps most impressive was that it achieved all this whilst commanding a significant price premium over every other comparable brand in the market.

Stella's advertising contributed to this success in two different ways. The first was to raise Stella's already high reputation amongst drinkers. The premium market comprises three different types of drinker – the 'Connoisseurs', whose interest is in flavour; the 'Style-Seekers', who go for novelty and fashion-appeal; and the 'Headbangers', who are interested only in strength. Stella's advertising was unique in that it appealed equally to all three of these drinker types. Evidence of this comes not only from the way in which Stella's image increased during the 1980s, but from the fact that by the end of the decade Stella was the *only* premium lager brand to be consumed above average by all three drinker types.

The second, perhaps more important way in which advertising worked, was by enabling Stella to increase its on-trade distribution. Advertising set up what might be termed a triangular relationship between Whitbread, the consumer, and the publican. Because advertising told the consumer that Stella was more expensive than other lagers, the publican knew he could sell it at a premium price; because this meant he earned a greater margin, not only was he keen to stock the brand, but he was prepared to pay a premium price for it himself; and the income generated by this premium price in turn paid for the cost of the advertising. In Stella's case, this triangular relationship was so successful that the premium income which was produced by the advertising was almost *twice the total cost of the advertising*.

At the end of the 1980s came further evidence to support the role of advertising. In 1987 heavy TV activity by the competition forced Stella's share of adspend below its sales share, and the sales share stopped growing. Two years later, with adspend now one-third of sales share, the sales share declined for the first time since 'Reassuringly Expensive' was run in the copy.

MARKET BACKGROUND

During the 1970s, a young man's fancy turned from the bitter beer his forebears had drunk to a new beverage called lager. Unlike bitter, lager was fizzy, light-coloured and served cold. But in order to counter accusations of it being a girl's drink, UK lager adopted two bitter characteristics: it was served in pints, and it was made weaker so that it could be consumed in greater quantity. Thus was created the anomaly called the UK standard lager market.

Some ex-bitter drinkers found standard lager so thin and tasteless, that they resorted to the handful of brands which retained lager's original premium strength. These 'Connoisseurs' were the first on-trade premium lager drinkers, and the focus of their attention was flavour.

In the mid 1970s, two unbelievably hot summers, rampant inflation and rising unemployment heralded the arrival of a new breed of premium lager drinker. These young men sought nirvana through bottles of Holsten Pils, or cans of Fosters, and their habit of falling over at the end of each session earned them the title 'Headbangers'.

However, few pubs outside London had cooling shelves, and only the most determined were prepared to seek oblivion via warm lager. Then in 1980 Bass launched Tennents Extra. It was nationally available, chilled on draught right from the start, had unequivocally macho advertising, and was not that expensive. Pretty soon, 'heads' were being 'banged' all over the UK.

The coincident arrival of affluence and cooling shelves in the early 1980s was a heaven-sent opportunity for both big brewers and small opportunists to trawl the world for premium priced cans and bottles to put on display. Suddenly lager became a fashion accessory, and a third type of drinker – 'Style-Seekers' – emerged. They would drink almost anything provided it wasn't there last week. Their interest was exclusivity first and product second. TV advertising was anathema to them, as it meant that everyone knew about the brand. They went for unadvertised bottled brands, like Grolsch and Becks.

Thus at the start of the 1980s you had three different types of drinker, all wanting something different, faced with a raft of different products, some available only in bottles, some only in cans, and some on draught. In the midst of this bubbling cauldron was Stella Artois.

STELLA ADVERTISING BACKGROUND

Stella Artois was brought to the UK in 1937. Even then it was expensive, but it was not until 1975 that it decided to advertise the fact in press. CDP's campaign was designed to attract the early lager connoisseur, who wanted a quality drink and was prepared to pay for it. Stella quickly established itself as a small but successful draught premium brand, but its growth levelled out towards the end of the 1970s: although the brand's volumes rose, they did so only in line with the market, and Stella failed to make any serious impression on the competition.

In 1981, Frank Lowe and Geoff Howard-Spink started their new agency and Whitbread was their first client. Surprisingly, they resisted the temptation to augment their income by switching to a new high-budget TV campaign. The only change they did make demonstrated just how well they understood the psychology of the market at the time; it was the addition of a new end-line:

'Stella Artois – Reassuringly Expensive'

This line became the backbone of two distinct strategies: one designed for the consumer, one for the trade.

THE CONSUMER STRATEGY

The basis of the original CDP campaign was quality of ingredients. What Whitbread and Lowe Howard-Spink recognised was that a quality message had relevance to all three drinker types, not just the 'Connoisseurs'. A quality lager to a 'Headbanger' is one which is stronger, and a quality lager to a 'Style-Seeker' is one which is fashionable and exclusive. But how do you convey quality to highly sceptical younger drinkers? The answer was to take what was the executional device of the original CDP campaign – the premium price – and use it as a 'quality reassurance' statement; hence the origin of the phrase 'Reassuringly Expensive'.

The clever thing about this line was that each user group could appropriate it for their own ends. The original 'Connoisseurs' could use it with the ingredients story to reassure themselves that the product had a distinctive flavour; the 'Headbangers', who knew that duty levied on alcohol made up a large chunk of the price, could use it to reassure themselves that because it cost more it was stronger; and the 'Style-Seekers', who sought exclusivity, could use the high price to reassure themselves that not many people would be able to afford the brand, and it would remain exclusive. Yet this three-way appeal was but part of the strength of the line; perhaps its greatest strength was in the way it could be used not with the consumer, but with the trade.

THE TRADE STRATEGY

The key to success in the draught lager market has always been distribution, particularly distribution in the free-trade. In 1981 most free-trade licensees would have stocked a range of draught beers and one or two draught lagers, and have had a further half a dozen bottled and canned lagers on the cold-shelf. Then along comes draught premium lager.

The first question the publican will ask is:

'Do I need it? Putting another font on the bar means dropping an existing product, perhaps one which sells slowly but has a popular core of users. Who is going to drink this new product, how much will I sell of it, will it be enough to keep the pipes clean?'

Whitbread and Lowe Howard-Spink knew that only one thing would help overcome the publican's concern, and that was the prospect of profit. Few can resist the temptation to replace a low margin product with a high margin one. However, they also knew that artificially reducing their own margins in order to increase the publican's was a short-term measure guaranteed to cause trouble as soon as they tried to raise the trade price. The extra profit had to come from the consumer. But how then do you convince the publican that drinkers will pay a higher price than normal?

The answer was to use advertising to forewarn the consumer that the product would cost more, and explain why. By doing this, the publican will perceive that the product will have a built-in high margin, and will be extra keen to stock it – perhaps so keen that he will pay a premium himself for it.

In effect what was being set up was a triangular relationship. The advertising tells the consumer the product is going to cost more; the publican stocks the product because he knows it will earn him extra margin, and pays a premium to do so; the premium price ideally pays for the advertising which tells the consumer the product costs more in the first place. But what was needed to make it work was a phrase which the salesman could use to convince the publican. Again, 'Reassuringly Expensive' fitted the bill, because it reassured the publican that this was not just a short-term ploy to get him to stock, but was a long-term positioning which would guarantee him extra profits.

THE MEDIA STRATEGY

If 'Reassuringly Expensive' was so effective, why could it not have been transferred onto TV in 1982? For two reasons. Firstly, in order to work it demanded that each type of consumer was able to consume the advertising in his own, almost private, way. If the advertising itself became widely discussed, it could end up being 'assigned' to one group to the detriment of the others. But secondly, and more importantly, such public discussion was guaranteed to drive off the 'Style-Seekers', an affluent group who perhaps more than any other would be likely to pay the premium required to finance the whole thing.

'Reassuringly Expensive' ran as an end-line from the start of 1982 onwards. A total of 18 press subjects have been run since then, averaging two new executions each year. A selection of these can be found on pages 130 and 131.

The media budget in 1982 and 1983 increased moderately, but in 1984 it increased significantly, and this rise held for four years. It should be noted that a TV test was run in HTV in 1985 but the results were disappointing and the test was discontinued after a second burst of advertising in 1986.

Details of Stella and competitive advertising expenditure are shown in Table 1.

TABLE 1: PREMIUM LAGER ADSPEND (£000)

Brand	1980	1981	1982	1983	1984	1985	1986	1987	1988	1989	1982-89 SOV (%)
Stella Artois	531	499	614	682	1,206*	1,034*	1,601*	1,205	721	694	9.6
Tennents Extra	67	568	683	562	598	529	599	2,020	2,762	4,549	15.2
Holsten Pils/ Export	1,340	1,986	1,284	1,319	3,114	1,842	2,363	2,284	3,811	4,064	22.2
Kronenbourg	1,021		996	368			235	1,103	1,771	2,241	8.3
Löwenbräu	280	1,186	1,242	1,477	741		869	1,558		1,956	9.7
Budweiser					726	1,458	1,344	1,792	1,637	1,270	10.1
Grolsch					333	490	194	319	868	1,391	4.4
Lamot	280				685	1,501	1,188	1,607	255	2,069	9.0
Others	314			105	267	585	1,121	1,912	2,110	1,229	9.0
Annual total	3,551	4,239	4,818	4,514	7,669	7,440	9,514	13,800	13,935	19,463	100.0
Stella SOV (%)	14.9	11.8	12.7	15.1	15.7	13.9	16.8	8.7	5.2	3.6	

Source: MEAL Digest

Note: *Includes TV area test expenditure

QUALITATIVE EVALUATION

The decision to stick to the price/quality campaign was a bold one, but was not taken with the assistance of research. Whitbread commissioned two qualitative research projects shortly after the incorporation of 'Reassuringly Expensive'. The first comprised four focus groups by Dr Terry O'Brien in December 1982; the second 15 depth interviews by Campbell Daniels Research in August 1983.

If the campaign was working correctly, it should have been building a strong image for Stella on the areas of *flavour, strength* and *fashion appeal,* as well as a reputation for being *more expensive than other lager* and *worth paying the extra for.* This is precisely what was found. Some of the more pertinent quotes were:

Strength:
'It's recognised as being very strong, and it is.'
'It's one of the strongest of all.'
'It's as strong as Pils or Special Brew.'

(The last comment was particularly apposite, given that Stella was significantly less strong than either of these brands.)

Flavour:
'The flavour is better.'
'The taste is better/stronger.'
'It's distinctive – you recognise it.'

Fashion Appeal:
'It is a stylish drink.'
'... a more classy lager.'
'It sounds sophisticated.'
'It's really trendy.'

Expense/Good Value
'Stella is not too badly priced – you get what you pay for.'
'It's not overpriced.'
'It's worth the money, more than most lagers.'
'It's good value.'

Dr O'Brien summed the value for money issue up as follows:

'Most respondents expressed the view that Stella Artois represents good value for money in that the premium price it commanded was offset by its higher alcohol content and stronger flavour.'

And his overall conclusions were as follows:

'The present research would suggest that an expense/quality platform is very viable for Stella Artois. It is clearly a memorable concept, and is seen to be very much in accord with Stella imagery.'

The same research also confirmed the wisdom of the choice of press media rather than TV. A devout 'Style-Seeker' said:

'It has become fashionable – and is becoming more so – it is something different, *and it's not advertised too much.*'

So the campaign was structurally correct, but how well did 'Reassuringly Expensive' fit within it? The findings of the Campbell Daniels research were clear on this point.

> 'Stella Artois has a classy and expensive image but an actual price that is within reach of most people, with the result that the brand represents an affordable aspiration, a drinker pedestal that is within easy reach. The advertising end-line, "Reassuringly Expensive", is a most apt way of encapsulating this affordable aspiration image aspect of Stella. More than that, it reminds the drinker that his aspiration is justified, to himself and to others.'

QUANTITATIVE EVALUATION

Whitbread did not track the Stella campaign, but the Millward Brown syndicated lager tracking study fortuitously commenced just before 'Reassuringly Expensive' was adopted. I have used tables from Jan/Feb 1982 as pre-data, and as post-data Jan/Feb 1987, one of the last periods before the syndicated lager survey underwent a major change which impairs comparability.

In 1982, courtesy of its previous advertising, Stella was already a well-established brand of lager with a 'premium price' perception and a good reputation for quality and flavour. However, it was neither brand leader in sales, nor the most highly-rated brand for strength. These honours were held by Holsten Pils. Also, hard on the heels of both Stella and Holsten Pils was the recently launched Tennents Extra, riding the wave of draught popularity amongst 'Headbangers'. For Stella's advertising to work it had to do four things:

1. It had to elevate Stella's image for *strength* above Holsten Pils, and maintain a lead over the 'macho' positioned Tennents Extra. This would secure the brand's appeal to 'Headbangers'.
2. It had to maintain the brand's lead on *flavour*, in order to maintain the loyalty of 'Connoisseurs'.
3. It had to create a *fashionable image* for the brand in order to appeal to 'Style-Seekers'.
4. It had to open up a lead between Stella and all other brands on *premium price* perception, without any deterioration in respondents' *willingness to drink* the brand.

This is precisely what the advertising achieved. I have summarised the performance in Table 2, showing Stella's scores on the five most relevant image dimensions and how they related to the premium brand with the next highest image in 1982 (Holsten Pils) and 1987 (Tennents Extra). Note that *Appeal to the young* is chosen as the most relevant fashion measure because the 'Style-Seeker' would not drink a brand which appealed to older drinkers. It was on this key dimension that Stella had its poorest score in 1982 and made its greatest improvement.

TABLE 2: STELLA IMAGE VS TOP/NO. 2 BRAND

	Jan/Feb 1982	Jan/Feb 1987
Strong in alcohol	46% –8% behind Holsten Pils	59% +9% ahead of Tennents Extra
Has a lot of flavour	38% +5% ahead of Holsten Pils	43% +14% ahead of Tennents Extra
Appeals to younger drinkers	10% –5% behind Holsten Pils	22% +5% ahead of Holsten Pils
More expensive	50% 1st equal with Holsten Pils	60% +20% ahead of Tennents Extra
Would like to drink	32% +5% ahead of Holsten Pils	40% +16% ahead of Tennents Extra

Regretfully, one of the most signficant image dimensions, *Appeals to those who keep up with the latest trends* was not asked in 1982. However, as Table 3 shows, by 1987 Stella was 6% ahead of the next most fashionable brand, a position it would certainly never have occupied in 1982. Not bad for possibly the oldest lager brand in the UK.

TABLE 3: 'APPEALS TO THOSE WHO LIKE TO KEEP UP
WITH THE LATEST TRENDS'

	Jan/Feb 1987
Stella Artois	21%
Holsten Pils	15%
Tennents Extra	11%
Holsten Export	7%
Löwenbräu	8%

Source: Millward Brown syndicated lager
tracking study – 'all aware of brand'

Were these movements simply a function of an increase in those who buy Stella on the tracking study? There was an 18% increase (from 39% to 57%) in those who claimed ever to have tried Stella between the two periods, and a 16% increase (from 13% to 29%) in those who claimed to now drink Stella. However, *Is particularly refreshing*, an image dimension which you could argue was not in any way influenced by advertising, rose just 2% from 25% to 27% during this period, which suggests that Stella's rise in image was prompted by advertising, not just by more drinkers on the study.

What this response demonstrates is that 'Reassuringly Expensive' fulfilled all the criteria required of it according to the consumer and trade strategies set: Stella improved its image and took leadership on all the key image dimensions pertinent to each of the three drinker groups; it also achieved the lead on premium price perception and willingness to drink, the two dimensions necessary to convince the trade to stock the brand and invoke the 'triangular relationship'. The only question which remains is whether or not the strategies achieved what was required of them.

Discover the breaking point of plastic.

A round of Stella? That'll do nicely. But the price? Even flexible friends have been known to crack. It's our insistence on using the very finest ingredients that so undermines your financial standing.

We give our buyers a blank cheque to obtain the most fragrant of female hops. (The Saaz variety from Czechoslovakia win by a nose.) We give them carte blanche to travel the length and breadth of Europe in their quest for the cream of the barley crop. As if that wasn't enough to cripple your credit, we then bump up the price even more by allowing Stella to mature for at least six weeks. Most beers are granted half that time.

We could cut corners in order to place less of a strain on your resources. But as we aren't about to lower our standards, may we suggest instead that you raise your credit limit? **Stella Artois. Reassuringly expensive.**

It's frequently accompanied by a good whine.

And who could blame a chap for carping? The cost of Stella *is* unnervingly high. But what would you have us do?

Wave goodbye to the buyers who roam the world sniffing out the most fragrant of female hops?

Abandon forthwith our pernickety insistence on Europe's choicest barley?

Cut short the 6 long weeks Stella languishes in maturing vats? (After all, many rival brews are deemed drinkable after a mere 3 weeks.)

Don't think that we haven't given suggestions such as these a great deal of serious thought.

Each one of them has been most carefully considered for at least 3 seconds.

For whilst they may well result in an adequate brew, it most certainly would not be Stella Artois.

And if that were the case, then, sir, you certainly would have something to whine about.

Stella Artois. Reassuringly expensive.

THE RESPONSE

The 1980s were a period of unparalleled activity in the premium lager market. No fewer than six major draught brands entered the market – Tennents Extra was the first, followed by Kronenbourg 1664, Lamot, Carlsberg Export, Budweiser, and Grolsch – as well as literally hundreds of minor brands in bottles and cans. Advertising spend on premium brands alone increased fourfold between 1982 and 1989 (Table 1).

Stella entered the 1980s in a relatively undistinguished way, with both sales and market share declining slowly despite an advertising share-of-spend between two and three times higher than brand share. In late 1981, 'Reassuringly Expensive' first appeared in copy, and Whitbread geared their sales force up for a major distribution drive. The results were dramatic.

Volume Sales and Share

Stella's volume sales increased 33% in 1982, and thereafter just kept on growing. By 1989 its volume sales were 406% up on the 1981 figure, having risen every year in the interim. This volume growth outstripped the market, and Stella's share of market grew every year to 1987, rising from 5.8% in 1981 to 11% by 1987 (Table 4).

TABLE 4: STELLA ARTOIS BRAND PERFORMANCE

	Premium Lager volume 000 BB	Stella volume 000 BB	Brand share %	Advertising share %
1978	1,525	101	6.6	11.8
1979	1,698	107	6.3	18.4
1980	1,754	103	5.9	14.9
1981	1,761	102	5.8	11.8
1982	2,069	136	6.6	12.7
1983	2,317	189	8.2	15.1
1984	2,693	238	8.8	15.7
1985	2,948	293	9.9	13.9
1986	3,480	377	10.8	16.8
1987	4,139	455	11.0	8.7
1988	4,536	500	11.0	5.2
1989	4,852	517	10.7	3.6
Total 1982–89	27,034	2,705	10.0	9.6
1989/81	+176%	+406%	+84.0	

Sources: Beer Market Survey, Whitbread Stats, MEAL

Distribution and Throughput

Between January 1983 and January 1989 total outlets stocking draught Stella more than doubled, with the biggest increases evident in the most competitive area of all, the free-trade, where Stella's distribution increased by 140% (Table 5).

TABLE 5: STELLA DRAUGHT DISTRIBUTION

	Tied-trade	Free-trade	Total
Jan/Feb 1983	2,961	2,041	5,040
Jan/Feb 1989	5,592	4,911	10,503
% increase	+89%	+140%	+108%

Indexing Stella's draught volume increases between 1982 and 1988 against draught distribution at the beginning of the following year shows that Stella's throughput per outlet rose by 56% over this period. Impressive though this is, it is less than the corresponding total market growth of 109% over the same period.

Two things are responsible for this shortfall. Firstly, Stella was already a successful draught brand in 1982, and its distribution would mainly have been in outlets which already had a high throughput of draught premium lager. Secondly, the total market includes a whole raft of new bottled, canned, and draught brands which would be competing directly for business with Stella in both new and existing outlets. On this basis a 56% increase in throughput is an outstanding achievement (Table 6).

TABLE 6: STELLA VOLUME VS DISTRIBUTION

	Stella Draught distribution	Stella Draught volume	Stella throughput index	Total Market growth index
1982/83	5,040	115	100	100
1988/89	10,503	373	156	209

Source: Whitbread Stats

Market Penetration

Stella's growth was impressive, but was it a phenomenon enjoyed by all draught premium lagers at the time, caused simply by the influx of new users to the category. Sales figures for competitors are not available, but TGI from 1984 onwards (1983 and earlier figures are not comparable) shows that only two brands grew significantly during this period – Tennents Extra and Stella – and Stella's growth was by far the greatest. At the end of the decade, even after three years without growth, Stella still had 80% more users than any other draught brand (Table 7).

TABLE 7: TOTAL USERS OF DRAUGHT PREMIUM BRANDS

	1984* %	1985 %	1986 %	1987 %	1988 %	1989 %	1990 %	1991 %
Stella Artois	8.5	10.5	11.4	13.9	13.8	13.9	14.9	14.8
Tennents Extra	2.1	2.9	4.3	5.7	6.7	7.2	6.9	6.6
Holsten Export	3.1	3.5	3.0	2.9	3.0	3.3	3.3	3.2
Löwenbräu	4.6	5.3	5.1	5.3	6.6	6.4	7.3	6.8
Kronenbourg	7.1	6.2	7.4	7.3	7.5	7.8	8.4	8.7

Source: BMRB TGI
Note: *Figures prior to 1984 are not comparable.

Penetration of Drinker Types

Evidence of Stella's success in appealing to the three groups of drinkers is available from TGI. A cluster analysis conducted on 1990/91 TGI data isolated a group of late 20s/early 30s up-market drinkers with clearly affluent quality-oriented tastes ('Connoisseurs'), a group of younger middle-market heavy drinkers with clearly hedonistic tastes ('Headbangers'), and a group of younger up-market drinkers, highly experimental and with fashion-oriented tastes ('Style-Seekers'). These three groups are the three most frequent consumers of premium lager, and the only *premium brand they all consume above average is Stella Artois* (Table 8).

TABLE 8: TGI CLUSTER ANALYSIS

Cluster:	1	2	3
Title:	Connoisseurs	Headbangers	Style-Seekers
% Lager drinkers	14.8	12.7	13.6
Most often index:			
Stella Artois	136	116	137
Tennents Extra	91	112	128
Holsten Export	49	126	174
Holsten Pils	66	173	145
Kronenbourg	140	71	139
Löwenbräu	96	143	176

Source: BMRB TGI 1990/91

Trade Price Premium

Finally, in order to make the triangular relationship pay off, it was necessary for Stella not only to be seen as expensive by the consumer, but to maintain a premium wholesale price to the trade. Whitbread, like all brewers, kept records not only of their own wholesale prices but those of their competitors. These records show that throughout the 1980s Stella sold to the trade at a consistently higher price than all its major competitors, and that this price-differential was indeed greatest at the time of Stella's most rapid growth (see Table 9).

TABLE 9:   AVERAGE WHOLESALE PRICE (£ per bulk barrel)

	Mar 1981	Jul–Sep 1983	Jul–Sep 1985	Jul–Sep 1987	Jun–Jul 1989
Average Stella	£101.70	£128.70	£151.40	£162.30	£184.50
Average competition*	£96.70	£121.20	£142.50	£156.60	£176.60
Stella Premium	£5.00	£7.50	£8.90	£5.70	£7.90
Stella % Premium	+5.2%	+6.2%	+6.2%	+3.6%	+4.5%
1983–1989 Average Stella premium price = +£7.50 per barrel					

Source: Whitbread Stats

Note: * Tennents Extra, Holsten Export, Löwenbräu. Full details of prices were supplied with original submission.

OTHER FACTORS

From 1982 onwards, Stella Artois produced the sort of results which brand managers frame and hang on their walls. Were there any other factors which might have contributed to this success?

Sales Force Activity

It is clear that a significant sales drive accompanied the introduction of 'Reassuringly Expensive' in 1982, but no extra salesmen were employed, nor is there any record of a significant rise in trade deals or distribution incentives commencing at this time.

Packaging

There is no doubt that Stella's font was a very impressive piece of machinery, made as it was of solid brass, and measuring over a foot tall. It contributed greatly to the brand's success, but since the same font was available before 1981 when the brand's share and sales were static, it cannot have been a primary cause of the brand's revival in 1982 and thereafter. The same is true of can and bottled packaging, which remained virtually unchanged throughout the 1970s and 1980s.

Sponsorship

One important factor in Stella's history is its sponsorship of the Queens Club Tennis Tournament. This prestigious event was and is one of the few occasions when the name of a sponsor actually enters the language of the game. However, the Stella Artois Tennis started in 1979, well before Stella showed signs of growth, so rather like the font design, this is unlikely to have been the cause of the brand's success in 1982.

Promotions

Was there some clever promotional ruse used to attract drinkers to Stella? There were during this period a number of off-trade promotions, but Stella's main volume growth was achieved in the on-trade, without the use of any consumer promotion.

Potency

Was the secret of Stella's success that it was stronger than other premium lagers? No. Holsten Pils was significantly stronger than Stella at 6.5% alcohol by volume (ABV). Stella was 5.0% ABV, just like Tennents Extra, Holsten Export, and the majority of bottled lager brands. Brands like Löwenbräu, Krönenbourg and Carlsberg Hof at around 4.5%, and Kronenbourg 1664 at 4.7% ABV, were not quite as strong, which might help to explain their relatively poor performance; but Stella's mythical potency was just that – a myth!

Product

Many people will swear that Stella's success was all down to a genuinely superior product with a genuinely better taste. There is a simple way to test this hypothesis, which is to test Stella blind against its competitors.

Served blind, Stella was *not* significantly preferred to other draught lager brands, indeed it frequently lost to them. The reason is that Stella is one of the most bitter-tasting of all lagers, and many people find a fuller, sweeter taste more to their liking. So despite the expensive Czechoslovakian female hops, Stella is not a significantly preferred pint... until of course, you put the *name* back on it.

CONCLUSION

Aside from the introduction of 'Reassuringly Expensive' into the advertising copy, nothing else seems to have happened that can account for the dramatic increase in Stella's sales from 1982 onwards. How could so small a change have possibly had so momentous an effect?

The answer is that all the factors necessary for Stella's success were already in place by 1981, and 'Reassuringly Expensive' acted as the catalyst. Stella had the image, the product, the sponsorship, and the packaging needed to become the UK's pre-eminent lager brand, but it had nothing to pull all this together. 'Reassuringly Expensive' gave the consumer a handle to attach to the brand, and even more importantly, gave the salesman a handle he could use to manipulate the publican into stocking the brand. But there is one final piece of evidence which supports the importance of the role of advertising perhaps more than any other, and that is what happened when its power was diminished.

Stella's share of advertising spend between 1982 and 1989 averaged 9.6% against a volume sales share of 10.0%. For the first five years Stella spent ahead of its sales share, and grew every year. By 1987, the launch of a heavy new campaign by Tennents Extra pushed Stella's share of adspend into single figures for the first time in nine years: that year, Stella's sales share peaked at 11%, and in 1989, with share of adspend down to just 3.6%, Stella's sales share declined for the first time since 'Reassuringly Expensive' was run (Figure 1). In other words, Stella's growth, which commenced when 'Reassuringly Expensive' was added to this advertising, ceased when the brand's advertising support was drowned out by the competition. Thus we have both a positive and a negative correlation between the advertising and Stella's achievement.

CONTRIBUTION TO PROFIT

The ultimate criteria for advertising effectiveness is that the advertising should not only contribute to the brand's success, but should also show a commercial return. Stella could not have maintained a price premium without the 'triangular relationship', and it could not have established this relationship without advertising. Stella's *average* cash premium per bulk barrel above competition between 1983 and 1989 was £7.50 (see Table 10). Multiply that by the draught

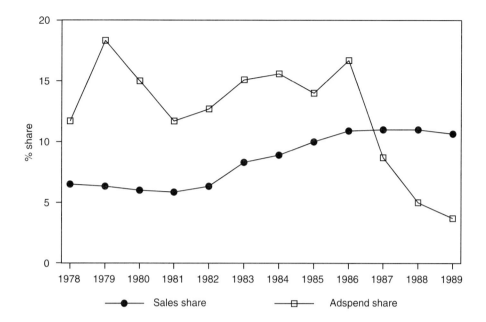

Figure 1. *Adspend share vs sales share*

barrellage sold between 1982 and it yields a total extra income of £15,650,000. This income could not have been earned without advertising, yet the media bill for advertising over this period was just £7,757,000, and the production bill is estimated at less than £400,000.

On this basis Stella's campaign earned Whitbread at the very least £7½ million clear profit after expenses even if you assume it *played no part whatsoever in earning a premium price for the canned and bottled product, and no part whatsoever in the brand's volume growth* (Table 10).

TABLE 10. STELLA CAMPAIGN RECONCILIATION

Average draught premium 1983–1989	=	£ 7.50 per bulk barrel
Total draught barrellage 1982–1989	=	2,087,000 bulk barrels
Total premium revenue	=	£15,650,000
Media costs*	=	£ 7,757,000
Production cost estimate	=	£ 400,000
Net profit		£ 7,493,000
Return on advertising investment		192%

Note: *MEAL figures, excluding discounts, including costs of abortive TV test in HTV 1985/86.

POSTSCRIPT

This case history covers the period up to 1989, which is the most recent data the Whitbread Beer Company will allow to be quoted. During this period, Stella's growth was spectacular, but as the period ended the brand showed signs of decline, and in 1990, the brand deviated from its self-imposed rules and went on TV. Does that mean that the original press campaign ran out of steam? Not at all.

In 1981, premium lager was just 16% of the total lager market, with a total media spend of only £4 million per annum; by 1990 premium lager had risen to 25% of total lager with advertising in excess of £20 million. Stella was still the brand leader, but there is a limit to how much money can be spent by one brand in the press, and this inevitably left the brand vulnerable to both new and existing competitors prepared to spend millions of pounds for a share of this valuable and prestigious market. Furthermore, the migration of Style-Seekers in the late 1980s to bottles meant that the value gained by the relative anonymity of press started to be marginal. Whitbread therefore made the decision to put Stella on TV. This decision was quite clearly correct for although we cannot quote sales figures, Stella's user base on TGI, which was static between 1987 and 1989, revived and reached a new all time high in 1990 of 14.9% (Table 7).

Finally, it should be noted for the record that Stella is still undisputed leader of the premium lager market, still has an image unchallenged by any other brand, and still uses the same 'Reassuringly Expensive' campaign, in the press, that it did in 1981.

8

An Eye to the Future

The Role of Advertising in Raising Optrex's Defences

INTRODUCTION

When Crookes acquired Optrex in 1983, it was the clear brand leader in the eyecare market, with a volume share of 83%, universal pharmacy distribution, high levels of consumer awareness and only three direct competitors, two of which were very small[1]. Optrex was thus a dominant brand without many obvious problems.

It may seem strange to increase significantly the advertising investment for such a dominant brand, but that is what Crookes decided to do. This paper attempts to explain why they did so and to evaluate the results.

SUMMARY

In 1983, there were good reasons to believe that another manufacturer might launch into the market and challenge Optrex's position of dominance.

Industry factors (which will be explained in more detail later) were forcing pharmaceutical companies to look at creating consumer brands in areas other than their traditional heartlands.

To those looking for new markets, the eyecare market would have appeared attractive in 1983. Product technology in the market was not high, and hence imitating products such as Optrex was neither difficult nor very expensive. In addition, the eyecare market was an attractive target because of its high value and profit margins as well as its lack of sizeable brands, other than Optrex.

Crookes were thus faced with the challenge of being in a market which was highly profitable, but which, at that time, had few barriers to entry. And they knew from their own experience that pharmaceutical companies were under great pressure to look for such markets in which to diversify.

---

[1]Competitors were Murine with 12.5% share, Visine and Optabs with less than 5% between them. Other products with different seasonal patterns and specified use (eg Brolene) have not been included in this market definition.

What's more, the whole 'Over the Counter' (OTC)[2] pharmaceutical industry was undergoing dramatic change. New distribution channels (other than the traditional pharmacies) were growing rapidly. Also a whole range of consumer marketing techniques (including consumer advertising) were beginning to be used much more seriously.

The eyecare market had yet to experience most of these changes. All of Optrex's sales were still through pharmacies and up to 1982, although Optrex had had consumer advertising, the amounts spent were very low. The average annual advertising expenditure in the 1970s was only £274k at 1991 prices.

Optrex was thus not only in a very attractive and relatively unguarded market, but the changing nature of pharmaceutical marketing provided the opportunity and impetus for any new rival to challenge the status quo by exploiting this situation.

Furthermore, reliance on Optrex's undoubted familiarity and historical consumer empathy as a defence appeared to be risky. Following price rises between 1979 and 1982, volume sales had been gradually slipping. This suggested that brand loyalty was not as high as in the past and was, if anything, likely to continue to decline.

Crookes decided to address this by investing heavily in consumer advertising, a decision which in itself could have made the market larger and even more attractive to a competitor.

What we shall see, however, is that since 1983, the market did indeed grow in size. Optrex reversed its decline, growing in both absolute volume and share. The majority of this growth, we will argue, was due to the advertising investment. We will show also that advertising increased the brand's strength in consumers' eyes and is continuing to do so. The result of this is that:

1. The brand responded well to the changing market with substantial growth in the newly available distribution channels, thereby eliminating this as a potential opportunity for the basis of a rival launch.
2. Real price rises enabled profits to increase.
3. The effects of the advertising on Optrex, and the very virtue of spending this money, have kept competitors away from the market (despite launches continuing to occur in other more crowded pharmaceutical markets). In fact, not only has Optrex kept rivals away, but Visine, the brand leader in Australia and the US, was squeezed out of the UK market as a result of Optrex's renewed brand strength.

The value of all this to Crookes Healthcare is that revenue has increased since both volume sales and real unit price are significantly higher than in 1982. Optrex has not been attacked by a competitive launch, and it has every chance of continuing to dominate the growing eyecare market in the future.

OPTREX'S ORIGINS

Optrex is a general purpose eyecare brand, first launched in the 1930s. Different stories abound about its past: one intriguing account suggests that it was invented by a New York dentist for his racehorses' eyes. Officially, however, its invention is

[2]Medicines available without prescription.

credited to a French chemist, Madame Famel, who spent time studying the medical practises of the North American Indians. This introduced her to the healing properties of Witch Hazel (Optrex's key ingredient), used by the Indians to treat a number of afflictions including bruises, piles, and eye disorders.

Optrex Lotion was first sold under licence in the UK in the early 1930s. Over the years, other formats were added to the range. Optrex Drops were introduced in 1955 (under the name of Optone). And in the 1970s, a further product was introduced to treat minor eye infections under the name of Clearine, now Optrex Clearine.

THE SITUATION IN 1983

At the time of Optrex's acquisition in 1983, it was a highly profitable brand enjoying considerable market share (Figure 1) and good levels of consumer awareness and trust.

Surprisingly, it had little competition. The only remaining competitors in 1983 were Visine Drops and Murine Drops, both similar to Optrex Drops, as well as Optabs, which, when dissolved in water, produced an eye lotion.

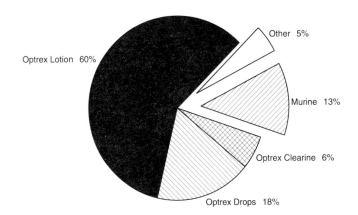

Figure 1. *Optrex market share 1983*
Source: Nielsen

There were, however, concerns that this situation could not be guaranteed to last. These included Optrex's own sales trend, the changing sales environment for OTC medicines, and the increased probability of competitive activity.

Declining Sales

Optrex's volume sales had declined from 1976 to 1982 (Figure 2), a period which had seen several large price rises. This implied that despite Optrex's dominant share, it did have consumer weaknesses. Loyalty towards the brand was more fragile than its share would indicate.

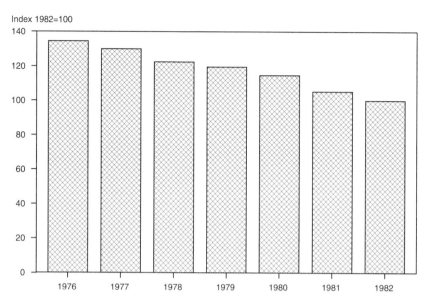

Figure 2. *Total Optrex sales volumes 1976–82*
Source: Nielsen

Changing Environment

The competitive environment for OTC medicines as a whole was changing quite rapidly.

1. Government health policies were forcing pharmaceutical companies to seek out new markets. At the beginning of the 1980s, the pharmaceutical market was undergoing fundamental change. Anxious about rising NHS costs, the government was actively encouraging a move towards self-medication. As an incentive, they restricted the prescription of many branded medicines in 1985 by the introduction of the 'Black List'.
    Unable to rely on prescription sales, companies were being forced to invest in developing consumer brands, either by actively promoting existing products, or by entering new markets. They were therefore under increasing pressure to create strong brand franchises.
2. Additionally, many medical products were no longer restricted to being sold in pharmacies. New distribution opportunities were thus on the horizon, and being actively developed by the grocery trade as they searched for higher margin sectors to exploit. OTC medicines were an attractive area for them. This provided an opportunity for existing brands to expand or a new product to be launched, since it presented an area of distribution which was not 'tied-up'.
3. Pharmaceutical companies were increasingly using classical marketing techniques (such as consumer advertising) to sell their brands. Their real expenditure on consumer advertising nearly doubled between 1979 and 1983 (Source: MEAL).
    In contrast, brands in the eyecare market had spent very little on advertising pre-1983 (Table 1). This market therefore presented a relatively easy

opportunity for a brand (either new or existing) to use significant levels of advertising to generate high awareness, as well as drive distribution and sales.

TABLE 1: TOTAL EYECARE ADVERTISING (1979–83)

	1979	1980	1981	1982	1983
£000s at 1991 prices	544	615	51	0	1,319

Source: MEAL

Increased Probability of Competitive Activity

There were additional reasons why pharmaceutical manufacturers were likely to be looking at the eyecare market as an opportunity.

1. *The eyecare market was profitable.*

   The eyecare market was worth c£6m in 1983. Although the more mainstream OTC markets for analgesics and cough and cold remedies were much bigger than this, in the context of many of the OTC medicine markets, the size of the eyecare market was not insignificant. Although we do not have data on other OTC markets for 1983, more recent data indicate the lack of large competitive brands in Optrex's market compared with other OTC medicine markets of comparable size (Table 2).

TABLE 2: CURRENT VALUES FOR OTC MEDICINE MARKETS

Market	Brands	Market size
Eyecare	Optrex Murine	£12.1m (1991) Sources: Nielsen, Crookes
Antiseptics	Dettol Germolene Savlon,TCP & others	£24m (1989) Source: AA
Laxatives	Senokot, Nylax Fybogel & 12 others	£18.7m (1991) Source: Nielsen
Hayfever	Pollon-Eze, Seldane Piriton, Phenergan Aller-Eze	£15.3m (1991) Source: IMS
Indigestion remedies	Rennie, Setlers Gaviscon, Bisodol, Asilone & 18 others	£36m (1989) Source: AA

In 1983, a market such as Optrex's might therefore have been expected to profitably sustain two or more 'big' brands, and so a competitor was likely to view this market as a potential source of important incremental profit.

2. *In 1983, barriers to entry in terms of legal and technical requirements were not insurmountable.*

    Although the process of licensing a pharmaceutical product might seem daunting to those outside the market, the most likely entrants were those already with pharmaceutical experience, for whom the regulatory requirements were relatively straightforward. Nor were competitors likely to be deterred by the complexity of production, since the active ingredients were generally available and the necessary technology not specific to eyecare[3].

    Additionally, many of Optrex's potential competitors already had suitable eyecare variants in other countries. These companies had the product, the technology and the basis of the clinical data required to launch – and to launch in a relatively short period of time. Indeed, Visine, brand leader in the US and Australia[4], was already a small player in the UK market in 1983.

3. *Funding research and development for innovative products was becoming less viable.*

    By 1983, the costs of R&D were rising rapidly. At the same time, patent periods were being restricted to as little as five years, giving less time in which to recoup any investment. As a result, it was becoming cheaper to spend heavily on advertising and marketing to launch a copycat brand, than risk investing in R&D to invent innovative prescription products. Overall then,

    (i) Optrex was perhaps showing some signs that its consumer franchise was becoming weaker, with some consumers leaving the market, others moving to competitors.

    (ii) Various factors suggested that:
         — there was a worrying possibility that some other pharmaceutical manufacturer might launch into the market;
         — Optrex's existing rivals might exploit the new distribution outlets, and the general lack of advertising to improve their positions at the expense of Optrex.

THE DECISION TO ADVERTISE

Crookes recognised both the potential for Optrex and its vulnerability. They had had experience of successfully supporting established brands against competitors, where advertising had been the key hard-hitting and immediate consumer influence available to them. They believed that this could work for Optrex.

---

[3]Current technical requirements – recently, Optrex has raised the technical barriers to entering the market by moving production to a sterile plant, something which would have to be matched by any company wishing to produce a similar product. Whilst other competitors do have a sterile plant, adapting them to produce a lotion variant would take considerable investment. The level of this investment is now likely to be well above what they could hope to recoup from the market in anything but the very long-term.
[4]Visine has a 50% share in the US and 45% in Australia.

OPTREX ADVERTISING CAMPAIGN

VO: Tired eyes?

Refreshing.

Gritty eyes?

Soothing.

Smokey eyes?

Optrex. What a sight for sore eyes.

OPTREX 'EYES' CAMPAIGN (1990–1992)

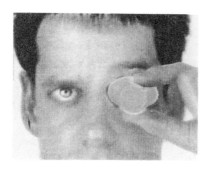

Eye 1: I'm singing in the rain,

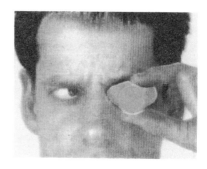

Eye 2: Will you hurry up in there.

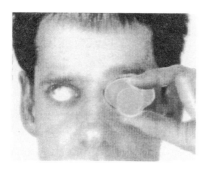

Eye 1: What a wonderful feeling,

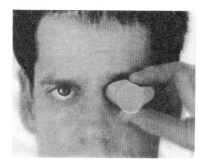

Eye 2: You weren't the only one out late last night.

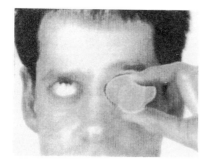

Eye 1: I'm hap, hap, happy again.
Eye 2: And don't forget to clean the bath when you've finished.

VO: Optrex. Are your eyes trying to tell you something?

The Advertising Objectives

1. To reverse volume and share decline.

2. To grow volume sales.

3. To increase the brand's consumer strengths, including:
    — awareness of and trust in the brand;
    — loyalty to the brand;
    — desirability for the brand particularly amongst the young – the future lifeblood of the brand.

4. To deter competitive launch.

Advertising Campaigns

Over the period concerned, different campaigns have run, each one focusing on appropriate usage occasions for Optrex. The first campaign involved a series of eye problem/solution scenarios. The most recent campaign involves the talking Optrex eyes, enthusing about the pleasures of using Optrex and featuring different 'Optrex Moments'.

Media Investment

£800k (MEAL) was spent in 1983 (which equates to £1,257k at 1991 prices). This level of investment has been maintained consistently to date. The majority of the money has been spent on TV, although latterly radio has also been used.

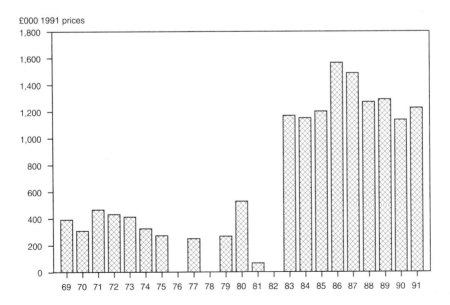

Figure 3. *Optrex real advertising spend*
Sources: MEAL, CSO

WHAT HAPPENED?

Volume and Share Growth

Immediately following the increase in advertising investment in 1983, there was a sharp uplift in sales, with volume in 1983 rising by 9.6% over 1982 levels, reversing the trend of 1979 to 1982.

Optrex sales have grown steadily since the rise in advertising investment (Figure 4) and the brand has increased its share of the market from 84% in 1983 to 91% in 1991.

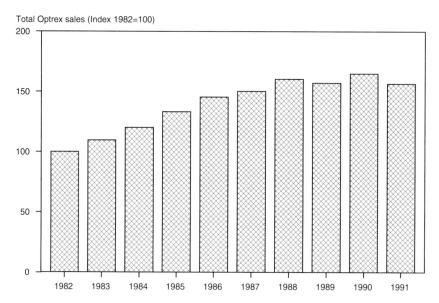

Figure 4. *Optrex sales have grown steadily since 1983*
Sources: Nielsen, Ex-factory

Market Growth

By 1991, the market was 33% larger in volume terms than in 1983.

Today Optrex is the eighth largest 'Over the Counter' (OTC) pharmaceutical brand in pharmacy (year to March 1991). Turnover through pharmacies is larger than that of well-known brands such as Lemsip, Night Nurse and Rennie. (Sources: IMS and Crookes' internal estimates.)

Grocery Sales Growth

Optrex Lotion is the variant which is sold in grocers. (Eye Drops are still restricted by law to pharmacies in the UK.) Lotion sales have grown steadily in grocers over the years and econometric analysis indicates that relatively little of this has been at the expense of pharmacy sales. It might have been plausible that increased distribution was the prime cause of the overall change in the brand's sales. This is actually not true – Optrex Drops, which are restricted to the pharmacy sector, have also shown steady growth (Figure 5).

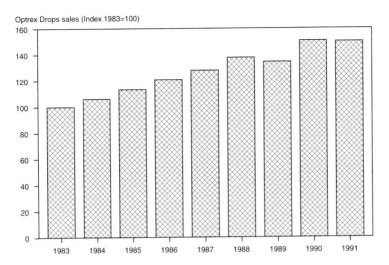

Figure 5. *The steady volume growth of Optrex Drops in pharmacies*
Source: Nielsen

Increased Brand Strength

The brand has strengthened its consumer appeal. Changes have occurred on the following dimensions:

1. *Brand awareness.*

   We have consistent tracking data only from 1988 to 1991 although there are some limited data for 1980 and 1986. These data nonetheless provide strong evidence that brand awareness is growing.

   Spontaneous brand awareness has shown steady improvements, almost certainly because of the advertising. This is corroborated by the high levels of correlation with advertising awareness. The latest figures (August 1991) show unprecedented awareness for both the brand and the advertising (Figures 6 and 7).

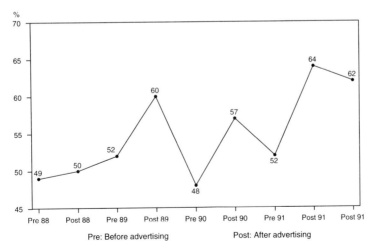

Figure 6. *Spontaneous brand awareness of Optrex*
Source: RSGB
Base: All adults

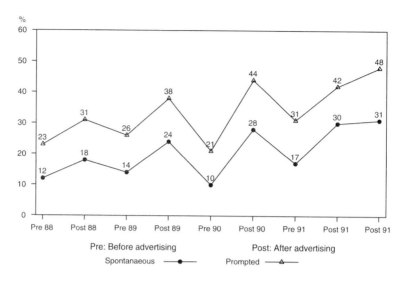

Figure 7. *Awareness of Optrex's advertising*
Source: RSGB
Base: All adults

Our earliest data in 1980 show prompted brand awareness to be less than 80%. Since 1986, awareness has been almost universal (Figure 8), again coinciding with increased advertising awareness.

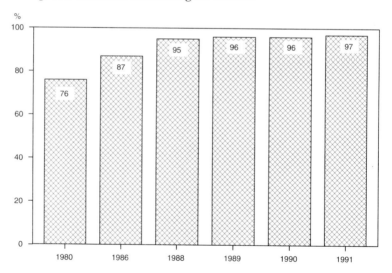

Figure 8. *Prompted brand awareness of Optrex*
Sources: RSGB 1986–91, Optrex Ltd 1980
Base: All adults

2.   *Consumer image and trust.*
     Evidence of the depth of consumer trust in Optrex can be found in the many qualitative studies conducted between 1984 and 1992.

     'I don't know who makes it, but it doesn't matter. It is a known brand name. Optrex is to eyes like Hoover is to vacuum cleaners.' (Male 20-40, 1984)

As one researcher summarised in 1991,

'No other brand was thought to exist, none was looked for, the subject <of other brands> was never, ever considered.' (Source: Winstanley Douglas Grantham, 1991)

The fact that Optrex owns this trust is obviously a fundamental asset in making the market less attractive to would-be competitors. We only have quantitative data from 1988, when the advertising had already been running for four years. However these show that increases are still occurring (Figure 9). We would suggest that this has been happening since 1983.

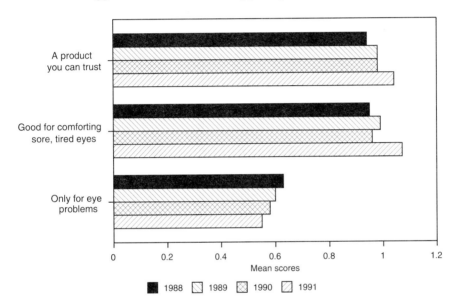

Figure 9. *Optrex brand image*
Source: RSGB
Base: All adults

3. *Usage/loyalty.*
   TGI reveals that during the 1980s, following the increase in advertising, there has been a marked downturn in people drifting away from the brand. Figure 10 illustrates how the number of triallists lapsing from the brand in any one year has dropped by almost 40% between 1983 and 1991. This coincides with the sustained sales lift seen when the advertising weight first increased in 1983 and demonstrates that loyalty to the brand is increasing.

4. *Penetration growth.*
   The number of users of Optrex had been declining since 1975 reaching an all time low in 1982. (NB TGI data refer to fieldwork in the previous year, hence what is dated 1983 refers to behaviour in 1982.)
   Penetration rapidly picked up from 1983 and is now well above its level before heavy advertising began.
   This increase in penetration was across all age groups, but it was particularly evident amongst the younger 15–24 age group. This was a group particularly targeted by the advertising (Table 3).

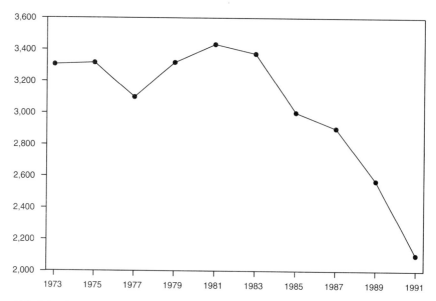

Figure 10. *The decline of lapsed usership of Optrex (non-users: used but not in last six months)*
Source: TGI
Base: All adults

TABLE 3: OPTREX PENETRATION (1983 = 100)

	1975	1983	1985	1991
All adults	121	100	118	113
15–24 year olds	118	100	121	119

Source: TGI

5. *Perceptions of value for money.*
Despite real price increases of 5.2% for Drops and 9.6% for Lotion between 1986 and 1991, fewer consumers now believe the brand to be expensive (Table 4). This suggests that the brand is held in increasingly high regard.

TABLE 4: PERCENTAGE AGREEING 'OPTREX IS EXPENSIVE FOR WHAT IT IS'

	1986	1991
Very expensive	10	5
Fairly expensive	29	16

Source: RSGB
Base: All adults

This change in consumer attitude is also reflected in Optrex's decreasing price sensitivity as measured by econometric analysis.

6. *Optrex's decreasing price sensitivity.*
    Over the period since 1983, Optrex has become considerably less sensitive to
    price changes.
    Two econometric studies provide the evidence for this. One examines price
    sensitivity in the period before Crookes' investment, the other looks at price
    sensitivity today.
    The first study using data for 1978–1982 showed a price increase leading to a
    once and for ever loss in sales. For each 1% that the price of Optrex increased
    in real terms, volume dropped by 0.4% and stayed down. The steep price rises
    over the period 1979 to 1981 were thus an important contributor to Optrex's
    loss in volume sales over this period (Figure 11).

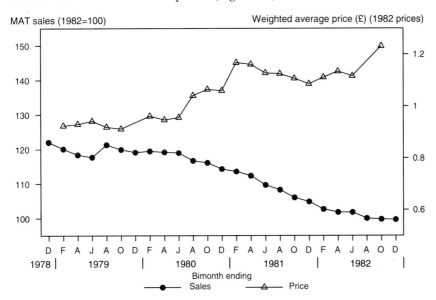

Figure 11. *Total Optrex sales vs real price*
Sources: Nielsen, CSO

    The second study, carried out in 1991, used data from 1983–1990, and shows
    that Optrex's current response to a price change would be short-run ie
    although there would be a small loss in sales in the month of the price increase,
    sales would return to their original level in subsequent months. This analysis
    also shows Optrex becoming gradually less sensitive to price over time,
    coinciding with the increased advertising investment. Furthermore, a model of
    Murine covering the period 1982–1991 shows that this decline in price
    sensitivity is not general to the market, and that Optrex is now less price
    sensitive than its main competitor.

7. *Decreasing sensitivity to stock levels.*
    One of the key factors thought to jeopardise sales levels in OTC medicine
    markets is a decline in pharmacists' stock levels. Received wisdom is that if a
    pharmacist has large stocks of a brand, he is more likely to actively promote it.
    Since the bulk of sales in this market involve asking for the products rather
    than selecting them from the shelves, this is entirely plausible.

The econometric model of Murine provides evidence that changes in stock levels are still important to Murine, ie consumers are not asking for Murine by name, and so its sales are heavily influenced by the pharmacist and his desire to shift stocks. However, this is not the case for Optrex. Consumers are asking for Optrex by name and hence the level of stocks in the stock room is not now a factor in Optrex's sales.

This has not always been the case. Between 1978 and 1982, a 1% decrease in Optrex share of stocks had a significant effect on overall sales levels, losing 0.7% of volume.

These results suggest that the salience of Optrex, its desirability, and consumer preference for it have increased since 1982.

No Competitive Launches

Since 1983, when Crookes recognised that a competitive launch was increasingly likely, none has occurred.

We believe that no launch has occurred for three reasons.

Firstly, the very act of advertising at significant levels has made it very expensive for competitors. No longer can a rival attempt to gain trial by outspending an unsupported Optrex.

Secondly, Optrex is now well-distributed in the grocery sector which was a potential entry point for rivals in 1983.

Thirdly, as already shown, consumer salience and brand appeal have increased substantially, thereby considerably raising the costs of gaining share for a potential new entrant.

As a further indication of Optrex's renewed strength, we should consider the history of Visine since 1983.

Disappearance of Visine

Visine was withdrawn from the market in 1987. This we believe was the result of Optrex's added strength.

Although Visine was never large in the UK market, it was owned by a multinational company. It did receive advertising in the UK in 1980 and 1981, and saw a subsequent rise in sales and distribution. However, it has not been advertised since and sales gradually declined until it was withdrawn.

We believe that its removal from the market is an indicator of how rival pharmaceutical companies *now* regard the likelihood of success in the UK eyecare market against a rejuvenated Optrex.

Summary of Effects

Overall then, between 1983 and 1991, Optrex's sales and share have risen. Awareness, image, usage and penetration have all increased and Optrex has become less sensitive to price and reduced stock levels. Competitive launches have not occurred and one of Optrex's rivals (and potentially its most dangerous competitor) has been encouraged to withdraw from the market.

LINKING PERFORMANCE WITH ADVERTISING

There are a number of reasons why we believe that this perormance is the result of Optrex's advertising.

1. *Regional upweight.*
   First of all, we can directly link the advertising with sales effects.
   In 1989 Crookes tested the effect of upweighting their television advertising spend in the HTV region. During the upweighted period which was May/June, sales grew twice as fast in the HTV region as in the rest of the country whilst all other variables remained unchanged (Figure 12).

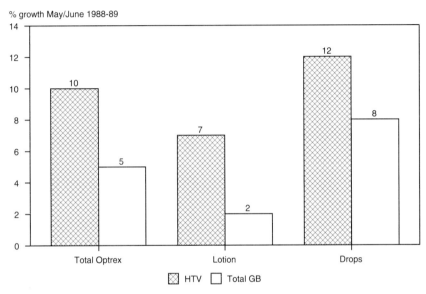

% growth May/June 1988-89

Figure 12. *Optrex year on year % volume growth – HTV vs GB*
Source: Nielsen

2. *Record penetration levels.*
   Secondly, record penetration levels were achieved in 1987 and 1988 (TGI) reflecting Optrex's highest levels of advertising (in real terms) which had occurred in 1986 and 1987 (Figure 13).

3. *Advertising awareness.*
   Thirdly, we have strong evidence that the advertising was highly visible.
   Although we have no data on advertising awareness prior to 1986, Figure 7 demonstrated that the advertising is being noticed. The increases in brand awareness and claimed usage seen earlier in the paper correlate with the increases in advertising awareness.

4. *Correlation of effects and advertising.*
   Fourthly, the changes in performance are well synchronised with the advertising.
   For example, Optrex advertising was at low weights and sporadic from 1975 to 1981. Penetration began to drop in 1975 and reached an all time low in 1982. However, following the increase in advertising expenditure in 1983, it leapt up and has maintained high levels ever since.

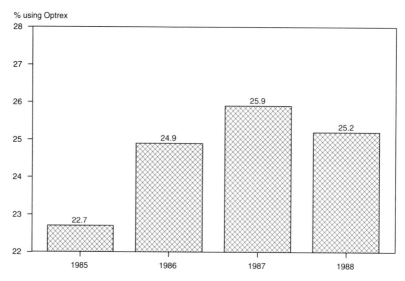

Figure 13. *Penetration increased in line with spend*
Source: TGI 1984–87
Base: All adults

Eliminating Other Variables

Finally, we can also show that no other factors are available to account for the improvement in Optrex's position.

1. *Distribution.*
   Distribution in new sectors has been gained. However, sales in pharmacies (where Optrex has had almost 100% distribution), have also increased over this period. We believe therefore that most of the increase in sales is not due to distribution gains.
2. *Sales force.*
   Optrex had its own direct sales force prior to being owned by Crookes and distribution in pharmacies was almost universal. After acquisition, Optrex's grocery sales were handled by a broker. The role of Crookes' sales force was therefore primarily one of consolidation, in what was becoming an increasingly tough marketplace as the pressure on pharmacists' shelf space grew.
3. *Consumer promotions.*
   Below-the-line marketing activity is restricted in OTC pharmacy markets by the PAGB code, and therefore any activity is almost exclusively limited to the trade.
4. *Packaging.*
   There was a packaging update in 1989 but econometric analysis showed that it did not have any impact on sales.
5. *Price changes.*
   Real price has risen since 1982.

We would conclude therefore that the increased brand strength and sales performance are due to the advertising investment. We would then suggest that this improvement in the brand's position, and the very act of advertising, deterred competitive launch.

We cannot prove that a launch was prevented as a result, but the evidence of Visine suggests that potentially serious rival manufacturers did reconsider the attractiveness of the market following Optrex's more aggressive performance.

THE FINANCIAL CONTRIBUTION

In calculating the value to Crookes Healthcare of advertising Optrex there are a number of components to recognise.

1. Sales growth which has led to increased revenue.
2. Reduced sensitivity to price has allowed Crookes to raise the real price of Optrex substantially and thus improve the profit margin per unit.
3. Reduced sensitivity to stock pressure has benefited Optrex Lotion directly in the period since 1983.
4. Exclusion of potentially share-eroding rivals.

We shall now attempt to put a value on each of these.

Assessing the Value of the Components

1. *Sales growth.*
   Total volume sales are almost 60% higher in 1992 than they were in 1982. The 24% rise in real price has meant that value sales have increased considerably more than this.
2. *The financial value of price insensitivity.*
   Price insensitivity increases revenue and profit for Crookes Healthcare.
   The real price of Optrex has increased by 24% since 1982. If Optrex had not succeeded in reducing its susceptibility to price changes, this would have meant that sales would have gradually declined. As a result, by 1991, volume sales for the year would have been 10% lower than they actually were. This would have been worth approximately £900k in 1991. Assuming no further real price rises and with all else remaining equal, sales at RSP will also be £900k greater per year in all future years too. But of course, the full value of the investment is yet to be realised. Sales should be robust against future increases in real price, thereby allowing substantial further increases in revenue and profitability.
3. *The financial value of reduced sensitivity to stock levels.*
   For Optrex Lotion this is particularly important. Over the last decade, drops products have grown in importance (offering the consumer more portable eyecare), thus reducing Optrex Lotion's share of stocks. Optrex Lotion's share of stocks fell by 10% between 1982 and 1991. Had Lotion remained as susceptible to stock pressure as it was pre-1983, this decline would have gradually produced less sales year by year, so that in 1991, 7% less Lotion would have been sold. This would have resulted in a substantial[5] loss at RSP in 1991, and as with the pricing result, would continue to do so in all future years.

[5]Confidentiality required actual figure to be removed for publication.

4.   *Exclusion of potentially share-eroding rivals.*
     It is impossible to put an accurate value on this. We do not know how much
     resource a rival would have invested in the market or how successful they
     would have been. However, Optrex's experiences in Australia serve to
     demonstrate what might have occurred – and hence what the advertising
     prevented:

     The Australian Experience
     Optrex had been the first real eyecare brand into the Australian market (as in the UK).
     The brand had received minimal advertising support since launch and unlike in the UK,
     this was never corrected. Visine was launched ten years later, and in 1984 undertook an
     aggressive head-on attack against Optrex, involving consistent and heavy advertising.
     The market grew by 28% and Visine grew by 49% to become brand leader. Optrex lost
     share and slipped ultimately to fourth brand. Visine now has a 45% share of the market
     whilst Optrex has 13%.

A similar or even much less pronounced decline for Optrex in the UK would
have been financially disastrous for the brand.
     Finally there is an added benefit which we had not anticipated.

Increased NPD Potential

Consumer response to a number of recent potential Optrex product ideas has led us
to believe that consumer appeal and trust in the brand is now of almost incalculable
value should Crookes Healthcare wish to expand the Optrex franchise via NPD.
     This is indicated by quotes from recent research:

'There's reassurance because you've heard of the Optrex name, anyway... if I thought well that's
Optrex, then I would try it.' (Winstanley Douglas Research 1990, 25-40 female)

It is also supported by a survey carried out in 1992. For every 100 people who
said that they would trust Optrex to launch a new eyecare product, only seven said
that they would 'definitely trust' Murine, Optrex's only remaining rival.

TABLE 5: INDEX OF CONSUMERS SAYING THEY WOULD DEFINITELY
TRUST THE BRAND TO LAUNCH A NEW EYECARE PRODUCT (OPTREX = 100)

	Optrex	Murine
I would definitely trust a new eyecare product launched by	100	7

Source: BMRB 1992
Sample: All adults

This is an added benefit and one which would have been eroded if a rival had
launched and undermined Optrex's consumer appeal.

CONCLUSIONS

Spending on advertising to defend against a competitive attack in many ways parallels a country's expenditure on defence. It is usually impossible to categorically demonstrate that higher expenditure lowers the risk of attack, or that stopping it would make attack imminent. Defence expenditure is geared to risk minimisation, to preserving the nation's external defences and to preserving the status quo and national prosperity.

In 1983, the risk of a successful competitive launch was much higher than it is today. Optrex has not only protected its borders but has also succeeded in annexing share from other brands in the market. Prosperity has been substantially increased through both rising volumes and margins.

The value of advertising therefore has been to ensure that not only does the market remain buoyant but also that Optrex can continue to dominate it now and in the future.

APPENDIX OUTLINING THE ECONOMETRIC MODELLING

The econometric results quoted in this paper are based on four econometric models using data from the Nielsen pharmacy audit together with appropriate economic and other data. A comparison of the significant variables and of the coefficients in the various models enabled the conclusions about pricing sensitivity and response to share of stocks to be drawn. The models used were:

1. A model of Optrex Lotion 1978–1982
2. A model of Murine 1982–1991
3. A model of Optrex Lotion 1982–1990
4. A model of Optrex Drops 1982–1990

Models 1 and 2 were produced specifically for this paper. Models 3 and 4 were produced for consultancy projects on behalf of Crookes in 1991 and have continued to predict sales well. All were subjected to a range of standard statistical tests for their fit and specification, all performed very acceptably against these.

It was not possible to produce a model for Optrex Drops covering the period from 1978–1982, due to missing data. All the early results quoted in the paper are thus extrapolated from model 1, the historic model of Optrex Lotion. The recent models 3 and 4, however, show Optrex Lotion and Optrex Drops responding almost identically to all main influences in the market. It seems very unlikely that their response paths would have diverged over time and thus it does not seem unreasonable to base estimates for the effects on the brand as a whole on the results obtained for Lotion.

Section Three

European

9

Jeans Sans Frontières
How Advertising Generates and Protects Levi Strauss Jeans Sales Across Europe

INTRODUCTION

This paper will describe the contribution that advertising has made to the continued development of the Levi Strauss jeans brand in Europe between 1988 and 1991.

We shall demonstrate how, despite a major economic recession and accompanying decline in numbers within Levi's core 11–24 target audience, the brand has prospered, generating enhanced profitability and stability for Levi Strauss and Co worldwide.

It will be our contention that a major contributor to this success has been the ability of advertising to generate consistent and enhanced brand imagery, the currency of this market, to such an extent that competitive image barriers have been established around the brand, thus protecting sales and share within an environment that forbode decline.

Lastly, and perhaps most importantly within this context, we shall demonstrate how this success has been achieved throughout Europe, utilising a solus campaign vehicle.

Background

The Levi's paper submitted in 1988 and published in *Advertising Works 5* concentrated upon the contribution of advertising to the successful re-launch of the Levi Strauss 501 jean from a predominantly UK perspective. It is, however, important to note that the same campaign helped to generate similar success throughout other major European markets (see Table 1).

TABLE 1: INDEXED LEVI STRAUSS 501 JEANS SALES GROWTH IN OTHER EUROPEAN MARKETS

		1985	1988
France	501	100	160
	Market	100	129
Italy	501	100	169
	Market	100	147
West Germany	501	100	413
	Market	100	138

Source: LSE Brussels

This paper will concentrate upon the continued development of the Levi Strauss brand and its advertising within the above markets, as well as describing the introduction for the first time of the same advertising campaign to the Spanish market, which Levi Strauss Europe (LSE) had previously developed without major advertising support.

The period 1988–91 has been selected because during this period LSE and the agency have acquired new learning about the way the advertising works across Europe. Equally from 1988 onwards, a major determinant of initial growth, new distribution, can be discounted, and lastly, but perhaps most importantly, in 1988 the brand and the advertising faced many new challenges.

1988 – FACTORS THREATENING CONTINUED SALES DEVELOPMENT

Despite the initial pan-European success of the 501 re-launch strategy, by 1988 LSE and the agency had become aware of several factors within the socio-economic and marketing environment which threatened the future growth potential of the company's European operation and as such forced a prolonged examination and re-evaluation of the advertising strategy.

1. *11–24 Population decline*
    Levi's core target is 11–24 year old males and females. Whilst purchases by this group account for no more than 60% of sales, because long-term jeans brand loyalties are established between 15 and 18, this group are critical in generating and maintaining brand share. Amongst Levi's core target audience, significant population declines were projected. By 1995 there would be 12m (15%) fewer European 11–24 jeans buyers. Despite these changes, could the advertising continue to grow sales and brand share?

2. *Economic recession*
    By 1988, economic downturn in the US gave LSE cause for concern. Due to the ability of the 501 to command price premiums well above the European market average and critically the domestic US market where jeans are much more of a commodity item, the company's profitability was disproportionately reliant upon Europe. Recession would undoubtedly place LSE's margins under intense pressure. Could the advertising protect the premiums it had helped generate?

3. *Resourcing and supply difficulties*
    During the previous downturn in the business in the late seventies, LSE had closed three plants, laying off 1,000 of the 4,500 workforce in the process. Renewed demand for the 501 was placing great strain upon the organisation's ability to deliver. In the words of LSE personnel management 'We knew we were killing our people'. LSE needed to invest, but if the above factors bit as hard as LSE had historically experienced, would this investment be wasted?

4. *Fashion change*
    Sportswear and bigger, baggier jeans fits were in. The retro American trend which had formed the basis of the initial advertising and, to some extent, helped to fuel the 501's early success appeared to be dying. Could advertising overcome this threat and maintain Levi's status?

5. *Distribution peak*
   Due largely to the prohibitive collection costs involved, distribution data are not accurately monitored in most European markets. However, it is felt by LSE that by 1988, driven by the initial growth of 501, Levi's distribution across all European markets had peaked. (Between 1988 and 1991, poor quality distribution has actually been 'culled' in order to protect the Levi Strauss image.) A major determinant of early growth had disappeared. Further volume would need to come from increased penetration and/or frequency of purchase, or brand switching. Given the above factors, could advertising deliver more Levi's buyers?

6. *Campaign wear-out*
   Due to high shares of voice and enormous additional PR, the campaign and its formula were exceptionally well-known. We worried that it was too well-known and in danger of rejection. Other youth culture developments such as environmentalism, pacifism, Eastern Europe, Apartheid seemed to point away from America, and especially the America of the 1950s. Was the existing campaign the right way forward?

7. *European expansion*
   LSE was anxious to increase its presence across Europe, immediately in Spain with the introduction of European advertising support, and in the longer term into other developing markets. Could the campaign continue to work across an increasingly broad spectrum of European cultures?

8. *Changes in the relationship between 501 and the brand*
   In 1985, following the success in the US of a similar strategy, the 501 was selected by LSE as the basis of its European re-launch of the Levi's brand. As the original denim jean, the 501 was capable of encapsulating and representing everything that Levi's stood for.
   The approach worked. Whilst sales responses were more acute upon the 501, there was a halo effect on sales of the entire Levi's jeans range.
   However, by 1988 several potential dangers of a 501-based strategy became evident. Major 501 counterfeit operations were flooding the market with cheap jeans of inferior quality. Equally, at a trading level, some retailers had taken to loss leading with 501s to drive overall store traffic. Could 501-based advertising continue to deliver results for the entire jeans brand?

Summary

The above recessionary economic, socio-demographic and fashion changes, in association with the distribution peak achieved, threatened at best to halt the brand's growth, and at worst to cause decline at a critical point within LSE's development aspirations.
   The remainder of this paper will concentrate upon the subsequent advertising action and effects upon the Levi's brand performance between 1988 and 1991.

DEVELOPING THE CAMPAIGN 1988–1991

Despite the above concerns, on-going campaign research amongst our target market across Europe gave us confidence. Despite growing familiarity with the advertising idea, campaign wear-out was not yet a factor. The campaign seemed to be maintaining its edge principally because of the ability of different advertising heroes and scenarios to deliver an ever broader, but still universal, spectrum of wearer imagery.

We developed the 'campaign chord' model illustrated below. The Levi's 'chord' was made up of a number of critical 'notes' – values and signals with which our young male target audience throughout Europe identified.

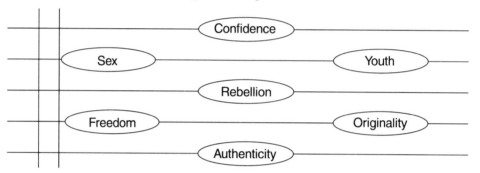

Intuitively, we felt that the 'notes' individual markets needed to hear within the campaign did vary across Europe. For example, in Northern European markets, tougher, more rebellious heroes were more aspirational, whereas in Italy, a softer, less macho personality was required. It was our view that if each new execution could appropriately accentuate different 'notes', we could begin to expand the role and meaning of the brand across Europe, simultaneously keeping the idea fresh. By broadening this territory, we would reduce that left for our competitors.

Equally, we were confident that this imagery could be attached to the brand as a whole, not just the 501. Because the market now understood the idiosyncrasies of the 501, there was no longer a need to 'educate' consumers. Whilst 501s would still be the only jeans worn in the ads, local affiliates were given freedom about range or 'corporate' brand-oriented endline tagging. We were confident of achieving the objectives that LSE had established.

LSE MARKETING OBJECTIVES 1988–1991

Over this four year period, the marketing objectives and advertising strategy have consistently been:

1. To maintain and increase brand shares throughout Europe.
2. To maintain the 501's price premium.
3. To introduce and establish the pan-European advertising support in Spain.
4. To achieve the above utilising a solus TV advertising vehicle.

ADVERTISING STRATEGY

—   To maintain and enhance Levi's and Levi's 501 image position.
—   To communicate core values through positive and appealing wearer imagery.

THE ADVERTISING EXECUTIONS 1988–91

The following executions were produced with a view to broadening and deepening the appeal of the brand's imagery across Europe. Whilst the creative campaign brief was virtually unchanged for these seven commercials, the specific proposition/support and tone of voice requirements were changed, in order to reflect the need to expand and appropriately rotate the delivery of key values and signals across each European market.

POOL HALL

FRIDGE

BEACH

TABLE 2: LEVI STRAUSS ADVERTISING EXECUTIONS 1988–91

Execution	Tone of voice
Fridge	Sexy, physical
Pick-up	Resourceful, classic, masculine
Pawnbroker	Sharing, mutual, jeans valued
Beach	Charming, resourceful, fun
Great Deal	Independent, successful, classic
Pool Hall	Tough, in-control, admired
Camera	Resourceful, independent

TABLE 3: LEVI'S COPY ROTATION THROUGHOUT EUROPE 1988–91

		France	Germany	Italy	Spain	UK
1988	Spring	Parting	Cochran	Cochran		Cochran
	Autumn	Fridge	Fridge	Cochran	Laundrette	Fridge
1989	Spring	Fridge	Fridge	Fridge	Parting	Pick-up
	Autumn	Pick-up	Pawnbroker	Fridge	Fridge	Pawnbroker
1990	Spring	Pick-up	Beach	Pick-up	Pick-up	Beach
	Autumn	Great Deal	Great Deal	Pick-up	Beach	Great Deal
1991	Spring	Great Deal	Pool Hall	Great Deal	Great Deal	Pool Hall
	Autumn	Camera	Camera	Great Deal	Camera	Camera

EVALUATING LEVI'S PERFORMANCE 1988–1991

As our initial paper and earlier sections here have described, the principal criterion of success within the European jeans market is motivating brand imagery.

The role of jeans within youth culture goes far beyond practical clothing benefits or the relatively limited differences that can be built into a pair of denim trousers. Jeans brands are used to communicate and to signal, often on public, and personally important occasions, the ownership on behalf of the wearer of specific and fundamental personality characteristics and values.

Hence *the means* to the end (sales) is the creation and enhancement of brand imagery. Shifting such attitudes which are often deep-seated and deeply-held does not usually occur rapidly.

Equally, product purchase occurs on average 1–2 times per annum, and given the relatively high purchase price, is rarely spontaneous. Examining sales data during and after specific advertising bursts for immediate sales effects is, therefore, unrealistic.

In evaluating the contribution of the advertising here, we shall report brand sales performance data from 1988, the watershed period when initial early growth determinants had stabilised, and a new and largely negative marketing environment challenged the brand. This will then be compared with the same data for 1991. The introduction phase of the campaign in Spain will be presented similarly.

DIRECT SALES EFFECTS

What Happened to the Market?

As predicted, between 1988 and 1991 the markets of each affiliate entered recession either flattening all growth or producing decline. (See Figure 1.)

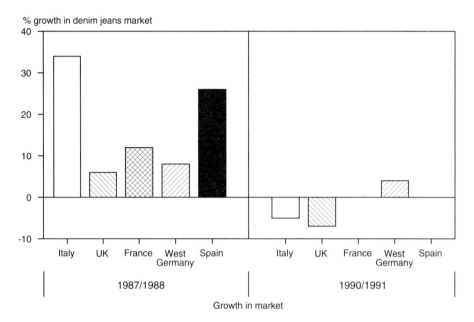

Figure 1.   *The impact of recession upon denim jeans sales in Europe 1988–1991*
Source: LSE Brussels

The extent of population declines within the 11–24 age groups are also demonstrated below. (See Figure 2)

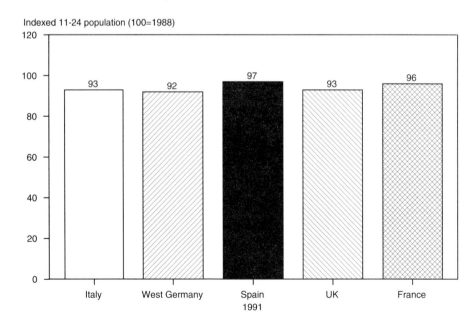

Figure 2.   *Indexed European 11–24 population declines 1988–91*
Source: LSE Brussels

Overall Sales Picture

Within all Levi Strauss established European markets, total brand sales increased well ahead of each local market. Equally, the re-launch in Spain produced significant sales increases, again larger than those seen within the rest of the Spanish market and comparable to the response seen in the rest of Europe in 1986.

TABLE 4: INDEXED LEVI'S SALES PERFORMANCE VS INDEXED
LOCAL MARKET GROWTH (1988 = 100)

	Levi's sales		Market (ex-Levi's)	
	1988	1991	1988	1991
Italy	100	177	100	82
France	100	188	100	118
UK	100	136	100	108
Germany	100	169	100	145
Spain	100	182	100	132

Source: LSE Brussels

Levi's Incremental Sales vs the Market

As mentioned above, the recession impacted upon each of the markets featured. Comparing Levi's actual growth performance against that which would have occurred had the brand followed the rest of the market (by no means an inconceivable scenario given Levi's price premium and the overall loss of potential new buyers) demonstrates the incremental volume the brand had achieved.

TABLE 5: INDEXED LEVI'S ACTUAL VS PROJECTED SALES
(100 = Levi's Sales Projected upon Market Growth)

	1991 projected Levi's sales	1991 actual Levi's sales	Levi's increment
Italy	100	216	116
France	100	160	60
UK	100	125	25
Germany	100	116	16
Spain	100	133	33

Source: LSE Brussels

For reasons of confidentiality, we are not at liberty here to describe LSE's jeans margins and hence to value the above incremental sales. The overall contribution LSE was able to make to Levi Strauss & Co's worldwide revenue is however described within the Financial Effects section, and establishes the incremental profitability of these sales.

Brand Share Growth

Obviously, such growth rate versus the market improved Levi's market shares significantly giving the brand market leadership in all the regions featured here. It is also important to note that Levi's *leading* competitor market shares were simultaneously being eroded. These changes appear on Figure 3.

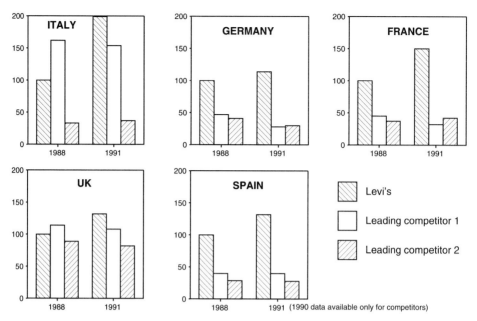

Figure 3.   *Indexed Levi's brand share increases vs competitors 1988–1991 (1988 = 100)*

CRITICAL FACTORS IMPACTING UPON LEVI'S PERFORMANCE ACROSS MARKETS

Quite clearly the differing local market and brand development conditions in each region have governed individual market responses and produced a spectrum of results. These are summarised in Table 6 and discussed in greater detail overleaf.

TABLE 6:   CRITICAL FACTORS IMPACTING UPON LEVI'S PERFORMANCE ACROSS EUROPE

Country	11–24 population decline	Levi's market position	Market health	Competitive activity	Levi's performance
Italy	High	Mature	Prolonged decline	Eroded	Exceptional
France	Low	Mature	Static	Minor	Good
UK	High	Mature	Decline	Intense	Good
Germany	High	Developing	Slowing	Intense	Moderate
Spain	Low	Young	Static	Intense	Good

Italy

Despite the significant declines in the 11–24 population and the local market as a whole, Levi's established itself as market leader benefitting from a substantially increased share of voice as leading competitors withdrew major spends. (In fact, Levi's increased its share of voice from 25% in 1988 to 62% in 1991.)

As a result of the recession, Italy's comparatively high number of premium priced designer jeans were particularly hard hit, and Levi's was able to capitalise upon downtraders in the market. The prolonged decline in the market also removed many smaller competitive brands.

France

Despite a loss of core target audience and a flat jeans market, Levi's increased its market share by 50%. In a similar situation to that occurring in Italy, higher priced fashion brands did not withstand economic pressure and several low volume, low price competitors ceased to trade.

UK

Levi's sales performance was remarkable as the brand faced its most intense competition in Europe within a difficult market environment where the recession bit very hard, and a significant fall in the 11–24 population occurred.

Levi's continued to increase market share at the expense of competitors who coped less well with the recessionary forces in the market.

Germany

Within the developing German market, Levi's sales and rate of share growth have been reduced by three critical factors.

1. Population decline amongst the target group occurred earlier, was more acute and occurred at a critical development stage for the brand.

2. Levi's share of voice during this period was reduced due to the entrance for the first time of competitive brands into the restricted commercial television marketplace.

3. Perhaps most importantly, the structure of commercial television in Germany is such that the rate of access of the advertising to the target audience is significantly impeded. This has undoubtedly reduced the speed of development of the brand and is reflected in other image performance measures presented later within this paper.
   The impact of this inhibition of the use of the brand's primary marketing vehicle – advertising – upon the development of the brand in Germany can be interpreted as further evidence of the effectiveness of the campaign overall.

Spain

The facts that in the Spanish market initial growth had flattened by 1991 and there were up to six other jeans advertisers using TV undoubtedly effected upon the re-launch. Despite these difficulties however, Levi's sales still almost doubled during the first three years of the re-launch.

Summary

Between 1988 and 1991, despite a major recession, accompanying population declines, and a static or declining distribution base across all of the countries featured, Levi's sales increases continued to outpace the performance of local markets. As a result, increased brand shares were reported across all markets. Equally, closest competitor brand shares were eroded over this period.

POTENTIAL EXPLANATIONS FOR THIS SUCCESS

In this section we shall examine alternative explanations of the continued success and development of the Levi's brand across Europe.

Reduction in Price

Between 1988 and 1991, in all the more established markets, the Levi's 501 price premium was not just maintained, but was increased, in some cases significantly (see Table 7).

TABLE 7: LEVI'S 501 PRICE PREMIUM OVER LOCAL MARKET AVERAGES 1988–1991
(100 = 1988 Levi's 501 Price)

	1988	1991
France	49%	51%
Italy	39%	45%
Spain	67%	60%
UK	47%	70%
Germany*	51%	56%

Note: * 1989–91 data available only
Source: LSE Brussels

The intensity of price competition from other brands and retailers, lack of overall market growth, and the already significant premium of the 501 in Spain, meant that the Spanish affiliate found it prudent to peg the 501 price during the re-launch. This led to a minor decline in the overall premium over this period, but still meant that the 501 retailed at an average 60% premium to the market average in Spain.

Distribution Growth

As described above, LSE's distribution base in Europe had peaked and was actually being 'culled' amongst poorer quality outlets in order to protect the brand's premium status.

Absence of Competitive Activity

During 1988 and 1991, the recession forced both competitive brands and the retail trade to price and in some cases position brands overtly against 501.

Increased Share of Voice

As a result of the above increased competition, Levi's share of voice levels *fell* in all markets with the exception of Italy, where a significantly increased share of voice delivered exceptional results for the brand, further evidence of the campaign's effectiveness.

Levi's Product Development

The Levi Strauss 501 jean has not changed for 30 years. Whilst the quality of Levi's products undoubtedly encourages brand loyalty, this alone could not account for the dramatic increases witnessed.

Fashion

As we have described earlier, during this period, the fashion for American retro items which may have aided the initial launch shifted away from Levi's towards baggier jeans fits, flares and non-denim products altogether, most notably towards sportswear. Equally, it is LSE's merchandising policy to avoid immediately responding to each new fashion trend within its range offer.

ACCOUNTING FOR THE SUCCESS

Having discounted the above factors, we are left with changes to the brand's image profile – the most dynamic element (excluding sales) within the immediate socio-economic and marketing environment of Levi's during this period.

It is our contention that the continued enhancement of the brand's appeal across European markets has been a direct consequence of the enhancement of the brand's image – the wearer values that we have already established represent a critical force within jeans wearing and specifically within jeans brand preference. Research presented below illustrates how Levi's has developed from being an also-ran in the market to becoming the definitive brand of the sector.

FUNDAMENTAL SHIFTS WITHIN LEVI'S BRAND IMAGE DEVELOPMENT

In order to understand the scale and long-term nature of the image shifts that have occured, it is valuable to establish the brand's development over a longer period.

1985 – Prior to the Initial Re-launch and the Introduction of the Campaign

In 1983, Marketing Week summarised the standing of Levi Strauss & Co thus:

'Like a surfer who has run out of wave, Levi Strauss found itself beached.'

Levi's research completed upon both the 501 product and the brand's image confirmed the difficulty of the task that lay ahead. Consumers felt that the brand had lost its way and reacted less than positively to the 501 concept. The following quotes from young jeans consumers further demonstrate the degree to which perceived brand and wearer imagery dominate brand preference and the nadir the brand had reached in this respect.

'The brand that led, and now everyone has overtaken them. A few years ago when skinheads were in, Levi's were *the* jean. Now it's Hard Core and Pepe.' (Burns Research Partners Ltd, UK 1985)

This view was shared across all European markets. Within a spectrum of consumer opinion across Europe at this time, Germany represented possibly the most negative market.

'The 501 concept generates negative feelings, bad look, bad fit.' (Imadi, Germany 1986)

1991 Image Status

By 1991, a fundamental and massive shift in consumer attitudes had been effected. From being a brand that was easily discounted, Levi Strauss had become Europe's definitive jeans brand. Commenting upon the brand's image in seven European countries in 1991, RDS International summarised the position thus:

> 'When consumers discuss jeans brands there is a feeling that Levi's *are* jeans, they don't even need to be named. Levi's are essential, conferring credibility on the wearer – "My Levi's are part of me".'

Levi's Image Power

During 1990, LSE instigated its first ever pan-European quantitative image track. Canvassing the opinions of 500 core target consumers in each of LSE's seven major European regions, including the five markets described here, this comprehensive study represents a substantial and unique data source with which to analyse Levi's image dominance of the European denim jeans market.

Using data from the above tracking study, it is possible to analyse the degree to which Levi's and competitive jeans brand images are defined. Consumers were asked to rank the brands that they were most aware of upon 60 different jeans wearer and jeans brand attributes. (See Technical Appendix, Notes 6 and 7) When combined, these data are in effect a measure of total brand image strength, breadth, depth and salience across Europe.

Figure 4 illustrates the extent of Levi's image dominance over competitors across all markets.

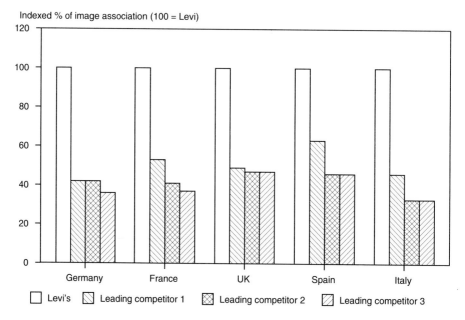

Figure 4.   *Levi's image power index vs leading competitors*
Source: Cenysdiam 1991

ADVERTISING AS THE SOURCE OF THIS IMAGE POWER

We have established that brand imagery is the principal criterion of success in this market. Equally, we have demonstrated Levi's rise to supremacy in this respect since the introduction of the campaign. Within this section we shall establish that the Levi's pan-European advertising campaign has been the single most significant driving force in creating, enhancing and directing this imagery.

The Role of Advertising in Directing the Brand's Image

Qualitative campaign development research conducted since 1988 has consistently reported the impact of the pan-European advertising campaign in generating, directing and enhancing the brand's image.

In describing the Levi's brand, consumers consistently referred to and effectively played back the notes of our campaign chord model. Quite clearly, consumers' vocabulary about the brand was almost entirely the *vocabulary provided by the advertising*.

Following the broadcast of Cochran and Fridge in 1988, Feedback Research commented upon groups in Paris.

'(About the Levi's wearer) …the modern, independent confident hero, a modern day adventurer.' (Feedback Research, Paris 1988)

Not surprisingly at this stage however, we were still very aware of sharing this territory with other brands. Within the same report Feedback commented:

'The campaign for Presse jeans was received favourably for its humour, romance and aesthetic value.' (Feedback Research, Paris 1988)

By 1989, further significant image shifts had occurred, with the campaign effect of Levi's being explicitly reported. Censydiam reporting on groups in London, Paris and Norway commented:

'Jeans have an immediate and extensive richness of images, feelings and associations. Basically these are reflections of previous commercials (mainly Levi's elements) based upon imitation of user groups.' (Censydiam, Antwerp 1989)

By 1991, following the broadcast of Camera and Pool Hall, the depth and breadth of Levi's imagery and the role of advertising in generating this was clear, even in Spain, where the campaign had only been on air for three years.

'For these youngsters, Levi's are the only jeans, cost is not a factor. They are regarded as part of their personality and a support which goes everywhere with them. Instead of saying jeans, people are saying Levi's.' (Inner, Madrid 1991)

Quite clearly Levi's was becoming the definitive brand. Other brands were being disregarded. This was directly attributed to the advertising.

'Jeans advertising is Levi's advertising. Levi's is the reference, the benchmark.' (Inner, Madrid 1991)

How the Advertising Created Relevant Imagery Across Geographic and Cultural Borders

In 1990 LSE and the agency conducted its most comprehensive qualitative research study of young European males, their attitudes and behaviour and the role of the Levi's brand and advertising within their world.

Almost 50 qualitative group discussions were completed with 400 core target 16–18 year old males in seven different countries including all five of those featured within this paper.

This extensive project shed important new light on the role the advertising played in developing consistent brand imagery across very different local markets. These findings are described below.

Common Target Audience Priorities Across Europe

The overriding value or priority for young males throughout Europe was freedom. This split into longer term aspirations for liberation from social and economic pressure and a conflicting desire for immediate escape and freedom in terms of sexual and physical release.

Desired Symbols and Props Delivered by the Advertising

In order to achieve the above freedoms, our audience perceived similar types of values, signals or props to be critical. These are illustrated below and represent a more sophisticated version of our original campaign chord model. RDS confirmed that the campaign's heroes were delivering these wearer values throughout Europe and that local 'note accentuation' was being achieved.

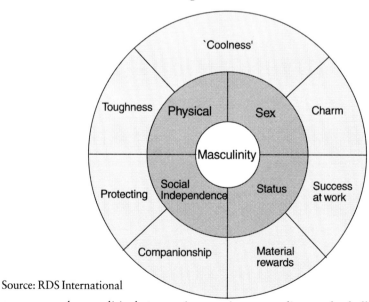

Source: RDS International

Whilst causes such as political oppression, environmentalism and rebellion were voiced, these had a low priority and were frequently held to be the responsibility of others.

A Universally Understood America

A more contemporary expression of America was rejected by the RDS research. Retro and Hollywood America delivered values that were complimentary to many of the required signals of our target.

This imagery was universally understood as it drew heavily upon the established imagery of film and music culture and uniquely embodied what it meant to be young – music, freedom, teenage angst, rebellion, non-conformity and fantasy.

Importantly, this mythical historic America imbued Levi's with an authenticity and integrity which its competitors (some of whom were equally qualified) could not now lay claim to.

Summary

RDS International summarised their evaluation of the campaign's impact upon the brand's imagery thus:

> 'The Levi's advertising campaign encapsulates the masculine core of physical prowess and sexual attraction. It is therefore powerfully relevant to the target. Within the campaign a range of ingredients is employed, all of which either enhance or invest in the masculine core.'

Equally, further analysis of Levi's specific image attributes upon Levi's quantified image track confirms that upon the critical image dimensions that the advertising was intended to enhance, Levi's dominates over its competitors (see Figure 5).

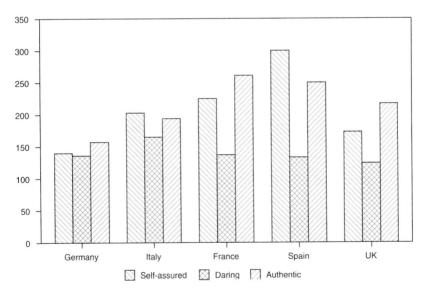

Figure 5. *Indexed Levi's brand image strengths*
Source: Cenysdiam 1991

This graph further illustrates the impact of advertising upon the brand's image. In addition, by virtue of the relative strength of this imagery, the above data confirm the existence of image barriers around the Levi's brand upon critical wearer values in the market. By consistently enhancing and broadening these strengths, the advertising is protecting the brand and the sales that this positioning generates.

CAMPAIGN EVALUATION – POSITIONING LEVI'S OPTIMALLY WITHIN DIFFERENT LOCAL MARKETS

It is our contention that advertising has positioned and protected Levi's within the optimum image and sales territory of each market despite different local marketing environments. The degree to which local jeans markets do differ is again confirmed by Levi's own tracking study data.

As well as asking respondents to rank brands against wearer and brand image attributes, the study also asks the same questions for jeans in general, ie generates an unbranded 'average' attitude to jeans wearing. Using cluster analysis of these responses, we have been able to map the positioning of the typical or average jeans brand on a country-by-country basis. Figure 6 reproduces the results of this analysis and confirms the differing orientations of jeans buyers within each market.

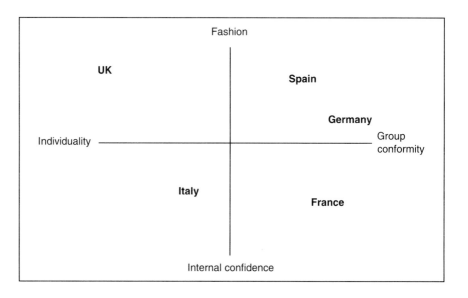

Figure 6.   *Average of values motivating jeans purchase across Europe*
Source: Cenysdiam 1991

Similar mapping exercises by country of Levi's and competitive brand image associations (see Figures 7–11) provide an interesting comparison with the above jeans 'average' map.

FIGURES 7–11: LEVI'S AND COMPETITIVE BRAND IMAGE MAPS BY COUNTRY

Within these maps, the closer an image attribute appears to a brand, the greater the degree of association with that brand.

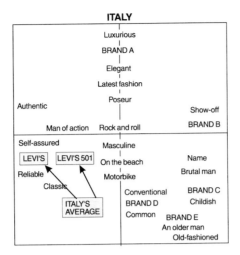

Figure 7.   *Italy*
Source: Cenysdiam 1991

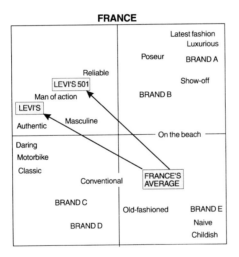

Figure 8.   *France*
Source: Cenysdiam 1991

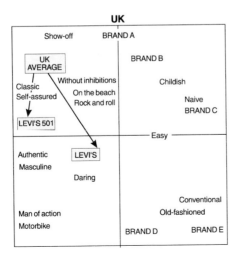

Figure 9.   *UK*
Source: Cenysdiam 1991

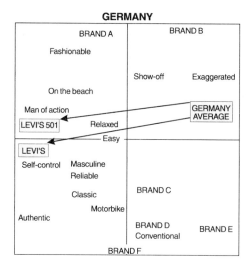

Figure 10. *Germany*
Source: Cenysdiam 1991

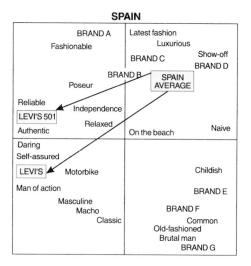

Figure 11. *Spain*
Source: Cenysdiam 1991

Analysis of these maps reveals four critical factors:

1. Despite the very different jeans 'average' start points of each market Levi's 501 position is unique and consistent in all countries. These 'shifts' between the average jean position expected versus the actual position of Levi's are illustrated.

2. The proximity of mapping of the Levi's brand to that of 501 would appear to confirm the halo effect of 501 imagery upon the brand as a whole.

3. Both Levi's and 501's territories are exactly in line with, and we believe a direct consequence of, the positioning objectives and values of the advertising.

4. As a result of Levi's higher image power described above, Levi's image mappings in each region are the strongest and most established in each country shown, thus prohibiting competitive entry.

HOW DO THESE POSITIONINGS OPTIMISE LEVI'S DEMAND?

Further confirmation of the link between the above image dimensions of Levi's and the brand's sales performance can be established by looking at the spontaneous brand purchase intention rankings canvassed by Censydiam.

These data, illustrated in Figure 12, are valuable for the following reasons:

1. Levi's position in the market clearly leads to the brand appearing at the top of jeans buyers' shopping lists throughout each market. This is the optimum market territory currently occupied, and reflects Levi's definitive status in all regions.
2. Where the data to make comparisons between 1990/91 or 1991/92 exist, Levi's position continues to strengthen.
3. Again, where comparative data exist, intention to buy from leading competitors appears to be eroding.

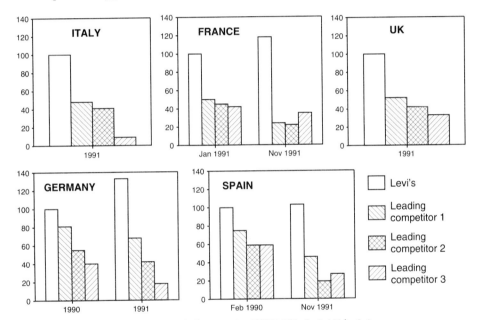

Figure 12. *Levi's purchase intention rating index vs leading competitors 1990/91 (100 = Levi's initial rating)*
Source: Cenysdiam 1991

Summary

The above data demonstrate that advertising imagery has consistently placed Levi's within the optimum and definitive position within each local market, and protects this territory via image barriers. It has also been shown that without advertising, previous consumer perceptions of Levi's and the differing 'average' jeans buying attitudes found in Europe would have placed the brand in significantly different territories.

In short, we have described how advertising has generated and enhanced competitive image barriers around the Levi's brand, thus optimising sales, brand share and premiums.

CAMPAIGN EVALUATION – EVIDENCE OF INDIRECT ADVERTISING EFFECTS UPON THE BRAND

In the following section, we shall describe other indirect benefits of the advertising which have added further value to the brand's image and its sales performance, and which support the view that a different strategy and campaign would not have achieved the same scale or scope of effect.

1. *Continued role and presence of the campaign within European youth culture*
    This effect, first described in our initial paper, has continued. The soundtracks from many executions have entered the Top 10 charts of the countries featured. Moreover, music of the same genre as our soundtracks did not tend to appear in the same charts, indicating that the advertising rather than music fashion regenerated these old tracks. Radio play and spin-off PR from these successes have obviously generated incremental awareness and credibility for the brand.

2. *Levi's advertising as a reference point for other marketers in the sector*
    Several youth advertisers and brands in Europe continue to refer to Levi's advertising within their own marketing, including Carling Black Label and Swissair. As imitation remains the sincerest form of flattery and logic would suggest that awareness of Levi's is reinforced by such activity, we believe this further adds to the campaign's overall effect.

    Most noticeable users of the advertising in a European context have been Genesis, who re-shot their own humorous versions of the Beach and Pool Hall commercials for the MTV (pan-European) promotional video of their single 'I Can't Dance'. Hit & Run Music, who produced the video for Genesis, kindly commented upon their reasons for choosing the Levi's films.

    'The 501 ads were probably the most famous and appropriate advertising reference point for young kids watching MTV in Europe. We drew on an American ad as well for the same reasons. Levi's have become part of their culture. Because the target audience for singles is not that dissimilar to that for jeans, by playing off the ads in the video, we knew that the whole point of the song and lyrics would be understood.'

3. *The continued media success of Levi's heroes and heroines*
    We have been very happy to see Tatjana Patitz, the girl from the Fridge commercial, go on to become one of the world's most famous models. Equally, Brad Pitt, the star of Camera, is now establishing his acting career in America, most notably thus far in *Thelma & Louise*. Both the above commercials were these performers' first advertising roles.

    These successes are indicative of the status of the campaign as a talent window that is seen internationally and evidence, we hope, of the quality of casting and execution present.

4. *The role of advertising within other pan-European promotional/merchandising activity*
    Apart from the intangible motivation and pride that most LSE personnel take from the advertising, additional value is gained from the advertising, particularly amongst the salesforce. LSE was quick to recognise the demand for and the value of campaign merchandise for the trade. This has enabled Levi's to use the wallspace of independent retailers as Levi's 'poster sites'. The pan-European economies of scale open to LSE through central sourcing of this critical material from one campaign has also been incalculable.

Equally (in an attempt to stop the illegal copying and display that retailers had undertaken), LSE now provides key retailers with 'a film of the film' to support the broadcast of each new execution. This provides Levi's with a unique presence at POS vs its competitors.

LSE also now produces selected limited edition ranges featuring the themes and stars of the ads which are of enough value to leverage the pricing, payment or stocking policies of key retailers.

THE FINANCIAL EFFECTS OF LEVI'S PAN-EUROPEAN SUCCESS

In this section we shall report the impact that the brand performance has had upon LSE's and LS & Co's worldwide profitability, structure and stability. In effect, these data provide an overview of the financial contribution advertising has made to the company.

The Role of the 501 Price Premium

The continued ability of the 501 to command a significant premium vs the European market average and domestic US 501, prior to and in particular *after* 1988 as the market entered recession and decline is illustrated in Table 8.

TABLE 8: INDEXED LEVI'S 501 PRICE VS EUROPEAN MARKET AVERAGE AND DOMESTIC US 501 PRICES
(100 = 1985 European 501 Price)

	1985	1987	1989	1991
Levi's 501	100	131	142	154
Market average	44	65	71	87
US 501	N/A	27	28	30

Given the simultaneous maintained growth of Levi's sales across Europe described above, the European affiliate contribution to worldwide earnings has increased fourfold since 1986, considerably re-balancing the company's revenue streams. This is illustrated in Figure 13.

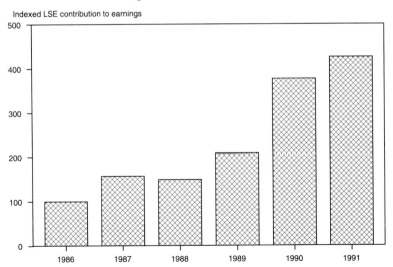

Figure 13. *Indexed contribution of LSE to worldwide earnings*
Source: LSE Brussels

Enhanced Profitability and Stability

The above success in Europe has considerably accelerated the repayment of Levi Strauss & Co's $1.587 billion LBO debt, adding not just profitability but enhanced stability to the company.

This dramatic shift in the contribution of the European Division, despite the recessionary forces present in the market has been commented upon within the American financial press and financial analysts' reports.

'We continue to view Levi Strauss Associates as an improving credit. Since the 1985 LBO, management has repaid its long-term debt ahead of schedule (reducing long-term debt from $1.587 billion in 1985). At the same time, Levi's management redirected its efforts into jeans with emphasis on the Levi's brand and on higher margin wash lines. By the emphasis on the 501, the jeans family has diversified into the designer jeans segment while at the same time increasing the company's operating margins.' (Source: Corporate Bond Research Report, Saloman Brothers Inc, NY, June 1989)

In 1992, the *Wall Street Journal* reported the following with regard to Levi Strauss & Co's performance.

'Levi Strauss posts 40% jump in profit for fourth quarter, San Francisco – Levi Strauss Associates Inc, parent of Levi Strauss & Co, said its fourth quarter profit jumped 40% to $105.5 million from a year-earlier $75.3 million, backed by the popularity of its jeans and Dockers label clothing. Revenue increased 17% to $1.36 billion from $1.16 billion. The US clothing manufacturer is privately held and doesn't report per-share earnings.
Levi continued to defy the recession with its fifth consecutive year of record sales. Domestic sales rose 17% to $3 billion and international sales gained 13% to $1.9 billion, but were partially offset by a strong US dollar. George B James, chief executive officer, said sales were especially strong in the company's European and Asia Pacific divisions.
Mr James said Levi's success was primarily due to strong consumer demand for its basic jeans, jeans-related clothing and other casual wear. Sales of its Dockers and 501 lines of clothing were especially strong, he noted.' *(Wall Street Journal, 22/2/92)*

By 1991, the company had reinvested in its manufacturing and personnel resource base, employing an additional 1,000 personnel in Europe.

SUMMARY

1. *The opportunity for future growth 1988–91*

   As the most expensive and developing mass market jeans brand of the late 1980s, LSE needed more young jeans buyers with disposable income. We had neither. One of Europe's most severe economic recessions and an accompanying decline in the 11–24 population threatened at best to halt the brand's growth, at worst to reverse it. In addition, fashion appeared to be turning away from denim to sportswear, and youth culture away from America towards Europe.

2. *Levi's performance 1988–91*

   Levi's jeans brand sales not only withstood the above factors, but grew significantly ahead of local markets, increasing brand share whilst competitors fell away. The price premium of the 501, a critical dimension of Levi Strauss & Co's worldwide profitability was simultaneously enhanced in all of its established European markets. The above performance was achieved from static or marginally-reduced distribution bases.

3. *The contribution of advertising*
   We have established that within a market whose principal criterion of success is brand imagery, pan-European advertising has been the single most important contributor in directing and enhancing the Levi's brand image.
   This has been achieved to such an extent, that Levi's now occupies and 'owns' the optimum positioning territory in each local market, protecting the sales volumes and price premiums that surround this definitive position. We have demonstrated that by understanding and reflecting the universal needs and values of young people throughout Europe, one cost efficient campaign vehicle has consistently positioned the brand in the above territory, despite differing local market environments.

4. *Enhanced profitability and stability*
   We have demonstrated the impact LSE's performance has had in enhancing and rebalancing Levi Strauss & Co's revenue streams, generating additional profit, employment and stability.

TECHNICAL APPENDIX

1. All market data have been supplied by Levi Strauss & Co's market research department, and are compiled from factory shipment data, and panel data collected within each local affiliate.
2. Population data are supplied by LSE, and are collated from analysis of government population monitoring statistics.
3. Personnel and employment data are from LSE's personnel department in Brussels.
4. Pricing data are supplied by LSE's market research department and are based upon panel data and LSE price lists.
5. Qualitative research information has been drawn from the following Levi's research reports:
   — Burns Research Partners Ltd, London, UK, May 1988.
   — Imadi, Instituut Voor Marketing – Diagnostiek, Antwerp, Belgium, February 1986.
   — Feedback Research, Paris, France, May 1988.
   — Censydiam NV, Antwerp, Belgium, March 1990.
   — Inner Research SA, Madrid, Spain, March 1991.
   — RDS International Ltd, London, England, January 1991.
6. Quantitative image tracking data are supplied by Censydiam, Antwerp, Belgium and are based upon research waves conducted as follows:
   — Germany, June 1990, October 1991.
   — France, January 1991, November 1991.
   — UK, May 1991.
   — Spain, February 1991, November 1991.
   — Italy, June 1991.
7. Image maps are based upon computer data cluster analysis completed by Censydiam and LSE.
8. Historical media data are supplied by Carat, London, and its subsidiary media monitoring agencies.
9. Singles chart data are supplied by Capital Radio.
10. LSE financial performance data are supplied by LSE Brussels.

Section Four

*New Consumer Goods
and Services*

10

Häagen-Dazs

*Dedicated to Pleasure –
Dedicated to Advertising*

INTRODUCTION

In 1991 Häagen-Dazs became the most talked about ice cream brand in the country. Every national newspaper wrote about it and its advertising.

This paper does not talk about that fame. Rather it talks about the thinking and facts behind that success, and describes how Häagen-Dazs became clear brand leader in its sector.

In the first section, we will put Häagen-Dazs into context vs its competitors and describe how the advertising strategy and creative work were developed.

Next, looking at the effect of advertising, we describe the sales growth from October 1990 to February 1992 and attempt to isolate the effect of advertising on sales, vs those due to distribution and seasonal growth. We do this using both econometric analysis, and analysis of sales from some 'core' outlets that stocked Häagen-Dazs both before and after advertising.

Finally, we will attempt to show how we believe advertising worked; first by creating high levels of awareness and trial, and second by positioning Häagen-Dazs successfully as a sensual and sophisticated adult treat and a new gold standard in the market.

THE UK TAKE HOME ICE CREAM MARKET

The UK ice cream market is underdeveloped compared to many in the world. In the USA consumption of ice cream is three times that of the UK.

The reason for this is not a lack of sunshine (see Sweden Figure 1). The problem has been that most manufacturers' vision of the potential of the market was limited to ice cream as a child's product.

Most take home brands, therefore, are designed; to act as 'default desserts'. Quality is not a key dimension. Format is more crucial. The products come either in large 'soft scoop' tubs, or multi-packs of hand-held products eg Cornetto.

By 1991 the market had started to change and recognised the potential for better quality adult products. Vienetta offered an adult version of default desserts, and in 1990 the Mars ice cream bar raised the quality stakes in the multi-pack hand-held sector.

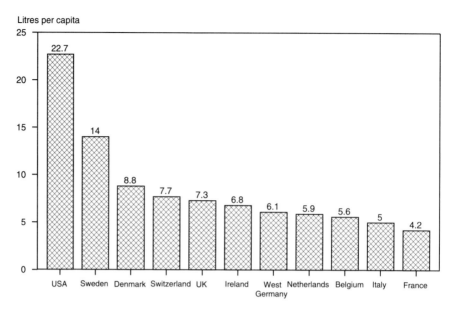

Figure 1.   *Ice cream around the world*
Source: Trade estimates
Note: These figures are underestimated by half due to the fact that much of these countries' ice cream is artisan produced and locally consumed so very difficult to measure

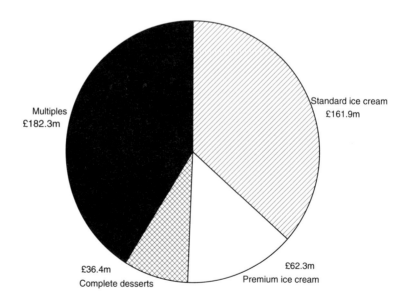

Figure 2.   *Sector shares by value of the UK take home ice cream market 1990*
Source: AGB

The market's premium sector proper (excluding complete desserts such as Vienetta, and premium multi-packs such as Mars) had also been showing signs of life for the last few years.

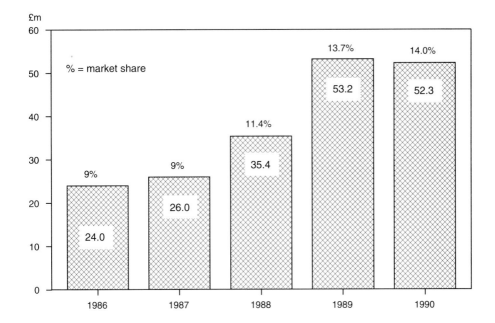

Figure 3.   *The growth of the UK premium ice cream market*
Source: AGB

AGB's definition of 'premium' ranges from products such as Wall's Gino Ginelli to the two brands that stood at the top of that sector and represented the premium ice cream sector proper – Loseley and New England.

These represented the gold standard of the ice cream market in the late 1980s, charging around £1.99 for half a litre.

Both brands had been available for many years (Loseley for 18 and New England for 15 years). Their marketing strategies had been classic 'seed branding', involving many years building credentials in delicatessens and premium independent food shops before then moving into multiple grocers.

It was against these two brands that Häagen-Dazs was primarily competing.

HÄAGEN-DAZS' MARKET OBJECTIVE

Häagen-Dazs believed the market for premium adult ice cream was still in its infancy and that there was the opportunity to raise the quality stakes even higher ie to develop a super-premium sector.

The company mission was to create a new gold standard and become the ultimate ice cream in the market.

At £2.99 per 500ml the intention was that Häagen-Dazs should command a massive premium of exactly £1.00 vs its two closest competitors.

The basis of Häagen-Dazs' self-belief lay both in its conviction that it had a superior product to its nearest competitors and, equally importantly, that both Loseley and New England had a number of image limitations which might be exploited.

The Image Limitations of Current Premium Brands

The initial quantitative research identified that the key users of current premium offerings were ABC1, 25–45 year olds, both male and female, with high disposable income (eg no kids) and high terminal education age.

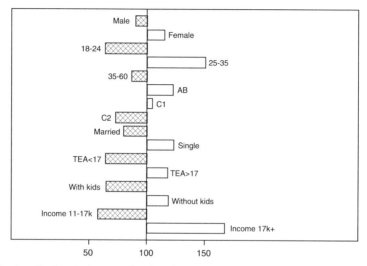

Figure 4.   *Index of usership of premium ice cream in last 12 months*
Source: BBH Quantitative Research May 1990

Qualitative research amongst this group revealed that existing premium ice cream was perceived to be primarily about formal, social occasions; dinner parties, Sunday family dinners etc.

In this restricted context a brand's role was to signal premium in a very overt way. The brand was about impressing others. Loseley, for example, was drawn by consumers as the epitome of traditional England – all Barbours, Range Rovers and country halls.

New England, though branded as American, carried many of the same signals eg pack graphics showing beautiful pictures of decanted ice cream.

The target identified was uncomfortable with this imagery. They were modern and sophisticated in their use of quality food. They did not feel it should be reserved only for formal occasions and for serving to others. They were just as happy eating good ice cream sitting around in an old pullover and relaxing privately.

There was an opportunity therefore to use advertising to rewrite the rules of premium ice cream by deformalising and contemporising its imagery.

THE HÄAGEN-DAZS ADVERTISING STRATEGY

After limited tests in Sainsbury the objective in 1991 was to embark on a full scale brand launch in the south of the country – London, Anglia and TVS – supported with full scale advertising. This area was the most competitive in the country but accounts for 51% of the market. It is at this point we helped develop the advertising this paper will analyse.

The advertising was designed to exploit our competitors' weaknesses. Early in the process we decided not to attempt to 'outbadge' Loseley and New England.

We avoided lifestyle images of Häagen-Dazs featuring in posh flats, sitting next to champagne glasses, or being eaten in the back of Rolls Royces!

Instead, we decided to concentrate on the product's credentials and the new type of individual premium experience created by it.

As a product Häagen-Dazs was associated primarily with richness, creaminess and smooth texture and intense flavour.

It created a distinct Häagen-Dazs moment, that was described by consumers as 'languorous', 'sensual', 'dream-like'. People described a feeling of hovering and a sense of 'time stopping still'.

Häagen-Dazs became not just another quality ice cream manufacturer but a very special purveyor of a particular mood or emotion.

This Häagen-Dazs moment was most often described as a moment to be savoured and enjoyed solus either as a reward or as compensation.

But this usage also carried some negative connotations of 'comfort eating' and guilty 'pigging out'.

However, in research there were hints of a different, more attractive, potential benefit; that of people sharing Häagen-Dazs and the Häagen-Dazs experience. Consumers talked of sharing a spoon, feeding each other, and of 'mellowing out' together in front of their favourite video with the lights off and curtains closed... and at this point people began to giggle knowingly.

This area offered Häagen-Dazs the chance to create a unique advertising language for ice cream. Solus reward eating was the cliché of premium food and would not have been as brave and as different as the product itself. The idea that Häagen-Dazs created a mood of sensual intimacy between adults was a far more interesting area for the brand to carve out and make its own.

The Creative Brief

Why are we advertising?
To position Häagen-Dazs as the new gold standard in the market by referring to the immense pleasure of the Häagen-Dazs experience.

Who are we talking to?
ABC1, 25 plus, single, male or female looking for new interesting quality tastes. They demand the best but are not precious or pompous about it.

What must the advertising say?
Häagen-Dazs – the ultimate in intimate pleasure.

Why should the consumer believe it?

What Häagen-Dazs put into the pot:	dedication to perfection
	extraordinary ingredients
What people take out of the pot:	an extraordinary personal pleasure

What tone of voice?
Adult, sensuous

Ripe Oregon strawberries are
especially selected as we

feel
it

best complements the rich cream
flavour of Häagen-Dazs.

Häagen-Dazs

Dedicated to Pleasure

Throughout the 1960's and 1970's
the sales of Häagen-Dazs
mounted steadily, relying purely on

word
of
mouth

Häagen-Dazs

Dedicated to Pleasure

The Creative Idea

The advertising idea flowed naturally out of the research.

We decided to juxtapose what Häagen-Dazs put in the pot (as evidenced by actual quotes taken from their company literature) with what consumers got out of the pot.

The approach was summed up in the line 'Dedicated to Pleasure' which was a tongue in cheek rewrite of the original company slogan 'Dedicated to Perfection'. In total four executions were developed

One of these, 'Feel It', we later recognised carried too many connotations of eating alone, and therefore was not used in the second phase.

The Media Strategy

87.5% of ice cream advertising in 1991 was on TV. TV was a budget option.

However, we decided to break away from this traditional means of media support, despite many attractive offers from TV companies for Häagen-Dazs as a new product.

Rather we chose to view media as part of the process of positioning Häagen-Dazs as a 'mood purveyor'.

First, we knew we wanted to achieve a feel with this advertising that could itself be savoured and enjoyed at leisure, just like the product.

Second, we believed the intimacy of the experience could be better illustrated through personal communication. Television is often a family or social medium. We wanted the communication to be private and not expose it to the comment and reaction of third parties.

Third, in keeping with the desired brand personality, we wanted to achieve a relationship with our target audience gradually, rather than blast them with a one-off message.

The solution we chose was to spend the bulk of our monies against the weekend colour supplements and in particular the weekend review sections of the up-market press.

Though we chose national titles these quality papers had a regional bias in terms of coverage. This coincided with the bias in our distribution and sales effort for the launch.

TABLE 1: TARGET MARKET COVERAGE OF PROPOSED SCHEDULE BY REGION

	Index of coverage
London	118
TVS	110
Anglia	101
National coverage	100

Source: NRS

The coverage achieved in the rest of the country was seen as investment for the (very near) future.

TABLE 2: HÄAGEN-DAZS SUMMER SCHEDULE

Week commencing	July 15	July 22	July 29	Aug 5	Aug 12	Aug 19	Aug 26	Sept 2
Review section								
IOS Review	✕	✕		✕	✕			
Times Review			✕	✕		✕		
Supplements								
Observer			✕	✕	✕	✕		
Independent			✕			✕	✕	✕
Sunday Times				✕	✕	✕		
Telegraph				✕	✕	✕	✕	
You			✕	✕	✕	✕		
Evening Standard				✕				
Women's magazines								
Vogue						✕ (Sept issue)		
Tatler						✕ (Sept issue)		
Elle						✕ (Sept issue)		
Marie Claire						✕ (Sept issue)		
Vanity Fair						✕ (Sept issue)		
Cosmopolitan						✕ (Sept issue)		

Source: BBH

This first burst started w/c July 15th and finished by w/c Sept 2nd. It achieved 67.4% coverage of ABC1, 25–45 year olds with an average frequency of 4.8 OTS.

TABLE 3: HÄAGEN-DAZS CHRISTMAS SCHEDULE

Week commencing	Dec 7	Dec 14	Dec 21
IOS Review	✕	✕	
Saturday Times Review		✕	✕
Sunday Times	✕	✕	
Guardian Wk	✕	✕	✕
Independent Wk	✕	✕	✕

Source: BBH

After the initial first burst we returned in December in anticipation of the Christmas season.

This second burst achieved 38.1% coverage with a frequency of just 2.5 OTS.

The MEAL estimate of the spend was £900,000, which gave Häagen-Dazs only a 6.0% share of voice across the whole year.

MEAL estimates are greatly exaggerated and, in fact, Häagen-Dazs' actual spend was roughly a half of this figure.

THE GROWTH IN HÄAGEN-DAZS' SALES IN 1991

In 1991 sales of Häagen-Dazs rose by 398% vs 1990.

Figure 5 shows Häagen-Dazs' overall retail sales, across the whole country, measured in terms of indexed ex-factory sales.

Figure 6 shows Häagen-Dazs' growth in multiple grocers in the launch area only using Nielsen Scantrack. We will use these data to examine the effect of advertising in more detail. It is a robust source based on EPOS data and therefore acts as a good proxy for the whole market.

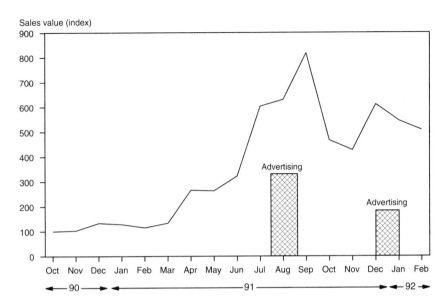

Figure 5.   *The overall retail growth of Häagen-Dazs*
Source: Häagen-Dazs accounts, revised to create equal monthly accounting periods

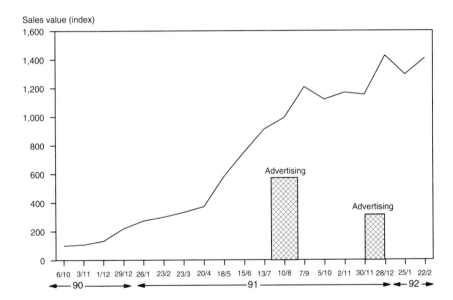

Figure 6.   *The growth of Häagen-Dazs in multiple grocers in launch area**
Source: Nielsen Scantrack – London/Anglia/Southern
Note: *Nielsen Scantrack splits GB into three areas: London/Anglia/Southern,   WWW/Midlands/Lancashire,   Yorkshire/Tyne
Tees/Scotland. Data cannot be broken into individual regions due to sample size

The Nielsen sales show a steeper incline than the sales overall. The multiples represented a new area for the brand and therefore sales grew from a smaller base. The result is that Häagen-Dazs multiple grocers in the area at the beginning of the launch accounted for less than 20% of Häagen-Dazs' overall retail sales. They grew to represent around 50% in the final periods.

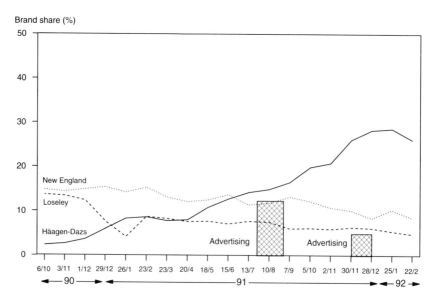

Figure 7.   *The growth in Häagen-Dazs' share vs key competitors*
Source: Nielsen Scantrack
Base: Dairy market, London/Anglia/Southern

Figure 7 shows this growth in the context of what was happening in the total market in multiple grocers in the launch area. Dairy market is Nielsen's equivalent to AGB's 'premium' ice cream sector and includes the same range of brands.

The tables show how Häagen-Dazs grew across the year in a number of distinct phases.

First, the brand sales gradually increased in the early part of the year.

This growth accelerates in the periods immediately before advertising, as distribution in anticipation of advertising is added, particularly by the multiples.

The first burst of advertising accelerates growth again.

Sales then fall as the market declines due to seasonality, though this happens at a much slower rate than the market overall. Thus brand share continues to rise.

The second burst of advertising in December increases sales growth again.

ISOLATING THE ADVERTISING EFFECT

We do not intend to claim that advertising created all the growth shown above.

Growth was, in fact, the result of three key variables: market seasonality, availability of product ie distribution, and finally, but by no means least, straight increase in consumer demand due to advertising effect.

Figures 8 and 9 show how the first two of these variables were also increasing during the advertising period.

It is clear that Häagen-Dazs benefitted from seasonal and distribution increases.

The effect of distribution and seasonality could be isolated by looking at Häagen-Dazs' rate of sale and Häagen-Dazs' brand share separately. However, both these measures look at the effect of the different variables in isolation from each other. Rate of sale isolates the effect of distribution but not seasonality, and vice versa.

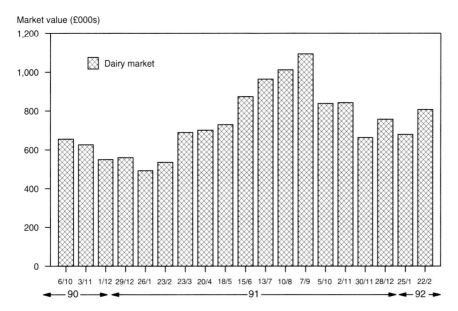

Figure 8.   *Market growth in Häagen-Dazs launch area*
Source: Nielsen Scantrack, London/Anglia/Southern

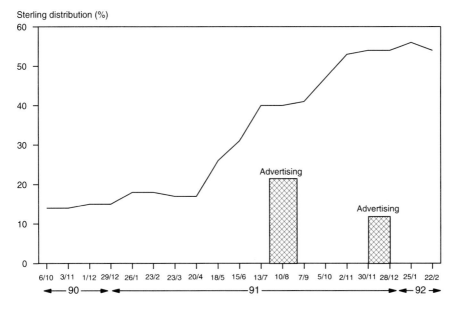

Figure 9.   *Häagen-Dazs sterling distribution growth in launch area*
Source: Nielsen Scantrack, London/Anglia/Southern

The simultaneous growth in the different elements suggests a far more complex interplay of variables. We therefore used econometric analysis to help disentangle them.

THE ECONOMETRIC ANALYSIS OF HÄAGEN-DAZS' GROWTH

It was first necessary to identify what we believed to be the underlying process that led to the brand's success. This theory was then tested against the data, and quantification of the relationships as derived using econometric methods. The diagram below attempts to show the hypothesis in a simplified pictorial form.

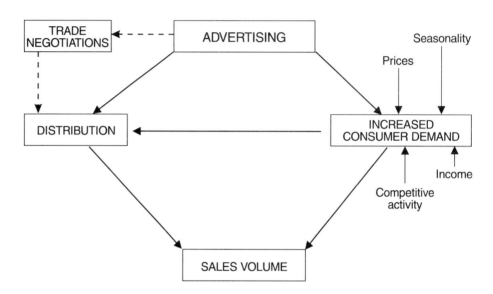

Figure 10. *How Häagen-Dazs advertising worked*

This theoretical model suggests that advertising had a number of direct as well as indirect effects on sales.

First, advertising for Häagen-Dazs, as with many new products, was part of the special trade negotiations which helped the brand secure the extra distribution before advertising even started (this distribution growth was seen in Figure 9).

Though it is tempting to claim advertising played some part in the securing of this distribution, we do not. The econometric analysis discounts any claim for sales due to direct trade negotiations by including these in the equation as a separate variable.

Second, advertising created direct increased consumer demand for Häagen-Dazs. The econometric analysis posits this as the first order effect of advertising.

Third, advertising's effect on consumer demand and the fame it created for the brand helped encourage trade buyers either to increase distribution, or provide distribution where before they had refused. In other words for every 1% of extra sales created by advertising x% of extra distribution was created. In effect this is a 'success breeds success' explanation of what happened, which has some appeal to common sense.

Häagen-Dazs' Director of National Accounts confirmed this change of attitude.

'Before advertising broke the trade were obviously wary. They were naturally suspect of our claims that we could create a new market for a different type of super-premium brand. After advertising doors opened that had been closed. Buyers started calling us. As a result test stores became full listings, and stores who had initially declined Häagen-Dazs changed their position.' (Mel Bugler, Director of National Accounts)

Two equations are suggested by the theory – one that explains advertising's role in volume sales, and one its role in distribution. The actual data fitted this theory well. Approximately 99% of the variation in both sales and distribution data is explained by the models.

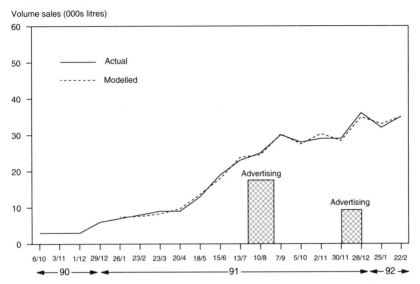

Figure 11.   *Häagen-Dazs sales: actual vs model*
Source: Econometric analysis

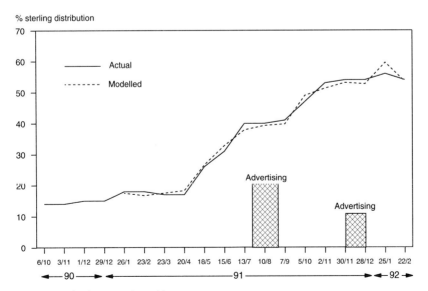

Figure 12.   *Häagen-Dazs distribution: actual vs model*
Source: Econometric analysis

In effect these two equations 'interact' creating a ripple effect. Advertising first creates extra sales, extra sales then create extra distribution. Advertising continues to create sales, but these are added to by the increased sales due to distribution. The result is yet more increased distribution and so on, and so on.

The effect of the advertising is shown below. Figure 13 shows sales due to direct consumer demand created by advertising. Figure 14 shows sales resulting from distribution growth due to advertising. These are estimated by looking at actual sales vs simulations of sales without advertising.

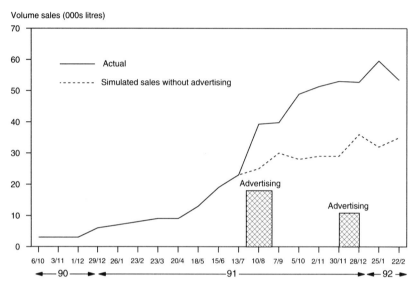

Figure 13. *Häagen-Dazs sales due to increased consumer demand*
Source: Econometric analysis

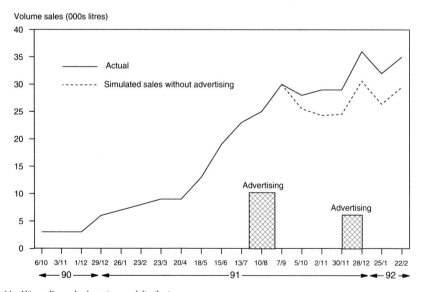

Figure 14. *Häagen-Dazs sales due to increased distribution*
Source: Econometric analysis

THE TOTAL VALUE OF SALES DUE TO ADVERTISING

Advertising created a 59.7% increase in volume over the eight month period since the first burst of advertising. 78% of this increase was due to the first order effect of advertising on consumer demand.

This is equivalent to a projected increase in value sales, as measured by Nielsen, across the full year of roughly £440,000.

This is a valid calculation as the model indicates that there is no evidence that the sales effect due to advertising has decayed. It is as if the demand for Häagen-Dazs has been shifted to a once and for all higher level.

The figures above relate to sales through launch area multiples only. Examination of the 'core' outlets (see next section) suggest sales increased across Häagen-Dazs' total distribution base. Distribution also seemed to grow across the country in roughly the same proportion (from around 3% to 32% on multiples across the country for example according to Nielsen). It seems fair to assume therefore that advertising achieved the same levels of sales increase across the country.

We have calculated earlier that multiple grocers accounted for just 50% of Häagen-Dazs' total retail sales. The sales effect due to advertising can therefore be roughly doubled.

This gives a figure which shows a sales uplift due to advertising within the first year of nearly two times actual negotiated media spend.

TESTING THE MODEL

In addition to the above evidence we have a totally different data source that externally validates the modelling analysis, and provides further supporting evidence as to the contribution of the advertising. This data source is a set of 'core' stores.

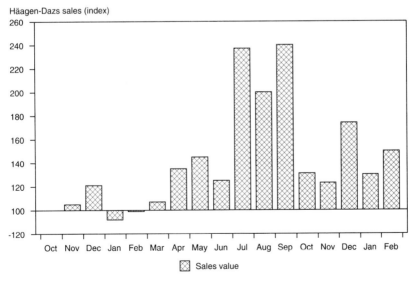

Figure 15. *Sales value growth in 'core' outlets*
Source: Accounts for London-based deli/grocer group

These core stores are those of a large deli/grocer group based in London. This group has over 20 stores and Häagen-Dazs was stocked in all of them from October 1990. Sales data were collected on a monthly basis.

This sudden rise in July cannot be attributed in any way to distribution growth. Seasonality played some part. However, it also represents some kind of once and for all leap in consumer demand. This is seen even more clearly if we look at year on year sales across the same monthly periods ie October on October, November on November etc. This discounts any seasonality effect.

TABLE 4: % INCREASE IN £ SALES YEAR ON YEAR

	+ %
Oct	51
Nov	18
Dec	44
Jan	41
Feb	51

Source: Accounts for London based deli/grocer group

Over the five months this represents an average 41% increase in rate of sale. This increase is roughly equivalent to that indicated by the econometric analysis of increased consumer demand excluding distribution effect.

DISCOUNTING OTHER FACTORS

The econometric analysis has discounted seasonality and distribution. This section will consider some of the other potential creators of consumer demand.

The Economy

The analysis did not include figures for the general economic climate. However, common sense tells us that the climate did not exactly work in the brand's favour.

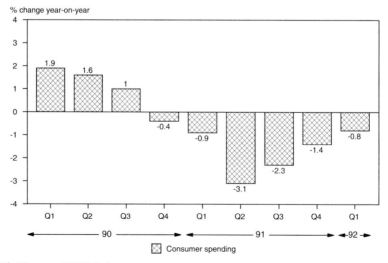

Figure 16. *The UK economy 1990/91, % change year on year*
Source: Government statistics 1985 prices

The launch took place in the middle of the longest recession since the Second World War. The result was a decline in consumer spending which, if anything, might be expected to have dampened the effect of consumer demand.

Market Growth

The econometric analysis works on share and therefore discounts general market growth effect. However, we should consider whether Loseley and New England in particular also increased share ahead of the market. In fact these two brands lost share over the year (see Figure 7).

There was no growth at the top end of the market that benefitted Häagen-Dazs.

COMPETITIVE ACTIVITY

Advertising and Promotion

General competitive activity increased dramatically in the years up to 1991

TABLE 5: ADVERTISING SPEND 1987 TO 1991

	£'000
1987	5,673
1988	7,275
1989	8,847
1990	16,814
1991	14,471

Source: MEAL

In terms of immediate competition, Loseley devoted its marketing activity to new packaging and POS. New England actually advertised for the first time in TVS, using TV. They achieved 837 TVRs: 68% cover at 4+ OTS (Source: DDS).

We can see from Figure 7 that the brand achieved no overall increase in brand share.

This is clear evidence that it is not just a case of any advertising achieving success. The advertising has to be right.

Distribution

Loseley and New England maintained the same levels of sterling distribution throughout the main part of the year (New England declined slightly in the last three periods).

Therefore it cannot be argued that Häagen-Dazs benefitted from the distribution decline of its nearest rivals. Haagen-Dazs won in terms of straight consumer demand. Häagen-Dazs' distribution lagged behind that of Loseley/New England making its brand leadership even more surprising.

Price

Häagen-Dazs' marked premium was maintained throughout the periods discussed. No price cutting or promotional discounting was employed to kick start the launch, nor at any point after.

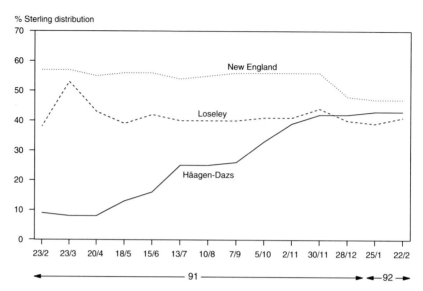

Figure 17. *Sterling distribution of Loseley/New England in launch area*
Source: Nielsen Scantrack
Base: London/Anglia/Southern

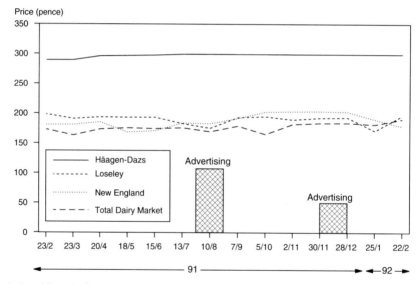

Figure 18. *Price differentials of key premium brands 1990/91*
Source: Nielsen Scantrack

Sampling and Shops

Through the period Häagen-Dazs opened further shops in Oxford, Bath and Heathrow. These acted as sampling points. Häagen-Dazs also carried out sampling to support the launch.

In order to measure the contribution of these elements we used tracking to monitor their effect. This took place before advertising, and then after each burst.

The proportion of the people receiving free samples remained roughly the same, or even dipped during the period of advertising.

TABLE 6: THE CONTRIBUTION OF SAMPLING (%)

	Pre		Post 1		Post 2	
	Total (300)	Aware of Häagen-Dazs (32)	Total (300)	Aware of Häagen-Dazs (75)	Total (300)	Aware of Häagen-Dazs (77)
Receipt of free sample in supermarket	—	4	1	5	—	1
Receipt of free sample elsewhere	1	10	1	5	3	10

Base: 300 ABC1 adults, 25–45 years, London/Anglia/Southern
Source: Consumer Focus Tracking Study
Note: ( ) = Sample size

We also asked respondents how they had first become aware of Häagen-Dazs.

TABLE 7: HOW FIRST BECOME AWARE OF HÄAGEN-DAZS (%)

	Pre (32)	Post 1 (75)	Post 2 (77)
Saw product in Häagen-Dazs shop	3	1	3

Base: All aware of Häagen-Dazs
Source: Consumer Focus Tracking Study
Note: ( ) = Sample size

The proportion of people who had come to the brand through the shops declined during the advertising.

Our conclusion is that the massive rise in demand was created above and beyond the contribution of sampling and shops.

THE EFFECT OF ADVERTISING ON HÄAGEN-DAZS AWARENESS

A tracking study was carried out amongst our core target market in London, Anglia and the South in three waves:

Pre   –   pre-advertising (June '91)
Post 1   –   post-1st burst (Sept '91)
Post 2   –   post-2nd burst (Jan '92)

This allowed us to look at rises in advertising awareness, awareness, usage, image and propensity to trial.

Advertising Awareness

Rises in advertising awareness were very strong (remembering the size of the budget), especially amongst those directly exposed to the advertising message (ie readers of papers/magazines on the actual schedule).

TABLE 8: AWARENESS OF HÄAGEN-DAZS ADVERTISING (%)

	Pre			Post 1			Post 2		
	Total (300)	Schedule readers (193)	Non-schedule readers (107)	Total (300)	Schedule readers (179)	Non-schedule readers (121)	Total (300)	Schedule readers (99)	Non-schedule readers (202)
Spontaneous awareness	0	0	0	7	10	3	4	11	1
Prompted by name	1	1	1	14	19	6	10	23	4
Prompted by pictures	2	2	2	24	32	12	22	38	4

Base: 300 ABC1 adults, 25-45 years, London/Anglia/Southern
Source: Consumer Focus Tracking Study
Note: ( ) = Sample size
Statistical error: 4-5% (see Appendix)

The total figure declines due to the reduced coverage of the advertising in 2nd burst (see media schedules) which was half that of the first. Awareness therefore holds amongst those potentially exposed to the campaign, but declines amongst those not on the schedule.

This effect is exaggerated as the market enters the Christmas season.

These two factors deflate the 'total' figures in the final wave of tracking.

It is encouraging, however, to see that awareness of those who had chance to see the 2nd burst of advertising (ie 'readers on schedule') stays high, or even increases.

Brand Awareness

The growth in advertising awareness was mirrored by growth in spontaneous and prompted awareness, again especially amongst schedule readers.

TABLE 9: AWARENESS OF HÄAGEN-DAZS PRE AND POST ADVERTISING (%)

	Pre			Post 1			Post 2		
	Total (300)	Schedule readers (193)	Non-schedule readers (107)	Total (300)	Schedule readers (179)	Non-schedule Readers (121)	Total (300)	Schedule Readers (99)	Non-schedule Readers (202)
Spontaneous awareness	2	2	0	11	14	7	5	12	2
Prompted awareness (name only)	11	12	8	25	33	13	25	43	17

Base: 300 ABC1 adults, 25–45 years, London/Anglia/Southern
Source: Consumer Focus Tracking Study
Note: ( ) = Sample size

Trial and Intention to Purchase

The growth in awareness for Häagen-Dazs was mirrored by increases in trial, with higher figures amongst readers on the schedule actually exposed to advertising.

TABLE 10:   CLAIMED USAGE OF HÄAGEN-DAZS PRE AND POST ADVERTISING (%)

	Pre			Post 1			Post 2		
	Total (300)	Schedule readers (193)	Non-schedule readers (107)	Total (300)	Schedule readers (179)	Non-schedule readers (121)	Total (300)	Schedule readers (99)	Non-schedule readers (202)
Eaten last 12 months	6	6	6	11	15	6	7	12	5
Eaten last 3 months	2	1	4	8	11	3	5	5	4

Base: 300 ABC1 adults, 25–45 years, London/Anglia/Southern
Source: Consumer Focus Tracking Study
Note: ( ) = Sample size

Claimed intention to purchase also increased amongst those aware of Häagen-Dazs.

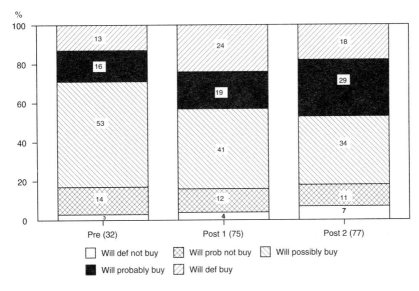

Figure 19.   *Propensity to purchase Häagen-Dazs pre and post advertising*
Source: Consumer Focus Tracking Study
Base: All aware of Häagen-Dazs

HOW THE ADVERTISING POSITIONED HÄAGEN-DAZS

The advertising also helped carve out a clear point of view for the brand.

First, the advertising positioned the product as the gold standard. In the tracking the consumers were asked whether they agreed/disagreed with a number of statements, such 'as best quality ice cream available'.

Häagen-Dazs achieved pole position vs its two closest competitors, after just 3 years in the market and six months of advertising.

TABLE 11:   % AWARE OF EACH BRAND AGREEING THAT PRODUCT
IS 'THE BEST QUALITY AVAILABLE'

Häagen-Dazs	51
Loseley	44
New England	32

Base: All aware of brands
Source: Consumer Focus Tracking Study
Note: Sample Size – HD = 75, L = 88, NE = 57

The objective of the advertising however was not just to ensure we became the new gold standard in rational terms. It was also to create a whole new set of image associations.

Qualitative research showed that we clearly achieved our objectives of creating a new language for Häagen-Dazs.

'The campaign has had considerable effect on perceptions of Häagen-Dazs' image. It clearly positions Häagen-Dazs as premium quality, special, adult, modern, worthy of attention, exclusive and a whole new different angle on ice cream.' (SRG Research, Oct '91, Base: ABC1 adults, 25-45 years)

The list of words below shows the initial reactions to the advertising in the groups. Respondents were asked to write down on paper the first words that came into their head.

TABLE 12:   INITIAL RESPONSES TO ADVERTISING COMMUNICATION

Sensual	Wicked	Fun	Naughty
Erotic	Irresponsible	Smooth	Sensation
Sexual	Natural	Youthful	Happy
Moving	Sexy	Seductive	Intimate
Pleasure	Desirable	Passionate	
Shared	Togetherness	Raunchy	
Cool	Private	Stunning	
Vibrant	Sophisticated	Indulgent	

Source: SRG Research, Oct '91
Base: ABC1 Adults, 25-45 yrs

The advertising succeeded therefore in positioning Häagen-Dazs as a sensual, sophisticated adult treat.

HOW ADVERTISING MADE HÄAGEN-DAZS FAMOUS

Before advertising there was little press coverage of Häagen-Dazs. Most was trade based except for two or three paid-for consumer advertorials in June.

After advertising national consumer press coverage soared (see Figure 20).

A content analysis of consumer articles reveals that, of the 263 consumer articles, 42% mentioned the advertising. Another 14% of the articles actually featured one or more of the advertisements, as well as then going on to discuss the brand and advertising. Extra PR gave 52% coverage, at 2.2 OTS (analysis by Biss Lancaster).

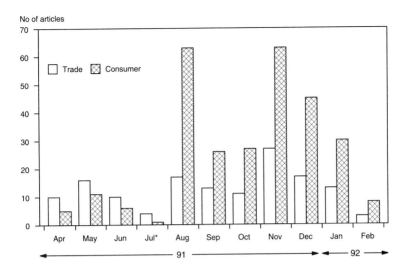

Figure 20. *Number of Häagen-Dazs articles pre and post advertising*
Source: Biss Lancaster Analysis
Note: First advertisement appeared July 15th

Press coverage continued well after the campaign finished. The latest piece of 'free' advertising was the National Press Association's use of the case history in their campaign on the benefits of press. This took place in March 1992. It is estimated that £1m at rate card was spent on this one execution. Its effect is, however, outside the periods covered by this paper.

CONCLUSION

This paper, we believe, has demonstrated how advertising helped Häagen-Dazs gain brand leadership of the take home premium ice cream market.

First, advertising with only a 6.0% share of voice, made Häagen-Dazs the most talked about ice cream brand of the year, indeed the 'New Product of the Year' according to The Marketing Society.

The advertising first created consumer excitement, then PR, then trade excitement, and consequently more and more consumer interest. The whole launch gained an unstoppable momentum.

On top of that, advertising helped create an absolutely clear brand point of view for Häagen-Dazs. Everyone who knows Häagen-Dazs knows what the brand stands for. Häagen-Dazs is 'Dedicated to Pleasure'. This was a completely new and unique point of view on the market, which redefined what 'premium' meant to consumers.

These brand values, both client and agency would argue, are Häagen-Dazs' future competitive advantage as new products attempt to follow. Certainly they help justify Häagen-Dazs' considerable premium vs rivals.

When we developed our advertising proposals we knew we were creating a new advertising language for ice cream in this country. We knew it broke many of the rules. Häagen-Dazs was willing to take that step and proved that they were as dedicated to producing good advertising as they were to producing great product.

We hope to have proved in this paper that they got the advertising they deserved.

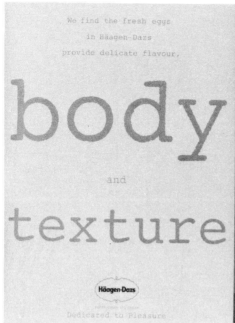

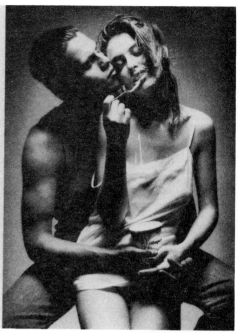

Daily Mail, Thursday, March 5, 1992

It is the

intense

flavour of
the finest ingredients
combined with

fresh

cream that is
essentially Häagen-Dazs.

Dedicated to Pleasure

Now it's on everybody's lips.

IF HÄAGEN-DAZS Ice Cream is dedicated to pleasure, their advertising is dedicated to success. Between July and September 1991, they advertised in newspapers and their supplements. During this period brand awareness doubled, rising from 9% to 21%. And sales in major outlets rose by a third. For the pleasure that only success can bring, why not advertise in national newspapers.

PEOPLE READ NEWSPAPERS

This advertisement was placed by the Newspaper Publishers Association.

TECHNICAL APPENDIX

The theoretical sales growth schema in the main text generates a number of testable predictions ie the dynamic structure, the form of the equations and bounds parameters of the variables.

Reliable Anglia/London/Southern Nielsen Scantrack four weekly data for Häagen-Dazs volume sales, distribution and total ice cream market data were available for the period October 1990 to February 1992.

Häagen-Dazs press advertising data were represented as +1 cover, for bursts 1 and 2 in the volume model, and as 0,1 variable in the distribution model. Competitive advertising was represented by TVRs.

The Häagen-Dazs advertising effect, over the available data did not decay, and entered the empirical model as zero decay adstock.

Distribution was increased by trade negotiations. The influence was captured by a 0,1 variable. The following mnemonics have been used to represent the variables.

L = logarithmic base e transformed. V = Häagen-Dazs volume. D = Häagen-Dazs sterling distribution. COMTVR = competitive advertising. COV1 = Häagen-Dazs first burst advertising. COV2 = second burst. HDMED = 0,1 variable for Häagen-Dazs advertising. TVOL = Total market volume. NEGOT = Trade negotiations.

The system can be shown to be block recursive and therefore if the Gauss-Markov conditions hold OLS will produce the BLU Estimates.

Variable	Sales volume model Parameter	t-ratio
Constant	-6.748	9.2
LD(t)	0.730	8.4
COV1(t-1)+ 0.5*COV2(t)	0.00528	5.1
COMPTVR(t-1)	-0.00058	3.4

$R^2 = 0.994$, $\overline{R}^2 = 0.992$, Regression standard error = 0.051

DW = 2.5 – this value is in the indeterminate region therefore Box-Pierce Q-statistics have been provided as tests against first and higher order autocorrelation. Short Chow parameter stability and constant variance = 0.393, f(4,6). Chi-squared Q statistics, Q(1) = 1.335, Q(2) = 4.854, Q(3) = 5.997, Q(4) = 6.131 cv 9.49, Q(5) = 6.624 cv 11.1, Q(6) = 6.700.

Variable	Distribution model Parameter	t-ratio
Constant	2.053	17.9
LV(t-1) - LV(t-2)	0.569	5.8
LV(t-2)	0.377	6.9
HMED(t-2)	0.242	4.9
NEGOT	0.399	6.9

$R^2 = 0.991$, $\overline{R}^2 = 0.988$, Regression standard error = 0.052. DW = 1.987. Short Chow parameter stability and constant variance = 0.207, f(4,6). Chi-squared statistics, Q(1) = 0.002, Q(2) = 0.122, Q(3) = 2.911, Q(4) = 2.914, Q(5) = 3.013, Q(6) = 3.266.

The models fit the data and theory very well. The SE of the models are consistent with the data sampling error. All parameters are statistically significant at the 99% level and some at the 99.9% level, and stable on the basis of Chow tests. The Gauss-Markov conditions are upheld by the diagnostics.

11

The Launch of Gini

This is a simple story about the launch of Gini into a crowded and, in advertising terms, undifferentiated market. It is a straightforward account of how advertising contributed to arousing interest in a new product launch and stimulating trial. It is not a mould-breaking case history nor a complicated one. However, its ability to clearly demonstrate the value of advertising in contributing to one of the most successful launches of recent years, makes it well worth writing.

BUSINESS BACKGROUND

Cadbury Schweppes bought the rights to the Gini label from a subsidiary of the Procter & Gamble company in November 1989. However, they did not achieve direct control over the development of the brand until the summer of 1990 when they bought the non-cola soft drinks business of Source Perrier. This brought with it control of Gini's bottling and distribution. Whilst these acquisitions were made with the intention of consolidating Cadbury Schweppes' French business, (Gini is a well-established major player in the French market), it also paved the way for a new product launch from Schweppes GB, eager to move their business out of the declining mixer sector and into the profitable and growing carbonated soft drink market. The acquisition of Gini completed the search for a successor to Sunkist which was launched by Cadbury Schweppes in the spring of 1989.

Reference is made to both Cadbury Schweppes and Coca-Cola Schweppes Beverages (CCSB) in this paper. It should be explained that the former own the brand and market it, the latter bottle and distribute it.

MARKETING OBJECTIVES

1. To take a 2% share of the fruit-flavoured carbonates' market by the end of Year 1. This market is highly fragmented with no one brand taking as much as 10% share. Of the well-established brands only four have over 5% share. A 2% share in year one would make Gini a major contender, already larger than Orangina, Citrus Spring or Dr Pepper.
2. To minimise cannibalisation of CCSB's fruit-flavoured portfolio (Sprite/ Sunkist/Lilt/Fanta).

WHAT IS GINI?

Technically it is a cloudy lemon, mildly carbonated drink. It contains quinine and 1.8% real lemon juice. Its taste delivery is sharper, cleaner-tasting and has a bit of bite – closer to bitter lemon than 7-Up. Its main pack format is the 33cl can but it is also available in the family-sized 1.5 litre PET bottle. Both standard and diet versions of Gini come in these two pack sizes. Its pack design is bright green and yellow, it is loud and attention-grabbing, consistent with the big players in this market against whom it will compete for 'share of throat' on shelf. It is also at price parity with the competition (28p for a 33cl can).

Despite slight product differences Gini essentially shares the characteristics of all other canned and carbonated soft drinks. Its lemon flavour places it firmly in the fruit-flavoured carbonates sector of the carbonated soft drinks market. This sector, 667.9 million litres in 1991, accounts for 32% of the volume sales of the market and includes brands such as 7-Up, Tango, Lilt, Sunkist, Sprite and Fanta. These brands had all been similarly marketed using a successful mix of sun, teenage fun and refreshment on the Coca-Cola model. Schweppes and CCSB used this well-worn soft drink formula for the launch of Sunkist and Sprite in 1989. They did not want another brand to compete on exactly the same terms. They were prepared to risk breaking the mould to establish a new franchise for Gini.

DEVELOPING A UNIQUE POSITIONING

There appeared to be opportunities for distinctiveness in three somewhat interrelated areas :
1. How we approached lemon.
2. Who we targeted.
3. The brand image.

How We Approached Lemon

The existing lemon soft drink sector is diverse. It straddles various marketing-defined sectors through bitter lemon, hi-juice and lime products, traditional lemonade, Citrus Spring through to Sprite and 7-Up.

Overall the 'lemon' offering is indistinctive: cheap, bulk family-purchase lemonades at one end to 7-Up and Sprite, safe brand choices that deliver effective refreshment.

'Real' lemon however, is perceived as fresh, zesty, revitalising, sharp and full of character. In the context of soft drinks this differentiates it from orange fruit-flavoured carbonates (Table 1).

TABLE 1: SOFT DRINK IMAGERY

Orange Imagery	Lemon Imagery
Mass market, everyday	Refined, occasion-specific
Teenage 'Coke gone orange'	Adult, stylish
Accessible, bright, cheerful	Natural, authentic, different
Frenetic activity, sporty	Casual, interesting

Source: CLK Qualitative Research

Gini delivers excellently against real lemon criteria. Its cloudiness suggests a greater degree of real lemon to consumers and its sharpness gives it character and bite. A drink that could be far broader in appeal than bitter lemon and more interesting and real than Sprite.

It seemed important that Gini capitalised on these distinctive image characteristics that are rooted in real lemon qualities.

Who We Targeted

Carbonated soft drinks are drunk by young people. 54% of volume is accounted for by under 24 year olds; this increases to 63% within the fruit-flavoured sector. However, most significantly nearly 70% of this under 24 year old volume is consumed by *teenagers*.

We could not ignore the heart of the market. To go after an older target audience would have risked a small niche volume. However, we felt that the current bland and superficial presentation of soft drinks opened up an opportunity to us. During those teenage years there is a between period of personal discovery, of enquiry, experimentation and stimulation.

This period of active interaction with the world also relates to soft drinks. We felt that most fizzy 'pop' ill-served this group in terms of product and image. We defined them as 'soft drink graduates'. They are less tolerant of the soft drink simple formula and seek products with greater flavour, taste and character.

They responded extremely positively to the product. It fitted with their criteria for a more grown-up tasting soft drink.

TABLE 2

Adult soft drink preferences	Gini product attributes
Not too fizzy	Lighter fizz
Not too sweet	Sharp
Not too heavy	Bit of bite
Clean tasting	Clean tasting
Refreshment	Reviving refreshment
More sophisticated	Authentic/natural
More demanding	Distinctive

Source: BMP DDB Qualitative Research

There was clearly an opportunity for a brand with a more grown-up taste and hence grown-up values that were more adult, more sophisticated and more demanding than 'pop'.

The Brand Image

'Soft drink graduates' were also tired of the image formula adopted by most mainstream soft drinks. Teenage Americana was becoming increasingly 'not for them'. They aspired to a more adult and sophisticated treatment. Whilst this clichéd soft drink vernacular of sociable 'solar' values is very recognisable, has a breadth of appeal and has been successful for brands such as Coke and Sunkist, it is automatically generic. Within this image territory you can either join them (ie be a lemon Sunkist) or parody them (Tonic/Irn Bru), but to differentiate yourself within this territory is likely to be a subtlety lost on consumers – after all Gini is still only a carbonated soft drink in a 33cl can.

We believed we needed to build a more adult alternative to teenage Americana which would capitalise on Gini's product character, differentiate it from 'pop' and intrigue and interest our soft drink graduates. What we needed was to find an image territory that had the substance to build a strong personality unique to Gini.

ROLE OF ADVERTISING

Advertising Objective

To stimulate trial of Gini.

Target Audience

Amongst carbonated soft drink users (12–24 year olds).

Advertising Strategy

1. *By arousing interest in the product itself*:
   — It's a new, major contender in the UK soft drinks market.
   — It's a mainstream, lemon drink but more sophisticated, distinctive and authentic than other soft drinks.

2. *By creating a unique brand image that differentiates it from other soft drinks*:
   — Via more adult rather than teenage imagery
   — Via a fresh (non-US mould) approach to soft drinks advertising

We believed that the *Mediterranean* could provide a rich source of imagery for the brand, a motivating alternative to Americana. In addition it could provide a provenance for the drink suggesting that it had authentic roots in the land of lemon groves instead of being a marketing invention.

In this context the name Gini was accepted whereas previously it was meaningless, had inappropriate associations and sounded apologetic.

Figure 1 shows how we believed Mediterranean could work.

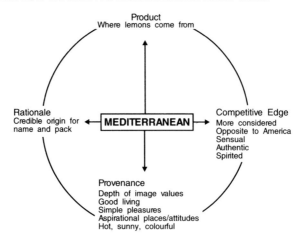

Figure 1

Qualitative research in the autumn of 1990 strongly endorsed giving the brand a Mediterranean heritage and provenance. It subtly expressed adultness, it suggested an honest, full-flavoured, thirst-quenching product and it was a distinctive territory not owned by any other soft drink.

This research also helped us to define what we meant by Mediterranean. It was not the Mediterranean of St Tropez, of yachts, white villas, blue seas and turquoise swimming pools. These 'lifestyle' images have become an advertising cliché. The Mediterranean needed to be expressed as more than just a style setting, it needed to be about the people, their way of life and their attitudes. The values which were relevant were authenticity, sense of community, sensuality, passion and spontaneity. The imagery also needed to be redolent of heat and lemon groves. This rooted our creative development in the Southern Mediterranean, away from sophisticated restrained Europe, closer to the rustic, Latin or Romany spirit. We believed we had found a more adult alternative to Americana that would attract core soft drink users (teenagers) who wanted to feel more adult.

The Balancing Act

It was vital that our imagery was sufficiently broad in appeal since non-mainstream imagery would lead to a small niche volume. Yet the advertising needed to work especially hard to differentiate the brand via a distinctive advertising style and more adult user image because this would be tempered firstly by the product which despite its differences was still a fizzy soft drink, secondly by its mainstream pack format and graphics and thirdly by its distribution presence – next to Coke and 7-Up on every shelf and therefore always 'within an arm's reach of desire'.

There would be nothing aspirational or distinctive about Gini's presentation except the advertising. Figure 2 shows this graphically – the advertising needed to be the most differentiated aspect of the mix in order to position Gini as a branded offering distinct from Sunkist, Sprite, 7-Up etc.

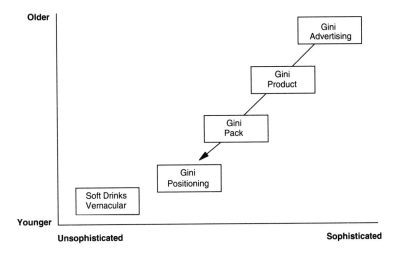

Figure 2. *Gini's competitive context*

It was vital to get the positioning absolutely correct to be competitive. If the mix of elements were to position Gini further away from the soft drink vernacular it would fail to establish its credentials as a mainstream soft drink and would not have been included in our target's repertoire. If it were to position Gini closer it would have failed to differentiate and become 'just another soft drink'.

THE CREATIVE SOLUTION

So much for the content of the advertising story, now we needed to tell it in order to provide the stature of a launch and create maximum impact.

The battlefield was clearly TV which had received 16,000 ratings from the carbonated soft drink sector in 1990 alone and we had high volume targets to achieve over a short period for Gini. However, we did not have the budget to compete in rating power with the 1800+ TVR brands so there was a need for an imaginative solution.

This solution centred on drama and intrigue. For the first two weeks three 10-second commercials ran. They were virtually unbranded, showed no product and did not attempt to explain themselves. They centred on the inexplicable Mediterranean loss of Gini although we are not told who or what Gini is: 'Gini est parti en Grande Bretagne'. Teasing people in this way was meant to serve as the base for the resolution and launch proper. Qualitative pre-testing highlighted the dangers of overkill. If people saw these ads too often they would become frustrated and possibly uninterested in hearing the answer. If they saw them too little we would have failed to create that initial drama. On the media front we therefore aimed to maximise coverage and minimise frequency.

The resolution came in the form of a 50-second ad, building on the idea of who/what was Gini, establishing that it had gone to Britain and was a lemon soft drink. This long timelength made the launch a significant event but could not be sustained throughout the summer on a relatively small budget. To extend the campaign a 20-second cutdown was used, alternating weeks of advertising to enable the campaign to continue until the beginning of September.

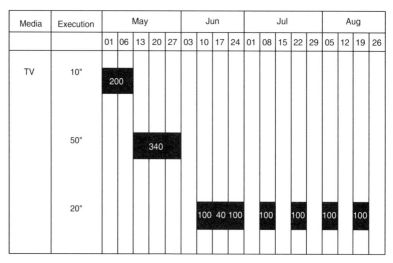

Figure 3. *Gini launch 1991 media plan (TVRs by week)*

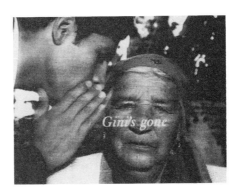

The creative and media solution was therefore to attempt to balance the demands of intrigue, stature and a sustained presence. Each timelength played a different role: teaser, resolution, reminder but were designed to work together to achieve a whole. The media plan is shown in Figure 3.

THE ADVERTISING EFFECT

In a market such as fizzy soft drinks one expects to see some sales as a result of shelf presence alone. Distribution is key to this market. It is not essentially brand loyal: consumers have a repertoire of brands they drink and so long as it is clear that a new brand is competing for a share of that repertoire, trial will be stimulated. What is therefore of prime importance is what happens to volume within the crucial first six months – can that initial interest be sustained to give the trade confidence in the future of the brand?

One factor which has helped us look more closely at the advertising effect was the existence of a non-advertised TV region, this was Tyne Tees. Whilst regional variations always exist, denying a non-advertised area the status of a pure 'control', Tyne Tees does appear to be representative in all but advertising. Similar levels of distribution were achieved at a similar rate by CCSB – a strength in the top-end grocery sector and weakness at the bottom end (where supplies are not controlled by CCSB) was replicated in the North East. Tyne Tees also shows the same brand share for existing fruit-flavoured carbonates and the same sector share of total carbonates as elsewhere.

Finally, all trade and consumer promotions were national. This has led both Schweppes and us to place some confidence in attributing most of the difference in Gini's sales and share achievement between Tyne Tees and the rest of the country to advertising.

Let's begin by looking at volume sales in Tyne Tees and in the rest of the country (ie the advertising regions).

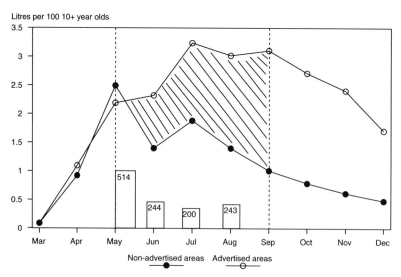

Figure 4. *Gini volume sales 1991*
Source: Nielsen

Because distribution is the same everywhere, this chart is effectively a measure of rate of sale. By dividing the total volume by the number of people over the age of 10 in each area we have arrived at a figure which indicates the litreage bought per 100 10+ year olds. This should control for the regional population differences.

What we see is a similar pattern of sales from the moment of sell-in to the start of advertising, in fact the closeness of the two lines pre-advertising demonstrates the ability of Tyne Tees to act as a control. From the beginning of May when the 10-second teaser campaign broke everywhere but Tyne Tees, followed by the 50-second campaign in mid May, the divergence in sales pattern is evident. In the advertised regions the initial sales uptake was not only sustained but also built upon during the summer months, whereas in Tyne Tees presence on shelf alone was not sufficient to keep up the early sales momentum.

The chart does beg the question of what happened in June when sales in Tyne Tees plummeted and looked quite flat elsewhere. Competitive activity was fierce but no more so than in May and July. The main contributing factor was the weather. June was an abysmal month – a comparison with the average for the last 22 years revealed that June 1991 had 30% less sunshine, 37% more rainfall and was 15% cooler than average. May, July and August were far more average months. Nothing affects soft drink consumption like the weather. The market was down 4% June 1991 vs June 1990. It seems valid to hypothesise that a combination of no advertising support and bad weather meant that sales in Tyne Tees suffered particularly badly in June whereas the advertising activity pulled sales through in the other areas.

Figure 5 shows us the share Gini achieved of fruit-flavoured carbonates.

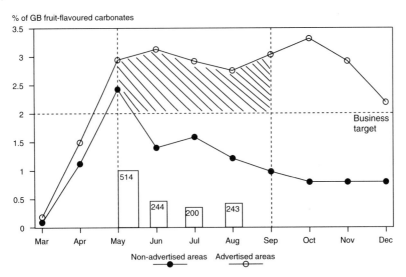

Figure 5. *Gini share of fruit-flavoured carbonates 1991*
Source: Nielsen

Achieving a 2% share of the fruit-flavoured carbonates sector was a marketing objective. As mentioned earlier, this was not an unambitious target in a fragmented market, a 2% share in Year 1 would establish Gini as a mainstream contender in the market.

An average brand share of 2.7% was achieved during the summer. This already made Gini a larger brand than Fanta (2.2%) and Orangina (1.8%).   ·

If we look at our advertised regions versus Tyne Tees we see, not surprisingly, that share reflects sales. Again the divergence is only apparent from the start of the campaign in May giving us faith in our 'control'. Brand share peaked at over 3% in the advertised areas whilst the campaign was on air. This puts Gini into the same size bracket as Sprite two years after its launch.

In Tyne Tees the brand share was less than half that of the advertised areas and dropped away to less than 1%.

From October we see share for Gini decline, this is indicative of the fact that the established brands tend to re-assert their dominance and take a bigger share of the market outside of the summer months when the smaller, newer brands are unsupported. This feature of the carbonated soft drinks market has been evident in previous years.

Different regional weights of advertising allowed us to split out the TV regions which received under 1,000 TVRs from the TV regions that received a heavier weight of over 1,000 TVRs. We banded these together with the under 1,000 TVR band (London and Anglia) having an average of 817 TVRs and the over 1,000 TVR band (Central, Scotland, TVS, HTV, Granada, Yorkshire) with an average of 1,370 TVRs. This is shown in Figure 6.

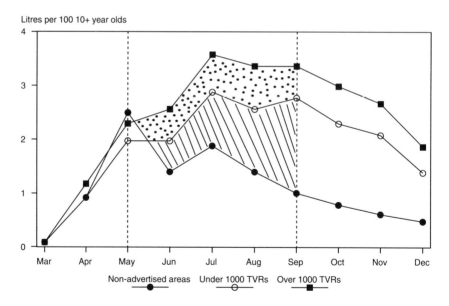

Figure 6. *Gini volume sales 1991 by advertising weight*
Source: Nielsen

Figure 6 clearly demonstrates that not only advertising but also weight of advertising contributed to the sales effect. The areas receiving over 1,000 TVRs took the lead in sales terms in May, the month the advertising broke.

Minimising cannibalisation of the CCSB fruit-flavoured carbonates portfolio was central to Schweppes' business objectives for Gini. Gini's source of volume is shown in Figure 7.

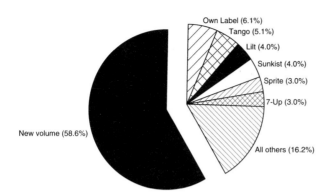

Figure 7. *Gini source of volume*
Source: AGB Superpanel 20 w/e 4 Aug 1991 vs 17 Mar 1991

Gini could easily have taken its sales exclusively from fruit carbonates. An analysis of the source of Gini's volume at the beginning of August revealed that actually less than half of Gini's volume came from this sector of the market and that the majority of the volume Gini brought to the sector was incremental. Cannibalisation of CCSB's fruit carbonates (Sunkist, Sprite, Lilt and Fanta) was therefore lower (at 13%) than their share of the sector would have suggested (20%). CCSB share of fruit-flavoured carbonates actually grew across the summer from 19% to 24%.

It appears that Gini was sufficiently differentiated to contribute to CCSB's strength in this sector of the market by not only being an additional rather than substitutional part of consumers' fruit-flavoured carbonates repertoire, but also by attracting new drinkers to the sector.

The final measure that we must look at, and that at the end of the day determines the fate of any new product launch, is how many people tried Gini. Stimulating trial was also the key objective of the advertising. Whilst awareness can often be attributed to presence on shelf and repeat purchase to product appeal, trial, above and beyond natural market promiscuity, needs to be promoted via marketing activity. Overall trial levels were good but not outstanding. It was a bad summer weather-wise which meant that Gini, (unlike Sprite and Sunkist in 1989), did not benefit from the usual seasonal uplift. In addition some distribution weaknesses at the bottom end of the trade meant that the desire for Gini could not always be satisfied. However, once again there were marked differences between the advertised areas and Tyne Tees.

TABLE 3: TOTAL PENETRATION 1991

	Standard Gini	Diet Gini
Non-advertised areas	4.7%	2.8%
Advertised areas	8.5%	5.8%

Source: AGB Superpanel

Nearly twice as many people tried the brand in the advertised areas. Once more we also see weight of advertising contributing to the levels of trial.

TABLE 4: TOTAL PENETRATION 1991

	Standard Gini	Diet Gini
Advertised areas (under 1,000 TVRs)	7.4%	2.6%
Advertised areas (over 1,000 TVRs)	9.1%	6.5%

Source: AGB Superpanel

If we plot the penetration achieved per month from the launch of the brand at the start of April we can see how it equates to the advertising period.

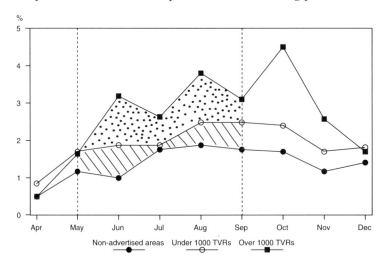

Figure 8. *Penetration by month 1991 total Gini*
Source: AGB Superpanel

Once again the divergence starts at the same time as the advertising.

HOW DID THE ADVERTISING WORK?

We believe that the advertising was successful not simply at launching a new product but at establishing Gini as a brand. It communicated that Gini was a soft, carbonated lemon drink and surrounded it with more adult, distinctive and sophisticated imagery. This emergent brand identity was appealing and motivating to our 'soft drink graduates' who not only appreciated a different approach but felt it was appropriate to the product.

So much for the assertions, let's look at the evidence.

The advertising awareness scores achieved on the tracking study were very encouraging. 36% of 12–24 year olds spontaneously recalled the TV advertising within two months of it being aired. This was an encouragingly high score and amongst our teenage core users it received the highest awareness scores on the tracking study (46%), higher than the familiar and popular campaigns of Coca-Cola (37%), Sunkist (44%), Irn Bru (45%) and Lucozade (41%).

However, given our desire to launch a new brand rather than a new product, one of the key scores on the Millward Brown Tracking Study was the branded recognition of the photoprompt. Half a dozen unbranded stills from the TV commercial are shown to the total sample who are then asked whether they have seen the commercial and if so, who it is for. The importance of this score is that if several brands share similar imagery than respondents wrongly attribute the unbranded stills. Given the generic nature of the 'soft drinks vernacular' (as discussed previously), few high scores are achieved on this dimension.

The branded recognition score for Gini two months after launch was 85%. A new campaign can only be compared with other new campaigns so if we take the scores achieved by Sunkist and Sprite two months after launch the comparison is as follows.

TABLE 5: BRAND IDENTIFICATION FROM PHOTOPROMPT

	%
Gini (amongst 12–24 year olds) 1991	85
Sunkist (amongst 12–24 year olds) 1989	51
Sprite (amongst 12–24 year olds) 1989	14

The scores for both Sunkist and especially Sprite were lower because of the 'me-too' nature of their brand imagery. Even with Coke, which you might argue 'owns' much of this image territory and has a well-established, well-liked campaign, the score is usually between 50–60%. This is an aspect of branding where we believe we have shown that a distinctive ad that challenges the 'norms' of the category can really pay dividends.

So, the imagery established for Gini was distinctive but what impressions did it give of the brand? Qualitative post-testing of the finished film in March 1991 addressed this area. What is revealed was that Gini, whilst sharing many soft drink category values – social, youthful, 'cool', popular and active, was seen as being a cut above the others – more stylish and exclusive. There was a strong consensus regarding the Gini drinker: in his/her 20s, sophisticated, cool, healthy, popular, confident, intelligent, good company and well-off. For most this image was highly aspirational. A projective technique which showed a Coke drinker facing a Gini drinker and required the respondents to fill in thought bubbles from each revealed some interesting perceived differences.

TABLE 6:

Coke	Gini
Common	Individual
Gassy, sugary/sweet & artificial	Natural, delicately fizzy
Cheap	Of the minute
Out of date	Fashionable
Entrenched/conservative	New and different
Not experimental	Classy
American	Upmarket
Same old thing	Better choice
For all and sundry	With-it

What emerged was that Gini pitied Coke whilst Coke was defensive yet intrigued by Gini. Although there was no intention on the part of Schweppes to take on the might of Coca-Cola with the launch of Gini, it was interesting that our soft drink graduates saw Gini as having sufficient stature and more exciting values to challenge the established brands. These values do appear to have been communicated by the advertising (these respondents had not tried the product) – by the character of the girl, the sub-titles, the cosmopolitan/Mediterranean imagery and the more demanding style of the execution.

Quantitative research also endorses this. A quantitative pre-test of the finished film showed the following levels of agreement with prompted statements about Gini:

TABLE 7

	% agreeing
Is a popular drink in the Mediterranean	79
Comes from the land of lemon groves	81
Would have a tangy taste	79
Would be a refreshing drink	78
Would be drunk by adults more than children	74
Would be a more natural drink	58
Would be a more distinctive drink	54

Source:　Millward Brown

Once on air the tracking study was able to look at Gini's image relative to other fruit-flavoured carbonates. On generic statements such as 'drink on its own', 'suitable for different occasions', 'quality' etc, Gini's scores were similar to other brands but there were some interesting differences:

TABLE 8

	Gini indexed on average of all fruit-flavoured carbonates*
Prompted brand image (Base: 8–69 year olds 　aware of advertising)	
Are less sweet than other soft drinks	186
Are international brands	152
Are for fashion-conscious people	289
Have good advertising	125
Are American drinks	*17*
Prompted statements on advertising (Base: Those aware of the advertising)	
More interested in drinking the product	150
Appeals to all ages	164
A soft drink really worth trying	175
Appeals specifically to teenagers	*50*

Note:　　*(Lilt, 7-Up, Sprite, Sunkist, Fanta and Tango)
Source:　Millward Brown Tracking Study

So, in image terms Gini appears to have been successfully differentiated but how well did the advertising convey the nature of the product? It would not be helpful to raise expectations only to disappoint consumers when they tried the product.

Qualitative research told us that the advertising suggested an adult, sophisticated, stylish, continental product. More 'limon' than lemonade:

'Like lemon you get abroad.'
'Made with real lemons, not artificial.'
'It's different because it's from the Mediterranean.'

When the animatic was quantitatively researched respondents were asked for their impressions of the product after seeing the advertising but before tasting the product and then again after tasting it.

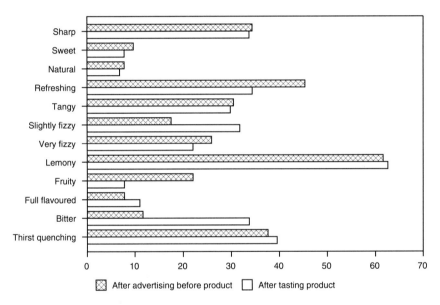

Figure 9. *Impressions of taste before and after tasting the product*
Source: The Research Business

What is encouraging is how closely expectations from the advertising fitted their response to the product itself. The advertising clearly delivered the soft drink values of refreshment, fizziness and fruitiness more than the product but this is an overclaim probably true of all soft drink advertising. The one discrepancy of some concern was the bitter score after trying the product. The quinine level was later reduced in order to ameliorate this rating.

We believe that the advertising worked hard to give Gini a distinctive and aspirational image that differentiated it in a crowded sector and yet was sufficiently credible and true to the product to encourage trial without disappointment. Qualitative research has shown that the more demanding nature of the film (the antithesis of most soft drink advertising) was very favourably received by our slightly more astute and discerning target.

ELIMINATING OTHER VARIABLES

The advertised period was May–September. No major factors in the marketplace changed during this period as far as we can tell. There were no other important new product launches and relative pricing remained constant. A trial-sized can of Gini was launched as a promotion but this was not until September and it was national.

Tyne Tees, our non-advertised area, has acted as our control. The similar build in volume sales, share and penetration that we saw in Tyne Tees and the other areas prior to the advertising breaking gives us confidence in Tyne Tees basic similarity. However, possible variables have been considered in order to eliminate other factors that may have contributed to the different sales effects.

Distribution

Regional levels of distribution from the introduction of Gini to the trade in March 1991 were within 10% of each other. They also built at a similar rate.

Trade Structure

Whilst Asda has a bigger share of the major multiple trade in the North East, the overall structure of major multiples/independents/corner shops is the same.

Demographics

12–24 year olds account for exactly the same proportion of Tyne Tees' population as they do nationally. There are no obvious demographic differences.

Competitive Activity

All above and below-the-line competitive activity was national.

Gini romotional Activity

Gini's promotional activity which included couponing and the trial can was national.

ADVERTISING CONTRIBUTION

If we attribute the full difference in sales volume between Tyne Tees and the rest of the country to advertising we can calculate a 140% uplift in sales accounting for 7,709,000 litres of Gini.

Whilst profitability figures are not available for confidentiality reasons, Schweppes are extremely pleased with their return on investment.

CONCLUSIONS

Gini could easily have been yet another can of 'pop'. There was nothing distinctive or aspirational about Gini's presentation apart from the advertising. We believe the advertising worked hard against the objectives set for it.

The drama and intrigue of the creative solution clearly signalled the arrival of a big, exciting, mainstream contender in the UK soft drinks market.

The advertising built a distinctive brand identity for Gini that set it apart from other soft drinks in image terms.

The evidence suggests that the advertising got the balance of the positioning correct – sufficiently distinctive to attract attention (ie differentiated) yet sufficiently mainstream to be included in consumers' repertoire (ie competitive).

We believe that the advertising sustained and capitalised on the initial interest that was created by its presence on shelf. Not only did the advertised areas benefit from higher levels of trial, consequently larger sales volume and a greater share of the market but the heavier advertised areas benefited most. We hope that this shows that in a crowded, undifferentiated market a fresh and unconventional approach to building a brand can pay dividends.

Gini's successful launch has endorsed the creative strategy and this year a new commercial is running which builds on last year's executions concentrating less on the arrival of Gini in the UK and more on the image values of the drinker, the drink and its provenance.

12

Renault Clio:
Adding Value During a Recession

INTRODUCTION

In 1991 sales of new cars in the UK declined by 20.7%, the worst annual fall for 17 years. [1]In March 1991 Renault UK launched the Clio, the successor to the long established Renault 5. This paper sets out to demonstrate the effectiveness of the advertising campaign; firstly helping to launch the new car, then creating a premium positioning for the Clio at the top of the small car sector and finally broadening Renault's appeal in this sector in terms of age.

Consequently, and despite the singularly unpropitious trading conditions, the Clio succeeded in recapturing volume share for Renault in the small car segment. At the same time, notwithstanding the economic recession, the Clio delivered increased profit to the company through its premium price positioning.

BACKGROUND

Small Car Sector

The small car sector accounts for c25% of UK new car sales and is the second most important sector in terms of volume.[1] It is also, alongside the executive/luxury sector, the most influential in terms of shaping the manufacturers' overall marque image.

The small car sector therefore, is of disproportionately high strategic signifiance. Furthermore, the sector is growing in appeal. This is due to a number of factors:

— The improving quality build (and thereby standing) of small cars.
— The effect of the recession in forcing people to trade down.
— Increasing road congestion and associated environmental concerns.
— The growth of the grey population ('empty nesters').
— The increasing incidence of two car ownership (now 22% of households compared with 15% in 1980[2]).

Competition is strong in the small car sector with the three 'domestic' marques –

---

[1]Source: SMMT. Methodologies, sample sizes etc for sources quoted throughout this paper are indicated in Appendix 1.
[2]Source: Department of Transport 1991.

Ford (Fiesta), Vauxhall (Nova) and Rover (Metro) – accounting for 57% of sales in 1990; of these, both the Fiesta and Metro launched new models in 1990 just prior to the Clio launch[1]. The other key competitor, the Peugeot 205, commanded a 10% share and was firmly established as the image leader in the sector[1] (Figure 1).

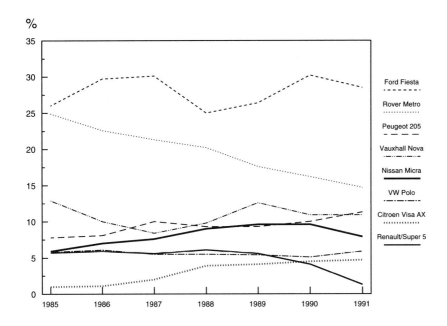

Figure 1. *Renault 5 and competitor performance in small car sector*
Source: SMMT/Renault UK

Renault's History in the Sector

Launched in 1972, the Renault 5 proved an extremely successful model for the company, accounting in its prime for 41% of Renault sales in the UK.

The introduction of the Super 5 in 1985, gave the now 10 year old model a new lease of life so that by 1988, the Super 5 had achieved a 6.1% sector share compared with Renault's total market share of 3.9%[1].

This highlights the twin legacies built up by the Renault 5, on the one hand, Renault's strong small car heritage and on the other, the company's historical dependency on this sector to deliver volume sales.

However, by 1990 the 5 was showing its age in the face of more dynamic competition; its sector share declining to 4.1% and its sector ranking falling to 9th position[1].

The Clio Product

It is important to note that the Clio was a *replacement* for the Renault 5, not a facelift. The Clio therefore, was a totally new car, the key features of which were:

— Completely new exterior styling.
— Luxury equipment levels normally only available in larger cars (eg power assisted steering, electric windows and door mirrors, 'Plip' remote control central locking).
— Enhanced interior space.
— Advanced build quality.
— New 'Energy' engine.

For the launch, three core variants would be available: the entry model 1.2 litre RL, the 1.2 litre RN and the 1.4 litre RT.

The Clio's main point of competitive difference therefore, was that it brought a new standard of refinement to the small car sector. However, as has often been proved, strong product advantage does not in itself guarantee sales success (cf Fiat Tipo); a developed brand image is essential.

ISSUES

Entry Prices

The Clio's price entry point was £1,191 more expensive than for the Renault 5 range (see Table 1).

TABLE 1: CLIO AND RENAULT 5 PRICING

	Renault 5 1990	Clio 1991	Difference
Lowest price	£5,494		
Plus 9% car price inflation 1990-91 to facilitate comparison with Clio	£5,999	£7,190	£1,191

Source: What Car?, 1990/91

Moreover, when compared with the other players in the small car sector, only the Honda Civic had a higher entry price (see Figure 2).

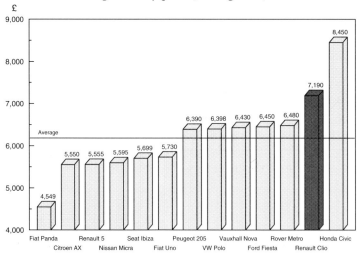

Figure 2. *Small sector entry prices at the launch of Clio*
Source: *What Car?*, May 1991

Prior to the launch of the Clio, Renault's price positioning was at the middle to lower end of the sector where it was perceived to offer good value for money. Indeed, price was the primary reason given for purchasing a Renault 5 in 1990 and significantly more important for 5 purchasers when compared with the segment as a whole[3].

In price terms therefore, the Clio would represent something of a conceptual leap and the advertising would need to play its part in justifying Renault's new premium positioning in the sector – without alienating Renault 5 owners.

The Recession

At the time of the Clio launch, consumer confidence for major purchases remained depressed – sales of new cars in the UK had been falling for 18 consecutive months[3]. (See Figure 3.)

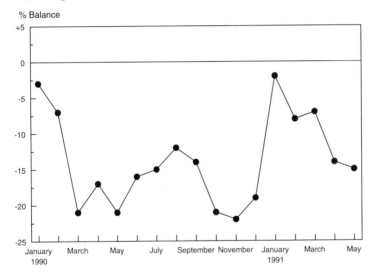

Figure 3. *Consumer confidence for buying major purchases right time minus wrong time*
Source: Publicis/Gallup

The first months of 1991 also saw a 'Price War' in both the small and lower-medium car segments, with prices in the lower-medium becoming competitive against small cars.

Certainly, these were not ideal conditions in which to launch a new car, particularly one carrying a premium price.

Health of the Renault Marque

The relationship between marque and model in the purchasing process is a complex one. Whilst the purchasing decision ultimately comes down to the individual model concerned, a marque that is neither desired nor respected can prevent a model being placed on a shopping list in the first place. Thus, the role of marque image plays an important part within the individual model purchasing decision (see Figure 4).

[3]Source: NCBS Model Year H.

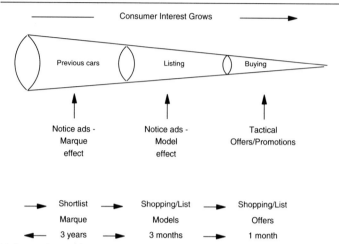

Figure 4. *Empirical car purchase model*
Source: Qualitative Research

In 1990, Renault's total market share declined to 3.36% – its lowest level for 15 years. Consequently an in-depth assessment of the marque was undertaken. Qualitative research[4] revealed that, although Renault had attained 'first division' status in terms of product acceptability, the key problem was a lack of *positive* image factors resulting in low desirability. Future opportunities were identified for the marque but, in the meantime it was clear that, at launch, the Clio would not benefit from strong parent brand endorsement. The parent and the model would have to develop in tandem.

THE OBJECTIVES

Sales Objectives

Renault UK set the Clio the following sales objectives.

1. To achieve 1.38% of the total car market (5.5% of the sector).
2. To account for 33% of Renault sales.

Both these objectives were to be achieved by the end of the first full year of trading. In effect, the Clio was required to emulate the Renault 5's 1989 sales performance from year one.

Marketing Objectives

The marketing objectives set for the Clio were:

1. To retain the loyalty of a high percentage of Renault 5 owners.
2. To steal share from key competitive models.

The marketing strategy set out to launch a highly specified Clio at a high entry price, supported by heavyweight theme advertising and substantial below-the-line activity.

[4]Source: Strategic Research Group 1990/91.

THE ADVERTISING STRATEGY

Advertising Objectives

1. To announce the new Renault Clio.
2. To establish a premium positioning for the Clio in the small car sector.
3. To broaden Renault's appeal in the small car sector in terms of age profile.

Targeting and Positioning

Core buyers in the small car sector are typically ABC1 professionals aged 25–44 years with a fairly even male:female split. In terms of age, Renault 5 had a purchaser profile four years younger than the sector average[3]. However, given the Clio's premium status, it was decided to broaden its age appeal. The target audience was expanded to all those aged 25 years plus and thereby included also those aged 45 years and beyond.

Given their high level of disposable income and their increasing numbers, these were vital people to attract.

In terms of the attitudes and motivations of potential Renault buyers, qualitative research identified them as:

— Individualists not extroverts, nor peer group clones.
— Appreciative of values concerned with quality of life, culture, comfort.
— Secretly aspiring to something different, more stylish.
— Relating emotionally as well as rationally to their cars.
— Pragmatic drivers who see the car as a means to an end rather than as an end in itself.
— Appreciating interior values and specification.

Thus, the potential Clio buyer was identified as being slightly out of the car-buying mainstream, coming out of a broader age spectrum and displaying greater attitudinal *joie de vivre* than his/her standard counterpart. This proved highly directive in developing a differentiating brand personality for the Clio.

Further research conducted across Europe revealed that, on the Continent too – though for differing reasons – small car buyers were increasingly demanding the 'extras' normally associated with executive cars. As a result, the following pan-European brand positioning was adopted by the entire Renault network.

'The Small car with the refinement of a Big car'

THE CAMPAIGN

The advertising campaign was planned in two phases:

1. *Announcement phase*
   To run for only two weeks, the announcement phase was restricted to two single objectives:
   (a) To create maximum awareness of the arrival of the new Clio from Renault.
   (b) To make a stylistic break from previous Renault advertising in this sector and so begin the process of consumer reappraisal.

The creative executions – adapted from a French campaign, titled 'Transformer' – were built around the concept of a car hatching from a technological egg (quite apposite as the UK launch was on Easter weekend), symbolising the birth of a new car.

The media solution was to use a multi-media approach calculated to achieve a very rapid build of coverage and maximise creative synergy. The week before launch, teaser posters appeared nationally, followed three days later by 10 second teaser TV commercials; both executions featured a solus, giant, red metallic egg with the strapline/voiceover 'Not just another hatch'. On launch day the posters were changed and in place of the giant red egg, a giant, red Clio was revealed with the headline: 'The New Renault Clio. Car of the Year 1991'.

NOT JUST ANOTHER HATCH

TRANSFORMER

On television, commercial breaks were 'top and tailed' featuring a reprise of the 10-second teaser and subsequently a 30-second reveal of 'The Hatch'. The reveal poster and solus 30-second TV execution continued to run for the next nine days.

In colour supplements and specialist car magazines, seven page gatefolds and colour double page spreads, with tip-on cards were used, together with three page colour advertisements in the national press.

2. *Positioning phase*

The role of this phase was threefold: to position the car, to build a long-term and lasting image for the Clio; to continue to enhance consumer awareness.

To this end a 60 second commercial, made specifically for the UK by Publicis London, was aired.

The storyline follows the supposedly clandestine extracurricular activities of a father (Papa) visiting his mistress and his daughter (Nicole) visiting her boyfriend. The Clio RT was featured in both instances in the role of an accomplice. In the commercial Nicole serves to epitomise the generic small car values of fun, youth and nippiness, whilst Papa serves to broaden the age appeal of the car and reflect the added refinement of the new Clio. The commercial ended with the new marque strapline; 'Renault: A Certain Flair'.

The commercial was aired for two more bursts in summer and autumn, and cut down to 40-seconds and 30-seconds respectively, to maximise media efficiency. During periods without television activity, two full page colour advertisements: 'How to take the Small car upmarché' and 'For something small, potent and tasteful, you have to know where to look', both featuring the Clio RT, were rotated in national press whilst DPS versions appeared in the colour supplements and specialist car magazines.

In all, 66% of the media spend in the first nine months of advertising activity was put in TV, 29% into press and 4% into posters (see Figure 5).

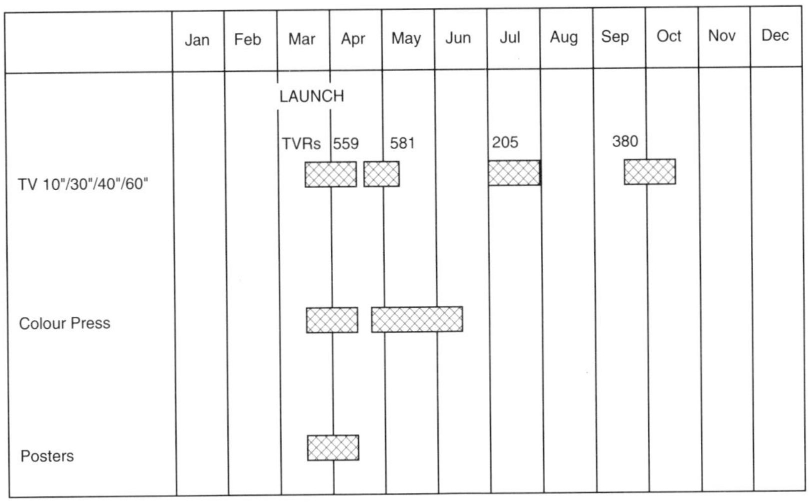

	Jan	Feb	Mar	Apr	May	Jun	Jul	Aug	Sep	Oct	Nov	Dec
			LAUNCH									
TV 10"/30"/40"/60"			TVRs	559	581		205		380			
Colour Press												
Posters												

Figure 5. *Clio media plan*

PAPA AND NICOLE

THE SALES RESULTS

Despite the depressed state of the car market in 1991, the Clio exceeded its first year sales objectives.

TABLE 2: CLIO SALES PERFORMANCE YEAR 1 (Year to March 1992)

	Objective %	Achievement %	Difference
Clio sector share of small cars	5.50	7.00	+1.50
Market share	1.38	1.82	+0.49
Clio's share of Renault total sales	33.00	41.50	+8.50
Clio/R5 sector share of small car		7.70	

Source: SMMT

The Clio's success boosted Renault's small car sector share to 7.7%, and its total marque share to 4.0%, in both cases Renault's best figures since 1981[1].

In attaining a total market share of 1.82%, the Clio surpassed the equivalent performance of both its predecessor, the Super 5, and its most immediate competitor, the Peugeot 205, which recorded first year market shares of 1.65% and 1.09% respectively.

Furthermore, the first year of Clio sales saw the middle and top of the range versions, (RN/RT), accounting for a higher proportion of the sales mix than had been the case for the Renault 5. This shift in the mix provided both an early endorsement of the changed positioning as well as increased profit to the company.

TABLE 3: COMPARISON OF CLIO AND RENAULT 5 SALES MIX
(excluding Turbo, Diesel, Limited Editions)

	Clio 1991 %	Renault 5 1989 %
Entry range	24	42
Mid range	26 ⎱ 76	10 ⎱ 57
Top range	50 ⎰	47 ⎰

Source: SMMT, 1991

EVALUATING THE CAMPAIGN

The Problem

Isolating the precise effects of advertising in the car market is acknowledged to be 'fiendishly difficult'[5]. This is especially the case when – as with a launch – the analysis is limited to identifying what are essentially short-term effects.

For the consumer, buying a car is broadly analogous to a house purchase. On both occasions, it is a protracted process, involving a high unit price and subject to a complex mixture of rational and emotional motivating forces aside from advertising; most importantly, the role of the dealer, governed by his own agenda of discounts, bonuses and product availability.

[5]Source: IPA Guide to Authors, 1992.

The task of isolating the effect of advertising is further complicated by the sheer amount of 'other' marketing activity which traditionally accompanies a major car launch. To illustrate the point, it is worth examining a chronology of events from the first week of the Clio launch:

1990	September	–	Birmingham Motor show
	December	–	'Quest for Clio', competition with Anneka Rice
1991	5th March	–	London Fleet Show
	21st March	–	VIP events at dealerships
	22nd March	–	Poster teaser (Egg)
	25th March	–	Launch mailing to 750,000 customers and prospects
	27th March	–	TV teaser (Egg)
	28th March	–	Manchester Motorshow
	29th March	–	LAUNCH
			Revelation TV (Transformer)
	6th April	–	'Open weekend' at dealerships
	12th April	–	New TV commercial, ('Papa and Nicole').

Other conventional means of evaluation are also not open to us. In other markets, such as fmcg, regional tests are often adopted in order to isolate varying weights of promotional activity. However, the nature of the car market and the structure of distribution means that it is rarely feasible for a national, 'first division' manufacturer to conduct such a test.

Whilst moreover, there is a suggestion of a correlation between the Clio's sector share and share of voice (SOV), at this stage, there are not enough data points to construct a meaningful econometric model (see Figure 6).

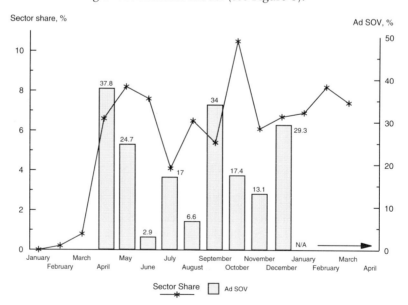

Figure 6. *Renault Clio sector share and ad SOV*
Sources: SMMT, MEAL

The Solution

It is necessary therefore to concentrate on the following traditional measures, in order to establish whether the advertising objectives were met and so attempt to draw a connection between the advertising and subsequent sales performance.

Advertising measures → Were the ads seen?
                     → Were the ads well branded?
              ↓   → Were the ads liked?
                     → Were the ads on strategy?
Brand measures   → Did awareness of the model increase?
              ↓   → Was the desired model image created?
Motivational measures → How important was advertising in creating
              ↓   interest?
SALES → The Buyers   → Fit between reasons for purchase and strategy?
                     → Was the desired level of loyalty achieved?
                     → Was the age profile broadened?

ADVERTISING MEASURES

Advertising Awareness

There was a considerable build of claimed awareness of advertising for the Clio in response to the launch and subsequent advertising, reaching a peak of 56%, which then stabilised to around 40% for the rest of the year[6] (see Figure 7).

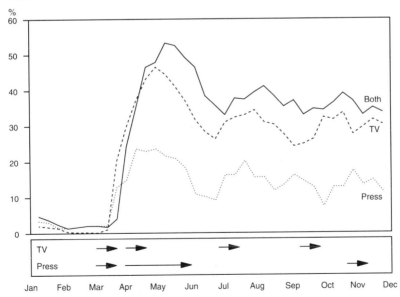

Figure 7. *Claimed ad awareness – Renault Clio (rolling eight weekly data)*
Source: Millward Brown

[6]Source: Millward Brown.

Since the amount of money spent on advertising car launches is so considerable, it is sometimes difficult to distinguish between advertising effectiveness and media weight. A model is therefore needed which measures the efficiency of a commercial in generating advertising awareness. There has been much debate about the use of the Millward Brown Awareness Index, which attempts to measure how much advertising awareness rises per 100 TVRs[7]. If this model is used in conjunction with other measures, then the Awareness Index can be a useful tool in helping to diagnose advertising performance.

Both the 'Transformer' and 'Papa and Nicole' commercials were highly effective at generating brand associated recall. Both commercials, attained an Awareness Index of 7, which was well above the average of 3–4 for all car advertising. Millward Brown's data also revealed that with the exception of the launch of the Rover 800, the Clio's score was higher than that of each of the last eight competitive car launches. Clio's Awareness Index also compared favourably with previous Renault advertising in the sector, and was equal to the highest index achieved by the famous Renault 5 'What's Yours Called?' campaign.

A further indicator to the degree of memorability of an advertising campaign is provided by Millward Brown's 'baseline' measure (the level to which claimed ad recall falls when the advertising stops). By the end of 1991, the Clio had recorded a base level of 9 which was above the median of 5–6 and still rising.

Branding

Figure 8 shows that both commercials succeeded in achieving higher levels of correct model and marque identification than the best performing advertising for the Renault 5: 65% correctly recalled the 'Papa and Nicole' commercial as being from Renault and 50% correctly recalled the model name 'Clio'.

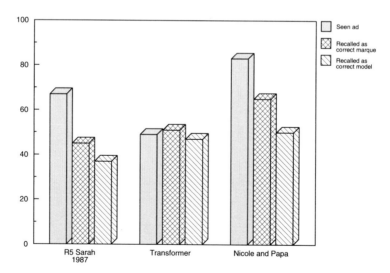

Figure 8. *Prompted recall of ads and branding*
Source: Millward Brown

[7]Source: P Feldwick, 'How Valuable is the Awareness Index?', MRS 1991.

Indeed, we believe that one of the key reasons for the success of this campaign was the use, in the 'Papa and Nicole' commercial, of 'Structural Branding'[8]

Having identified that the potential Clio buyer was attitudinally different from the majority of the car buying public, it was critically important, in terms of casting, that the central characters in the commercial reflect this attitudinal difference. In conclusion, strong branding was created and achieved for the Clio by successfully 'marrying' the personalities of the main characters with the inherent personality of the marque.

Attitudes

In this context, it is interesting to examine the recent Copy Research Validity Project carried out by the American Research Foundation in which they concluded that, 'undoubtedly the most surprising finding in the study was the strong relationship found to exist between the likeability of the copy and its effect on sales'[9].

What is known also, is that the behaviour and attitude of personnel in the dealerships is often directly linked to what they perceive to be (or not be) 'effective' and 'consumer-liked' advertising (for this reason a close relationship with a 'Dealer Panel' was maintained in the development of the campaign).

In terms of prompted attitudes, both commercials were favoured by consumers, especially 'Papa and Nicole' (see Table 4). 80% of the sample positively endorsed the commercial compared with an average figure of 58% for all car commercials in 1991.

TABLE 4: PROMPTED ATTITUDES TO RENAULT CLIO TV ADVERTISING

	Nicole & Papa %
ANY POSITIVE ENDORSEMENT	80
Made the car seem attractive	43
Humorous	43
Quite appealed to me	25
Made me more interested in the car	15
I learned something from it	7
Convincing	3
ANY NEGATIVE ENDORSEMENT	28
Didn't tell me anything new	13
Silly	13
Found it hard to believe	7
Dull	1
Put me off the car	1
Base: All definitely recalling	(276)

Source: Millward Brown, 1991

Qualitative research[4, 10], since the launch, has confirmed how well liked the Clio advertising has become; a point further endorsed by the large PR and press coverage the campaign has attracted.[11]

---

[8]Source: R Langmaid, W Gordon, 'A Great Ad – Pity They Can't Remember the Brand', MRS 1988.
[9]Source: *Journal of Advertising Research*, April/May 1991.
[10]Source: Carne Martin Research Company 1991.
[11]See Appendix for examples of press coverage.

Communication

Both phases of the campaign fulfilled their specified objectives.

The main message gathered from the 'Transformer' phase was that Renault had launched a new small car called 'Clio'. At a lower level, 'Car of the Year' and an association with 'acceleration' were also noted.

In the positioning phase of the campaign, the 'Papa and Nicole' commercial spontaneously communicated 'nippiness', 'small', 'for everyone' and 'stylish'. Indeed on prompting, further dimensions of 'comfort', 'quality', 'for younger people with no commitments' and 'would appeal to people over forty' were also communicated.

BRAND MEASURES

Brand Awareness

Two months after launch, spontaneous brand awareness of the Clio compared well with other competitors' car launches (see Figure 9) and exceeded that achieved by the Renault 19, two years earlier.

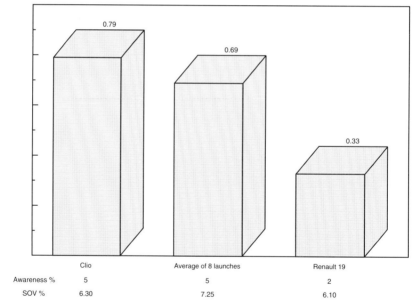

	Clio	Average of 8 launches	Renault 19
Awareness %	5	5	2
SOV %	6.30	7.25	6.10

Figure 9. *Ratio between SOV and spontaneous awareness, Clio vs previous car launches (two months after launch)*
Sources: Millward Brown, MEAL

As we have acknowledged, advertising is obviously not the only contributor to brand awareness. Other communication channels such as dealer promotions, PR, direct marketing etc, all play a significant role. An analysis of model awareness by advertising recall however, shows a marked increase in awareness of the Clio brand by those claiming to have seen the advertising against those who have not (Figure 10).

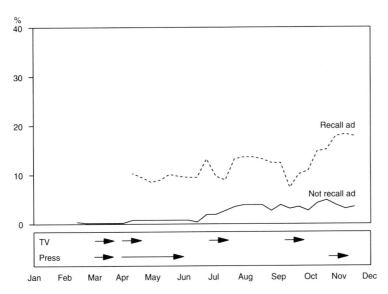

Figure 10. *Spontaneous model awareness – Renault Clio (rolling eight weekly data)*
Source: Millward Brown

Image

Brand image was also monitored by the Millward Brown Tracking Study. One might have expected the Clio, as a new car, to take some time to establish an image profile, but in fact this was quickly achieved. Figure 11 shows the perceived strengths and weaknesses of the Clio relative to other cars in the small car sector. This reveals a strong and differentiated image centred around style but also driveability and roominess; in other words, 'Big Car refinement'.

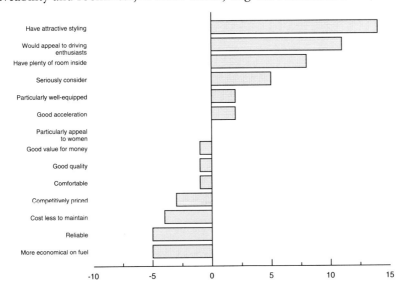

Figure 11. *Clio image strengths and weaknesses (deviations from predicted values)*
Source: Millward Brown, 1991

MOTIVATIONAL MEASURES

Renault's Customerlink Survey uncovered that television advertising received the highest number of mentions for prompting buyers' initial interest in the Clio and was the second most influential source of additional information (once initial interest had been aroused). These scores for the Clio were well ahead of those achieved by other Renault models (see Figure 12).

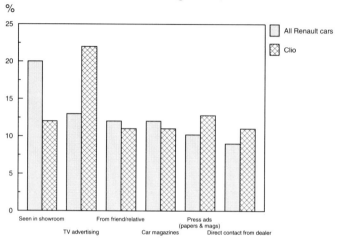

Figure 12. *First thing that started interest in Renault – finally bought (Base: all purchasers; all Renault 562, Clio 188)*
Source: Renault Customerlink, May-June 1991

PURCHASE

New Car Buyers Survey (NCBS) asks Renault buyers why they bought what they did. The reasons given for purchasing a Clio show key strengths to be: 'style', 'spaciousness' and 'equipment'. This contrasted strongly with the reasons given for purchasing a Renault 5 and highlighted how a distinct different overall positioning for the Clio had been created so justifying its high entry price point (see Figure 13).

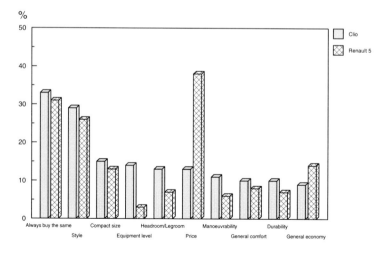

Figure 13. *Main reasons for purchasing*
Source: NCBS H model year

Source of Business

In terms of source of purchase, purchaser data for the first five weeks of sales showed that 52% of Clio sales were bought in replacement of another Renault and 44% were conquest sales. First-time or additional buyers accounted for the remaining 5% of sales. These early results indicated that a reassuring level of loyalty to the marque was being achieved despite the Clio's different positioning from the Renault 5.

Driver Profile

A key objective was for the advertising to extend the Clio's appeal to a broader and therefore older age group than the Renault 5.

Figure 14 shows that this was clearly achieved with Clio drivers on average being seven years older than the segment and 14 years older than Renault 5 buyers.

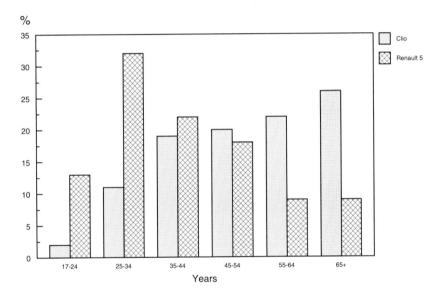

Figure 14. *Clio age profile vs Renault 5 and segment*
Source: NCBS H Model Year

CONCLUSION

The Clio not only met but also exceeded its first year sales targets. This was achieved in a marketplace which, in 1991, saw sales down a fifth on 1990 and in which, over the same period, the small car sector declined by 17.9%. In all, in its first full year of trading the Clio helped Renault to achieve both its highest small car sector share and its highest overall marque share in a decade.

The advertising campaign for the Clio proved impactful, well-branded, involving and successfully communicated the desired strategy.

Specifically, the advertising contributed to the development of a new premium positioning for Renault in the small car sector, in mid-recession and without alienating Renault owners, thus helping to meet a major and difficult marketing objective whilst generating increased profit for the company. Furthermore, the advertising evidently assisted in widening the age profile of the actual buyers, in a sector where Renault had historically attracted younger owners.

Whilst it is acknowledged that it is not easy to isolate the effect of advertising in the car market, it was shown that the advertising for the Clio had proved the key source of initial interest for eventual buyers.

It is our opinion that this stemmed from the correct identification of the attitudinal motivations of an 'individual' target audience and its consequent application in the course of the positioning phase of the campaign through the adoption of 'Structural Branding'. This factor created an empathetic and desirable brand image for the Clio in a market where inter-product differentiation is becoming increasingly unlikely to be accomplished and even where it can be accomplished is, more often than not, insufficient.

Results from all aspects of evaluation reflect positively on the Clio and suggest that the effectiveness of the advertising campaign has played a major role in the successful launch of the car.

APPENDIX

Sources

The sources referred to in this document are:

SMMT:	(Society of Motor Manufacturers and Traders) – sales figures, market and sector share figures.
NCBS:	(New Car Buyers Survey) – a pan-European study conducted in the UK by MIL. 30,000 questionnaires processed annually.
Renault Customerlink Survey:	A postal questionnaire to all buyers of new Renaults.
Millward Brown Car Tracking Study:	A tracking study reporting for 8-week periods, rolling weekly. About 100-200 respondents a month for each sector, although booster sample used initially for Clio launch.

Car girl drives men wild

FRENCH actress Estelle Skornik, who plays naughty Nicole in the Renault Clio TV advert, has made British men go weak at the knees.

The 21-year-old has had hundreds of letters from admirers declaring their love.

"We were extremely surprised," said Douglas Thursby-Pelham, account director for Publicis, the advertising agency which dreamed up the ad.

"But I suppose Nicole epitomises all that is French."

Estelle has also had letters from women wanting to know about the spotted sun dress she wears.

The response was so big that Selfridges reproduced the £450 Lolita Lempicka Parisienne number in a £37.99 version.

Estelle, who innocently kisses her father then drives off to a secret liaison with a lover in the original ad, can currently be seen in its sequel for the Clio 1.6 model.

There are also plans for her to star in further adverts for Renault.

LOVE LETTERS: Actress Estelle Skornik

On course for success: Ms Skornik in the Renault advertisement

Estelle drives her fans wild

THE young French actress Estelle Skornik has been a hit in the advertisement she made for the new Renault Clio.

Hundreds of viewers have been writing in for information not about the car – but about her. Men want to fix up dates with her and women want to know where she buys her dresses. Shot on location in France, the ad shows Estelle sneaking off in her car for a tryst.

Renault said that it was delighted at the way it turned out. Its spokesman added: "We hope to continue a long relationship with Estelle..."

TV CAR CHIEFS PUT KATE IN TOP GEAR!

Renault lend out £3,000 ad frock for school ball

By DAVID NEWMAN

PRETTY Kate Richards loved the little black dress in Renault's TV ads so much that the firm is setting her wear it.

Our DRESS: Little charmer Kate in the stunning outfit

Naughty, but Nicole

Step out in style — win a 'Clio' party dress and take-off for France

MAGICAL: Kate shall go to the ball

THAT DRESS!

● I AM not surprised the television advertisement for Renault is a success. Actress Estelle Skornik (above) looks like a girl should look — feminine. Young girls these days have no dress sense. They wear ugly boots, black leggings, jackets too large for them and have untidy hair. Do they think it's wrong to look feminine and attractive?
Joy Bradshaw, Christchurch, Dorset

EXCLUSIVE: How Nicole's sexy new ad is set to drive us wild again

What would Papa say?

By LORRAINE BUTLER

FILCHING FILLY

● Full of fun — and typically French ●

13

Call Waiting –
A New Service From BT

INTRODUCTION

Since BT was privatised, and started to face competition in its key market of communications network usage, the company has made great strides forward in its aim to become more marketing oriented. A prime example of the new philosophy was the launch of BT's Call Waiting service in London.

This paper examines the launch of this new service to BT's residential customers. It will argue that the advertising campaign played a key role in generating high levels of applications to take up the service. The advertising built awareness, understanding and, crucially, communicated a motivating benefit for the service to a significant section of the target audience.

The provision of new services such as Call Waiting to its residential customers is an important element in BT's response to its increasing competitive threat.

BACKGROUND

Call Waiting is one of a group of new services that BT can offer to its customers when an exchange is modernised. The services are 'network based', that is, although they are accessed through a customer's telephone, the technology that provides them resides within BT's network. Customers pay for the services either on a per usage basis – as with Charge Advice (a service which automatically tells the customer the price of the call just made) – or by renting the service – as with Call Diversion (all your calls diverted to another number of your choice whilst you are away from your base phone) and Call Waiting. Call Waiting is a service that alerts a person if someone is trying to call them whilst they are on a call to someone else. They hear a bleep in their earpiece when someone else is calling them; by pressing the 'R' and '2' buttons on their phone (to access the service customers need a phone with 'Touchtone' dialling) the customer can switch from their original call to the new caller; the same operation takes them back to the first call. Thus effectively doing away with the engaged tone.

BT has always advised their customers when their exchange is being modernised; an element of this notification has been to announce the new services that were going to become available with modernisation. However, the programme for the introduction of modernised exchanges was largely driven by the localised needs of BT's business customers. Hence, the penetration of modernised exchanges for residential customers has been patchy, the consequence of this has been that promoting any network service through advertising has always run the risk that the majority of people seeing the advertising would not be able to avail themselves of the service.

It is only now that the company can promote the services to customers on a more macro basis, taking advantage of the above-the-line promotions and building synergy between various elements of the marketing mix.

The decision was taken to test launch network services in London, an area with a high penetration of modernised exchanges. In addition a control area, Edinburgh, was established simultaneously in order to identify the incremental sales attributable to the advertising.

THE MARKETING TASK

BT wanted to increase the penetration of its network services amongst its residential customers. This would have three key benefits to the company:

1. The direct revenue provided through rental and usage fees.
2. The indirect revenue provided through the increased usage of BT's network.
3. Increased loyalty to the company in the face of a growing competitive threat through the communication of the measures that BT is undertaking to provide its customers with a better service.

MARKETING STRATEGY

Previous test mailings of the services pointed to an increased level of response when a single-minded approach was taken, ie just announcing one service rather than the whole range.

This analysis was supported by qualitative research which suggested consumer confusion when they were confronted by more than one service at a time. (Source: David Douce.)

Hence, BT decided to adopt a staged approach to the launch of the services; starting with Call Waiting which had been identified in several pieces of research as being the most widely appealing of the services available for rental. This would then be followed up by the marketing of other services to a market that had already started to accept the concept of network based telephone services.

In order to encourage take up of the services BT decided to offer a three month free trial to anyone applying. This offer had also been tried in the past with encouraging results with approximately 60% continuing with the service after the trial. However, in the past customers had to contact BT to say that they wished to continue with the service; for the London trial it was agreed that customers would need to contact if they wished to discontinue the service. It was estimated, based upon experience in related fields, that this change together with pro-active calling to trialists to welcome them to the service and help overcome any problems would take its retention levels to at least 75%.

DIRECT MARKETING

BT only has limited opportunities to offer its services to customers. Although it does have a high street presence, this is currently not national in its coverage. Hence, the only really feasible means to sell the service to customers was through direct marketing and specifically direct mail. Additionally, and importantly, direct mail enabled BT to only mail those customers on a modernised exchange and to tailor the mailing according to the equipment that the customer was known to have available.

TARGETING

Previous work on the appeal of the services had identified households with high call bills as offering the best prospect for the take-up of the service. This fits with common sense, those households with high call bills will have their phone in use more of the time and so will see more benefit from Call Waiting. The distribution pattern of BT's customers' phone bills meant that groups with phone bills smaller than £100 start to become very large and expensive to mail and, given their lower predisposition towards taking the service, it was therefore believed that mailing to those customers with call bills of below £100 would not be cost effective.

For this reason it was decided that, initially, the trial offer would be mailed to BT customers with call bills over £100 per quarter or more. This group is known as the Top Residential or 'Top Res' audience. They are fairly diverse in terms of attitudes and demographics, high call bills tending to be a function of circumstances such as having teenage children at home, having friends or relatives abroad, working from home or just really enjoy talking on the phone.

THE ROLE FOR ADVERTISING

Advertising had two objectives in the launch of Call Waiting.

Primarily: to build awareness of the service amongst the target audience and persuade customers of its benefits, thereby increasing the take-up of the trial offer amongst those who were mailed.

Secondary: to stimulate enquiries for the service amongst those who are not mailed the offer (ie those with phone bills below £100).

ADVERTISING STRATEGY

The first stage in the development of the advertising was a qualitative research project undertaken by David Douce. This looked at existing promotional material for Call Waiting together with a series of concepts to help identify the ideal positioning for the service and the most motivating advertising proposition.

Concepts

The concepts explored a range of different benefits that Call Waiting could bring to customers. These explored the benefit to the caller and the callee, benefits to different types of people (men/women, young/old etc) and rational and emotional benefits. For example, rational benefits were missing out on events or opportunities because the caller always found the phone engaged; emotional benefits explored the frustration of not getting through and evoked concern amongst people of not being available when needed.

CONCLUSIONS

The key conclusions from this work were:

— Interest in the service when it was promoted through rational benefits was limited.
— Customers saw Call Waiting as a service that, although superficially appealing, was unlikely to get much usage – 'a bit like a cucumber shredder' according to one respondent. As such they quickly started to view it in the context of BT's profits and felt that they should be offered it for free.
— Customers found it hard to think of personal calls which were important enough to be worth interrupting a call that they were currently involved in. Vitally important calls were felt to be very rare and other callers finding the line engaged would try again.
— These barriers disappeared when the communication presented an emotional rather than a rational benefit. The concept board that most persuaded customers to review their feelings about the service showed a girl in a phone box outside a station on a dark wet night trying to call her parents.
— This moved the service from being viewed simply in terms of the rational function that it brought the bill payer to it being seen in emotional terms. Basically, it pointed to the power of an emotional benefit to fire the imagination over possible needs and therefore sell the service more effectively.

Once the power of the emotional benefit had been identified work was needed to look at the best interpretation of this for our target audience.

David Douce's research pointed to the relationship between parents and older children as being a powerful trigger. An examination of the 'Top Res' audience pointed to 46% of them having teenage children. As discussed previously, those who did not fall into this group were largely either businesses on a residential line or people making a lot of international calls. It was known that people in business could understand the benefits of Call Waiting to them very easily and so would respond to any communication about the service fairly readily. International callers use the phone largely because of circumstance – they have close friends or relatives abroad.

For these reasons it was decided that advertising would be most effective targeted at that group of the high user audience consisting of parents with teenage children. Additionally, the approach adopted had the potential to work with people who do not use their phone as much as the Top Res group – most people want to be easily available for at least one other person.

Key Message

With Call Waiting you need never miss out on important calls because you are on the phone.

MEDIA STRATEGY

The timing of the media was designed to build awareness and interest in Call Waiting immediately prior to customers' receipt of their mailshot. Hence, the campaign started on 28th October 1991 and ran to 18th November 1991 with the mailing starting to go out on the 12th November. The mailing was sent out Mailsort so should be received by customers within seven days.

Running a regional test combined with a limited budget severely limited the media options, effectively ruling out our ideal image building medium of television. Attempt to use posters proved to be unsuccessful as we could not communicate the complicated product story in what is essentially a very simple medium. The only real options available were radio and press. This limited our targeting and reach capability quite seriously but within these constraints we put together the best schedule we could. As far as possible the target was BC1 adults with children.

We decided to opt for a combination of both press and radio, assigning clear roles to each medium. Radio was felt to be an excellent medium to dramatise and build awareness of Call Waiting. Press, on the other hand, was there to support the radio, to work in synergy reinforcing the emotional message and importantly providing a means for people to enquire about the service.

The ratecard cost of the campaign was £296,126 and it is estimated that the premium that we paid for regional editions could be over 50%. In addition, this severely limited positioning options and our opportunities to use colour.

TABLE 1: MEDIA SCHEDULE

Radio Stations	Press	Press region
Capital AM and FM	Evening Standard	
LBC AM and FM	Daily Mail	London and South East
Jazz FM	Mail on Sunday	London
Melody	News of the World	London and South East
	Sunday Mirror	London and South East
	Sunday Times Magazine	London
	Daily Telegraph Magazine	London and South East
	TVTimes	London

CREATIVE EXECUTIONS

The executions brought the advertising strategy to life by depicting people in miserable situations trying to call home but unable to get through because someone is on the phone. Great care was needed to ensure that the situations were emotionally powerful enough to motivate customers but not so worrying that the response would be to call the emergency services. The following situations were shown in press or demonstrated in a radio commercial.

Swimming finished early.

He was told off for shouting.

If you had, he wouldn't be getting the engaged signal time after time after time.

You see, a new service called Call Waiting - available rental free for a limited period only - would mean he'd hear an announcement asking him to hang on.

At the same time your darling daughter would be interrupted by a gentle bleep letting her know that there was another call trying to get through.

A couple of pushes of the phone buttons later and your youngest would be through.

Allowing you to give him the reassurance he needs.

It's almost like having two phone lines, in fact.

Call Waiting is available, using a tone dialling phone, wherever a telephone exchange has been modernised.

What makes it even more attractive is that if you contact us within the next fourteen days, a three month trial of Call Waiting is yours with no rental to pay.

So contact us now. And find out how to free up your phone.

He bashed his knee.

He's lost his bus pass.

His big sister's at home on the phone catching up on some crucial gossip.

And he can't believe you didn't accept this free offer.

CALL FREE 0800 800 848 DAY OR NIGHT

FREE TRIAL OFFER

Call Waiting

I am a BT customer. Please send me details of the Call Waiting offer.
My first three months will be rental free.

Title: Mr/Mrs/Miss/Ms   Initials

Surname

Tel no (inc dialling code)

Address

              Postcode

Please send to: BT Call Waiting Offer, FREEPOST 800 (BS3333), Bristol BS1 6GZ (No stamp required.)   FFO 521

This service is in addition to your standard telephone service. Normal rental charges for Call Waiting are £4 per quarter inc VAT for a minimum period of 12 months.

RADIO COMMERCIAL

SUZIE – 60 SECONDS

Boy 1	It's getting late. We'd better phone home to say we've lost Suzie.
Boy 2	What are they going to say? If only she hadn't run off.
SFX	*Dialling. Engaged tone.*
Boy 2	*(Groans)*. That'll be my mum ringing yours to find out where we are. They're gonna be really worried.
Boy 1	I'll try mine.
Boy 2	Don't be stupid! If they're talking to each other, yours will be engaged too.
Boy 1	No. We've got this new Call Waiting thing on *our* phone.
SFX	*Dialling. Sorry the number is busy. We're trying to connect your call. Please hold the line. Sorry the number is busy…*
Mum	Hello?
Boy 1	Mum, it's Colin.
Mum	Oh, thank goodness. Where are you?
Boy 1	Suzie's gone missing.
Mum	What!?
MVO	With Call Waiting, when you're on the phone you'll hear a gentle bleep when another call is trying to get through. BT's Call Waiting service is now available rental free for three months, on our *digital* telephone exchanges. You'll need a tone dialling phone to use the service. For details call us free now on 0800 800 848.
Mum	Now, calm down and we'll sort it all out. Hang on – what's that outside?
SFX	*Door opens*
Mum	Suzie!
SFX	*Dog barks excitedly*
Boy 1	Wicked!
MVO	BT. You're more than just a number.

Eight o'clock at night.

Rain pouring down.

Your train's cancelled.

Your shoes leak.

Your son's on the phone at home discussing where to meet on Friday night.

And you're cursing yourself for turning down this free offer.

If you'd accepted it you wouldn't be listening to an interminable engaged signal.

Because with a new service called Call Waiting - available rental free for a limited period only - you'd hear instead an announcement asking you to hang on.

At the same time, a gentle bleep would let your prodigal son know someone was trying to get through.

With a few pushes of the buttons on his phone, you'd be through and the original conversation would be on "hold."

A choice word or two from you, and he could organise your rescue from the station. Then return to his friend.

It's almost like having two phone lines, in fact.

Call Waiting is available, using a tone dialling phone, wherever a telephone exchange has been modernised.

Sounds good? It's even better when you consider that you can try out Call Waiting for three months rental free, as long as you contact us in the next fourteen days.

So don't get left out in the cold. Contact us today.

CALL *FREE 0800 800 848 DAY OR NIGHT*

FREE TRIAL OFFER

Call Waiting

I am a BT customer. Please send me details of the Call Waiting offer. My first three months will be rental free.

Title: Mr/Mrs/Miss/Ms _____ Initials _____

Surname _____

Tel no (inc dialling code) _____

Address _____

_____ Postcode _____

Please send to: BT Call Waiting Offer, FREEPOST 800 (BS3333), Bristol BS1 6GZ (No stamp required.)

This service is in addition to your standard telephone service. Normal rental charges for Call Waiting are £4 per quarter inc VAT for a minimum period of 12 months.

RADIO COMMERCIAL

EMMA AND MARCUS – 60 SECONDS

SFX	*Rain, wind.*
Station PA	We regret to announce the cancellation of the 7.14.
1st woman	*(To herself)* Great. I'll ring home when the phone's free.
SFX	*Pay phone door opens.*
2nd woman	Here, come and wait in the phonebox!
1st woman	Oh, thanks!
SFX	*Pay phone door closes. They go inside. Button dials number. Engaged signal.*
2nd woman	*(Groan)* As usual. Here, try yours. My son Marcus is probably chatting up that Emma girl again.
1st woman	My daughter's always on the phone too, so we've got this new Call Waiting service.
SFX	*Dialling. Sorry the number is busy. We're trying to connect your call. Please hold the line. Sorry the number is busy…*
Daughter	Hello?
1st woman	Hello love, sorry to interrupt. Can you ask Dad to pick me up from the station at eight please?
MVO	With Call Waiting, when you're on the phone you'll hear a gentle bleep when another call is trying to get through.
	BT's Call Waiting service is now available rental free for three months, on our *digital* telephone exchanges. You'll need a tone dialling phone to use the service.
	For details call us free now on 0800 800 848.
1st woman	*(Lowers voice)* And Emma? If you're talking to someone called Marcus, tell him to hang up. I think his mum's trying to phone home.
MVO	BT. You're more than just a number.

These types of scenarios were also translated through into the direct mail pack that consumers received. Even ultimately through to the script of the telesales people who called customers who took up the trail, to enquire as to whether they found Call Waiting useful and if they had any problems. The consistency of message was a key component of the campaign, leading consumers sequentially through the purchase process.

TEST AND CONTROL

In order to provide a control for the London advertising test, the mailing was also sent out to a sample of 25,000 'Top Res' customers in Edinburgh. The Edinburgh customers saw no other promotion of Call Waiting than this mailing.

In order to ensure that any differential responses were not due to different attitudes to the telephone in the different parts of the country we have profiled 'Top Res' customers in the two areas. The on-going customer tracking system that we used to do this does not allow us to look exclusively at Edinburgh but we can look at the East of Scotland region of which Edinburgh accounts for over 40% of the population in that region and probably a much higher proportion of Top Residential customers.

The results show some differences in usage and attitudes but nothing that would influence the results dramatically one way or another. If anything East of Scotland customers are slightly more pro-BT and therefore more positively disposed towards their products and services. Their ownership of phones is almost exactly the same as that of the London customers (Figure 1) as is their ownership and usage of technological products such as personal computers and mobile phones.

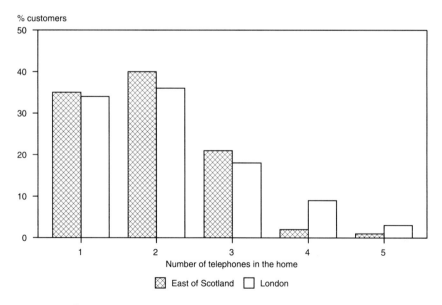

Figure 1. *Comparison of equipment ownership between the two regions*

TABLE 2: SATISFACTION WITH BT SERVICE (SEPT 1991)

	London	East of Scotland
Completely satisfied	20%	29%

Source: FDS

EVIDENCE

The key sources for our results are BT's own response figures together with its on-going advertising tracking study conducted by BMRB. Where appropriate these sources have been supplemented by other supporting information.

RESULTS

The paper will look at the advertising results in terms of the objectives set of raising awareness, understanding and persuading customers of the benefits of the service. We will then look at how this converted through into product take-up.

Awareness and Understanding

We attempted to measure spontaneous awareness of Call Waiting by asking customers if they were aware of any additional facilities that could be used with their phones; for those who replied 'yes' we asked what those services were. The most popular responses to the question were for memory buttons and answering machines. However, the proportion describing Call Waiting nearly quadrupled during the campaign.

TABLE 3: COULD YOU DESCRIBE EACH OF THE SERVICES YOU CAN THINK OF?

	London		Rest of UK	
	Pre campaign (45)	Campaign (88)	Pre campaign (150)	Campaign (225)
Call Waiting described	4%	15%	1%	4%

Sample sizes do not allow us to compare spontaneous awareness between London and East of Scotland. However, prompted awareness of the service was measured on BT's Customer Satisfaction Monitor. This has a larger sample than the BMRB monitor and thus enables examination of the two regions (Figure 2). The analysis points to a rise in awareness during the campaign which, after a slight dip in the two months after the advertising finished, has continued to build as the service has started to capture the public's imagination. The BMRB monitor also measured prompted awareness with even more impressive results.

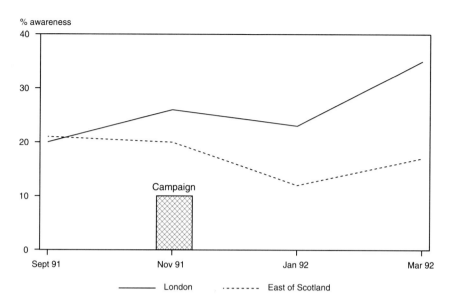

Figure 2. *Awareness of Call Waiting*
Source: FDS

TABLE 4: AWARENESS OF CALL WAITING AFTER PROMPTING WITH A BRIEF DESCRIPTION

	London (221)	Rest of UK (598)
% aware (post campaign)	31	17

Source: BMRB

Motivation

The BMRB monitor was used to measure customer's interest in the service. As discussed previously the service is initially superficially appealing to people, but when it comes down to it they do not feel that it is worth applying for. Hence, although we get high levels of interest this does not convert directly through to responses.

The campaign built successfully upon this initial superficial interest, converting it through to a deeper level. This is indicated by the difference in levels of interest between those who remember seeing the advertising and the population in general.

TABLE 5: USEFULNESS OF CALL WAITING

	Total (170)	Any recall of advertising (49)
Very/fairly useful	40%	54%
Not very useful	24%	22%
Not at all useful	34%	23%

Another indication of interest in the service is the amount people are prepared to pay for it. To a degree this is influenced by affluence but that effect should be partly cancelled out by comparing responses in London between those recalling and not recalling the advertising. Additionally, looking at the proportion not prepared to pay anything for the service gives an indication of its value to people.

TABLE 6: HOW MUCH PREPARED TO PAY FOR CALL WAITING PER QUARTER

	Total UK	Total London	London recall advertising
	(170)	(66)	(49)
£1.99 or less	2%	1%	–
£2-£3.99	1%	1%	–
£4-£4.99	1%	2%	3%
£5 or more	15%	20%	26%
Nothing	54%	56%	36%
Don't know	18%	12%	28%

Source: BMRB

With the actual cost at £4.00 this is a reasonable argument to suggest that the advertising not only created desire for the product but created the possibility of higher margins.

Applications

The increased awareness and interest in the service converted through to a significant increase in take-up of the offer.

Figure 3 shows the response levels to the mailing by week. At the end of the campaign the responses to the mailing in the London region were more than double those seen in the Edinburgh region. Therefore, as advertising was the only major difference between the two regions, we conclude that it must have acted as a powerful catalyst to trial.

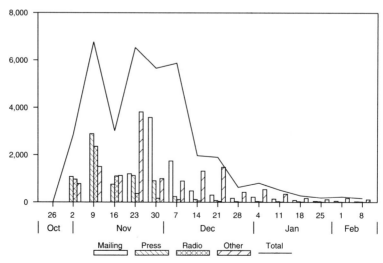

Figure 3. *Weekly response totals by media*

TABLE 7: MAILING RESPONSES

	%
London	9.0
Edinburgh	4.2

In addition the advertising in London produced 23,304 responses in its own right (over 60% from the press advertising). It was not anticipated that the advertising would generate responses on this scale, so this response level caught us somewhat unaware and systems had to be put in place rapidly to handle them. A key part of this was to identify which of the responders to the advertising were on modernised exchanges and so had Call Waiting available to them.

A significant number of responses (6,289) lived in parts of the region in which Call Waiting was not available.

We have not been able to profile the advertising responders but it seems reasonable to conclude that a large proportion of them would have phone bills of below £100 and would have not received the mailing. Thus the advertising enabled us to reach groups to whom the service is relevant but it would have been difficult to address cost effectively through direct mail.

In total there were 28,934 customers who took up the offer (there were a few hundred unattributable telephone applications). If it is assumed that the Edinburgh result is typical of a mailing response without the benefit of advertising support, then the number of these responders attributable to the advertising alone is as follows.

Directly responding to advertising	23,304
of which not available	6,289
(a) Responders	17,115
(b) Mailing responders	11,048
(c) Of which those attributable to mailing ((b) x 4.2/9.0)	5,156
Total attributable to advertising ((a)+(b)-(c))	23,007

At the time of writing, it is not certain what proportion of customers will keep the service after their trial is over. The volume of responses resulted in it frequently taking over a month between the customer's initial enquiry and BT connecting the service.

Results up to the end of April 1992 suggested a retention level of over 90%. Even on the basis of the initial estimate of 75% that would result in 17,250 people taking up the service directly as a result of the advertising or (on the basis of £4 per quarter rental fee) an income stream of £276,000 per year.

TABLE 8

Retention levels	Directly attributable customers	Income
60%	13,800	£220,800
75%	17,250	£276,000
90%	20,700	£331,200

Suggesting that the campaign will cover its regional ratecard costs in just over a year and quite probably much faster than that!

Work is still being undertaken to identify the increase in phone usage attributable to Call Waiting and so it is not possible to include an estimate for the additional revenue resulting through this route. However, it will undoubtedly be positive and add significantly to the rental income.

CONCLUSIONS

From our analysis we conclude:

1. That the dramatisation of the benefits of Call Waiting via emotional advertising was an important step forward in the promotion of the service.
2. That the advertising developed effectively communicated this emotional benefit.
3. That the communication of the benefit through the advertising was effective across the board in creating interest and desire for the service.
4. That this converted through into increased levels of applications for the product among those mailed than would be expected without the advertising.
5. That the advertising enabled BT to cost effectively generate applications from those customers positively disposed towards the service with phone bills lower than £100 per quarter.
6. That this increased level of application resulted in incremental revenue to BT that covered the direct costs of advertising in under 18 months.

On the basis of these results BT made the decision to roll the campaign out nationally in exactly the same form.

Section Five

Small Budgets

14

Whipsnade Wild Animal Park

How TV Advertising Helped Reverse a 30 Year Decline

INTRODUCTION

The advertising brief for Whipsnade Wild Animal Park was very simple: dramatically increase the number of visitors to Whipsnade (and in doing so, reverse a 30 year trend of declining attendances).

Despite an annual media budget of well under £300,000, we nevertheless recommended advertising on television.

This paper will show that this bold strategy has proved an extremely successful one. We have reversed the 30 year trend; visitor numbers were increased by 25% in the first year and that increase has been sustained over a second year despite adverse economic conditions which have seen all of Whipsnade's major competitors in decline.

WHIPSNADE'S DECLINING FORTUNES

Whipsnade Wild Animal Park is the 'country home' of the Zoological Society of London. (London Zoo is the Society's London base.) Set in 600 acres of rolling parkland near Dunstable in Bedfordshire, Whipsnade is home to over 2,800 animals, including many rare and endangered species.

Whipsnade has seen annual attendances decline from 750,000 in 1961 to below 400,000 in the late 1980s (see Figure 1).

Whipsnade's management attributed this decline to the failure, over many years, to attract new generations of visitors to Whipsnade. In turn, this was attributed to two main factors:

— The growth in local, heavily advertised, competitors such as Windsor Safari Park and Chessington World of Adventures. These combined wild animals with the added attractions of rides and amusements.
— By contrast Whipsnade had suffered from chronic lack of investment in advertising and promotion, and was believed, consequently, to be virtually invisible in the market place.

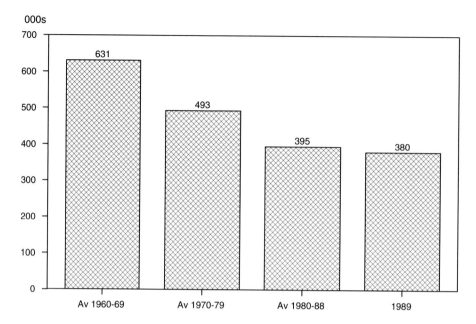

Figure 1. *Annual visitor numbers*
Source: Whipsnade Wild Animal Park

THE ADVERTISING CHALLENGE

Lowe Howard-Spink was appointed in January 1990. The advertising brief was very simple: to help increase visitor numbers.

1989 had been Whipsnade's worst-ever season for attendances. Despite the favourable circumstances of a long, hot summer – the first of two – visitor numbers had fallen to 380,000. This was down 11% on the previous year.

Whipsnade's marketing objective was to reverse the long term decline and raise attendances to 480,000 in 1990. This would mean a year-on-year increase of 26% and would represent an increase of 33% over the number of visitors predicted by the 30 year trend.

THE ADVERTISING STRATEGY

Both Whipsnade's own visitor records and market data collected by the British Tourist Authority (BTA) indicated that Whipsnade competes in a category of visitor attractions that can best be described as 'The Family Day-Out'.

Although easy to recognise, the market for family days-out is extremely difficult to define precisely as it embraces an enormously diverse range of destinations and experiences, from theme parks such as Alton Towers, through to a trip to the zoo, or a day at the seaside.

Strategic qualitative research[1] revealed, however, that such days-out fall broadly into two categories: those initiated by children and often described by parents as 'junk' entertainment; and those initiated by parents and seen by them as having more 'nutritious', that is, educational, value.

DAYS OUT/TRIPS FALL INTO TWO CATEGORIES

Initiated by children Approved (very occasionally) by parent	Initiated by parents Approved by child
Examples:	Examples:
■ Ghostbusters II ■ Macdonalds ■ Alton Towers	■ Museums ■ Theatre ■ Zoos, Wildlife parks, Sanctuaries
'Junk' entertainment	More 'educational' entertainment

We had no ambitions to try to re-locate Whipsnade in the 'junk' sector competing on the same terms as theme parks. This would not only have grossly mis-represented the nature of the Whipsnade experience but would also have conflicted with its scientific role as a centre for conservation and rare species breeding. The strategy, therefore, was to boost its performance in the educational sector.

The key decision makers in this sector are parents not children and so it was parents who were to be the primary target of the advertising campaign. However, we also needed to take care not to alienate children, since they still have power of veto in such situations!

In the light of that decision, we then had to ask where Whipsnade stood in the market place.

The belief of Whipsnade's own management that it had very little presence in the minds of parents contemplating a family day-out was only partially confirmed by an omnibus telephone survey commissioned in January 1990[2].

Prompted recognition of the Whipsnade name was in fact quite high (89% in London and 79% in Central). Although the levels of spontaneous mentions were naturally much lower (34% in London and 15% in Central), they were broadly comparable with Windsor and Chessington. Windsor and Chessington, however, each receive roughly three times more visitors than Whipsnade, so the problem was not simply one of awareness.

Qualitative research[3], comparing the views of Whipsnade visitors with demographically similar groups of non-visitors, revealed the extent of the problem more fully.

Although the name 'Whipsnade' itself was familiar enough, potential visitors had only the haziest idea of what kind of day-out Whipsnade would offer. Many still thought of Whipsnade as a zoo (which, had indeed been its official title until recently). This conjured up images of Victorian menageries and animals in cages. Equally, the term 'Wild Animal Park' was for many people indistinguishable from 'Safari Park' – of which Windsor was by far the best known example and already widely visited.

The role for advertising was not simply to make Whipsnade more 'top of mind' among parents planning a family day-out, but also to create a strong and distinctive character for the place, which would earn it a unique position on their list of 'places to go'.

THE CREATIVE SOLUTION

The key features which give Whipsnade its unique character, are essentially the animals themselves and their environment. That is, over 100 species of wild and rare animals, in a naturally beautiful setting, where they live in their natural social groups, behaving as though in the wild. We believed that this strongly differentiated Whipsnade from purely commercial theme parks, where the main attractions are rides and amusements and the animals are essentially a sideshow.

In the creative brief, the appeal that we wished to communicate was summarised as:

'A walk on the wild side'

A 40 second TV commercial was created to capture the beauty and excitement of the Whipsnade experience. Based on the film *Out of Africa*, it comprised a series of shots of wild and exotic animals moving across the screen, accompanied by the original film sound-track. The viewer sees wild animals behaving completely naturally, apparently in their native habitat, and only at the end is it revealed that the entire film was shot on location at Whipsnade Wild Animal Park; 'Out of Bedfordshire'.

THE MEDIA STRATEGY

The advertising was required to deliver a year-on-year increase in attendances of 26%. Because Whipsnade is an outdoor attraction, the vast majority of these new visitors would need to be attracted between April and September. Moreover, there are for Whipsnade (in common with most other domestic visitor attractions in the UK), 20 key days a year which can account for up to 30% of the year's total visitor revenue. These are the bank holiday weekends, beginning with Easter and ending with the last weekend in August.

Although Whipsnade was operating on a very tight budget, we believed nevertheless that only television could provide both the impact and the rapid coverage build necessary to achieve our objectives.

The initial TV plan for Whipsnade was based upon a number of important assumptions about timing and geographical targeting:

— Typically, the decision to visit an attraction is not made until the day before, or even the morning of the visit itself. The more weather-dependent the appeal of the attraction, the more likely this is to be the case.
— Given very limited funds, tight targeting of bank holidays was likely to generate the greatest return on investment.
— Most visitors live within a radius of one hour's drive from Whipsnade, so activity would concentrate on those TV stations serving that locality.

WHIPSNADE WILD ANIMAL PARK
'OUT OF BEDFORDSHIRE' 40"

Music: Soundtrack to *Out of Africa*

Whipsnade lies in the middle of a large overlap between London, Central and Anglia TV regions. When preparing our initial TV schedule we assumed that the majority of new visitors to Whipsnade were more or less equally likely to be coming north from the London area or south from Birmingham and Coventry.

On our limited budget we could not hope to target both regions adequately, so we decided to concentrate our spend in Central (using the Central West transmitter) where pound for pound, we would be able to achieve much greater frequency than in the London ITV region and so get a better return on our investment. (Anglia TV region we initially discounted altogether as having insufficiently large centres of population to provide us with significant numbers of new visitors.)

However, with the benefit of a new market research programme[4] which for the first time gave us a breakdown of Whipsnade visitors by ITV station usually watched, we very quickly discovered a much higher than expected proportion of visitors from the London and Anglia TV regions and relatively few from Central. This made the likely return on an advertising investment in Central look much less attractive, so we decided to re-deploy the second half of our planned TV spend from Central into London and Anglia.

Thus, the final deployment of TV funds for 1990 is illustrated below:

	April	May	June	July	August
Central TVRs (West)	137	97	93		
London TVRs				67 69	38
Anglia TVRs (West)				209	

Total			
	Central:	£125,800	327 TVRs
	London:	£124,600	168 TVRs
	Anglia:	£ 30,000	209 TVRs

Meanwhile, a second stage of qualitative research[5] commissioned during the summer of 1990 had further clarified our understanding of the role for advertising: the belief that the choice of where to go for a day-out is made less than 24 hours before the visit itself appeared to be only partly true. Our qualitative work suggested that although the *final* choice of destination is made only a very short time in advance of the visit, there is a crucially important list of candidate destinations drawn up a few days beforehand – from which the final choice is made, depending on mood and, frequently, weather.

We were concerned that our very tight targeting of bank holidays and other key weekends meant that Whipsnade was not being considered at the point, generally a few days earlier, when families were drawing up their short-lists. We therefore planned, for the following season, to try to extend our periods of on-air activity.

A 10 second commercial was created to run with the original 40 second film in the ratio of 1:1. This enabled us to buy more spots in the London region and also to extend our TV presence back earlier into the week preceding a bank holiday.

Accordingly, the 1991 TV schedule looked like this:

	March	April	May	June	July	August
London TVRs	106	118	128		97	122
Anglia TVRs (West)	44	45	53		47	62

Total			
	London:	£180,000	571 TVRs
	Anglia:	£ 20,000	251 TVRs

Although less than half of competitive spend levels, this budget of £200,000+ represented a tenfold increase on Whipsnade's historical advertising spend. This had previously concentrated on attracting visitors from the immediate locality by promoting special events such as Birds of Prey displays, Easter Egg Hunts, etc on Chiltern Radio.

However, whereas the TV advertising was intended to attract *new* visitors, it was felt that the promotion of special events on Chiltern Radio still had a complementary role to play in giving local and regular visitors a reason to re-visit. Accordingly, Whipsnade's spend on local radio has been maintained at a level consistent with its pre-TV advertising weight.

WHAT HAVE WE ACHIEVED?

In 1990, the number of visitors to Whipsnade increased by 25%, from 380,000 in 1989 to 473,000[6]. This marked a dramatic reversal of the long-term decline in attendances (see Figure 2).

Regular surveys of visitors[7] indicated that a major element of this growth had come from an increased proportion of 'new' visitors (ie those who had never before visited or not visited for over 10 years), which had risen by a quarter from 48% at the beginning of the season to 60% by the end.

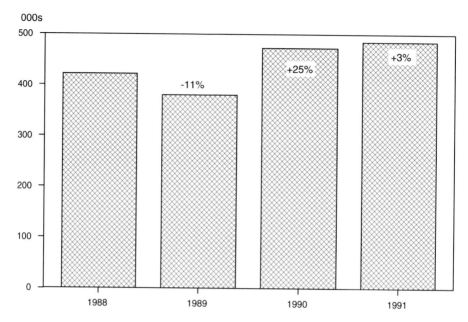

Figure 2. *Reversal of fortunes (annual visitor numbers)*
Source: Whipsnade Wild Animal Park

In 1991 visitor numbers rose to 485,000 despite the adverse economic conditions (principally high mortgage rates) which saw a real reduction in leisure spending in 1991 of nearly 2% over 1990 (see Figure 3).

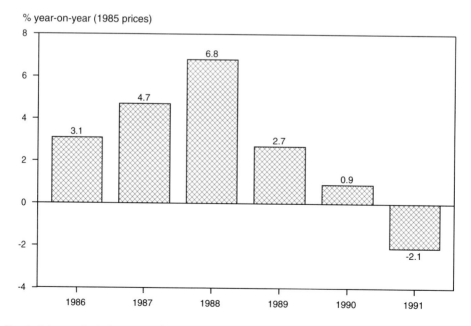

Figure 3. *Leisure spending (real year-on-year change)*
Sources: CSO, Henley Centre

This sustained improvement by Whipsnade over the two years is in marked contrast to the fortunes of Whipsnade's strongest local competitors:

TABLE 1: WHIPSNADE OUTPERFORMS THE COMPETITION
(Visitor Numbers Indexed Against 1989)

| | Whipsnade | | Windsor | | Chessington | | Thorpe Park | |
	000s	Index	000s	Index	000s	Index	000s	Index
1989	380	100	1,100	100	1,235	100	1,280	100
1990	473	125	1,070	97	1,515	122	974	76
1991	485	128	899	82	1,424	115	921	72

Sources: BTA, WWAP

Only Chessington comes close to Whipsnade's 1989/90 increase in visitors and no competitor managed to hold firm from 1990 to 1991.

Furthermore, this achievement was sustained despite a 32% increase in the gate price, from Easter 1991, which took the price of an adult admission from £4.50 to £5.95.

HOW DO WE KNOW IT WAS TV ADVERTISING THAT MADE THE DIFFERENCE?

Evidence for the central role of TV advertising in increasing Whipsnade's attendances is derived primarily from visitor surveys[8], conducted at regular intervals throughout the 1990 and 1991 summer seasons. Each survey wave sampled 300 visitors around key weekends such as bank holidays and at the beginning of school summer holidays in July.

This research provides three key indicators of a correlation between advertising activity and visitor numbers:

1. Profile of visitors by ITV region;
2. TV advertising awareness by ITV region;
3. Claimed 'influence of advertising on decision to visit' by ITV region.

Most importantly the data shows, not just that each of these indicators moved in line with the others, but also that the change in media strategy during 1990 was accurately reflected in changes across all three indicators.

1. *Profile of Whipsnade visitors by ITV region*
   From mid-May 1990 onwards, each wave of visitor research included the question 'Which TV station do you watch most often?' This enabled us to estimate the profile of visitors by ITV region.
   As shown in Figure 4, the percentage of visitors sampled who watch Central TV reached its peak of 20% at the end of May 1990. This coincides with the last of the three bursts of activity on Central. Since that time there has been no further advertising on Central, and the proportion of visitors from that region fell very rapidly, to settle at roughly half the peak.

Correspondingly, the percentage of visitors who claim to watch London or Anglia TV stations most often has grown significantly since the change in media strategy, from the low 70s to the mid 80s.

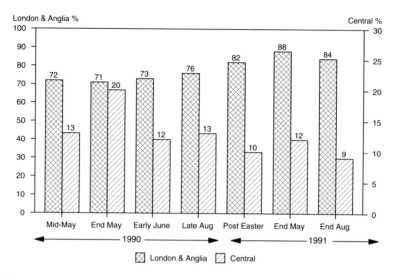

Figure 4. *Changing profile of Whipsnade Visitors by TV region ('Which TV station do you watch most?')*

2. *Awareness of TV advertising*

   Awareness of TV advertising has mirrored the pattern of results that we saw with regard to visitor profile. When we were on-air in Central claimed awareness of TV advertising built to 41%. Since coming off-air in Central, awareness has declined to around 14%. In London it rose very quickly from 8% to 35% and has remained at around that level. Awareness in Anglia meanwhile has grown steadily from a baseline of 4% to 33-34%.

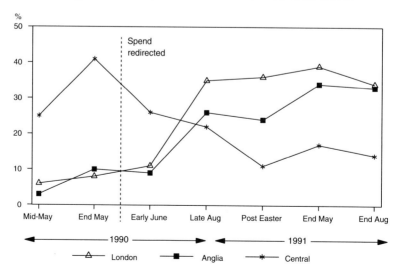

Figure 5. *Claimed TV ad awareness amongst visitors by ITV region*

3. *Influence of advertising on decision to visit*

Although in some respects this is a naïve question and one which many advertising practitioners believe will inevitably produce a serious under-estimate of the true influence of advertising on purchase behaviour, we decided to go ahead and ask it nonetheless.

What the results suggest is that the advertising has had a long-term as well as a short-term effect.

The earliest results, at the beginning of the first season, suggest that the advertising was influential whilst on air, but that this influence was rapidly eroded between bursts. By the end of the 1990 season, the erosion between bursts seems to have been diminishing.

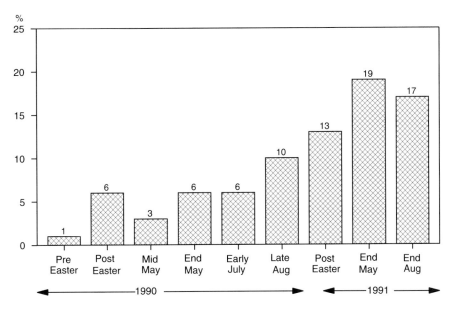

Figure 6. *Did advertising influence your visit here today? (total visitors)*

The 1991 results (which only in effect measure post-advertising periods) suggest that the commercial has gained in influence with repeated exposure over two seasons and our expectation would be that residual influence is also stronger between bursts than it was initially.

Again, a comparison between results for visitors from the different ITV regions, receiving different weights of advertising support over time, indicates that this influence is associated with TV advertising rather than any other promotional activity.

In particular, the Anglia airtime appears to have been very cost effective – all the more remarkable considering that in choosing the Anglia West transmitter, we were restricted to only seven spots a week when on-air. These spots were always, however, immediately after the regional news, and it can be argued that this particular programme environment found audiences in an especially receptive mood.

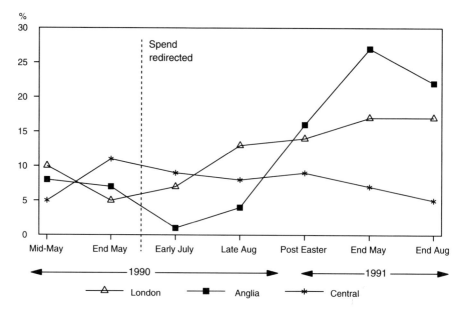

Figure 7. *Did advertising influence your visit here today?*

WHAT ELSE COULD HAVE CONTRIBUTED
TO THE RISE IN VISITOR NUMBERS?

There are three additional factors whose importance needs to be evaluated:

— Weather;
— Relative price;
— 'Product' quality and delivery.

   Each of these factors plays an undoubted part in the decision of where to go for a day-out. Nonetheless, they can all be eliminated as important agents of the growth in visitors to Whipsnade.

Weather

The summer of 1990 was one of the sunniest periods on record, and this is certain to have had a positive effect on visitor numbers. However, as Figure 8 shows, 1989 had been at least as good a summer as 1990; yet it marked the nadir of Whipsnade's fortunes. Equally, the summer of 1991 was one of the dullest on record, yet Whipsnade suffered no loss in attendances.

   We believe that weather – particularly, short-range weather forecasts – must be an important factor influencing the final choice of destination for a family day-out. However, advertising Whipsnade on television appears to have achieved its aims in 1990 unaided by any improvement in the weather versus 1989 and to have sustained visitor numbers in 1991 despite the largely negative influence of the weather that year.

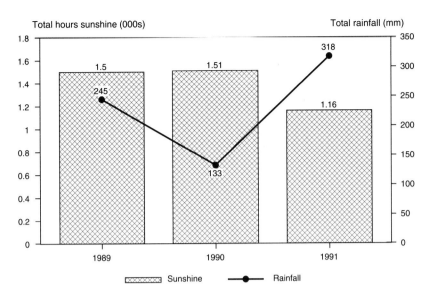

Figure 8. *Sunshine and rain – three summers* compared*
Source: London Weather Office
Note: * March to September

Relative Price

Whipsnade has not reduced its prices in order to attract more visitors. On the contrary, in 1991 it raised its ticket prices by 32%, taking the price of an adult admission from £4.50 to £5.95. No competitor has raised its admission prices by more than 12% since 1989.

'Product' Quality

Can the increase in visitor numbers be attributed to any significant improvements in the quality of the 'product'? Regular surveys of 'visitor satisfaction'[9] over the 1990 & 1991 seasons show that visitor satisfaction levels have remained virtually unchanged over the period (see Figure 9).

THE PAYBACK

The primary aim of advertising Whipsnade on television was to dramatically increase visitor numbers and consequently to increase revenue.

A media investment of £500,000 over two years has generated the major part of a 26% increase in attendances over the same period and the incremental revenue from these extra visitors has taken Whipsnade from a financial loss of £1.3 million in 1989 to an anticipated profit of £0.4 million this year.

Although this forms no part of our case for the effectiveness of Whipsnade's advertising, the Chief Executive, Mr Andrew Forbes, also believes that the increased visibility and popularity of Whipsnade 'has awakened the corporate sector who now see us as a positive proposition'. This has enabled Whipsnade to negotiate a number of important sponsorship deals with major UK companies to help fund new visitor attractions and also build a Conservation and Breeding Centre.

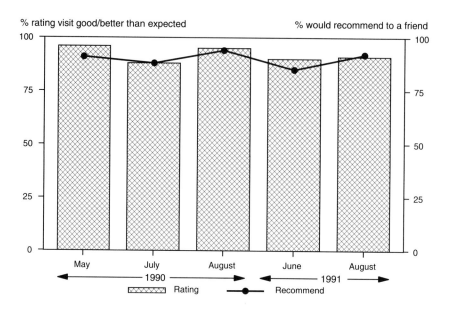

Figure 9. *Visitor satisfaction*

APPENDIX

Research Studies Referred to in the Case Study

1 & 3.   Four qualitative group discussions amongst BC1 women with children in the South East; two with zoo-goers and two with non-goers (Lowe Howard-Spink, 1990).

2.   Telephone omnibus survey amongst a nationally representative sample of 1,000 adults (NOP Market Research, January 1990).

4,7,8 & 9. Series of surveys across the 1990 and 1991 seasons, each of which drew a random sample of 300 visitors over a three day period, who were interviewed as they entered the site. Sample was then weighted to reflect known gate figures (Feedback Consumer Consultancy, 1990 & 1991).

5.   Two qualitative group discussions, sample as for 1 above (Kate Watts, The Planning Department, July 1990).

6.   Self-completion questionnaire distributed to sample of 300 interviewed at site entrance (see 4,7 & 8 above). Return rate for questionnaires averages 30% (Feedback Consumer Consultancy, 1990 & 1991).

15

The Launch of K Shoes
Washable Leather Trainers

INTRODUCTION

K Shoes is both a manufacturer and a retailer. The shoes it manufactures are sold through its own 230 K Shoe Shops and some 900 independent shoe retailers.

In 1991 the High Street was gripped by recession and the adverse trading conditions forced the company to focus its marketing activity on retaining and consolidating its existing market position – and customers. One way of achieving this was to widen the nature of its product offer to its customers.

K Shoes had long been tantalised by the huge growth in sales of trainers, an area in which the company had not been involved, either in retail or manufacturing terms. The women's trainer market had grown 70% in value from year end 1989 to year end 1990. At the end of 1990, it was estimated to be worth £254.4 million. In 1991 the company entered this market.

The trainer market can be split into two; trainers for sports wear and trainers for casual leisure wear. Among K Shoes customers – largely women aged over 35 – the sports wear trainer market is extremely limited. Thus K Shoes specifically targeted the leisure wear trainer market.

In entering such a developed market, K knew it needed a product that was not only in keeping with the K brand name but also one that had a competitive edge to attract customers into this new area for the brand. Until this was available, no market entry would be contemplated.

THE K WOMAN AND TRAINERS

Qualitative research revealed that the K woman saw a role in her wardrobe for a trainer as a versatile, modern, casual shoe. However, on the whole, because of the colour (ie predominantly white) of trainers, the K woman felt most comfortable viewing them as a spring/summer shoe. Her conservative tastes tending away from white shoes in the autumn/winter.

The K woman is concerned about her appearance, but is not overly fashion conscious. Thus a known trainer brand name has less importance for her. She has a practical streak and wants both looks *and* performance from a shoe.

For her, the important selection criteria for trainers were comfort and looks whilst the 'problem' areas were keeping the trainers looking good/clean and smelling fresh. Trainers were notorious for becoming unpleasantly smelly!

The company had developed a new way of treating leather which allowed it to be machine washed and still keep its looks. Using this leather, K designed a machine washable trainer for women, thus overcoming worries about keeping trainers clean and smell-free.

With this product the company was able to take its first step into the market with a shoe which the company felt exactly matched the needs of its sort of customer.

However, K Shoes recognised that simply having a good product was not enough. K Shoes are known for comfortable, well-made, well-fitting shoes but trainers were a new market for them. For the K washable trainer to be considered, K first had to get women to register that K had actually entered the market.

Even though the target audience was existing K customers, not all of these women would be regular K shoppers, many would shop at K only infrequently. We could not, therefore, simply rely on them seeing the shoe in store. Among regular K shoppers, there was a need to raise awareness of the merits of the new washable trainer. The product advantages might well have been lost in store given that it was a single style in a shop full of shoes. K Shoes felt, therefore, that without advertising it had little chance of success.

Thus, despite the underlying economic conditions, the company committed advertising money to the launch of washable trainers. A modest media budget of £268,000 was set aside for this task.

The target audience was existing K shoppers, both regular and irregular. These were the women for whom the shoe had been designed. The task was to consolidate the existing customer base by getting these women to consider K Shoes for *trainers*.

K Shoes was looking for short-term success in terms of sales of the washable trainer but also long-term effects in gaining a foothold in the trainer market, thus allowing it to expand its range in the future.

DISTRIBUTION

For the washable trainer to be successful, it was essential that it was stocked not only in K Shoe Shops (230 outlets) but also in the much larger pool of independent shoe retailers who stock K Shoes (900 outlets).

Advertising had a key role to play in achieving this distribution. The structure of the K operation is such that K Shoe Shops are not obliged to stock any one particular product. Without advertising support it might not have been possible to persuade K Shoe Shops to stock this new product and, even if they had, it is almost certain that independent retailers would not have followed suit in significant numbers.

THE STRATEGY FOR WASHABLE TRAINERS

In developing the advertising strategy it was necessary to take into account not only the nature of the K woman but also the way she responds to advertising. It was essential that the advertising was direct and simple in its message. The K woman was unlikely to respond to clever imagery. She wanted a clear demonstration of the product benefit to satisfy her practical streak.

We therefore decided that whilst visually reassuring the K woman about the look of the shoe, the advertising should focus in as simple and direct a way as possible, on the K product plus of *washable leather.*

THE ADVERTISING

The single page press advertisement devised by BBH featured the washable trainer in a washing machine with the headline 'The first leather trainer capable of 1,000 circuits a minute'.

It was our intention to show the K woman how good the shoe looked whilst demonstrating succinctly the product benefit of washable leather.

This one advertisement ran in spring and autumn of 1991. In the spring it was also adapted into a four sheet poster.

THE TIMING OF THE ADVERTISING

In general, the trainer market is a year round market. However, the spring was thought likely to be the easiest time of year to get K Shoes shoppers thinking about trainers. It was decided therefore that the main push of the advertising should fall in the spring, launching the product as loudly as possible.

It was also acknowledged, however, that if K was to succeed in gaining a year round presence in trainers, ie maintain distribution, the washable product would need some additional support later in the year.

MEDIA STRATEGY

Choice of media was important in achieving the maximum effect from a limited budget.

Women's press was selected by virtue of its ability to talk more discreetly to our core K customers.

The media task was to target the K woman as directly and efficiently as possible. To augment what was already known about our core K customer and her reading habits, we carried out our own qualitative media research project within K Shoe Shops. We interviewed 16 K Shoe Shop customers in in-depth interviews in two locations.

Not surprisingly, women's weeklies, domestic monthlies and home interest titles were avidly read by these women.

The research also revealed why and how they read their magazines. Based on these results, we only bought positions which faced their three favourite articles ie horoscopes, letters' page and features highlighted on the front cover.

Single pages were used in order to achieve the best balance of impact in relation to coverage and frequency. Single pages allowed us to stand out whilst being in the right position to be read by our desired target audience.

In the spring, in addition to the women's press campaign, we also used selected four sheet poster sites which were used as 'outdoor point-of-sale' to attract women out shopping – possibly for trainers – into a K outlet.

We selected individual poster sites near competitive outlets which did not stock K Shoes but which were within shopping centres or high streets close to a K shop.

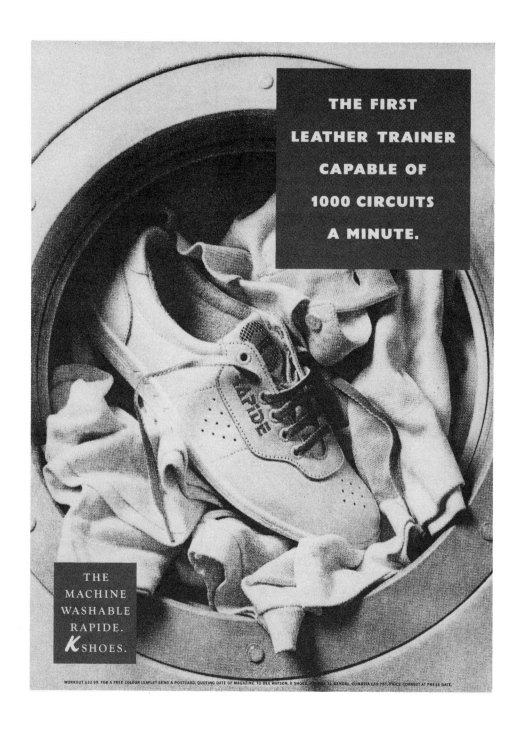

THE FIRST LEATHER TRAINER CAPABLE OF 1000 CIRCUITS A MINUTE.

THE MACHINE WASHABLE RAPIDE. **K**SHOES.

WORKOUT £32.99. FOR A FREE COLOUR LEAFLET SEND A POSTCARD, QUOTING DATE OF MAGAZINE, TO DEE WATSON, K SHOES, SPRING BANK, KENDAL, CUMBRIA LA9 7BT. PRICE CORRECT AT PRESS DATE.

THE MEDIA PLAN

The resulting media plan for 1991 is as illustrated and represents a media spend of £268,000.

Spring 1991 media plan

	4th Mar	11th Mar	18th Mar	25th Mar	1st Apr	8th Apr	15th Apr	22nd Apr	29th Apr	6th May	13th May	20th May	Total no of insertions
National newspapers													
Daily Mail	●												1
Women's weeklies													
Woman's Weekly			●	●									2
Woman's Realm			●	●									2
Woman			●					●					2
Woman's Own				●					●				2
Domestic monthlies													
Family Circle				●				●					2
Living				●				●					2
Prima				●									1
Woman & Home						●				●			2
Good Housekeeping						●				●			2
Essentials							●					●	2
Home interest													
Country Living	●					●				●			3
House Beautiful		●					●				●		3
Feature monthlies													
New Woman		●				●				●			3
Options		●											1
Woman's Journal			●										1
Outdoor		←			1,209 sites (4 sheets)						→		**31**

Autumn 1991 media plan

	9th Sep	23rd Sep	30th Sep	7th Oct	4th Nov	11th Nov							Total no of insertions
Women's weeklies													
Woman's Weekly					●								1
Woman			●										1
Domestic monthlies													
Family Circle				●									1
Living	●			●		●							3
Prima		●											1
Woman & Home	●			●		●							3
Good Housekeeping				●									1
													11

THE EVIDENCE OF AN ADVERTISING EFFECT

Given the financial constraints, the expenditure on any data capture was very limited. For this reason we tried to be as ingenious as possible with the restricted funds available.

Not only was research limited but we were also constrained in that all sales data on individual styles had to be counted manually. The cost (in time and money) of such an operation severely limited the number of variables that one could look at. In addition these sales data were only available from K Shoe Shops.

The evidence we have falls into two categories: evidence relating to advertising performance and evidence relating to sales effect. We will start with advertising performance.

ADVERTISING AWARENESS

Our advertising was noticed. During 1991 we conducted seven research 'dipsticks' in the form of street interviews among women claiming to read the publications in which we advertised. We asked respondents to pick from a prompt card the brands of shoes/shoe shops they had seen advertised recently.

TABLE 1: PROMPTED ADVERTISING AWARENESS
(Base: Regular readers of publications advertised in)

	Spring				Autumn	
Pre			Post	Pre		Post
1	2	3	4	5	6	7
Mar	Apr	May	Jun	Aug	Oct	Dec
Sample size:						
(153)	(151)	(155)	(168)	(174)	(157)	(148)
%	%	%	%	%	%	%
7	14	12	11	17	18	14
	Advertising Activity				Advertising Activity	

One can see that following our advertising in the spring, prompted advertising awareness rose significantly. The memorability of the advertising is reinforced by the fact that levels remained high, even after the break in advertising over the summer (ie between stages four and five).

When prompted with the advertisement itself, levels were obviously higher, but followed a similar pattern. Although we see a drop over the summer, it by no means falls to the pre-advertising level of stage 1.

TABLE 2: ADVERTISING RECOGNITION
(Base: Regular readers of publications advertised in)

	Spring				Autumn	
Pre			Post	Pre		Post
1	2	3	4	5	6	7
Mar	Apr	May	Jun	Aug	Oct	Dec
Sample size:						
(153)	(151)	(155)	(168)	(174)	(157)	(148)
%	%	%	%	%	%	%
5	21	23	36	14	19	16
	Advertising Activity				Advertising Activity	

The figures demonstrate that our advertising was gaining awareness – an essential first step – but was it motivating?

WHAT THE PEOPLE WHO BOUGHT THE SHOES SAID

The research budget was extremely limited so we looked for an inexpensive way of getting some feed-back from those women who were buying washable trainers. We devised a small card questionnaire which was put into the washable trainers' shoe boxes at point of purchase. This questionnaire offered a monthly draw with a prize as an incentive for returning the card to K Shoes. Results were then hand counted.

Obviously one must apply some caveats here as the sample is self-selecting ie those interested enough to return the card; but we feel that they do give valuable additional insight.

TABLE 3: CUSTOMER RESPONSE CARDS

	Spring (758) %	Autumn (201) %
Where did you first see this shoe? Those saying 'an ad'	30	18
What prompted you to buy? Those saying 'an ad'	18	13
All claiming to have seen any K advertising	65	56
All claiming the ad seen showed washable trainers	42	32

Firstly an extremely high proportion of purchasers had seen some K advertising of which a very high proportion claimed to have seen an advertisement for the washable trainer.

Clearly in comparison to our street interview data, there is a much higher level of advertising awareness here. When one looks at this in the context of the advertising having achieved some 65% cover of ABC1 women aged 35+ in the spring and 44% in the autumn, these levels are extremely encouraging.

A number of our buyers specifically claimed to have first seen the washable trainer in an advertisement or even to have been prompted to buy the product from an advertisement.

We feel this is an indication that our advertising was motivating – particularly given people's reluctance to admit to being influenced by advertising – and reinforces our case that advertising had a direct influence on sales.

Certainly the single insertion in the *Daily Mail* which launched the washables campaign caused the K switchboard to be jammed all day by customers and traders alike.

So if our advertising is both noticed and motivating, what evidence do we have that sales followed?

SALES

Looking at sales of washable trainers through K Shoe Shops, one can see that there was an uplift in both spring and autumn that correlates with the timing of our advertising activity. Figure 1 clearly shows this.

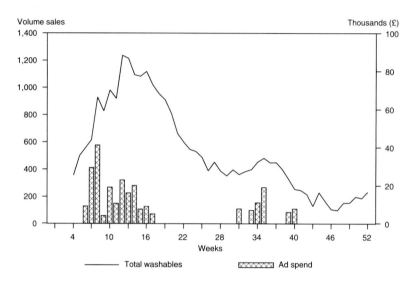

Figure 1. *Sales of washables through K Shoe Shops v ad spend*

The spring burst appears to have had a greater effect, even taking into account the larger media spend. This was not wholly unexpected, as indicated earlier, as K Shoes was aware that spring was likely to present a greater opportunity. The role of advertising in the autumn was to maintain distribution and to try to start to slowly overcome consumer conservatism concerning white shoes in the winter months.

QUANTIFYING THE EFFECT OF THE ADVERTISING

While Figure 1 suggests that there is a relationship between advertising and sales we recognised that it is possible that factors other than advertising caused the sales movements.

We wanted to isolate and quantify the sales effect of the advertising in terms of the extra sales that resulted from specific levels of advertising. We did this by hypothesising the potential 'polluting' factors, investigating them and either quantifying their influences or discounting them. A brief discussion of this process follows.

Distribution

Distribution through K Shoe Shops remained constant across 1991. Numbers of shops remained static. All shops stocked washable trainers and there were no out of stock problems. For the purposes of our analysis we can therefore discount distribution changes.

Price

The price of washable trainers rose by £2 during 1991 representing an increase of 6%. Overall there was a 2% rise in average footwear prices, taking into account competitive pricing, and a 4% rise in the Retail Price Index.

This fluctuation in real price makes it difficult to assess the influence of price and we therefore included it in our econometric analysis of the data. The findings of the analysis eventually discounted price as an influence.

Consumer Incomes

Consumers' real disposable income remained almost constant during 1991, as did consumer spending, and so can be ignored as an influence.

Fashion

K Shoes does not operate in the high fashion market. The washable trainer was no exception. It merely made an existing 'fashion' trend, ie trainers, accessible for mature women with a practical streak. We contend therefore that the fashion aspect of the product can be ignored as an influence.

Competitive New Product Launches

The only sort of competitive launch which could conceivably increase K sales was another washable trainer which might raise the saliency of the product benefit. There was no washable competitive launch and we therefore discounted the influence of competitive activity.

Seasonality

Assessing seasonality presented a difficult obstacle. A cursory glance at the washable trainer sales data suggests there may be a seasonal pattern. The total trainer market sales are seasonal with sales peaking in the summer and tailing off during the colder months. However, if one looks at the 35+ women's trainer market it has a flatter seasonal profile. To complicate things further, K Shoes felt its customers had their own seasonality profile. We needed to take seasonality into account. But how?

We knew that the K woman viewed trainers as 'white, casual shoes' and saw them as a largely spring/summer item. We therefore looked at sales of all (non-advertised) white casual K Shoes sold through K Shoe Shops as a proxy for the seasonality influence.

We have confidence in this proxy for three reasons. First, the knowledge of the K Shoes marketing staff suggests that it mirrors the seasonal demand for light, casual shoes. Secondly, it is data based on our target customers – with all their foibles – ie the K woman. Thirdly, it is data based on the same outlets as our washable trainer sales data – K Shoe Shops.

So sales of white casual K Shoes through K Shoe Shops were used to quantitatively account for seasonality in our econometric analysis.

A MODEL

Having looked at all the possible influences we concluded that the elements we needed to investigate were price, seasonality, sales and advertising spend.

It was our hypothesis that once we had taken seasonality into account and calculated a seasonally adjusted base sales level, the advertising would be seen to increase sales by a fixed percentage from this base level. If our hypothesis was correct, this percentage sales increase and indeed decay, would be the same for both bursts of advertising.

As can be seen from Figure 2, the model that we produced fitted the data very well and the diagnostic details of the model (see appendix) suggest that the quantification of the advertising effect is robust. We therefore feel confident in using this model to determine the sales, revenue and profit implications of the advertising.

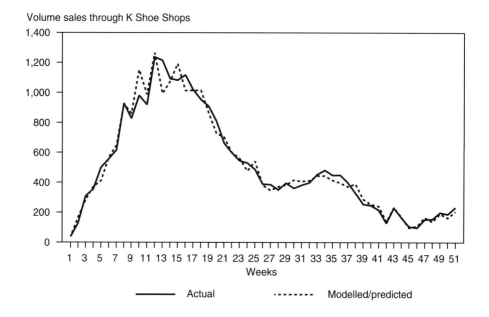

Figure 2. *Sales model: actual v model predicted*

The analysis finds that there was indeed an advertising effect in both the spring and the autumn.

Although the sales effect looked greater in spring, when seasonality was taken into account, the sales effect generated was identical for both bursts of advertising.

Both bursts had identical percentage increases in sales per percentage increased in coverage of our target audience and identical decay rates. Our hypotheses were correct therefore and this gives us considerable confidence that we have correctly isolated the effect of the advertising. Figure 3 shows what the model predicts sales would have been in the absence of advertising.

Volume sales through K Shoe Shops

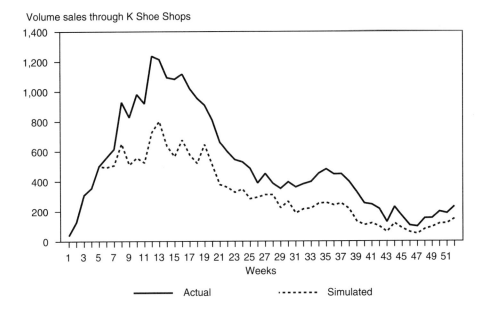

Figure 3. *Sales model: simulation without advertising*

Looking at the data another way, Figure 4 shows the weekly effect of the advertising, in terms of additional sales.

Volume sales through K Shoe Shops

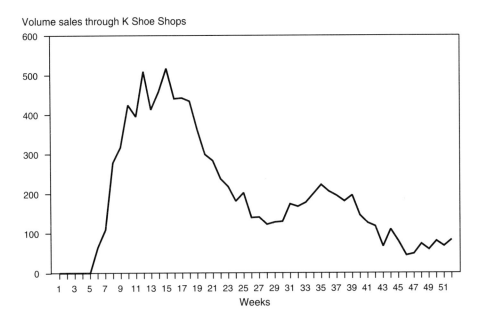

Figure 4. *Sales model: sales caused by advertising*

SALES OUTSIDE K SHOE SHOPS

So far we have only looked at sales through K Shoe Shops. We believe there was also an advertising effect in the independent retailers.

As has been said, we have no 'sales out' data except for K Shoe Shops. However, we do have a guide, albeit partial, to the pattern of sales outside of K Shoe Shops. It is possible to look at washable trainer sales on an ex-factory basis but two caveats need to be applied to these data. Firstly they record only about 50% of actual washable trainer sales as they exclude the initial options placed by stores at the beginning of each season. The ex-factory data are therefore measures of re-ordering once the initial options have been taken up and sold. Secondly, ex-factory sales obviously precede any sales out of the shops.

Having highlighted its flaws, we still believe ex-factory data are valid in examining the *pattern* of sales in comparison with those through K Shoe Shops.

Figure 5 shows ex-factory sales (including those through K Shoe Shops) compared with consumer sales through K Shoe Shops.

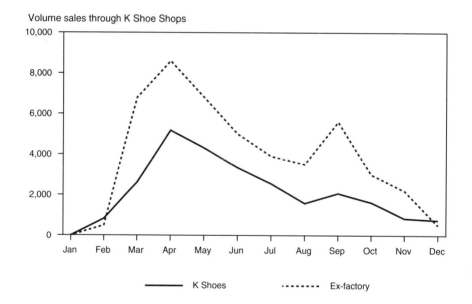

Figure 5. *Ex-factory sales v K Shoe shop sales*

One can clearly see that the total market pattern mirrors that of sales through K Shoe Shops. There are peaks in sales in spring and autumn, albeit greater in spring.

This strongly suggests that a similar advertising effect to that shown through K Shoe Shops was working in the independent retailers.

DID THE ADVERTISING PAY FOR ITSELF?

Given that the econometric analysis provided a model that fits the sales data extremely well, is stable, consistent across the year and takes seasonality into account we can have considerable confidence in its accuracy. The stability of the analysis allowed us to undertake further work to *quantify* the effect of the advertising.

Using the econometric analysis it is possible to estimate the number of pairs of washable trainers sold over and above what could have been expected without advertising.

In total we generated 10,000 extra sales of K washable trainers through K Shoe Shops, representing a 61% increase over expected sales across the year. If the same pattern occurred in independents this would represent 46,730 extra sales. Thus, 56,730 extra pairs in total. In order for the advertising spend of £268,000 to be covered we would need therefore an average marginal contribution of £4.72.

Although for reasons of confidentiality we cannot divulge the exact level of contribution, we can state that the average is considerably greater than £4.72.

We recognise that it could readily be argued that the effect of advertising would be less in independent retailers as they would have many priorities other than K. Yet, even if one assumes *half* the effect in independent retailers (ie 30%), the advertising more than covered its cost.

(We believe a 30% increase to be extremely conservative as K stockists tend to be similar in nature and customer profile to K Shoe Shops.)

IN SUMMARY

— Against a difficult market background, K Shoes decided to launch washable trainers – a new product, in a new market for K – aimed at existing K customers.

— The key to the advertising strategy was understanding the K woman. We recognised the need for a direct, simple communication of the product benefit – washable leather.

— The advertising itself reassured on look whilst forcefully demonstrating the product benefit.

— Media selection and buying was key to maximising the efficiency of the budget. Qualitative research helped us pinpoint the optimum locations for our advertising.

— Our advertising was noticed. Advertising awareness increased encouragingly given the modest spend.

— There was evidence that the advertising was motivating from research among women who had bought K washable trainers.

— Sales of washable trainers increased around the time of our advertising activity. This sales increase could be seen in K Shoe Shops and independent retailers.

— Econometric analysis showed identical patterns of lift and decay for both bursts of advertising.

— The analysis suggested the advertising had generated some 10,000 extra sales through K Shoe Shops.

— Even if one were to assume a considerably lower level of effect in independents, the advertising more than paid for itself.

THE FUTURE

As a result of the success of the launch of women's washable leather trainers in 1991, K Shoes has expanded its range for 1992 and now has six women's styles, two men's styles and three styles for children (including styles for boys).

TECHNICAL APPENDIX

This appendix outlines the statistical quantification of the effect of advertising on K Shoes washable trainers' sales via K Shoes Shops. Full technical detail is available in the original paper kept with the IPA.

Based on *a priori* reasoning and evidence discussed elsewhere it can be shown that:

1. Distribution, consumer incomes and prices could be ignored.
2. Fashion effects and the structure of the market could be ignored.
3. Seasonality could be quantified.
    Against this background it was hypothesised that:
4. As +1 cover builds, +2, +3 etc builds. Advertising would increase sales more proportionally as coverage built.
5. Advertising would increase sales by some percentage from the non-advertised base and the effect would decay geometrically.
6. Both bursts per unit of cover would show identical sales increases and decay profiles.

The above hypothesis can be encapsulated in the following model:

$$Ln(V) = a + b*Ln(S) + c*(A) + d*(E)$$

Ln = log base e transformed, V = volume sales, S = seasonality, A = advertising measured in terms of +1 cover and decayed through time, ie $A(t) = C(t) + f*C(t-1) + f^2*C(t-2) + + + f^i*C(t-i)$ where C = +1 cover, E = estimated season extension, f = retention rate.

This model was tested against the 1991 sales data (51 weekly data points), using ordinary least squares. The parameters of the model and validation diagnostics were:

Variable	Parameter	t-ratio
a (constant term)	1.480	13.4
S (seaonality)	0.716	46.1
A (advertising)	0.008789	12.0
E (extension)	0.282	9.1

$R^2 = 0.979$, $\overline{R}^2 = 0.978$, ESE = 0.102, DWS = 1.71

Split sample varince ratio – f-test 1.46. Parameter stability split sample Chow f-test 2.00. Parameter stability & equal variance – alternative Chow f-test 1.57.

Higher order autocorrelation is rejected on the basis of numerous orders of LM & Q statistics.

The advertising has two quantitative aspects. The decay (10% per 4 weeks) and the sales uplift for a given level of advertising 'stock'.

The 'uplift' parameter can be interpreted as a percentage increase in sales generated for a given level of cover. For example at 50% cover the sales are increased by about 55% (ie $(\exp(0.008789 \times 50) - 1) \times 100 = 55\%$). Both bursts have identical percentage 'uplift' per unit of cover, and identical decay rates (see split sample Chow test).

A total increase in sales of 10,062 units, a 61% annual increase, is directly attributable to the advertising.

16

The International Fund for Animal Welfare –
How a Single Advertisement Saved 500,000 Lives

INTRODUCTION

This paper examines the role that advertising played in averting a bloodbath; the unjustifiable killing of hundreds of thousands of seals off the shores of Canada.

It explains how a campaign conceived in a very short space of time, with a very small budget, caused a government to effect a very big policy U-turn, saving the seals.

The campaign was created in London to address an international problem.

THE CLUB IS RAISED

In February 1992 the Canadian representatives of the 'International Fund for Animal Welfare' (IFAW) became very concerned over their government's intention to allow widespread seal hunting to start again. Widespread culling had ended in 1983 after sustained campaigns by IFAW and Greenpeace, though the government allowed a low level of culling each year (in 1991, 50,000 pelts were taken). The seals were being blamed for the dwindling cod stocks in the North Atlantic waters around Canada and the government intended to permit a cull of roughly 500,000 to address the problem.

But the seals were not to blame.

IFAW's Canadian supporters needed help. They contacted their head office in the UK for advice on how to take on the Canadian government. The UK operation was in the middle of stirring up public debate about another animal welfare issue, fox-hunting in the UK. It was felt that its experience and resources needed to be mobilised to address the Canadian situation.

IFAW is, as its name suggests, an organisation committed to preventing cruelty to animals wherever it occurs in the world. Founded in 1969, it became best known for helping to stop the infamous Canadian whitecoat seal hunt in 1983 after a prolonged battle. IFAW is funded entirely from voluntary donations.

IFAW UK is the only office in the organisation to retain an advertising agency; BBH in London. Although it was not initially clear that advertising could assist with the seal cull problem, IFAW UK asked its agency to join the think tank on what action could be taken.

A FISHY PROBLEM

'Canada is set to re-open the hunt for harp seals' (headline in *International Herald Tribune*, February 26, 1992)

'The cry goes up for a renewed seal cull' (headline in Canada's *Globe & Mail*, February 29, 1992)

Canada was in the middle of a cod crisis. Its $700 million a year cod industry, employing 31,000 people, was insisting on drastic measures to save dwindling cod stocks in the North Atlantic (780,000 tonnes of spawning cod down from 1.1 million in 1991).

The fishing industry has considerable economic and political clout; it contributes greatly to Canada's exports and has a large constituency of voters that cannot be ignored. The Fisheries Minister, John Crosbie (whose own family made its fortune through seal hunting), was determined not to lose the support of the industry he represented.

The cod problem had been evident for several years. In 1990, Canadian government scientists had warned of the impending crisis, publicly announcing that:

'failure to take appropriate steps to reduce current levels of fishing mortality will most probably lead to a significant continuing decline in the spawning population' (Harris Report on Northern Cod Stocks, 1990)

The problem was quite simple; over-fishing. The recommendation in the Harris Report was for substantial cuts in cod fishing quotas in 1990 and 1991. The Canadian government chose not to implement these recommendations.

Instead it waited until cod stocks had reached crisis levels, and in February 1992 it singled out three culprits; domestic trawlers, foreign fishing vessels, and the harp seals. In respect of the former, fishing quotas for 1992 were slashed by 35% on February 24th.

Foreign fishing vessels were less easy to control – their catches were mainly outside Canada's 200-mile exclusion zone. Diplomacy was the government's first course of action, but there was talk of introducing extensive fish quota reductions outside the 200-mile limit and of enforcing the reduced quota by use of gunboats if necessary. That, at least acknowledged the real problem.

As for the third of the accused, the harp seals, two misinformed statements by the Canadian Fisheries Minister gave IFAW grave concern; firstly, that the seal population had risen from 2 million in 1985 to 3.5 million in 1992, and secondly, that this expanding herd was responsible for consuming vast quantities of cod.

On February 29th, the Fisheries Minister, John Crosbie, was quoted in the Canadian press as saying 'In my recent discussions with representatives of the fishing industry they have been unanimous in their advice that measures should now be taken toward controlling seal populations. Acting on this advice, the federal government *will* initiate measures to encourage harvesting of seals. Amongst other steps, we will be seeking to assist groups such as the Canadian Sealers Association in developing seal products and markets for these products. The issues for discussion with the industry are *how* to do this, *not whether* to do this. On that issue, the fishing industry has made its position clear'.

The government had clearly made up its mind on its course of action. It needed to be seen to be taking action; culling seals was an easy way to achieve this and could be implemented quickly for short-term political gain. John Crosbie announced that 510,000 harp seals would have to be killed each year to control the growing population, and a press release on February 29th from the Fisheries Ministry announced that sealing licences would be made available immediately to registered commercial fishermen and that new entrants would work under the supervision of experienced sealers.

Equally alarming for IFAW was the media reaction. The fishing crisis was big news, but although the media carried reports on the proposed cull, editorial opposition to it was virtually non-existent. The press, largely pro-government, appeared in favour of any action to save the Canadian fishing industry and not one newspaper investigated possible flaws in the Minister's argument. The conspiracy of silence was not breached even by a barrage of press releases by IFAW and Greenpeace asserting that seals were not to blame for eating stocks of cod.

IFAW'S BAIT

IFAW was in a frustrating position. In front of it was evidence from the Royal Commission for Seals and Sealing showing that in a sample of 555 harp seal stomachs *only four* contained cod (less than 1%). Not only do they rarely eat cod, but seals are migratory for half the year, meaning that for 6 months their diet is consumed *outside the boundaries* of the Canadian fisheries in the Northwest Atlantic. So, of the little cod that seals do eat, for only six months are they competing for it with Canadian fishermen.

The government's assertion that seal populations had 'exploded' was also disputed by IFAW – estimates of the population size ranged from 1.4 to 4.2 million, but in the absence of any evidence, IFAW believed it was dangerous to assume it had 'exploded'. It was quite possible that the population had self-stabilised.

These facts had already been published and scientists had made their views clear. In February 1991, scientists from the Department of Fisheries and Oceans (Mr Crosbie's Ministry!) had said:

'At present there is little reason to believe that the harp seal is having a serious impact on the cod stock' and as late as January 1992 they were to write:

'... interactions between seals and fisheries are complex and often misunderstood... The truth is we do not know what the effects of a change in seal numbers would have on commercial fisheries.' (I.H.Ni, W.D. Bowden and D.G. McKinnon)

These startling facts were simply being ignored by those that mattered. They had to be made aware of them.

SELECTING THE RIGHT TACKLE

IFAW's head office in the UK and BBH isolated various options to combat the proposed cull. These were:

1. Continued press-relations in Canada.
2. Political lobbying in the Canadian Parliament.
3. Political lobbying in the US and European Parliaments in the hope of persuading the outside world to boycott Canada's fish products or even Canada as a tourist destination.
4. A consumer advertising campaign in the US and Europe to encourage a boycott of Canadian produce.
5. A consumer advertising campaign in Canada to stop the cull.

The first two were already being pursued, but to little effect. As we have seen they were not working; the Minister was in favour of the cull; the media was behind the Minister.

IFAW's key problem was time. The government had made it clear that the issue was not 'if' but 'when' and 'how'. IFAW had to create an immediate impact, ruling out options 3 and 4. Although lobbying and awareness generation outside Canada might well have had an eventual effect – time was not on IFAW's side. On a practical level, the cost of effectively advertising to encourage a consumer boycott of Canadian fish produce across the US and Europe was beyond IFAW's means.

The only route deemed likely to be effective enough, quickly enough, was option 5. There were strong reasons why advertising was the right choice. 'Issue' advertising is extremely rare in Canada. As Howard Hirschorn, Advertising Research Manager at the *Toronto Globe and Mail* (Canada's only national newspaper) said:

'Advocacy advertising, as we call it, has occasionally been used in a very limited way, usually small spaces. I can vaguely remember one or two examples from human rights groups, but not for some years now.'

Advertising had the potential to ensure that the issue could not be ignored.

Additionally, its speed of communication and its ability to reach a variety of audiences simultaneously would be extremely valuable. Those key audiences divided into two broad groups; 'direct influencers' and 'indirect influencers'.

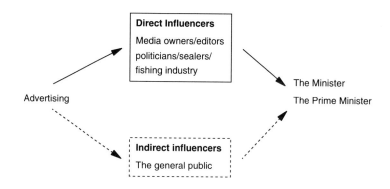

If swayed, the 'direct influencers' could put real pressure on the government, and in turn the government would feel additional pressure if it believed the public was concerned.

THE ADVERTISING TASK

The principal role of advertising was to increase debate about the issue by putting the record straight. It needed to create more media coverage of the seals' point of view and more opportunities for IFAW representatives to put the facts into the public domain. Such action would, at least, increase pressure on the government to review its decision. As Brian Davies, founder of IFAW said on March 9th:

> 'In recent weeks we have grown frustrated that time and again people have trotted out the old lies that seals are responsible for the cod crisis so the hunt should be expanded. We are at the eleventh hour and so drastic action is needed. The government continues to blame seals and apparently forgets its own statistics. We hope that our advertising campaign will make people sit up and take notice.'

THE ADVERTISING IDEA

On March 5th IFAW presented BBH with a great deal of scientific evidence supporting the seals' case. The most difficult decision was what to use?

The obvious route for issue advertising (often witnessed in the UK) was that of shock tactics; using disturbing images to arrest attention and change opinion. (A man clubbing a seal would have been an obvious image.)

Given the frequent use of such images in relation to anti-sealing campaigns in the past, a deliberate decision was made to avoid this now clichéd approach. Not only did we want to avoid clichés, we were very concerned to avoid any backlash through being accused of sensationalising the issue. The ensuing media debate might then have been about the 'disgraceful' use of shocking pictures instead of the content of the message.

Instead, wouldn't humour allied to the irrefutable evidence create a more potent creative idea? The need to involve as many people, as easily as possible, in order to maximise interest, lent itself to humour. It could make the issue more accessible and memorable and by presenting the evidence in this way we felt would make the government look more ridiculous, increasing their discomfort. It was also important, we felt, to give the seals a voice, something they had so far been denied. A clubbed seal, although arousing sympathy, is very much just an object. If somehow we could turn the seals into the subject of the advertisement and imbue them with human characteristics, not only would it be more distinctive, it would hopefully arouse more direct sympathy.

Press was the chosen medium, as advertising of a political nature is banned in broadcast media in Canada. But this necessity gave us additional benefits. The advertising could be produced and placed quickly and its very presence in those titles we wished to influence could act as a strong catalyst to getting press coverage for IFAW's side of the argument.

THE ADVERTISING EXECUTION

One fact was selected from all the scientific evidence; that less than 1% of a seal's diet is cod. Its simplicity was its advertising strength. We chose to use double-page spreads, unprecedented for issue advertising, to try and make sure the message could not be missed.

The 2-page advertisement was briefed, written, produced and approved in 48 hours. The space was booked from the UK and the artwork flown over to Canada on the weekend of 7th/8th March. It appeared in two newspapers on Tuesday March 10th and one more on Wednesday 11th, at a low media spend of just £30,349.

Of the three papers that carried the ad, two, *Halifax Chronicle & Herald* and *St John's Evening Telegram*, were selected because they covered the main fishing ports threatening to resume seal culling and were widely read by the fishing industry. The third paper, the *Toronto Globe & Mail*, is the leading business paper in Canada and the only national. It was chosen because of its readership among the opinion formers and general public right across the country.

MEDIA SCHEDULE

Date	Title	Circulation	Size	Cost
10/3/92	Toronto Globe & Mail	305,723	DPS	£22,250
10/3/92	Halifax Chronicle & Herald	150,000	DPS	£4,628
11/3/92	St John's Evening Telegram	39,754	DPS	£3,471
			Total cost	£30,349

Who had cod for dinner?

There is a crisis in the East coast northern cod fishery, and the reason isn't seals, it's overfishing.

The fact is, harp seals rarely eat cod. Less than 1% of the harp seal's diet is cod.

But although the government has recently cut quotas for northern cod, the Fisheries Minister and many fishermen seem reluctant to accept responsibility for the current situation.

They are quick to blame others – including seals.

However, the Royal Commission on Seals and Sealing reported that, in a sample of 555 harp seal stomachs which contained food, only 4 stomachs (0.7%) contained cod.

Harp seals are migratory and only overlap with the northern cod stock for a few months of the year. More than half of their annual diet is consumed outside traditional Canadian fisheries in the Northwest Atlantic.

Nor do harp seals have the voracious appetites for which they are usually credited. For their size, they eat the same amount of food as other mammals, including humans.

Despite this evidence, there have, in recent weeks, been calls for an increased seal hunt to reduce the size of the harp seal population.

You may be surprised to learn that Canada still has the largest seal hunt in the world totalling over 60,000 last year.

But some in the fishing community are not satisfied with that.

They claim that the Canadian harp seal population has 'exploded' since the European community banned the importation of pelts from whitecoat harp seal pups and since Canada banned the large-vessel commercial hunt for whitecoats.

However, the Government's own results indicate that pup production did not increase markedly between 1978 and 1990.

They also claim that the seal population may have increased from 2.0 to 3.3 million animals since 1983. There is no data to support this assumption.

Even if it were true, there's no evidence to suggest that seal populations have any effect on fishermen's catches.

Government scientists, and many others, have admitted for years that they do not know what the effect of reducing the number of harp seals would have on fishery yields.

In February 1991, I.H. Ni, W.D. Bowen and D.G. McKinnon, of the Department of Fisheries and Oceans, said:

"…at present there is little reason to believe that the harp seal is having a serious impact on the (northern) cod stock…"

Most recently, Dr. W.D. Bowen of the Department of Fisheries and Oceans, wrote, in January 1992, that, "…interactions between seals and fisheries are complex and often misunderstood. … The truth is we do not know what the effects of a change in seal numbers would have on commercial fisheries".

Fishermens' anecdotes aside, there is not one documented case, anywhere in the world, where it has been demonstrated that seals are competing with commercial fisheries for common prey species.

Even National Sea Products

WHAT HAPPENED?

The campaign immediately created extraordinary interest, receiving widespread news coverage; it featured in 38 newspaper articles, and 30 radio and TV programmes that IFAW monitored (there may have been more).

Most importantly, the content of the media coverage represented a marked change from the previous pro-government stance of complicity in seal-culling. Most articles at last began to question whether seals were to blame and gave exposure to all the points made in IFAW's advertisement. Editorial in the pro-government press suddenly sat up, took notice and urged the government to move carefully.

On March 12th in an editorial headed 'Call it off John!', the *Evening Telegram* exclaimed:

'... If Ottawa really wants to expand the seal hunt by a magnitude of six to eight times, something that, in the circumstances, seems as far-fetched as it does foolhardy, it will have to do so over the substantial financial resources to oppose it of IFAW...A new statement from Mr Crosbie is needed and at once: He needs to come out and declare that there will be no enlargement of the current minimal landsmen harvest until large-scale destruction of northern cod or their food source is substantiated absolutely.'

On the same day, the *Halifax Chronicle & Herald* ran a leading editorial piece entitled 'Sealed Fate'. It began:

'Canada should think long and hard before authorising an expanded seal hunt which could trigger a ban on fish products in Europe. The risk may not be worth the benefits; given the advertising campaign against seal hunting organised by IFAW. As frustrating as the campaign is – informed by half truths... it is proving effective.'

(Not half-truths in our eyes, of course. The whole truth.)

It continued...

'Canada should move cautiously then. A first step would be the compilation of credible evidence on whether seals really are seriously depleting groundfish stocks. And even if they are, Canada must be wary about the unfair effects of the anti-sealing campaign on its international markets and image.'

Even those Newfoundland titles strong in their resentment of IFAW like *The Evening Patriot*, could not help acknowledging that they were winning the argument. In an editorial titled 'Vegetarian Seals' the following comment appeared:

'It is correct that no large scale killing of seals should take place in an effort to transfer blame to a species that has only public opinion to defend it. It is exceedingly manipulative to lend seals the human ability of speech to stir warm and cuddly thoughts about the doe-eyed seal pups ... '

The desired debate was happening. The seals' voice had been heard, the true facts were being aired, and even if some newspapers were disputing the facts and criticising our methods, their resentful coverage of the story was elevating it right to the top of the political agenda.

The reaction was immediate; a government U-turn on their imminent cull policy which had been announced 18 days earlier. On March 12th, the day after the advertising campaign ended, John Crosbie, the Fisheries Minister, announced that he was 'appalled' at the advertisements. He stressed that *no* decision had been taken on resuming the seal hunt and he didn't appreciate IFAW's attempt at a pre-emptive strike.

A real change in tune.

He shifted the blame for the cod crisis to the real culprits, humans, stating:

'Fish are animals and the International Fund for Animal Welfare should be taking out a 2-page ad in the European newspapers in Brussels and Spain and Portugal explaining what's happening to Northern Cod as a result of those countries overfishing actions.'

He was also quoted as saying:

'It's a disgrace that the International Fund for Animal Welfare will run a seal advertisement now when nothing new has happened ... No one has suggested we go back to the white coat hunt of young seals for the simple reason that opportunists like the IFAW would seize on that to start another campaign to make money for themselves from people who are impressed by the kind of images they portray.'

'In fact there has been nothing new done with respect to sealing this year. We've simply said, it's a problem and we have to assess it.'

Reassuringly for the seals he called for more scientific data on their diet.

Newfoundland's Fisheries Minister, Walter Carter, shared Crosbie's anger at the campaign but concluded with exactly the response IFAW had hoped for. He contested the facts contained in the advertisement and was widely reported as saying:

'I can only say the author of the article, the people they're quoting and the seals are all a bunch of damn liars.'

Would the government therefore match IFAW's campaign? Carter replied:

'No, but later this month the provincial government will launch a nationwide campaign against foreign overfishing.'

He also stated that:

'worldwide emotionalism over the seals will obscure a much larger problem – that cod stocks have been routinely overfished by foreign vessels and mismanaged by Ottawa.'

Even the Prime Minister, who had hitherto kept out of the debate, though tacitly supported Crosbie, joined in, aware that the issue was growing in importance. He tried to shift the spotlight away from the seals, repeating calls for action to curb foreign overfishing. As recently as March 4th he had said he had no intention of stopping foreign overfishing, reportedly through fear of jeopardising trade relations with European countries.

Astonishingly the Canadian Sealers' Association, who would be responsible for carrying out the proposed cull, announced that they did not wish to be involved:

'We're opposed to a cull. There's no economic benefit and no justification for it.' (Art Pearce, executive of the Association)

On February 24th the Fisheries Minister had made it clear that a cull was imminent and irreversible. Within 48 hours of the advertising appearing it was not even being contemplated.

IFAW's representatives were suddenly in demand and were interviewed extensively during the rest of the week, so much in fact that within three days of the first ads appearing IFAW's UK public relations company, The Jenkins Group, (who had been flown out from the UK) deliberately wound down their efforts and stopped interviews with the media, for fear of generating a backlash. Nick Jenkins of the Jenkins Group said:

'A general decision was taken with Brian Davies that as the media attention had achieved as much as we could hope, that IFAW would now wind down its active PR approach in respect of press, radio and TV in Newfoundland and Nova Scotia. The concern being that this could provide a platform for the sealers and that IFAW had made its point and could gain only limited value from such continued publicity.'

A HAPPY ENDING

Prior to the advertising, the media were reporting the issue from a pro-fishing, pro-government stance; the seals' point of view was simply not being heard, despite the wealth of supporting evidence. The advertising gave the seals' point of view, caused debate, created millions of dollars of press coverage from a tiny budget of £30,000 and made the government think again. At least 500,000 seals were saved as a result.

The advertising effected change. Even politicians admitted that. Patrick Bowyer, MP for Ontario (an opposition MP, sympathetic to IFAW), explained:

'Had that advertisement not run, I can't conceive that the government would have changed its mind. It was a very clever, witty and bold statement by IFAW that was talked about across Canada right up to the highest levels. It worked because it was an original and unprecedented means of criticising government policy, but also because of the content of the ad. By giving seals the power of speech you struck a note of sympathy amongst the public who, in general, love the seals, and by the public I include members of the government who of course aren't without emotions themselves.'

Truly an example of the pen being mightier than the sword.

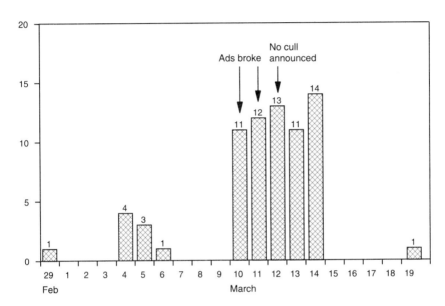

Number of times IFAW's case mentioned in press, radio and TV

CHRONOLOGY OF EVENTS

February 29th	Fisheries Minister announces proposed seal cull. Canadian IFAW supporters contact UK headquarters.
March 5th	BBH receive scientific data. Brief prepared. Advertisement written and approved by IFAW.
March 6th	Space booked. Artwork prepared and approved by IFAW.
March 7th	Artwork flown to Canada.
March 9th	Artwork delivered to newspapers. Press releases on the advertisement sent to Canada's media.
March 10th	First two insertions appear.
March 11th	Third insertion appears.
March 12th	Fisheries Minister announces 'no cull'.
March 13th	PR company winds down activities.

17

Marketing 'Desperation': The Launch of Limelite

INTRODUCTION

This case study shows how advertising can create a dynamic and profitable category from what had been a small specialist cleaning sector. A sector that attracted little consumer interest, and so generated minimal revenues for manufacturers and retailers alike.

So, this paper will demonstrate:

1. That the limescale removal market existed prior to the advertising launch of Limelite, but was small, and experiencing very limited growth.
2. That the advertising launch of Limelite single-handedly resulted in:
   — a significant growth in the market
   — and a dramatic increase in the hard surface limescale removal sector.
3. That the advertising established Limelite as the clear leader in limescale removal; and began the process of brand building.

MARKET BACKGROUND

The Limescale Problem

The limescale problem is restricted to those areas of the country that receive a supply of hard water.

The effects of limescale vary according to location in the home, in toilets, for instance, limescale will form chalky deposits under the rim of the bowl and around the water line.

Moreover, limescale will build up on electrical elements, making appliances less effective, more costly to run, and reducing their life.

However, the locations that concern Limelite are general household surfaces, where limescale manifests itself as:

— chalky deposits/crusts around taps, on sinks, on tiles, on showerheads.
— staining and dulling on work tops and other surfaces where water lies.

Note, as Table 1 illustrates, limescale predominantly affects southern England.

312

TABLE 1:   UK HOUSEHOLDS 1989 BY WATER COMPOSITION, 1989

TV regions	% population	Total households	% soft water	% medium hard water	% hard water	% total hard water	No of homes total hard
London	24	5,239,200	4	9	87	96	5,029,632
Manchester	14	3,056,200	85	13	2	15	458,430
Birmingham	14	3,056,200	28	47	25	72	2,200,464
Leeds	10	2,183,000	60	27	13	40	873,200
Wales & West	9	1,964,700	56	14	30	44	864,468
Scotland	8	1,746,400	99	1	0	1	17,464
Southern	6	1,309,800	9	36	55	91	1,191,918
Tyne Tees	5	1,091,500	15	49	36	85	927,775
Anglia	4	873,200	1	24	75	99	864,468
Westward	3	654,900	74	17	9	26	170,274
Border	1	218,300	97	2	1	3	6,549
Total	100	21,830,000	40	21	37	58	12,604,642

THE MARKET

In spite of the number of homes that are clearly affected by hard water, and hence limescale, the market that existed prior to the launch of Limelite was small.

Unfortunately, the available data on the marketplace at this time is limited. However, the key brands were Oz, Scaleaway and various own label products. Limelite had listings in the multiples from September 1990 and was very much a minor brand in the period prior to the advertising launch. Table 2 shows the composition of the market prior to the launch of Limelite's advertising.

TABLE 2:   BRAND SHARE IN THE TOTAL LIMESCALE REMOVAL MARKET

	Volume	Value
Limelite	3.8	4.4
Own label	8.3	11.9
Scaleaway	22.3	23.3
Oz	51.6	47.9
Others	14.0	12.5

Source: NMRA 4 weeks ending March 2nd 1991

There had been attempts by Oz to generate extra consumer interest in the category through the media activity, but it had little effect on the overall market size.

TABLE 3:   OZ ADVERTISING EXPENDITURE 1989 TO 1991, £

	1989	1990	1991	Totals
TV	-	91,514	159,519	251,033
Press	83,820	2,552	6,700	93,072
Total	83,820	94,066	166,219	344,105

Source: Media Register

Although this activity is small scale, it should be noted that the Limelite launch media budget was only £145,000.

THE PRODUCT

As for the product itself, Limelite has an acid base formulation which starts to dissolve limescale on contact. It is thus a fast and effective way of removing limescale – both chalky deposits and hard water stain dulling – from household surfaces.

The formula has a distinctive fresh pine fragrance, it is packaged in a lime green bottle and is available in both a 250ml and 500ml format.

This combination of features allows Limelite to command a price premium in the context of the limescale removal market, at £1.39 for 250ml.

MARKET CHALLENGE

The limescale removal market existed but it was not experiencing significant growth, and moreover, the brand leader had attempted to generate extra volumes by media expenditure, (not dissimilar to that planned for Limelite), with minimal success.

In this context we must consider the central challenge which was to help Limelite grow the product category. Sufficient volumes could not be provided by stealing market share, rather they could only come from an expanding market.

In short, limescale removal had to become a mainstream rather than a specialist cleaning task, so the category had to be expanded by new users.

ADVERTISING STRATEGY

The agency conducted informal qualitative research amongst housewives, from this two facts became increasingly evident:

1. There was some irritation with limescale deposits and, to a lesser extent, hard water stains. But most housewives recognised that their neighbours suffered from the same problems, which in turn made limescale more acceptable.
2. In occassional circumstances, particularly where the housewife appeared especially houseproud, efforts to remove deposits from areas like taps would involve unorthodox means of removal: one housewife had tried a nail file and scissors!

The combination of these two factors led to the development of an advertising strategy.

Since this was clearly a relatively low interest product category, we had to put limescale removal on the housewives' agenda. It was imperative that the advertising should create an environment in which the removal of limescale made a positive statement about the housewife and the thoroughness of her cleaning routine.

In effect, this meant that we had to educate the end user that limescale was a *major* problem in the home, before we could introduce Limelite as the perfect solution.

At the same time there was a secondary issue, re the perceived efficacy of some of the product category. This fact, combined with the difficulties some housewives would have experienced in removing limescale deposits, meant that the strength and efficiency of Limelite had to be communicated.

ADVERTISING OBJECTIVES

To deliver this strategy, there were three objectives:

—   Firstly, and fundamentally, advertising needed to generate awareness of, and interest in, the limescale removal market.
—   Secondly, there was a need to communicate the efficacious credentials of Limelite as a limescale remover.
—   And thirdly, advertising should begin the process of brand building. It should strive to create a personality/identity that was capable of development and continuation into the future.

MEDIA STRATEGY

The medium chosen to deliver the strategy and objectives was television. It was also decided that to maximise test area discounts and to give the product good visibility with the trade, the London TV region would be utilised.

The test exercise was designed to provide solid usable results re advertising effectiveness.

The actual media strategy recognised the limitations of a low budget, and the difficulty of targeting houseproud housewives. This targeting issue was fundamental to the whole campaign. Obviously, houseproud housewives are not defined by BARB!

However, we considered that those housewives who spent most time at home were most likely to have a particularly vigorous cleaning routine. This belief is supported by BMRB TGI 1991 data, which shows that heavy users of household cleaners, disinfectants, lavatory cleaners, etc are most likely to be non-working or working part time housewives.

In addition, we recognised that as consumers had to be educated that limescale in the house is a problem, we needed good levels of frequency within a defined target audience, to ensure that our message really hit home.

So, the end result was a strategy that targeted housewives but utilised a heavy daytime off-peak schedule that delivered high levels of frequency versus our core target: the housewife who did not work full time.

CREATIVE SOLUTION

The creative solution that capitalised upon this media strategy, and fulfilled the advertising objectives is entitled 'Desperation'. It is a classic product demonstration commercial, in that it shows a problem which the *hero product* then solves. It successfully communicates the consumer proposition of:

'Limescale build up, and hard water stains are a *major* irritation. Limelite will solve this problem fast.'

However, 'Desperation' takes the product demonstration format and enhances it. Adding humour, interest and beginning the process of brand building.

The 30-second film and its 10-second cut down depict 'over the top' ways of removing limescale from a set of taps, methods that ranged from an electric sander to an oxyacetylene blow torch!

The success of this creative approach in establishing an empathetic link with the consumer is clear, and detailed later in the paper.

MEDIA PLAN

Test Campaign

The executional detail of the media plan that delivered the creative solution to our target audience is detailed below:

Commercial lengths:	30 and 10 seconds
Commercial rotation:	1 : 1
TVR target:	625
Contractor:	Thames solus
Timing:	20 February for four weeks
Target audience:	Housewives
Coverage:	1+ 79%
	4+ 45%
OTS:	7.3
Campaign length:	4 weeks
Strike rates:	Emphasis on 30 second commercial in first two weeks; 10 second commercial the last two weeks.

(SFX) Psycho type screeches

(FVO) No matter how hard you try, ordinary cleaning will never

get rid of limescale and hard water stains

But now there's Limelite from 1001

Limelite gets to work in seconds...

To bring back that good as new shine.

And regular use will make sure limescale never comes back.

So if you're still struggling with limescale...

(FVO) Limelite removes limescale fast.

Daypart was designed to target the heavy viewer, and in terms of programming there was a natural emphasis on the soaps.

Note that although the original plan targeted 625 housewife TVRs, the overwhelming success of the product meant that the commercial had to be taken off air. The net result was the achievement of 575 ratings.

Coupon Book

The timing of the coupon book coincided approximately with the airtime. Using a full page, full colour advert, a coupon with a face value of 20p was door-dropped to all homes in London, TVS and Anglia.

Television Roll Out

The success that Cussons believe the advertising had resulted in the use of television on a wider scale, as Figure 1 shows.

The plan for the new TV areas followed the formula established in the London test, although rating achievement levels were higher for each of the regions.

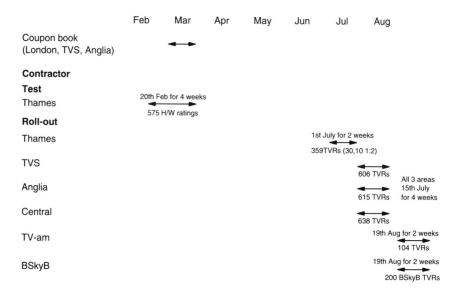

Figure 1.   *Media schematic 1991*
Note: All ratings are a mix of 30 and 10 second commercials rotated 1:1 unless stated

THE EFFECT OF ADVERTISING ON SALES

The marketing challenge, was to help grow the total market, and consequently, the primary advertising objective was to generate awareness of, and interest in, the limescale removal market.

Figure 2 demonstrates that, prior to advertising, sales were stagnant. In particular, the hard surface sector of the market was small, accounting for only around 15% of sales.

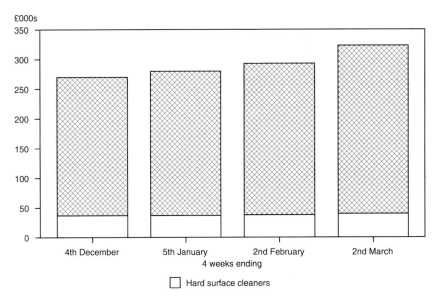

Figure 2.   *The limescale removal market – pre-advertising*
Source: NMRA

Growing the Limescale Removal Market

The Limelite advertising went on air week commencing February 20th, and had an immediate effect.

Figure 3 shows the limescale removal market sales from the launch of advertising onwards.

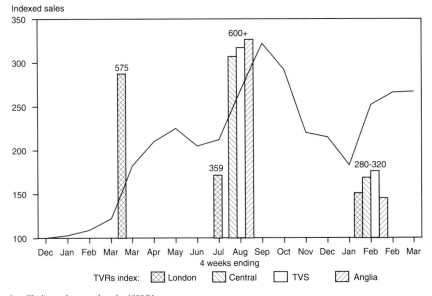

Figure 3.   *The limescale removal market 1990/91*
Source: NMRA

The limescale removal market took off such that between March and May, sales grew by 24%, and this was from advertising in the London region only.

Once the advertising was rolled out to Central, TVS and Anglia, sales rose even further. By September, sales were 222% higher than the previous December.

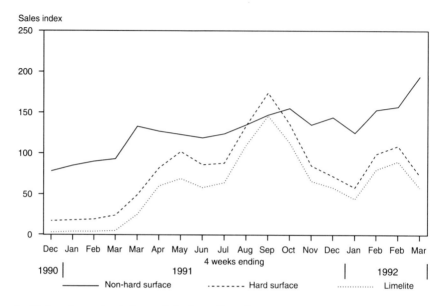

Figure 4.   *The limescale removal market by sector (indexed on total limescale remover market, December 1990)*
Source: NMRA

The Regional Picture

The evidence so far does not conclusively prove that advertising was the cause of Limelite's growth.

However, because the advertising was tested regionally, and then rolled out, it allows an accurate evaluation of its effectiveness.

Figures 5–8 compare the regions, using AGB Superpanel's recording of Limelite's sales. Sales have been weighted according to the number of households in the region, this then allows a direct and valid comparison between the regions.

The method for weighting has been to treat each region as if it were the size of London. Thus, the sales shown for TVS, Central and Anglia are their 'London equivalent sales'.

The effect of splitting Limelite's sales by region is striking.

According to AGB, sales in the London region, where advertising ran, went from next to nothing in January, to £300,000 in the four weeks to 14th April. At the same time, London equivalent sales in the TVS and Anglia regions, where only the coupon book was distributed, showed only a small rise in sales, each achieving a London equivalent of only £50,000.

Consequently, the advertising had boosted Limelite's sales by 500% over the coupon book's influence.

Sales in London then settled at a much higher level than in the other regions, and so advertising was rolled out.

The Roll Out

In July and August, the advertising ran in TVS, Anglia and Central.

Each region received around 600 TVRs over a five week period, slightly more than the original London test.

Sales in these regions performed significantly better than in London itself. London equivalent sales in TVS were 126% higher at the beginning of September than in London itself; the figure for Anglia was 77% higher.

These figures are all the more impressive given that London already had a high level of sales stemming from its earlier bursts of advertising.

In Central, a region that had received no support prior to July, London equivalent sales exceeded London by 3%.

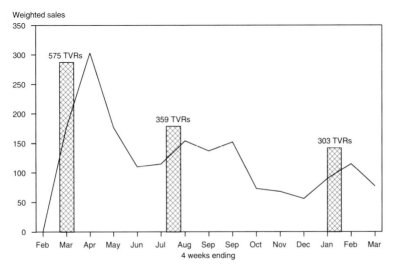

Figure 5.   *Weighted sales vs housewife TVRs by period – London*
Source: AGB Superpanel

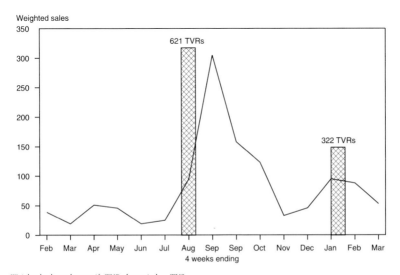

Figure 6.   *Weighted sales vs housewife TVRs by period – TVS*
Source: AGB Superpanel

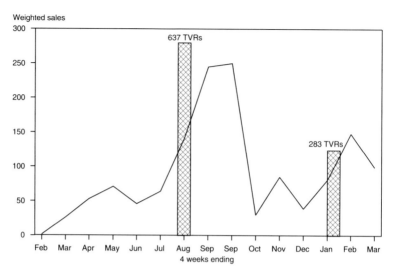

Figure 7.   *Weighted sales vs housewife TVRs by period – Anglia*
Source: AGB Superpanel

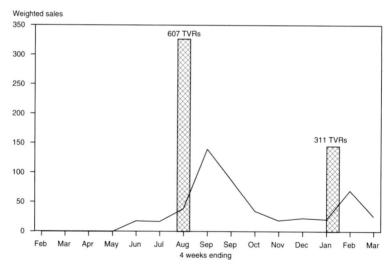

Figure 8.   *Weighted sales vs housewife TVRs by period – Central*
Source: AGB Superpanel

The Market After Limelite Advertising

The argument for advertising being the sole contributor to the increase in Limelite's and the market's sales, whilst not complete, is certainly persuasive.

Since Limelite's advertising first ran, the total limescale removal market's sales have increased by 144%*, the hard surface limescale removal sector's share of that market has risen to approximately 35%* as sales have risen by 320%, and sales of Limelite itself have risen dramatically to the point where Limelite, as Figure 9 shows, is now the clear brand leader with 37% of the market.

* AGB year-on-year figures, four weeks ending December 1991.

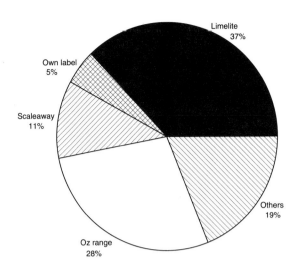

Figure 9.   *Brand slices of the limescale removal market*
Source: NMRA 16 weeks ending December 1991

Furthermore, the regional analysis showed that sales only grew where the advertising ran, something which occurred on two occasions.

Directly Linking the Advertising to Sales

When the decision was taken to promote Limelite using different methods in different regions, a quantitative study was commissioned by Cussons and undertaken by MAI.

The objectives of the tracking study were twofold:

— To monitor the levels of brand and advertising awareness of Limelite.
— To assess any difference between pre- and post-advertising and couponing.

Six waves were conducted. They were street interviews amongst 300 to 400 housewives per region, with TVS and Anglia counting as one region and London as the other.

The timing and structure of the waves were as follows:

Wave 1	Pre all advertising	13-15 February	Both regions
Wave 2	During London	6-8 March	London only
Wave 3	Post London	10-12 April	Both regions
Wave 4	Post London	25-27 June	Both regions
Wave 5	Post London	8-12 August	London only
Wave 6	Post Anglia	3-5 September	Anglia only

As Figure 10 shows, the awareness levels on a spontaneous and prompted basis, for both brand and advertising measures, increased significantly after the advertising ran in each region.

Figure 11 shows that, in a similar way to awareness levels, purchasing also rose significantly after the advertising had run.

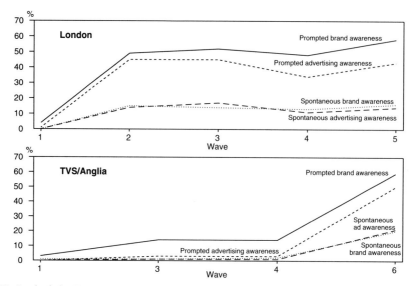

Figure 10. *Brand and advertising awareness*
Source: MAI Tracking study

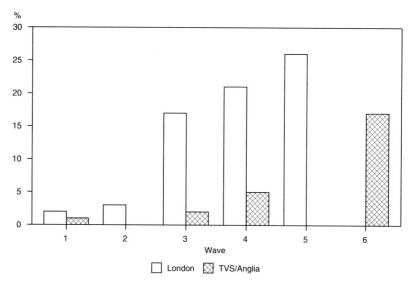

Figure 11. *Percentage of respondents ever bought*
Source: MAI Tracking Study
Base: All respondents

Also prior to the advertising, the number of purchasers was extremely low, at best 2% of the sample. Their main reason for purchase was that they either 'just picked up to try' or that they 'had a problem with limescale'.

Once the advertising had aired, not only did the number of purchasers increase, but also 'I saw the advertisement' became a major response as a main reason for buying. This far out-scored the 'use of money off coupons', and in London, immediately after the campaign had finished, remarkably, out-scored 'had a problem with limescale'!

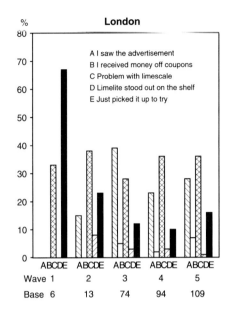
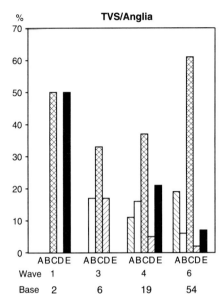

Figure 12. *Main reasons for buying – prompted*
Source: MAI Tracking study
Base: All purchasers

DISCOUNTING OTHER FACTORS

This section shows that other possible factors such as pricing, distribution, packaging and other promotions were consistent across the whole period in question.

That is to say, advertising has been the only fluctuating variable in the marketing equation.

Pricing

Price has remained consistent at £1.39 for a 250ml bottle since launch in September 1990.

This is a premium price for the limescale removal market, and as such, pricing cannot have been the driving force behind the sales growth.

Distribution

At the time of launch in September 1990, Limelite had distribution in each of the major multiples. As Table 4 shows, prior to the advertising, Limelite had listings in 1,681 stores.

However, sales were poor. It was not until the advent of advertising in March 1991, that sales began to grow.

Since then, distribution has increased only by existing stockists extending the product's listing in new TV regions. Thus, distribution cannot be a factor in sales growth in the original TV regions.

TABLE 4: DISTRIBUTION – ADDITIONS BY MONTH (NUMBER OF STORES)

	Tesco	Sainsbury	Asda	Safeway	Superdrug	Kwik Save	Gateway	Running total
September 1990	200	0	150	110	570	300	150	1,480
January 1991		201						1,681
May 1991		99						1,780
June 1991				100				1,880
August 1991		(55)		118				1,998
September 1991	169						500	2,667
							(145)	
March 1992			56					2,723
Total listings to date	369	300	206	328	570	300	650	2,723

Source: Cussons
Note: Figures in brackets indicate listings for the 500 ml bottle.

Promotions and Packaging

The couponing aside, there have been no other promotions on the brand. Similarly there have been no changes to the packaging since the September 1990 launch.

Thus these factors can also be discounted.

Seasonality

Because Cussons only have access to one year's data, we have no method of accounting for seasonality. However, the problem of limescale build-up is not seasonal, it affects everybody with equal vigour at all times of the year. Thus, there is no reason to believe there is any seasonality in the market.

CONCLUSIONS

The effect of advertising is indisputable.

Advertising had grown the limescale removal market, and virtually created a whole new sector.

When advertising occurs, sales increase.

The tracking study showed that as advertising and brand awareness grew, so did the number of purchasers, and also those who claimed to purchase because of the advertising.

We have discounted other potential influencing factors.

HOW DID THE ADVERTISING WORK?

Although 'short termism' and instant payback demands are regular problems for advertising agencies, it would appear here that advertising successfully delivered immediate sales results.

However, Cussons recognise the value of strong brands. So, after the initial success of Limelite an attempt was made to better understand both the relevance of the creative treatment and its role in brand building.

Of course, this is not an exact science, but both quantitative and qualitative data do exist which strongly suggest (they cannot prove) that the advertising 'adds value' to the product in terms of brand and image creation.

Three pieces of research work are most relevant to this assessment; they are each considered individually; and each was conducted post the successful London test.

TABS Data

Tracking Advertising and Brand Strength data were commissioned post the advertising test in London. It has provided data since June 1991.

TABS measures both the classic advertising standards of brand and advertising awareness; and the respondents' levels of agreement with a battery of image statements.

Brand and advertising awareness
Figure 13 plots brand and advertising awareness levels by four weekly periods.

Since the first burst of advertising on London, both measures have increased in unison at a constant rate. Brand awareness has risen between June 1991 and March 1992 from 34% to 45% and advertising awareness from 10% to 19%.

This is a definite upward trend in each awareness measure. Moreover, a simple correlation between the two variables shows an almost perfect match. In mathematical terms, the correlation coefficient is 0.8, where 1 means perfect correlation and 0 means no correlation.

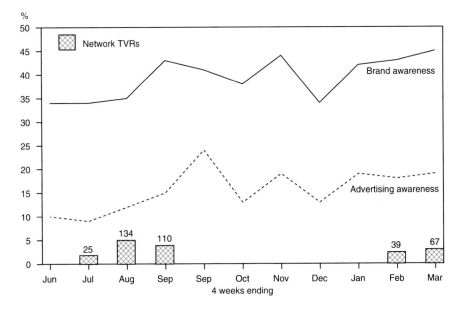

Figure 13. *Limelite brand awareness vs advertising awareness*
Source: TABS
Base: All respondents

Image statements

Clearly, brand awareness increases at the same time, and at almost the same rate, as increases in advertising awareness. Advertising has simply improved perceptions of the brand, see Figure 14.

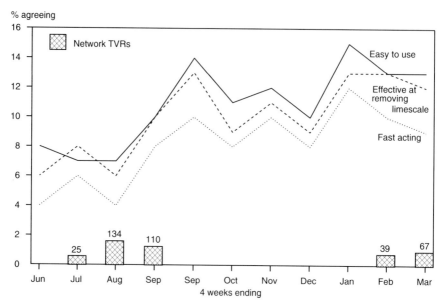

Figure 14. *Limelite image statements*
Source: TABS
Base: All aware of Limelite

Figure 14 plots the image statements amongst those aware of Limelite using four week ending data. It suggests that the advertising is delivering the key product characteristics of efficacy and speed that constitute the consumer proposition.

In fact, TABS has stated that:

'Goodwill is steadily rising in all regions; seen as easy to use, effective, fast acting product. Ads communicated all these messages.'

Millward Brown 'Link' Test

The second of three supplementary, post campaign pieces of research provides further evidence of why the advertising was working. In particular, it gives a clear guide as to how the communication was influencing goodwill scores positively. The Millward Brown Link test quantitatively provides:

— an assessment of the likely performance of film
— an indication of areas of interest and involvement
— detail on the communication points in the ad

Its format is basically: respondents view five ads on a reel, before being questioned.

In the case of Limelite, the Link test provides key results in terms of both the empathy generated by the advertising and its main communication points. Obviously, this test was conducted in an area that had not been exposed to the advertising.

Firstly, in terms of empathy it made the respondents feel positive about the product:

TABLE 5: PHRASES THAT APPLY TO THE AD

	Total sample %	Limescale sufferers %
Humorous	34	51
Lively	25	30
Eye-catching	21	28
Interesting	15	19
Stylish	5	7
Told me a lot about product	20	42
Made me want to buy product	36	51
Base: verbal sample	*(105)*	*(43)*

Clearly, the humour in the creative work was striking a positive chord, and the product demonstration was both well understood and motivating.

Secondly, and importantly, the efficacy of the brand, and so the credibility of the proposition was delivered. In that, respondents when asked about spontaneous impressions given by the ad overwhelmingly mentioned efficiency.

TABLE 6: SPONTANEOUS IMPRESSIONS GIVEN BY AD

	Main %	Total %
Any mention efficiency	68	76
Removes limescale	40	43
Keeps limescale away	5	6
Effective	22	28
Works quickly	4	6
Strong/powerful	2	3
Removes hard water stains	2	3
Brings back shine	1	3
Any mention cleans	15	20
Cleans	6	9
It's a cleaner	5	6
Base: verbal sample	*(109)*	

Given our original concern re consumer acceptability of the Limelite proposition as an effective limescale remover, this was an excellent result.

In fact, Millward Brown conclusions confirmed much of our original strategy:

'Story understood and involving. Strong in communication – single-minded message. Thought to be persuasive. Generates high interest in the product.'

Sarah Nelson Qualitative

Although this third piece of research is qualitative, and involves only two consumer groups of trialists it does provide further support to the brand building qualities of the advertising.

Conducted post the successful London test, it was designed to explore the brand in terms of potential for further product development.

The results were extremely encouraging both in terms of potential brand development and the success of the strategy to date.

We know that the advertising gave off the right messages about the product, with the result that considerable trial was generated. What Sarah Nelson's work appeared to confirm was that the overall strategy had worked, at least with these trialists. Remember we stated as the fundamental objective our attempt to grow the brand and as such there was a requirement to expand the market. And, that this would realistically only be achieved by making limescale a *real* problem: its removal represented a positive statement about the individual's cleaning routine.

Sarah Nelson stated that:

> 'Housewives fear that the unsightly appearance of limescale will reflect poorly on their domestic efforts, which are frustratingly undermined by the persistent growth of the problem.'

Since these people were not buying limescale removal products prior to the launch of Limelite, the role of advertising seems clear.

Moreover, in these groups consumers also acknowledged their faith, goodwill and brand loyalty. Indeed in terms of new product development Sarah Nelson stated that

> 'They are protective about the credentials that the brand has earned but are ready and willing to support and follow Limelite in its development.'

But, she notes that this development can only be within the limescale removal market.

SUMMARY

So, Limelite advertising has generated a short-term sales response. It also has added value to the product, and helped make the product a brand with potential.

Certainly, the advertising clearly communicated product efficacy in a way that is extremely motivating to the housewife. But importantly in the long-term, this has given Limelite a specialist positioning within the limescale removal that can be built upon.

THE FUTURE

The success of the advertising launch for Limelite in terms of sales is proven.

However, the key for the product's future is the continued development of a brand identity that will help resist the inevitable pressure of own label and other branded competitors. Limelite starts from a solid base, with the beginnings of specialist limescale removal brand values for speed of action and total efficacy.

Section Six

Special

18

Scottish Amicable

How it Paid to be Amicable

INTRODUCTION

The market for 'life' products (pensions, endowments, life assurance, savings plans etc) is dauntingly complicated and specialist – AVCs, PHIs, SERPs, premium waivers, unit-linked funds – need I say more?

Consumers can count on one hand the number of purchases they make in an entire life. Unsurprisingly therefore they lack both understanding and interest. Hence the old adage that life policies are sold and not bought.

The broker or salesman has almost total influence over which policy the consumer is sold.

Under such conditions, identifying a role for advertising is difficult, establishing its effectiveness even more so. Nevertheless, in this paper we will attempt to illustrate how advertising helped make the Scottish Amicable name more *sellable*, which in turn has contributed to increased policy sales.

THE DISTRIBUTION CHANNELS

Following the 1986 Financial Services Act, brokers were obliged to declare their status as either 'Independent Financial Advisors' (IFAs) who are free to select policies from any office or 'Appointed Representatives' (ARs) who are 'tied' to one single life office, selling only their policies.

Scottish Amicable's strength lay in the independent sector. This route offered the consumer the reassurance of being recommended a product from an unbiased and accountable expert. The quality of its products and performance ensured it a steady supply of recommendations without the direct costs of maintaining its own sales network.

Scottish Amicable did begin to cultivate a 'tied' network but this grew only slowly (accounting for less than 20% of sales in 1990).

THE SALES PROCESS

The advising process begins when a customer first approaches the broker. Generally independent brokers do not advertise themselves but rely on word of mouth or referrals from other professions or the life offices themselves. (For example, the modest number of enquirers who approach Scottish Amicable directly are referred to a choice of five local IFAs.)

Brokers are generally not obsessed with seeking out business, since it is normally the customer who decides for himself to seek advice. Normally this is prompted by specific circumstances – he or she changes job and needs to switch pension, finds a dream house and needs a mortgage, starts a family and needs life cover etc.

After thanking them for their approach and explaining his independent status, the broker thoroughly examines his new clients' financial situation – income, outgoings, policies owned, future plans etc.

Under the Act the broker is obliged to give the client 'best advice', meaning the most suitable policy in the marketplace for that client's particular circumstances. He is liable to be investigated by the authorities at any time and must be able to justify each recommendation.

Simplistically the process is as follows:

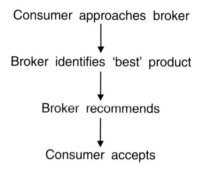

APPARENT ROLES FOR ADVERTISING

There appear two obvious routes for advertising to influence this process:

1. Directly influence consumers' approach.
2. Directly influence brokers' selections.

However, on examination, it becomes obvious that neither is viable.

Direct Influence Over Consumers

Consumers are notoriously unresponsive to invitations to seek help – apathy and unease combine to make contemplating their financial situation even less appealing than visiting the dentist – they generally only take action when they have to.

Drumming up sales is therefore not a realistic task for advertising.

Direct Influence Over Brokers

Direct advertising influence over recommendation is practically against the rules governing IFAs' commitment to select the 'best' product for each client's circumstances. Rational, objective facts – such as product specification, company performance, cost etc must dictate the choice.

Indeed, when IFAs are asked to rank factors in order of importance, advertising is last on the list.

TABLE 1: BROKERS' STATED IMPORTANCE OF FACTORS
Which of the following factors are most important in your choice of a company?

		% stating as important
1.	Good investment performance	78
2.	Financially sound	64
3.	Good underwriting service	22
4.	Prompt documentation	22
5.	Good/helpful inspectors	18
6.	Prompt and efficient quotations	17
7.	Specialist in life and pensions	13
8.	Particularly helpful	9
9.	Available for queries at local office	7
10.	Prompt settlement of maturities/claims	6
11.	Produces innovative products	6
12.	Well known to the general public	6
13.	Keeps brokers up-to-date	5
14.	Sympathetic to brokers' views	4
15.	Pays favourable commission	3
16.	**Promotes its policies to consumers**	**1**

Source: Taylor Nelson Investment and Insurance Monitor

Naturally, therefore, brokers have a low view of advertising in this market and strongly refute its direct effect on either consumers or themselves.

Which advertising, if any, do you feel has been most effective with consumers?   None   91%

Which advertising, if any, do you feel has encouraged you to place more business with that company?   None   86%

Source: Taylor Nelson Monitor

So, direct advertising influence was ruled out. However, by examining how the advising process works in practice, we were able to identify an opportunity.

IDENTIFYING A ROLE FOR ADVERTISING

This emerged from four key observations.

1. There's rarely such a clear cut thing as the 'best' policy.
2. Brokers, being human, have preferences.
3. Consumers, being human, have concerns and preferences too.
4. Brokers are inclined to recommend the names consumers are inclined to accept.

No Such Thing as 'Best'

In reality, 'best advice' narrows down the choice to a handful of companies, not one outright. Products are by and large similar, particularly for the popular contracts such as mortgage endowments or personal pensions. Prospective return specified in quotations, is restricted by rules limiting anticipated growth rate. The 'cost' (largely determined by management charges) is effectively hidden from the consumer. Hence competitive illustrations are broadly similar.

Of course, the broker may well have an informed insight into which companies are likely to perform better in the future, but this can be no more than an indication ('past performance should not be taken as a guide to the future'). Anyway, differences between the top ten companies are small compared to their performance over the worst.

TABLE 2: VALUE OF A TYPICAL ENDOWMENT OVER 25 YEARS

	£	% Below Best	% Above Worst
1. Standard Life	44,004	–	+49.7
2. Commercial Union	43,844	–0.4	+49.2
3. General Accident	43,535	–1.1	+48.1
4. Scottish Life	43,163	–1.9	+46.9
5. Royal London	42,418	–3.6	+44.3
6. Friends Provident	42,311	–3.8	+44.0
7. Scottish Amicable	41,924	–4.7	+42.7
8. Equity & Law	41,726	–5.2	+42.0
9. Eagle Star	41,433	–5.8	+41.0
10. Scottish Widows	41,182	–6.4	+40.1

Source: *Financial Times*, 1992

Human Nature

Given little to choose between products, the choice frequently hinges on the IFA's preference for particular companies. We found that brokers developed preferences for a variety of reasons – previous good experience, rewarding companies committed to their business, respecting the company's representative, 'better the devil you know...' etc. Above all, however, we found brokers were frequently mindful of the need to sell themselves and their recommendation to the client. The client is, after all, under no obligation and could go elsewhere for this or future business.

'You've got to win their confidence, they've got to feel happy with what you've sold them'.
(IFA, BMP Qualitative Research)

Clearly the manner and professionalism of the broker are crucial, but when it comes to signing his life away the client must trust the proposed company.

Consumer Concerns

For consumers, in an uncertain area and without much solid knowledge, the only real distinction to be made between companies is on the basis of awareness. Consumers assume companies they've heard of are big, established and likely to be secure. Unheard of companies, on the other hand, are a significant worry. Both qualitative and quantitative data support this (Figure 1).

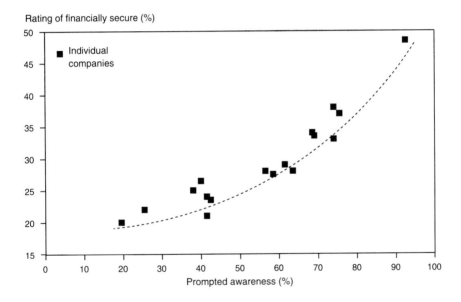

Figure 1. *Security vs awareness (across all insurance companies)*
Sources: Millward Brown, FRS

'Yes, you've heard of them, you're not dealing with any old Tom, Dick or Harry that might take a bath sometime soon.'

'We've all heard of the likes of Norwich Union and Scottish Widows but who'd ever heard of Barlowe Clowes or BCCI before?' (Consumers, BMP Qualitative Research)

To investigate this further, we measured consumers' 'willingness to accept'. Ad hoc quantitative research posed the hypothetical question, 'Imagine you were about to take out a new policy of some sort, like a pension, life assurance or an endowment. Which companies from this list would you feel most happy about accepting a policy from?' The results confirm consumers' inclination towards companies they've heard of (Figure 2).

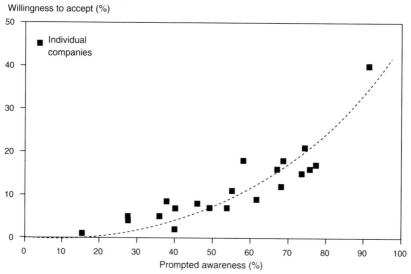

Figure 2. *Willingness to accept vs awareness (across all insurance companies)*
Sources: Harris, FRS

Moreover, qualitative work suggests that being *familiar* with a name is more reassuring than simply having heard of it once or twice.

'I'm definitely *more* aware of them than that other company. It's a name that's around a lot.' (Consumer)

In the light of that, the following data are fascinating. They show that when prompted with a list of names, consumers select the same companies as if there were no list and they were asked for names off the top of their head (Figure 3).

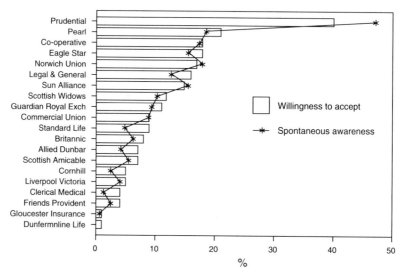

Figure 3. *Willingness to accept vs spontaneous awareness*
Sources: Harris, FRS, August 1991

Brokers Mindful of their Clients' Perspective

IFAs, for their part, know from experience that recommending, say, Norwich Union is a lot easier than Provident Mutual or Skandia. Moreover, they also suspect that the client feels better about their professionalism when the recommendation sounds familiar and secure.

'You do have your work cut out to sell a name like Skandia. The punter's usually sceptical about them at the outset <because> he doesn't know them from Adam. You have to woo them round.' (IFA)

CONFIRMING THIS INSIGHT

This hypothesis was not borne out by brokers' stated reasons for recommending (Table 1).

In order to resolve this, we conducted a special analysis of our broker tracking data, reconciling brokers' perceptions of companies' image with brokers' claimed usage of them.

The analysis yielded six clusters brokers tended to classify companies into. One very large group was of companies brokers see little worth in and have very few dealings with. One group was of offices brokers do deal with, but when they do, encounter bad service problems. There was a group of companies largely used for life assurance contracts where speed and cost of quotation were important. The smaller slightly more specialist companies such as NPI or Prudential Holborn, also formed a cluster and there was a group of perceived leaders which was largely a function of the large volume of business dealt with those companies.

However, one group (group 3) accounted for the majority of regular business as Figure 4 shows.

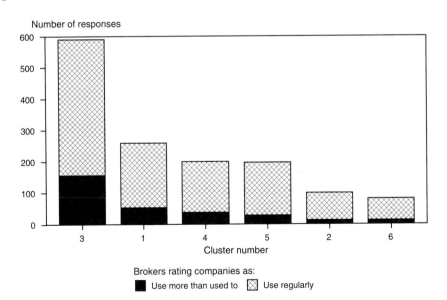

Figure 4. *Profile of clusters by amount of business accounted for*
Sources: Taylor Nelson, Digitab analysis

A good rating across a number of statements is important to be included by brokers in this group. In particular the company needs to be rated for 'Good inspectors', 'Financially sound' and '*Well known to the public*'.

Comparing these *inferred* results with brokers' *direct* ratings, the differences in emphasis are enlightening. When asked directly, brokers give tangible, rational and professional responses. By analysing implied importance we can see what our qualitative insight had been telling us – ie that brokers, all other things being equal, are actually influenced by such things as consumer awareness and the quality of inspector who services them.

TABLE 3:   IMPORTANCE OF IMAGE MEASURES ON SELECTION

Method: Asked *directly*	**Method:** *Inferred* from usage
Rank:	**Rank:**
1. Good investment performance	1. Good/helpful inspectors
2. Financially sound	2. Financially sound
3. Good underwriting	3. **Well known to the public**
4. Prompt documentation	4. Prompt documentation
5. Good/helpful inspectors	5. Prompt and efficient quotes
6. Prompt and efficient quotes	6. Good branch support
7. Specialist in life and pensions	7. Innovative new products
8. Particularly helpful	8. Specialist in life and pensions
9. Available for queries at local office	9. Good investment performance
10. Prompt settlement of claims	10. Sympathetic to brokers
11. **Well known to the public**	11. Poor after sales service
12. Innovative new products	(negative)
13. Sympathetic to brokers	
Base: Whole sample	**Base:** Whole sample, commenting on Cluster 3 companies.

Sources: Taylor Nelson Monitor, Digitab analysis

Armed with this, we developed a more realistic sales model as follows:

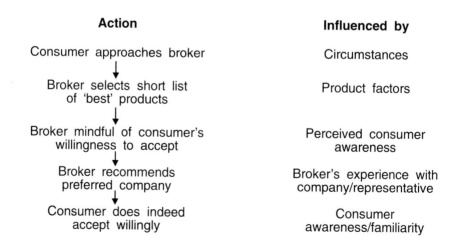

Action	**Influenced by**
Consumer approaches broker	Circumstances
↓	
Broker selects short list of 'best' products	Product factors
↓	
Broker mindful of consumer's willingness to accept	Perceived consumer awareness
↓	
Broker recommends preferred company	Broker's experience with company/representative
↓	
Consumer does indeed accept willingly	Consumer awareness/familiarity

We concluded that awareness (real and perceived) is a crucial element in business success. We can show that the bigger and better known life companies appear to be growing at a faster rate than those with lower awareness.

TABLE 4: AWARENESS RANKING AND SALES RESULTS

Rank in awareness	Average new premium growth
Top 10 companies	18.1%
11th-20th companies	10.3%
21st-30th companies	5.7%

Sources: FRS, LAMRA, 1989–91

This therefore provides advertising with a role in generating business.

SCOTTISH AMICABLE'S STANDING

Scottish Amicable was well rated on all practical factors. Its products were competitive, its service excellent, its long-term investment consistently good, its products good, its staff helpful and effective etc.

However, having no high street presence and no form of direct consumer contact (except with its existing policy-holders) awareness of Scottish Amicable's name was low.

TABLE 5: CONSUMER PROMPTED AWARENESS

	% heard of
Prudential	92
Legal & General	76
Pearl	75
Norwich Union	74
Abbey Life	70
Eagle Star	60
Commercial Union	58
Sun Alliance	58
Scottish Widows	53
Standard Life	41
Sun Life	41
Scottish Amicable	36
Guardian Royal Exchange	36
Liverpool Victoria	32
Allied Dunbar	30
Clerical Medical	17

Source: FRS, 1987–88

To compound this brokers were highly conscious of this. They rated key competitors Norwich Union, Standard Life and Scottish Widows as better known.

TABLE 6: BROKERS' PERCEPTION OF CONSUMER AWARENESS

	Well known to the general public %
Norwich Union	71
Prudential	50
Commercial Union	48
GA Life	47
Legal & General	46
Standard Life	46
Royal Life	42
Guardian Royal Exchange	42
Eagle Star	33
Scottish Widows	31
Sun Alliance	29
Cornhill	17
Abbey Life	15
Friends Provident	15
Scottish Amicable	**14**
Allied Dunbar	12
Sun Life	10
Clerical Medical	4

Source: Taylor Nelson, 1988

ROLE FOR ADVERTISING

There was therefore a clear role for advertising to directly increase consumers' awareness of Scottish Amicable (and hence their pre-disposition to accept it), and hence indirectly influence brokers' preference to recommend.

The following diagram charts precisely how we expected advertising's influence to percolate up to brokers.

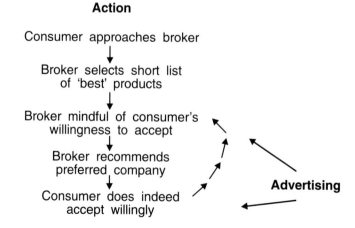

ADVERTISING DEVELOPMENT

With awareness approaching 40%, despite relatively good advertising, it was becoming increasingly difficult to push it further upwards (Figure 5).

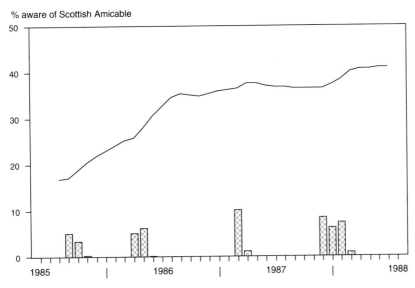

Figure 5. *Prompted name awareness (moving annual total)*
Source: FRS

Initial awareness gains are amongst people with an interest in the market (eg they've recently bought or are currently buying), beyond them the average man in the street is largely indifferent. Figure 6 illustrates.

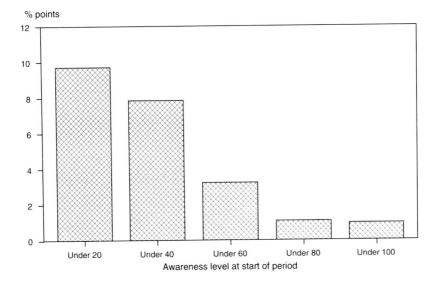

Figure 6. *Awareness gains per 1000 TVRs (all insurance companies)*
Source: FRS, 12 monthly periods 1987–91

In 1988 BMP DDB Needham was challenged to cut through this consumer indifference and boost awareness of Scottish Amicable beyond 40%. The Amicable Man was born. Two commercials showed Amicable Men shrugging off the tribulations of typical, if rather unfortunate days (one at work, the other looking after triplets).

Pre-testing indicated that this was the most enjoyed insurance advertising around at the time. However, despite this, awareness continued to grow only modestly. It was clear that a new perspective was called for.

A fresh look at the problem shed two important insights.

1.   What we really wanted was not a few points more prompted awareness, but *fame* and familiarity in the most general sense.
2.   All insurance advertising, being eager to reassure, was simply too pleasant. The scenarios presented are generally too perfect to gel with the man in the street.

It appeared the trap we had fallen into was to regard our commercials from the point of view of insurance companies rather than advertising generally. This meant that, unintentionally, we were reflecting the standard 'rules' of this genre:

—   Life is rosy
—   We make it ever rosier
—   Showing (what inevitably turn out to be) stereotypes of our ideal 'consumer'
—   Depicting 'ideal' scenarios
—   Being sensibly pleasant but not too wacky (they must trust us after all).

Specifically the misfortunes of our Amicable Men appeared somewhat scripted and unreal. This allowed consumers to feel the advertising wasn't particularly 'right' for them and to overlook it as just another insurance company.

We needed advertising with a currency and popularity that would overcome consumers' usual apathy towards the big, faceless institutions. Encouraged by the potential strength of the Amicable Man idea we formulated the following brief.

ADVERTISING BRIEF

What is the advertising trying to do?
Make Scottish Amicable famous (and hence a more reassuring choice).

Who are we talking to?
Broadly everyone 25–44, mass-market, who may embark on financial decisions in the future. Most importantly, the man in the street must feel the advertising is talking to him. Indirectly we need to be 'seen to be seen' by Independent Financial Advisors.

What's the main thought we want to put across?
Amicable Men are not troubled by the little things life springs on them.

Support
Because they have the reassurance of being 'covered' by a Scottish Amicable policy.

Guidelines

Scenarios work better when they look like they're observed from life, not made up or too 'cosy'.

Our competitors are other famous adverts generally, not other 'staid' insurance ads.

Amicable Man should mean mankind generally, not just males.

DEVELOPING THE CAMPAIGN

Like all good advertising, the 'Out-takes' campaign that emerged appears obvious in retrospect. The real life 'bloopers' of real people, captured on home video, were not only hilarious but related directly and personally to our audience.

In pre-testing, the ads were noticed and enjoyed as adverts generally, not just as financial ads. One respondent even offered to buy the tapes off the moderator there and then! Tonally, an insurance company with the straightforwardness to admit that life doesn't always run to plan was seen as very refreshing.

'The rest <ie competitors' advertising> are all sort of rose tinted, you know, 2.2 children and everything perfect. But this is real people like us.'

'They talk to us at our own level, not like all the others, kind of looking down their noses at you...<as if to say… "if you haven't got ten grand then bugger off".' (Consumers, BMP Qualitative Research)

In pre-testing amongst professionals, IFAs applauded the advertising for being a single-minded and unmissable name awareness exercise. Their customers were bound to notice it.

THE CAMPAIGN IS LAUNCHED

The first executions were duly aired in November/December 1990. Since then, thanks to low production costs, no less than 14 variations on the theme have run across four bursts.

(Our campaign preceded the top rating Jeremy Beadle out-takes programme by two months.)

Expenditure over the period (£3m) was in line with previous years' and with competitive activity. Each burst of activity received roughly the same number of ratings. (Thanks to the use of 10s, we were able to run two full bursts in 1991.)

TABLE 7: MEDIA EXPOSURE
Compared to Competitors and Previous Activity

	Average of 5 previous Scottish Amicable advertising bursts	'Out-takes' advertising		
		'90 Nov-Dec	'91 Feb-Jun	'91 Aug-Dec	'92 Mar-May
TVRs	809	751	752	676	374
Share of all life insurance advertising (%)	18.1	29.7	9.8	15.5	8.8

Source: BARB

TV SCRIPT

SONG: No matter how life goes,
         with all its joys and woes,

I never feel in a jam.
I guess I'm just an Amicable Man.

Got no worries financially,
got a pension policy,

My future's in good hands.
No wonder I'm an Amicable Man.

MVO: With a pension from Scottish Amicable
        you won't have to worry…

…no matter what life throws at you.

Scottish Amicable. Pensions, life assurance, endowments, investments…

CONSUMER AWARENESS

Prompted awareness of Scottish Amicable grew from 39% in 1990 to a peak of 60% in 1991.

Looking at moving annual data the growth in awareness, beginning with the new campaign, is most obvious (Figure 7).

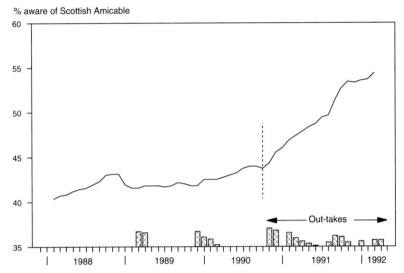

Figure 7. *Prompted name awareness (moving annual total)*

This is the fastest awareness growth achieved by any life office over the period and has only ever been exceeded by companies with much lower starting awareness. Compared to the expected gain for this level of awareness, the result is exceptional (Figure 8).

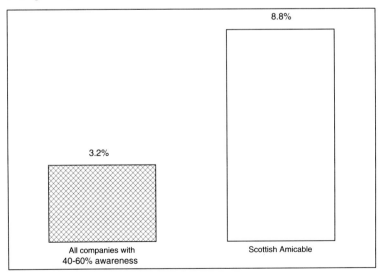

Figure 8. *Comparison of gain per 1000 TVRs with companies at same awareness level*
Sources: FRS, BARB

On a monthly basis, the synchronisation of awareness hikes with bursts of advertising is immediately apparent suggesting very strongly that advertising was the cause (Figure 9).

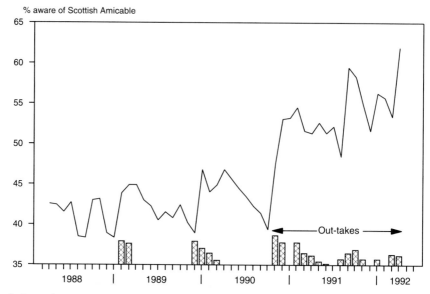

Figure 9. *Prompted name awareness (monthly)*
Source: FRS

A regional analysis of awareness rises shows a correlation with weight of advertising activity, again indicating that advertising was causal (Figure 10).

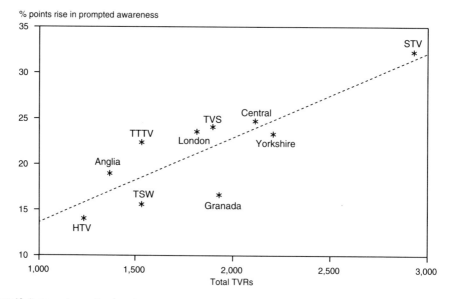

Figure 10. *Awareness rises vs ratings by region*
Sources: BARB, FRS, Nov 1990 to Nov 1991

It is worth pointing out, at this stage, that companies who did not advertise over this period or withdrew advertising, lost awareness, refuting any possible claim that rises were due to an industry-wide phenomenon caused by increased consumer exposure to financial matters (Figure 11).

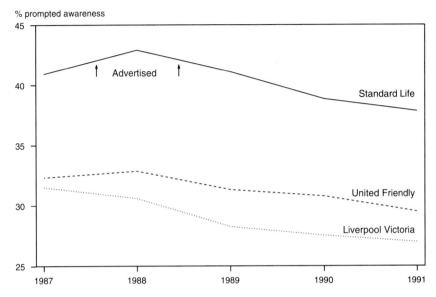

Figure 11. *Non-advertised companies*
Source: FRS Annually

It seems likely, therefore, that without any advertising, awareness of Scottish Amicable would have fallen below 40%.

CONSUMER FAMILIARITY AND IMAGE

Earlier we explained how our ultimate aim was familiarity rather than simple name recognition.

Through continuous qualitative evaluation we have found not only consumers who had heard of Scottish Amicable for the first time from the advertising, but also others who felt them *better* known as a result of the advertising.

'They're more of a familiar name than perhaps a year or so ago. If you say "Scottish Amicable" to anyone nowadays they go <sings tune>"... Amicable Man".' (Consumer)

Much of this we attribute not just to pure impact of the advertising but also its 'for real people like me' approach and obvious popularity.

This effect can be seen in spontaneous awareness data. The absolute scores are low, reflecting consumers' lack of interest and the great number of companies they could name (they only venture 2–3 names on average). However, the wholesale rise following 'Out-takes' advertising is highly significant, beyond the bounds of what we might have considered statistically likely (Figure 12).

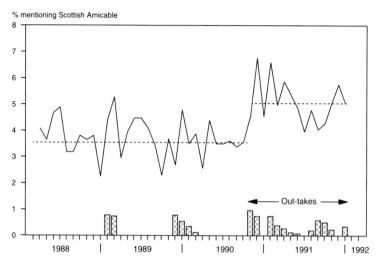

Figure 12. *Spontaneous awareness (monthly)*
Source: FRS

We have also detected the beginnings of 'brand values' – somewhat remarkable amongst such traditionally generic and distant institutions. Syndicated quantitative image statements are too general to reveal much, but we have observed distinctive and positive 'Amicable' traits in qualitative projections of the company.

'You imagine them as more normal somehow, not all stiff shirts and suits.'

'Feet up on their desks and laid back!'

'You do feel that if you did ring them they wouldn't be so hard-sell, you know, letting you decide in your own time.' (Consumers)

CONSUMERS' WILLINGNESS TO ACCEPT

Unfortunately there is no earlier analysis to compare the 1991 willingness to accept figure with. However, given the strong correlation with companies' awareness, it seems reasonable to contrast Scottish Amicable with companies that have now, only the same level of awareness that Scottish Amicable *used* to have in 1988 (and the level that it would have had without 'Out-takes'). On this basis, it seems likely that our 'willingness to accept' rating has doubled.

TABLE 8: AWARENESS AND WILLINGNESS TO ACCEPT

Name	Spontaneous awareness %	Prompted awareness %		Willingness to accept %
Scottish Amicable	5.5	57	⟷	7
Scottish Amicable in 1988	3.4	36		Not measured
Cornhill	2.6	40	⟷	3
Friends Provident	2.5	39	⟷	4
Liverpool Victoria	3.9	29	⟷	4
Clerical Medical	1.5	29	⟷	3

Sources: FRS, Harris, November 1991

CONSUMER SUMMARY

It seems probable that advertising has made Scottish Amicable more familiar, improving consumers' predisposition to accept a broker's recommendation of it.

Given the 'sold rather than bought' nature of the market, however, for advertising to have worked we need to establish that these perceptions have lodged with and influenced brokers.

EFFECT ON BROKERS' PERCEPTIONS

Since 1988, perceived consumer awareness has risen. Notably the largest rise comes immediately after the beginning of 'Out-takes' (Figure 13).

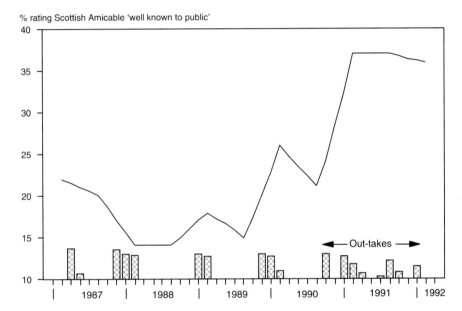

Figure 13. *Brokers' perceived awareness*
Source: Taylor Nelson

When the same data are looked at relative to key competitors we can see that Scottish Amicable's perceived disadvantage has been eliminated (and turned to a slight advantage) during the 'Out-takes' campaign (Figure 14).

Certainly brokers were highly conscious of the advertising (Figure 15), which explains the jumps in perceived awareness.

'Those ads have definitely done the trick for them, they're a household name now.' (IFA)

Brokers have also directly experienced increased consumer awareness. Many have reported cases where their recommendation has been well received by a client who has remarked on the advertising. In other cases brokers have included reference to the advertising in their 'sell', to help the client 'place' the company.

Overall, brokers seem to believe that Scottish Amicable is now easier to successfully recommend as a direct result of the advertising.

'They're definitely easier as a name. You used to have to go through all the spiel about "they're a mutual company, been going since 1826…" Now they <clients> are all happy about them.' (IFA)

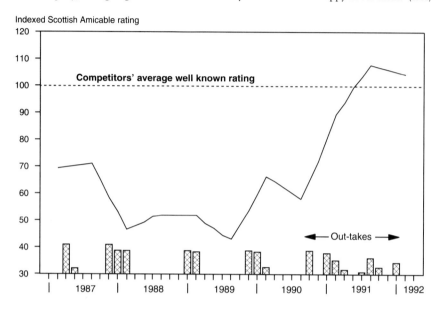

Figure 14. *Relative perceived awareness compared to competitors*
Source: Taylor Nelson

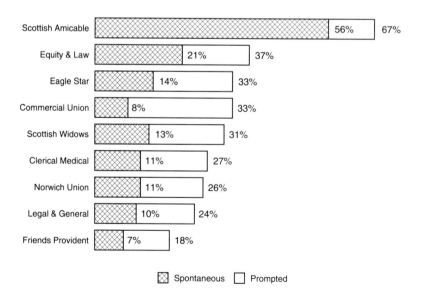

Figure 15. *Brokers' recall of advertising*
Source: Taylor Nelson, 1991

BROKERS' PREFERENCE TO RECOMMEND

It would be impractical and ethically dubious to conduct 'willingness to recommend' research amongst brokers. But we can examine claimed usage data.

Scottish Amicable already sits in the top five companies brokers use regularly. The number of brokers recommending them has not therefore risen significantly. However, within this group, a greater proportion of brokers claim to be placing more business with Scottish Amicable than they used to following the 'Out-takes' campaign.

TABLE 9: PREFERENCE TO RECOMMEND

	% of brokers dealing regularly with	% of those placing more business than used to, with
Standard Life	57	18
Norwich Union	52	21
Scottish Widows	37	19
Scottish Amicable	37	25
Scottish Equitable	34	15

Source: Taylor Nelson, 1991

SALES RESULTS

New premium income for Scottish Amicable was up 15% in 1991 to £489 million. Within this, sales of pensions were up 18% and, in a mortgage market down 3% (Source: BSA), endowments were up 8%.

To look at these results relative to total market sales we have two sources: companies' reported results and consumers' reported purchases.

Reported premiums from personal pensions fell by an estimated 13.5% (due to the recession). Scottish Amicable was the only company to buck this trend.

TABLE 10: PERSONAL PENSIONS SALES 1991 VS 1990

	% change
Scottish Amicable	+18
Scottish Equitable	−4
Standard Life	−6
Prudential	−15
Scottish Widows	−17
Allied Dunbar	−20
Legal & General	−34
Norwich Union	−38

Sources: Company reports, *Money Marketing*

Consumer data also report recent growth in Scottish Amicable's share of all life policies immediately following the 'Out-takes' campaign (Figure 16).

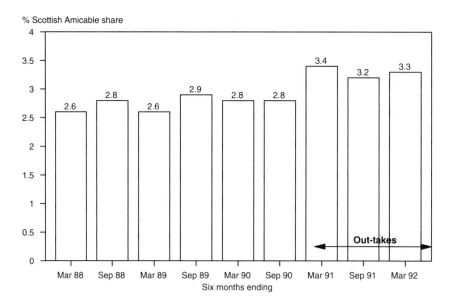

Figure 16. *Share of all life policies (consumer reported)*
Source: NOP

Within this broad category Scottish Amicable share of endowments, personal pensions and life assurance all show rises following the 'Out-takes' campaign (Figures 17 and 18).

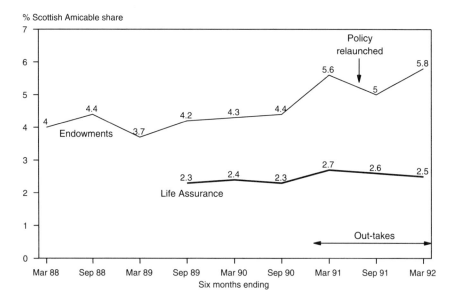

Figure 17. *Share of all life policies by type (consumer reported)*
Source: NOP

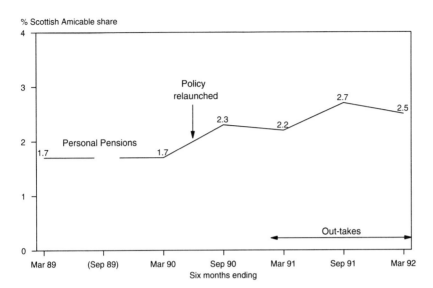

Figure 18. *Share of all life policies by type (consumer reported)*
Source: NOP

ESTABLISHING ADVERTISING'S EFFECT

What evidence do we have to isolate advertising as a cause of these effects?

Synchronisation

All the effects we have identified happen simultaneously with 'Out-takes' advertising. For this to happen in all three areas (consumer awareness, brokers' perceived awareness and sales) seems beyond coincidence.

Everything Worked to Plan

We constructed a role for advertising that was both reasonably complex and exactly specified. Furthermore we established quantitatively that both real and perceived awareness had influences on predispositions to accept and recommend.

Given that each element of the plan responded exactly as hoped, it seems highly probable that the plan as a whole worked. Expressed the other way round, it seems highly improbable that all the elements responded to plan and yet something other than advertising was wholly responsible for the sales rises.

Brokers Acknowledge the Advertising's Effect

Despite brokers' reluctance to concede direct influence we do have evidence that, albeit marginally, they have personally responded to the advertising.

We have seen levels of awareness of the advertising were high. We know too that the 'Out-takes' campaign was very well received by brokers. Qualitatively, they appear to enjoy the ads through the eyes of consumers, rather than as professionals. (This is useful given their suspicion of advertising they feel is directly aimed at them.) Quantitatively the advertising is clearly the most preferred in the marketplace, both now and compared to previous years (Figure 19).

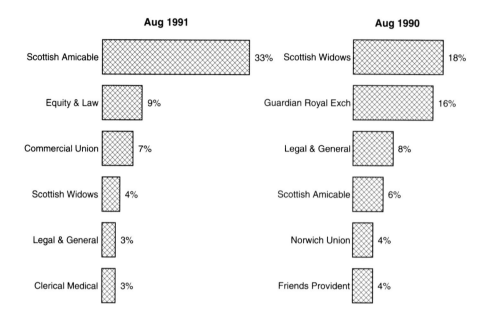

Figure 19. *Has particularly good advertising (brokers' nominations)*
Source: Taylor Nelson

These results were confirmed in 1991 when IFA readers of *Money Marketing* and *Money Week* voted Scottish Amicable 'Best Advertising' awards.

One effect of such high profile advertising seems to have been to raise the status of Scottish Amicable as a serious player in the market.

TABLE 11: COMPANIES THOUGHT PARTICULARLY ACTIVE IN THE MARKET

	% nominating
Scottish Amicable	26
Norwich Union	18
Commercial Union	14
Clerical Medical	13
Equity & Law	13
Eagle Star	11
Friends Provident	10
Standard Life	9
Scottish Widows	8

Source: Taylor Nelson, 1991

Although the absolute level is (predictably) low, Scottish Amicable is the only company to receive significant scores indicating that advertising encouraged brokers to place business with them (Figure 20).

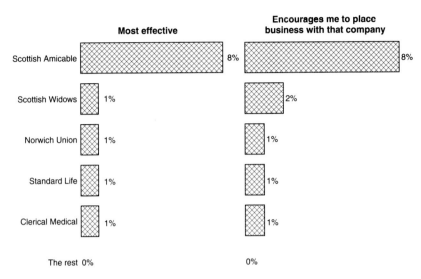

Figure 20. *Perceived advertising effectiveness (brokers' nominations)*
Source: Taylor Nelson, August 1991

Representatives Acknowledge the Advertising's Effect

Scottish Amicable's own inspectors have also reported the positive effects of advertising on the brokers they service.

> 'Yes, it's good PR for us...They <the brokers> like to joke about it with us − "watch out, here comes the Amicable Man!" I think it presents us as on the ball and geared up to the public.'
> (Inspector)

Allowing for Other Variables

It is unreasonable to claim advertising as the sole cause of good sales results.

Since 1987 Scottish Amicable has grown its base of *Appointed Representatives*. Also, like many life offices, it has tied with a building society (The Alliance & Leicester). However, for 1991 the proportion of its sales accounted for by IFAs changed only slightly (79% vs 81% in 1990), not enough to account for substantial sales and share increases

Without doubt the quality of Scottish Amicable's operations across the board have formed the backbone for their performance. *Investment* performance, financial *security*, broker *service* and *literature* have all been first class as ever. The point here, however, is that they have always been first class since the early 1980s. The company is no stranger to accolades. Such factors should lead to steady share growth but not the sudden uplifts we have seen or the bucking of falling sector sales.

The main *policies* have been revised and relaunched recently (pensions in July 1990, endowment in July 1991). However, note that the rise in endowments share (Figure 17) occurs before the policy relaunch, and pensions share (Figure 18), which does rise after the relaunch, rises for a second time 12 months later at the time of the 'Out-takes' advertising. Note also that share of life assurance also rises with the advertising when there are no significant product improvements.

We can conclude therefore that excellent investment performance, products and service have been a major influence on Scottish Amicable's continued success. However, no variables other than advertising can be found to explain the rises outlined in this paper. The fact that response to the advertising occurred as hoped and when planned, and that brokers are, unusually, willing to recognise the role that advertising played, suggests strongly that the rises were primarily due to the 'Out-takes' campaign.

WAS IT WORTH IT?

Of Scottish Amicable's £489m 1991 business almost a quarter was annual policies running for a typical term of 20–25 years. Hence, the income is 'worth' nearer £3 billion.

In terms of sales increases, pensions were up 18% in a market down 13.5%, a real gain of 31.5%. Endowments were up 8% in a market down 3%, a real gain of 11%. Consumers' reported share was up 18% (3.3% vs 2.8% Source: NOP). Total premiums were up 15%, a real gain of 10% compared to all companies (Source: ABI).

Hence it seems advertising was instrumental in causing increases between a pessimistic 10% and an optimistic 31.5%.

Even assuming the 10% figure, the extra income would be £300 million. This represents 100 times the advertising cost making it profitable even at conservative estimates of margin.

In addition, it seems reasonable to anticipate further sales rises over subsequent years, due to the increased 'sellability' of the Scottish Amicable name.

SUMMARY

This case is unusual in that direct advertising influence was not feasible. Instead, we relied on indirect and perceived influences with the aim of making Scottish Amicable more familiar, hence a more acceptable recommendation to both consumers and brokers.

Consumers' distance from and disinterest in life assurance companies forced us towards a single-minded, fame-oriented approach that broke the rules of conventional life assurance advertising. The extraordinary empathy and enjoyment we achieved appears to have been the decisive factor. It helped us be 'seen to be seen'. Amongst brokers, being perceived as effective is ultimately what made the advertising effective.

The result is dramatic improvements in sellability – consumers more willing to accept and brokers, consequently, more willing to recommend. This, on top of already excellent products, investment performance, service etc has helped tip the balance of recommendations Scottish Amicable's way.

Even if this only partly accounts for the increase in one year's premiums, the investment will pay back handsomely. We expect the effects of increased sellability to run over into subsequent years' results too.

We think it has paid, and will continue to pay, to be Amicable.

19

Alliance & Leicester
Building Society

Advertising Effectiveness 1987–1991

INTRODUCTION

In many markets, companies are faced with the problem of long purchase intervals that can be measured in years rather than weeks.

In some of these markets the problem is compounded by the products themselves being of little or no interest to the consumer, except around the time of the actual purchase decision.

As a result, at any one point in time, the vast bulk of potential future customers are unlikely to listen to anything a particular company might be saying about its products. This would appear to limit a company's ability to influence its potential future customers to those who are actually making a purchase decision.

This is exactly the situation faced by building societies. While total penetration of building society products is high, annual penetration is low – ie purchase intervals are long.

In addition, savings and mortgages are boring. Unlike cars or hi-fis, few people would cite 'mortgages' as an interest or hobby.

This case study aims to show how the Fry & Laurie campaign for the Alliance & Leicester enabled the society to talk to potential future customers, despite their lack of interest.

We hope to demonstrate how the Fry & Laurie campaign has achieved the long-term effect of increasing the *acceptability* of the Alliance & Leicester to its potential customers – and by doing so has enabled it to achieve dramatic growth in an otherwise slow-moving market.

BACKGROUND

Growth in the building society market tends to be a very gradual process. As we will see, consumers are in the market only very infrequently which means that changes in attitudes are only very slowly converted into changes in brand share.

Furthermore, the total value of all existing savings and mortgages is so much greater than the value of new accounts in any one year. In 1990, for example, net new money represented only 4% of total savings balances (source: BSA). Hence to achieve a slight change in your share of the total market requires a dramatic change in your share of new business.

This is why merging is the most commonly used means of achieving growth in the building society market. Since 1970, the number of societies in the UK has fallen from 481 to just 91.

NOTE ON DATA

Throughout this paper we will make reference both to net receipts and total savings balances. The former is the difference between the amounts of money invested and withdrawn in a given period of time. It represents, in effect, new business. The latter is the total value of all savings accounts held in a society. The corresponding measures for mortgages are net advances and total mortgage balances.

Building society assets, a measure published by the Building Societies Association, are the combination of liquid assets, outstanding mortgages and other investments, plus branches and other buildings owned. In effect, 'total assets' is a measure of the overall size of a society.

Because of the conversion of the Abbey National from a building society to a bank in 1989, it is excluded from some published data after this point. We will make it clear in each case whether data we use include or exclude the Abbey.

THE CONSUMER

— Building society products are purchased infrequently (eg average mortgage has a lifespan of around five years) but have high *total* penetration.

— There is a high level of perceived potential risk with building society products. Consumers have a nagging worry that it could go horribly wrong.

— Building society products are not intrinsically interesting (unlike say a car or hi-fi). They are just a means to an end. The 'product', such that it is, is just a number: an interest rate, sometimes with a discount or notice period attached.

— No-one ever went window shopping around building societies if they didn't need a product.

Taking all of these points together, we see that building societies' business depends on consumers who are very rarely in the market, and who have no interest in the product at all other times.

In the particular case of advertising, it suggests that the potential benefit of advertising *products* is very limited. To achieve a long-term advertising effect requires finding a way of talking to people who aren't making a purchase decision now and who aren't interested anyway. This requires an understanding of how consumers arrive at their decision.

OUR VIEW OF THE PURCHASE DECISION

Qualitative research (BMP 1986–1990) enabled us to understand the purchase process for the bulk of consumers:

— Consumers would only consider products from a limited number of institutions which they believe to be 'acceptable'.
— The key criterion for acceptability is security. A 'safe' name comes before everything else.
— Perceived security is a function of size. The bigger, the better – consumers are happiest when their savings or mortgage are an insignificant speck in the society's total assets.*

From this research we developed a simple model of the market:

— Building societies are, in effect, retailers of own label products.
— Their branches are shops where you buy own label mortgages or savings accounts.
— Before you buy the product, you must first 'buy' the retailer.
— People have a view of which retailers are acceptable regardless of whether they intend to go shopping in the near future.
— Only when they are actually buying will they be interested in product details.

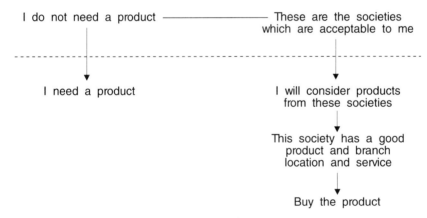

THE PROBLEM FACING THE ALLIANCE & LEICESTER IN 1987

— The Alliance and the Leicester Building Societies merged in 1985.
— From a position of being the 9th and 10th largest societies in terms of total assets, the merged society was 6th largest.

It was hoped that this increase in size would result in a greater share of new mortgage and savings business. Unfortunately, it did not. Market share of net receipts fell. Interest rates had to be improved in order to attract more money. The profit margin was squeezed.

*86% of people would only use a top ten building society or major bank for a mortgage or savings account. (Source: *Money Marketing*/NOP, November 7, 1991)

WHY DID THEY HAVE THIS PROBLEM?

We have already indicated how the acceptability of a society is an essential prerequisite for consumers entering the market for a product.

The proportion of all consumers who find a given society acceptable is in effect the 'pool' of potential future users of that society. It will then draw business from that pool as and when the consumers enter the market.

The larger the pool, the easier it should be to gain business: if there are a hundred people who would consider buying from you then it should be fairly easy to sell a product to five of them. If there are only six who find you acceptable, selling five products will be more difficult!

The pool of potential users is clearly an exploitable asset. The measurement of the size of the pool requires finding out how many consumers would consider using a given society – either for a mortgage, or for a savings product. This 'propensity to use' variable has been measured both for the Alliance & Leicester and its immediate competitors but unfortunately this has not been done consistently and only a limited number of data points are available.

We find that although it tends not to change very quickly, it is a reasonably accurate predictor of a society's share of the market (Figures 1 and 2). The correlation is not exact, but we would not expect it to be. Factors such as relative price (ie interest rates) and, importantly, branch location will modify the extent to which potential use is converted into actual use.

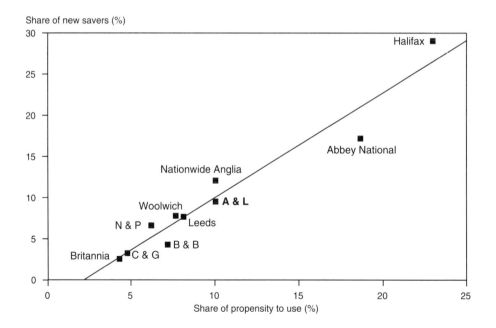

Figure 1. *Share of propensity to use for savings and share of new savers (1990)*
Source: FRS, April 1990 (propensity)/full year (new business)

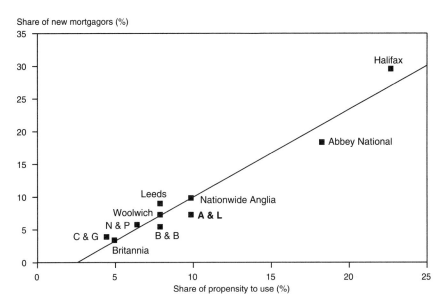

Figure 2. *Share of propensity to use for mortgages and share of new mortgagors (1990)*
Source: FRS, April 1990 (propensity)/full year (new business)

Note: in the above charts the share of propensity to use has been calculated by taking the percentage of adults who would 'consider using' a given society and dividing it by the total of each of the top eight societies' 'consider using' rating.

We also find that propensity to use correlates well with awareness; in particular, with spontaneous awareness (Figures 3 and 4). This continues the intuitive reasoning which says that people are happiest using household names.

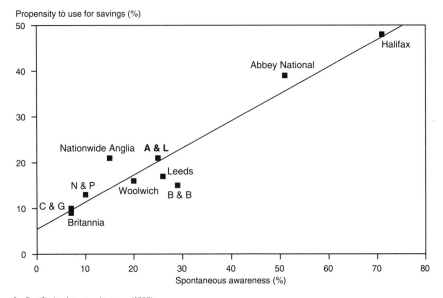

Figure 3. *Familiarity & propensity to use (1990)*
Source: FRS, April 1990 (propensity)/full year (awareness)

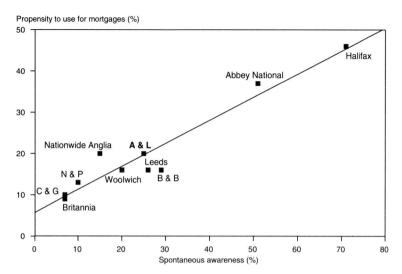

Figure 4. *Familiarity & propensity to use (1990)*
Source: FRS April 1990 (propensity)/full year (new business)

In August 1987, the Alliance & Leicester was only ninth in terms of both propensity to use and awareness, but sixth in terms of size (ie total assets, including Abbey National). This difference indicated that fewer people found the Alliance & Leicester acceptable than would be expected purely from its size, despite a product-focused TV advertising campaign. For the majority, the merged Alliance & Leicester was merely the equivalent of whichever of the two constituent societies they were previously more familiar with. It was clear that a different strategy was needed.

THE ADVERTISING STRATEGY

We needed to persuade people who weren't at all interested, that the Alliance & Leicester was big, safe and secure. Because of their indifference to the market it was clear that a message which relied for its persuasiveness on an involvement in the details of the products was bound to fail.

The solution to this problem was in fact a creative one. However, the springboard for that creative 'leap' was the need for a differentiated positioning for the Alliance & Leicester which would build on the generic market values of security. We needed to set the Alliance & Leicester apart from other societies and so give consumers a reason to consider it in the place of equally 'secure' alternatives. We wished it to become seen as a different kind of retailer.

The origination of the differential positioning resulted from the prevailing environment of public attitudes towards finance at that time.

In 1987, there was an unprecedented level of activity and publicity in the financial services arena. High profile flotations of public companies, the resultant popularisation of stocks and shares and events such as the 'Big Bang' deregulation of the stock market had combined to challenge the established perception of finance as being dull and slow-moving.

Against this background, there was a nagging suspicion that you were 'copping out' if you didn't make use of the complicated schemes which were now available.

We decided to add respectability to simple finance and to debunk the glamorous mystique of the complicated alternatives. In effect, we wanted to suggest it was 'smart' to be simple.

By making the claim that the Alliance & Leicester makes your financial life simpler we believed that the average consumer would have a reason to consider us instead of otherwise equally acceptable competitors.

Hence we claimed simplicity as our differential advantage over and above the generic values of the building society market (ie security):

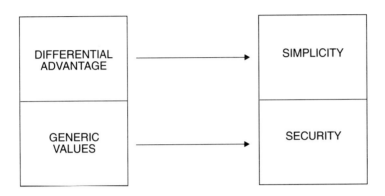

CREATIVE BRIEF

Marketing Objectives

1. Increase the number of people who would consider the Alliance & Leicester an acceptable choice for a mortgage or savings account.
2. In the longer term, increase the Alliance & Leicester's share of mortgage and savings business so as to drive growth (although no specific targets were set).

Advertising Objectives

— To increase people's perception of the Alliance & Leicester as a large, established and secure building society.
— To position the Alliance & Leicester as 'the sensible choice because it makes your financial life more simple'.

Strategy

By asserting that if you arrange your finances the complicated way it can lead to unexpected disaster whereas if you go to the Alliance & Leicester you get a reliable result without the fuss.

Target Market

All potential future customers of the Alliance & Leicester (including existing customers).

Proposition

Going to the Alliance & Leicester is the simple way to avoid your finances becoming unstuck.

Support

Because the alternatives are risky or absurd:

> eg the futures market
> the stock market
> the over complicated mortgage deal
> small, 'dodgy' financial institutions

MEDIA STRATEGY

1. We needed to change the perception of the Alliance & Leicester amongst a mass audience in a short space of time.

2. We had to be intrusive because most of our audience had no need at that time to use a building society and so would not be seeking out building society advertising.

Television was the only medium that could meet these objectives. Since the beginning of the campaign, the Alliance & Leicester has spent around £5m per full year in two (or sometimes three) bursts. The total spend from 1987–1991 was £22m.

THE ADVERTISING

The resultant advertising was the now-famous Fry & Laurie campaign. Each execution contrasts the simplicity of the Alliance & Leicester with the complexity and risk of the alternatives.

In each case, Stephen Fry represents the over-confident, pompous and arrogant buffoon who tries to do things the complicated way but becomes unstuck – either because his deals fall flat, or he is made to look a complete fool. Hugh Laurie, on the other hand, represents the sensible Alliance & Leicester customer who gets a reliable result with none of the fuss. They all have the same end-line 'You get a smarter investor at the Alliance & Leicester'.

Over the following five years, eight executions have been aired in total. These have struck a contrast with the following:

1987	'Restaurant'	Futures
1988	'Golf'	Stock market
	'Flat'	Dodgy mortgages
	'Control'	Alternative plastic card accounts
1989	'Young Ones'	Not sorting out a mortgage before house hunting
	'Complicated Animal'	Dodgy investments
1990	'Sproggit & Sylvester'	Small building societies
1991	'Old & Young'	Alternative investment products

FLAT

COMPLICATED ANIMAL

SPROGGIT & SYLVESTER

OLD & YOUNG

THE RESULTS

We intend to demonstrate that since the beginning of the Fry & Laurie campaign, the acceptability of the Alliance & Leicester has increased dramatically. This has resulted in an increased share of new savings and mortgages. Consequently, over time, the Alliance & Leicester's share of total savings and mortgage balances has increased. Overall, its share of total building society assets has increased such that the Alliance & Leicester is now the third biggest building society. We then intend to show that it is the advertising which caused the increase in acceptability.

1. *Increasing the acceptability of the Alliance & Leicester*
   Over the five years of the Fry & Laurie campaign, the 'pool' of consumers who would consider using the society has roughly doubled (Figure 5).

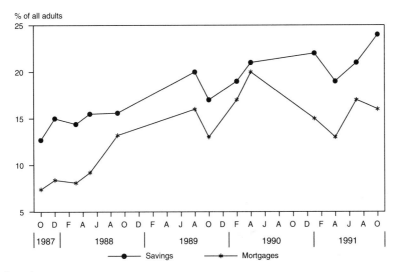

Figure 5. *Propensity to use*
Sources: FRS (1987–90), RSGB (1991)

> Whereas, in 1987, there were around six million adults who would consider using the Alliance & Leicester for a savings account, this had increased to around ten million in 1991. For mortgages, the increase was from around three and a half to seven million (understandably, mortgages require a greater degree of trust in the society).
>
> In other words, there are now twice as many people who would be prepared to do business with the society compared with five years ago.
>
> Furthermore, we would make the point that this is not a general market change. The Alliance & Leicester's *share* of 'consider using' has increased by 53% for savings and 103% for mortgages across the period of the campaign.
>
> It cannot be overstated how key this change in acceptability is. Its effect on the society's business was dramatic as we shall now show.

2. *Driving growth of the society*
   We would expect the clearest effect of increased acceptability on the society's business to be seen in its share of *new* mortgage and savings business – because total balances are so vast that they change only very slowly (as noted in the Background).

We have indeed seen a progressive increase in the society's share of net receipts which has paralleled the growth in acceptability (Figure 6).

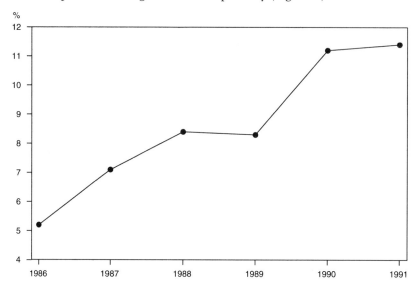

Figure 6. *Share of net receipts of major building societies*
Source: Alliance & Leicester

If a society's share of net receipts is consistently larger than its share of total balances, then over the long-term its share of balances will grow.

In 1987, the Alliance & Leicester's share of net receipts overtook its share of balances. The gap has progressively widened over the course of the Fry & Laurie campaign.

Consequently its share of total building society saving balances has grown (although less rapidly, since total balances are so large), as shown in Figure 7.

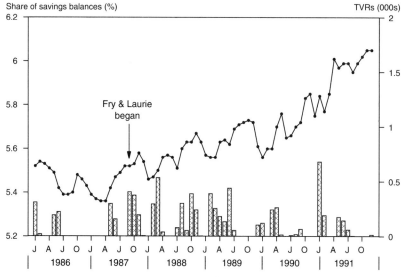

Figure 7. *Share of industry savings balances*
Sources: Alliance & Leicester, BARB

While the Alliance & Leicester's share of net mortgage advances has also outperformed its share of mortgage balances, the long-term picture is complicated by the variation in the extent to which it has made use of the wholesale money markets and the extent of commercial rather than residential lending.

Nevertheless, we still see the effect on growth in the society's share of total mortgage balances (Figure 8).

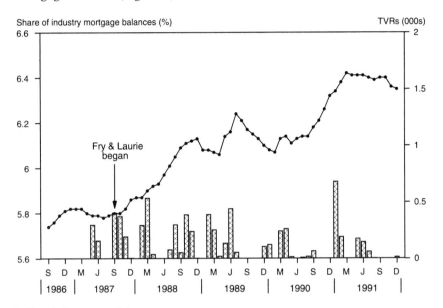

Figure 8. *Share of industry mortgage balances*
Sources: Alliance & Leicester (residential mortgages), BARB

We would also expect to see the Alliance & Leicester's share of building society customers increase: the greater number of people who find it acceptable will be translated into a greater number who actually do business with it, as and when they come to enter the market for a product. It must be stressed that the data we are looking at here is the share of *total customers* – a variable which, like share of total balances, moves very slowly. Hence, in 1986, 6.2% of all people who had a savings account, had one with the Alliance & Leicester. By 1991, this had increased to 7.2% (Table 1).

TABLE 1: ALLIANCE & LEICESTER'S SHARE OF TOTAL CUSTOMERS (%)
(based on top ten societies' customers including Abbey National)

	1986	1987	1988	1989	1990	1991
Savers	6.2	6.0	5.7	6.3	6.9	7.2
Mortgagors	6.9	7.6	7.5	8.0	7.7	8.2

Source: FRS

The combined effect of growth in share in its core markets is a growth in share of total building society assets.

It was noted in the Background to the paper that it is very difficult to increase a society's asset share other than by merging. Of the top nine societies (excluding Abbey National – data for later years are unavailable), the only one to achieve share growth from 1986–1990 without merging was the Alliance & Leicester (Table 2).

TABLE 2: SHARE OF TOP NINE SOCIETIES' TOTAL ASSETS

	1986 %	1990 %	% change
Halifax	31.7	31.5	−0.6
Nationwide[1]	13.5	18.1	−11.7
Woolwich[2]	9.3	10.6	+14.0
Leeds	9.1	8.7	−4.4
Alliance & Leicester	**9.0**	**9.4**	**+4.4**
National & Provincial	6.7	5.4	−19.4
Bradford & Bingley[3]	4.9	5.3	+8.2
Britannia	4.7	4.3	−8.5
Cheltenham & Gloucester[4]	4.3	6.7	+55.8

Notes: [1]1986 figure is combination of Nationwide and Anglia
[2]Merged with Gateway in 1988
[3]Merged with three societies 1987–90
[4]Merged with ten societies 1987–90
Source: BSA

Note: this *excludes* the extra assets which the Alliance & Leicester gained by acquiring Girobank in 1990. Had these been included the increase would have been even greater.

We have seen that, over the course of the Fry & Laurie campaign, the acceptability of the Alliance & Leicester has doubled. This has been paralleled by increases in its share of net receipts, total mortgage and savings balances, and total assets. Overall, the Alliance & Leicester has grown from being the fifth to the third largest society in the UK.

3.   *Evidence that the advertising caused this*

It seems unlikely that you could consider a society to be acceptable without first being aware of it. As we showed earlier, there is a very strong correlation between awareness and propensity to use.

Over the course of the Fry & Laurie campaign we have seen substantial increases in the level of awareness of the society. In 1986, the average levels of spontaneous and prompted awareness were 18% and 52% respectively. In 1991 these had increased to 24% and 86%.

We find that increases in awareness coincide with the periods of Fry & Laurie advertising and that awareness started to increase exactly when Fry & Laurie first appeared (Figures 9 and 10).

NB: The substantial uplift in awareness which occurred at the beginning of 1990 is not due to a discontinuity in the data (although there is one in January 1991, when the source changes from FRS to RSGB). It in fact corresponds to the first airing of the 'Sproggit & Sylvester' execution which has proved to be the most well-liked commercial in the campaign to date.

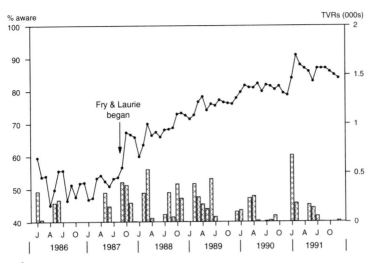

Figure 9. *Prompted awareness*
Sources: FRS (1986-90), RSGB (1991), BARB

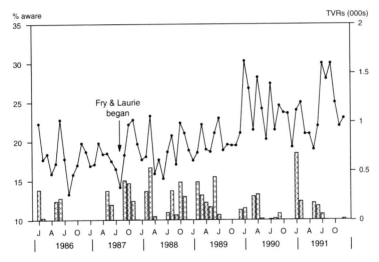

Figure 10. *Spontaneous awareness*
Sources: FRS (1986-90), RSGB (1991), BARB

In addition to increasing awareness of the society, there is evidence that it has increasingly been perceived as large and established (Table 3). This was the way the advertising was intended to work.

TABLE 3: % APPLYING STATEMENT TO ALLIANCE & LEICESTER

	1989	1990	1991
Established	24	28	30
Large	18	23	25
National	25	31	30
Lots of branches	15	19	23

Note: Image data are not available for other years
Source: RISU Image Monitor
Base: All adults (differences of 2% or more are significant)

It was noted earlier that the campaign was intended to influence a mass audience, not just the narrow subset of consumers who actually need a product at a given time.

Evidence that this happened comes both from awareness of the advertising (Figure 11) – ie its visibility – and from measures of its 'likeability'.

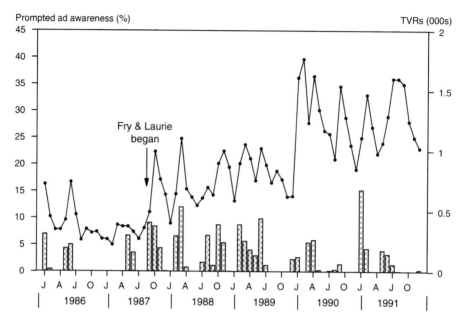

Figure 11. *Advertising awareness*
Sources: FRS (1986-90), RSGB (1991), BARB

In fact, the Alliance & Leicester's advertising awareness was disproportionately high when compared with its competitors who were spending more (Table 4).

TABLE 4:   SHARE OF PROMPTED AD AWARENESS VS SHARE OF VOICE %

	1986	1987	1988	1989	1990	1991
Share of ad awareness*	6.1	6.5	10.9	10.4	16.7	16.5
Share of voice*	7.6	7.2	10.9	9.3	11.7	8.4

Sources: FRS, RSGB, Media Register
Note: *Both calculated relative to all top ten societies including Abbey National. Before the Nationwide Anglia merger (1987) the separate Nationwide and Anglia data were combined.

The 'likeability' of the Fry & Laurie ads has been measured during the course of quantitative hall tests on each of the finished films. In this research, respondents are shown an Alliance & Leicester ad as part of a reel of ten commercials for a variety of product categories, eg food, personal care, automotive.

We find that respondents rate the Fry & Laurie ads very highly (Table 5).

TABLE 5: AVERAGE LEVEL OF AGREEMENT WITH DESCRIPTION
FOR EACH OF EIGHT FRY & LAURIE ADS

	%
Original	73
Amusing	76
Very/quite like to see again	61

Source: Sample Surveys Hall Tests. (Sample was recruited
to be representative of all adults).

NB: As noted earlier, the 'Sproggit & Sylvester' execution achieved the highest
scores on each of these measures.

Furthermore, there is evidence from building society image tracking that the
Alliance & Leicester is noted for its enjoyable advertising, while its competitors
are not rated as highly in this respect (Table 6).

TABLE 6: % AGREEING WITH STATEMENT
'HAVE ADVERTS I LIKE'

Alliance & Leicester	15
Halifax	9
Nationwide	4
Bradford & Bingley	8
National & Provincial	2

Base: All adults
Source: RISU Image Monitor 1991
Note: This survey did not include any other building societies.

So, we have shown that all of the necessary prerequisites to increased
acceptability have also increased. Moreover, we have shown that these increases
seem to coincide with the new advertising and that the advertising appears to be
sufficiently well liked and well known to be a credible cause of the changes.

Eliminating Other Variables

It is clear that, over the course of the Fry & Laurie campaign, both acceptability
and market share have increased. Apart from the advertising, what else could have
caused these changes?

1. *Price*

   We know that consumers who are not in the market for a building society
   product have little interest in product details. Since there are only very few
   'interested' consumers at any one time, it is unlikely that pricing could have
   influenced the overall acceptability of the society to the general public.

   Nevertheless, pricing does have a significant effect on business performance.
   Throughout the Fry & Laurie campaign the Alliance & Leicester has
   consistently enjoyed a cost of funds advantage over its competitors in the top
   13 building societies (ie the average rate they pay investors on their savings
   account is less than the average of the competition). While this premium has

fluctuated over the five years it has not declined overall. Similarly the Alliance & Leicester has enjoyed a mortgage yield advantage over the top 13 (or been at parity) for three out of the five years. In the other two years it has had a slight disadvantage – but this has never occurred in consecutive years.

Hence we can deduce that pricing has not caused the growth of the Alliance & Leicester: in fact, all other things being equal, we would have expected it to have caused a decline.

2. *Product*

As with price, we do not believe that product changes could have influenced the society's acceptability.

While the Alliance & Leicester has launched many new products over the course of the campaign, so have its competitors. However, these new products tend only ever to be repackaged versions of old products – and this difference is highlighted in the rate (ie the price) which we have already considered.

In the rare cases of genuine NPD (eg TESSA accounts), all societies tend to launch similar products at the same time and no one society can maintain a difference for any length of time. The Alliance & Leicester has not been the first to launch an innovative account over this period.

Hence, there is no reason to conclude that product differences have benefited the Alliance & Leicester disproportionately compared to its competitors.

3. Distribution

The Alliance & Leicester branch network has in fact shown a net decline over the course of the campaign. Nor has its share of the top nine societies' total branch networks changed significantly over this time (Table 7).

TABLE 7

	1986	1987	1988	1989	1990	1991
No of A & L branches	421	413	407	407	409	410
A & L share of top nine (%) (excl. Abbey)	10.6	10.4	10.0	10.1	10.5	N/A

Source: BSA

No significant long-term changes have occurred in other distribution channels (eg mortgage brokers) except for agencies (often located in estate agents' offices) which have halved in number from 1986–90.

4. *Competitive advertising*

The Alliance & Leicester's competitors have continued to advertise at a high level throughout the campaign. As we have seen earlier, the Alliance & Leicester's share of voice has fluctuated slightly but has not increased dramatically.

Hence the Alliance & Leicester's growth in acceptability and business cannot be attributed to lack of marketing effort by other societies.

5. *The effect of merging*

In 1987, the newly merged Alliance & Leicester had clearly not settled down from the short-term effects of the merger. As we have seen, awareness and propensity to use were very low for a society of its size.

However, would these measures have increased naturally over time, without the assistance of Fry & Laurie? Would consumers have become accustomed to the new, larger society through experience alone – and consequently have come to consider it a more acceptable choice?

We strongly believe that this would not have happened. Consider the analogous case of the merger between the Nationwide and the Anglia in September 1987.

Before the merger, these societies were the third and the seventh largest respectively (including Abbey National). After the merger, the combined society was third largest, not far behind the Abbey and way ahead of the Woolwich.

Unsurprisingly, it too suffered from low awareness and propensity to use. Consumers had no reason to perceive it as any larger than whichever of its constituent parts they were previously more familiar with (Table 8).

TABLE 8

	Pre-merger (August 1987)	Post-merger (October 1987)
Propensity to use for savings	Nationwide 27% Anglia 14%	Nationwide Anglia 22%
Prompted awareness	Nationwide 75% Anglia 68%	Nationwide Anglia 66%

Source: FRS

As a result, its pool of potential customers was smaller than it 'deserved' on the basis of its size (Table 9).

TABLE 9

Share of propensity to use (Top 10 excluding Abbey)	Asset share (Top 10 excluding Abbey)
13.6%	20.5%

Sources: FRS, BSA (1987)

Over time this has resulted in a relative decline in the Nationwide Anglia's business (Table 10).

TABLE 10

	1987	1988	1989	1990	1991
Share of mortgagors of top 10 excl Abbey (%)	19.4	19.0	18.3	16.9	16.6
Share of savers of top 10 excl Abbey (%)	19.6	19.3	19.0	17.2	16.2

Source: FRS

Its asset share of the top ten societies (excluding Abbey) fell from 20.5% in 1987 to 17.9% in 1990.

This dramatic decline indicates that the Alliance & Leicester's success was far from inevitable. The consequences of a merger between two similarly sized societies are potentially disastrous. Clearly, the Fry & Laurie campaign achieved an unusual reversal of fortune.

Having looked at the range of other possible causes for the increases in the Alliance & Leicester's acceptability and market share, none can explain the changes we have observed. In fact, they would seem to suggest that the opposite should have occurred.

Hence we are left with the conclusion that it must have been the advertising.

DID THE ADVERTISING PAY FOR ITSELF?

We have examined the size of the effect in two ways.

1. *Econometrics*

   The econometric analysis is explained in detail in the Appendix. This analysis effectively provides us with an estimate of the *short-term* effect of advertising, ie blips in net receipts caused by advertising. The model estimates that in the short-term the advertising generated £656 million additional net receipts for the society.

2. *Total effect*

   We have estimated the total effect of the advertising (ie both the short-term blips and the longer term effect of increasing acceptability) by assuming that without Fry & Laurie, the Alliance & Leicester's share of total industry savings balances would have remained at the pre-advertising level of around 5.45%. On the evidence of Nationwide Anglia's experience this is probably an optimistic assumption. On this basis (and assuming about 8% of balances are due to interest credited), the Alliance & Leicester now has an extra £1.21 billion of savings balances over and above what we would have expected.

   Taking these two calculations, we arrive at the following long- and short-term effects of advertising:

Long-term	£554 million
Short-term	£656 million
Total	£1,210 million

This £1.2 billion was additional money the Alliance & Leicester could lend as mortgages. Across an average five years' lifespan it will/has generated £93 million of additional gross profit.

This, however, still underestimates the total value of the advertising. The increase in acceptability today will generate enormous amounts of additional business in the future as potential customers become actual customers.

For a spend of £22 million, the society has made a profitable investment in its own future.

SUMMARY

A building society's future depends on its acceptability amongst the millions of consumers who have no need for its services *now*, but who will have a need at some time in the future.

Without this acceptability, the society will fail to achieve its due share of new business and it will decline relative to its competitors. But by increasing this acceptability it will claim a disproportionate share of new business and hence achieve real growth.

The problem is that this mass of potential future users have no interest in building society products. Hence it is very difficult to change their attitudes towards the providers of those products.

The Fry & Laurie campaign for the Alliance & Leicester achieved this difficult task. By persuading the mass of disinterested consumers that the Alliance & Leicester was established, safe and secure, and furthermore positioning it as the society that makes things simple, it doubled the pool of potential users who would consider using it.

As a result, the Alliance & Leicester has achieved an increasing share of mortgage and savings business which has enabled it to grow from the fifth to the third largest society without merging.

APPENDIX

Econometric Analysis

In order properly to isolate and quantify the short-term effect of advertising on Alliance & Leicester's savings business, an econometric model was constructed. Alliance & Leicester's net receipts were estimated for the 71 monthly periods from February 1986 to December 1991 (the longest period for which all the data were available) using ordinary least squares regression. The resulting model fits the data well, as Figure 12 shows, explaining 89% of the variation in net receipts, with no tendency either to over or under predict.

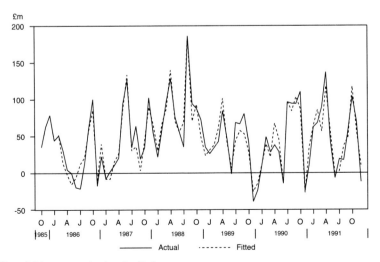

Figure 12. *Alliance & Leicester net receipts (actual vs fitted)*
Sources: Alliance & Leicester, BMP model

The model has been subjected to a range of statistical tests for both fit and specification, and passed each test satisfactorily at the 95% confidence level. Full details of these tests are given at the end of this appendix.

The econometric analysis shows that Alliance & Leicester's TV advertising has had a significant effect on net receipts. A burst of TV advertising produces a surge of net receipts one month later, with the effect dying away over the following months at a rate of 30% a month. The effect is illustrated in Figure 13.

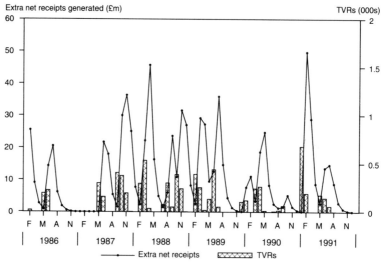

Figure 13. *Effect of TV ads on net receipts*
Source: BMP model

It is important to realise that this only represents the short-term effect of advertising. At least part of this effect is due to new account openings, and provided these customers are retained they will increase the base level of net receipts, as well as producing short-term increases. It is impossible to account for such long-term effects explicitly in the model, and so the model will tend to *underestimate* the effect of advertising on net receipts.

Furthermore, looking at the periods before and after the Fry & Laurie campaign began, it is possible to detect a fall in interest rate sensitivity. Before September 1987, a 1p decrease in cost of funds would have produced a 4.6% fall in net receipts. After the new campaign began, a similar reduction in interest rates would have only produced a 2.2% fall in net receipts. It cannot be conclusively proved that this was wholly due to advertising, but it does suggest another possible advertising effect over and above the one we have measured.

Bearing in mind these two caveats, it has been estimated that between September 1987 and December 1991, TV advertising generated at least £656m in extra net receipts.

The effects of press advertising are more difficult to quantify. Press advertising is usually used to support product launches or announce interest rate changes and promotions. It is therefore difficult to separate the effect of press advertising from these other factors. Press ads used to support the bond issues in 1986 and 1987 do seem to have boosted net receipts over and above the effect of the launches themselves, however.

No consistent effect of competitive advertising on Alliance & Leicester's net receipts was found.

Variables used in the model

Mnemonic	Meaning	Data Source
T16NR	Top 16 Net Receipts (adjusted for Abbey National)	A & L
ALADR	A & L Cost of Funds	A & L
T16ADR	Top 16 Cost of Funds	A & L
BOND2	Bond Issue 1987	Dummy variable
ALBRPS(-1)	Real Press spend on bond issue ads	Media Register, CSO
PROMO	A & L Promotions	Dummy variable
INVPLUS	Investment Plus improved return	Dummy variable
SPRET	Special Return improved return	Dummy variable
L4	Launch of Capital Choice	Dummy variable
L6	Launch of Midas & 90-day	Dummy variable
PRIV	Government Privatisations	Dummy variable
ADSTOCK	A & L TVR's adstock, 30% decay rate	BARB
C1	Closure of Prime Plus & Premium Plus	Dummy variable
C4	Closure of Capital Choice, Bank Save Plus, & Gross Account	Dummy variable
C5	Closure of Gold Plus, Ready Money Plus	Dummy variable
C	Constant Term	–
ALNR	A & L Net Receipts	A & L

Preferred Form of the Model

The dependent variable was ALNR. The equation was linear with the following coefficients:

Variable	Coefficient	T-Statistic
C	88.50	3.2
T16NR2	0.06	8.6
ALADR	1284.68	3.0
ALADR(−2)	10266.11	3.7
T16ADR(−2)	−12642.73	−4.4
BOND2	83.53	6.1
ALBRPS(−1)	0.0003	5.6
PROMO	18.14	2.4
INVPLUS	87.17	4.3
SPRET	67.30	5.0
L4(−1)	40.45	3.9
L6(−1)	120.77	6.1
PRIV	−20.09	−3.6
ADSTOCK(-1)	0.07	5.5
C1	−20.73	−2.5
C4	−53.09	−2.9
C5	−38.39	−3.2

Statistical Tests

The model performed well against all the standard diagnostic tests, with the following test statistics:

Number of observations = 71
Number of parameters = 17

Test Statistic	Value	Critical Value
R^2	89%	–
Adjusted R^2	86%	–
Durbin Watson	1.94	–
Standard Error	17.11	–
Mean of Dependent Variable	48.83	–
LM(1)	0.03	3.84
LM(6)	6.65	9.49
Arch (1)	1.56	3.84
Arch (6)	4.35	9.49
Variance Ratio Test	1.29	2.01
Chow Test for parameter stability	0.43	1.86
Chow Test for post sample predictive failure	1.27	1.91

20

Direct Line Insurance

Direct Response and Brand Building is Possible!

INTRODUCTION

By 1989, in order to achieve its goal of becoming a major motor insurer, Direct Line had to find a way to make a significant increase in its new business levels, and to make a definitive break away from the growing number of 'lookalike' direct insurers, who were all advertising in the same newspapers with a similar offer of cheaper motor insurance by going direct.

Adding TV to press advertising could be expected to build up the brand values – but could it generate the required increase in response levels?

This case study demonstrates that when Direct Line moved into TV, within three months they had not only seen their brand imagery transformed – they had also generated a massive increase in response. It is this joint development of the brand and direct response which has helped to drive the company up into the top ten UK motor insurers.

This study also shows that Direct Line's move into TV was far from 'a leap in the dark': careful use of planning, research and response monitoring ensured that the various components of the advertising could be evaluated at any stage. The effectiveness of the advertising was specifically designed to be demonstrable.

THE CHALLENGE TO DIRECT LINE

Market Background

For many years the motor insurance market had been dominated by the major brands, selling through the traditional outlet of high street brokers.

On paper, the opportunity for direct insurers looked very promising: by cutting out the middleman and dealing direct with consumers, Direct Line could easily undercut the established insurers who pay up to 20% commission to brokers – and motor insurance is a market where consumers *are* prepared to shop around to get a better price.

Because of this widespread practice of shopping around, motor insurance margins had already become somewhat leaner; Direct Line therefore had to be absolutely certain that the market gap would be profitable. To achieve this, they implemented two key management policies from the start:

1. *Automation*: paperwork is minimised at every stage of Direct Line's operations; this obviates the huge clerical overheads endemic in traditional insurance houses; computerisation also ensures first-class up-to-the-minute information for management and marketing.

2. *Low-risk business*: the most profitable insurance policies are those where the fewest claims are likely to be made; Direct Line's pricing is specifically designed to be most attractive to those drivers who fall into the underwriters' lower-risk categories.

Against this background, and with these policies firmly in place, Direct Line set itself the goal, in 1985, of becoming a top ten motor insurer by 1990. The first three years proved to be very successful; as well as cross-selling to Royal Bank of Scotland account holders, the company used off-the-page advertising in national newspapers which proved to be effective in generating good levels of response.

However, by 1988 other companies had begun to realise the opportunity in the direct market, and they began to advertise in the same newspapers, offering a very similar product – even using the same slogans and space sizes.

Not surprisingly, this diluted response rates for Direct Line and, while they had successfully established themselves as the largest of the direct insurers, it was clear that competition from these 'lookalike' advertisers was going to slow the growth of their business. Inquiry levels from press advertising failed to improve, even when the company experimented with larger space sizes.

A quantum leap was required: Direct Line had to break away from the pack and position itself clearly in consumers' minds as *the* direct motor insurer.

Some Important Questions Facing Direct Line

In 1989, when Direct Line Insurance first approached the advertising agency, they had already taken an important decision – to break into TV in order to build the brand. But there were some vitally important questions which were unanswered:

1. Direct Line was primarily a direct response advertiser, so response rates were crucial:

    —   could TV itself generate response at all, and if so, how quickly?
    —   would TV work by supporting press response?
    —   what sort of TV response mechanism was required (eg 'See Press for Details', etc)?

2. It was not clear how consumers would react when confronted in their sitting rooms with this product:

    — How readily could consumers distinguish between 'direct' insurance and other insurance?
    — What did consumers think 'direct' meant in terms of insurance? Was it seen as a potential benefit?
    — What were the key motivators of the Direct Line offer – lower prices alone? Speed? Less hassle?
    — How could these give Direct Line an advantage over the main insurance giants, as well as the other direct insurers?
    — What should the corporate tone of voice be? How important was it to be reassuring?

To answer these questions, a qualitative research study was set up (conducted by Winstanley Douglas), which looked at attitudes to the overall sector as well as consumer reactions to a number of potential positionings. The key findings were:

1. Unlike (say) estate agents, insurance brokers were not readily seen as exploitative middlemen, and consumers were not clear about what separates a broker from an insurer:

    We would have to explain 'direct'.

2. The Direct Line name was virtually unknown and did not sound authoritative or well-established; this led consumers to believe it might be local, or a small business, which did not engender a sufficient level of trust in the company:

    We would have to reassure them of our size and stature.

3. The offer of cheaper prices, although the prime motivator for shopping around, soon raised fears of a second class service, especially from an unknown or minor company:

    We had to show that we offered first class service as well as lower prices.

These findings from the qualitative research gave very clear guidance on the positioning and proposition for the advertising.

The questions about response, however, remained largely unanswered: the biggest unknown quantity was whether TV would generate direct response in its own right, or whether its effect would be to enhance press response.

However, the research had made us much more certain about the likely effect on response at an overall level. Perceptions of brand stature and credibility were absolutely crucial to consumers' propensity to insure with the company; we therefore concluded that, even if TV did only boost response to the press advertising, the brand's enhanced stature should ensure that the boost was very significant indeed.

ANSWERING THE CHALLENGE

The Advertising Solution

The task for advertising was to put Direct Line squarely onto consumers' mental candidate list of motor insurers – preferably in the 'must get a quote from them' category. Credibility and stature would need to be strongly implied (the Royal Bank of Scotland parentage was a useful component here), but what had to be demonstrated in the action of the commercials were the actual selling points – ie the benefits of first class customer service, and the associated benefits of going direct, including better prices.

Unlike in the press campaign, we could not list the conditions of eligibility, so we had to imply as far as possible that Direct Line Insurance was for the lower risk category of driver. This was expressed in the creative brief as follows:

Proposition

Direct Line Insurance – the easy way for you to get the best possible motor cover at the best possible price.

Target Audience

Sensible private motorists aged 25+ who drive sensible cars sensibly.

The Commercials

Research had emphasised that consumers only think about insurance at certain times – basically when they have to. The drama of the advertising executions was therefore deliberately rooted in 'high interest' situations in order to get maximum impact (see scripts).

The first, 'Showroom', depicted a man who had just bought a new car being inveigled into accepting the salesman's rather daunting-looking 'recommended' insurance policy. The second, 'Bump', showed a woman who was involved in a minor car accident in a car park – another classic 'high interest' scenario.

In addition, there was a clear requirement for the advertising to maximise the branding for Direct Line, so that consumers would come away with a memory of Direct Line rather than of a commercial which simply demonstrated the benefits of direct insurance.

The solution, both to this advertising problem and to the consumer insurance problems in the commercials, was the little red telephone. In both executions the little red telephone comes hurtling to the rescue. Importantly, in both cases, what is being demonstrated by the action is not cheaper prices but better insurance – speed, convenience, less paperwork – while the price message is kept to a supporting role.

The executions were also designed to give maximum emphasis to the fact that consumers are being encouraged to respond by telephone for a quotation. Not only is the dramatised problem solved over the telephone, and a telephone number given at the end, but the whole persona of the company is represented by the heroic little red telephone.

Finally, to maximise the credibility of Direct Line, the fact that they are members of the Royal Bank of Scotland Group was included as a sub-title in the end-frame.

Targeting

As previously discussed, Direct Line have a clear policy of targeting low-risk drivers, so the commercial had to imply as far as possible that we were addressing 'sensible people, aged 25+, who drive sensible cars sensibly'.

This was achieved on two levels. Firstly in terms of casting – the actors used were typical of everyday people, epitomising Direct Line's target market. The cars shown were also normal middle-market British models. Secondly, in terms of tone of voice: although the executions derived much humour from exaggeration (eg the larger-than-life oleaginous car salesman) the underlying agenda was always firmly rooted in consumer reality – ie sensible solutions of real life car insurance problems.

Response Monitoring

Every time a consumer telephones Direct Line for an insurance quote, their details are directly entered into the central computer: these details include information on source of inquiry – consumers are asked 'How did you hear about us?' and one of the many answer-codes is for TV advertising.

Because these data are continually updated on computer, management can analyse patterns of response very quickly indeed – when Direct Line talk about the 'latest' campaign response statistics, they mean three minutes old!

This meant that the effect of TV in terms of response could be analysed straight away, and the media mix adjusted accordingly.

Client:	**Direct Line Insurance**	**Date:**	**6.12.89**
Product:	**Motor Insurance (Cover)**	**Time Length:**	**40 secs**
Title:	**'Showroom' (Revised)**		

Reasonably smart car showroom, where an amiable, ordinary man of about 40 is sitting in a shiny family saloon with the door open. A smooth salesman stands beside him and drops the car keys into his hands.

Salesman: ...there's the keys, sir...

The salesman reaches into his jacket for the insurance forms.

...now what about insurance?

Cut to little red telephone on wheels coming over a street horizon.

SFX: US cavalry charge played on small motor horn.

Cut back to showroom as salesman whips out an application form which rapidly unfolds to a quite ludicrous length, reaching down to the ground. The red phone enters, does a couple of manoeuvres round the salesman's legs, bumping away the tail of the application form, and comes to rest by the driver, who picks up the receiver. He listens intently.

Salesman: ...may I draw your attention to our Whizzo Megacover Superplan?

MVO: If you want to save time and money on motor insurance...

Phone: (Girl's voice, telephone effect) Hello, this is Direct Line...

MVO: Call Direct Line, where you deal with a human being, not a blank form ...

Cut to CU of Direct Line girl talking into her headset.

Girl: What model is the car, sir?

Cut to CU of her VDU screen as she types in the data.

MVO: ... and a computerised system that already provides low cost insurance for more than a quarter of a million motorists.

Cut back to showroom, where the salesman is looking disgruntled amid his cars.

Cut back to CU of Direct Line girl.

Girl: Right, Mr Hampel... you're covered.

Cut back to driver listening to phone with grumpy salesman eavesdropping.

Driver hangs up and speaks to still disgruntled salesman.

Driver: Thank you...

...what's wrong, haven't you seen a carphone before?

Reprise shot of little red telephone coming over horizon.

SFX: US cavalry charge played on motor horn.

MVO: For cheaper motor insurance with a human voice, call Direct Line on 081-686 2468.

Super: Logo, phone number and Royal Bank of Scotland Group line and logo.

Client:	Direct Line Insurance	Date:	6.12.89
Product:	Motor Insurance (Cover)	Time Length:	40 secs
Title:	'BUMP' (Revised)		

Open-air car park, possibly outside hotel or superstore. The car park is fairly full but there is one space near the centre into which two cars back simultaneously, and collide.

SFX: Crash

Man: Keep calm … nobody panic!

Immediately, one driver, a man, leaps out and starts flapping his arms about in obvious hysteria. The other driver gets out calmly and surveys the slight damage.

Cut to little red telephone on wheels coming over a street horizon.

SFX: US cavalry charge played on small motor horn.

Cut back to woman, surveying damage. She speaks to the man who looks pained.

Woman: Hmm … looks like an insurance job.

As he speaks, the little red phone arrives on the scene, whizzing round his feet and causing him some astonishment.

Man: Great …a claim form as long as War and Peace…

…estimates…

CU of little red phone as it trundles merrily across to the woman. She picks up the receiver as it stops, and she listens.

MVO: You only find out how good an insurance company is when you make a claim…

Phone: (Girl's voice, telephone effect) Hello, this is Direct Line …

Cut to Direct Line girl at her VDU terminal talking into her headset.
Cut to CU of her screen as the data is typed in.
Cut back to CU of woman listening, with man trying to eavesdrop.

MVO: With Direct Line, you deal with a human being, not a blank form…

Girl: Can you describe the damage to me?

Cut back to CU of Direct Line girl's face.

MVO: …with a computerised system that already provides low cost insurance for over a quarter of a million motorists.

Girl: …so we can authorise the repair immediately…

Cut back to woman. She hangs up the receiver and hands some documents back to the man, before starting up her car.

Woman: Thank you … well, I must be off. Nice bumping into you…

Reprise shot of little red telephone coming over street horizon.

MVO: For cheaper motor insurance with a human voice…

Super: Logo, phone number and Royal Bank of Scotland Group line and logo.

MVO: Call Direct Line on 081-686 2468.

Media Strategy

Given the unknowns concerning direct response, press advertising presence was initially maintained while TV was tested. This entailed an exploratory approach by Yershon Media (who were responsible for all media planning and buying) using constant updates on response data from Direct Line's central computer to assess whether number of spots in a given TV area should be increased (if response was slower than other areas) or decreased (if there was a danger of overloading the Direct Line switchboard). This sensitivity to response is one of the major factors underlying the 'front-heavy' shape of the TV campaign below.

The campaign was launched in Direct Line's stronger regions – Scotland (generating business for the Glasgow office) and London/South (for the Croydon office).

	Jan 90	Feb 90	Mar 90	Total
Television				
30" network equivalent ratings	285	131	20	436
Press				
Ratecard spend (£000s)	244	181	79	504

Sources: BARB/AGB, MR/MEAL

The move into TV entailed a 93% increase in Direct Line's total TV/press spend, and the company's share of voice rose from 13% to 22%.

Image Monitoring

In order to measure the effect of the advertising on consumers' awareness and image of Direct Line Insurance, we needed some form of tracking survey. One candidate for this was the widely-used Millward Brown Syndicated Insurance Tracking Study, but this proved too inflexible for our purposes, so Millward Brown were asked to design a dedicated tracking study instead.

This involved telephoning every week a sample of 100 private motorists (within given regional and demographic constraints) in order to assess their awareness of Direct Line versus other insurance brands, their perceptions of the company and the service it offered, and their broad reactions to the advertising.

Results from this survey naturally took longer to come through than the computerised response statistics, but this was not a problem, for two reasons:

1. Shifts in awareness and imagery of companies (especially imagery) don't happen overnight.
2. We had already tested the impact and communication in a series of Millward Brown LINK-tests, conducted before the advertising went on air. (These are written up in some detail in the Market Research Society 1991 Conference papers – S Ashman and K Clark 'Ensuring the Sales-Effectiveness of Advertising'.)

EFFECTS OF THE CAMPAIGN

With our measurement systems in place, we could assess the effect of the campaign in both dimensions – the effect on inquiries and the effect on awareness and imagery.

The Effect on Inquiries

The results of the campaign were dramatic, as the following graphs indicate.

It soon became clear that TV was not only capable of generating response in its own right, but it was also doing it immediately. Inquiries to Direct Line from consumers (ie requests for a motor insurance quotation) rose at such a rate that the company had to take steps to avoid clogging the switchboard.

Figure 1 shows (within the seasonal variations in demand at this time of year) that where the December business levels were only slightly ahead of the previous year, inquiries jumped during the TV campaign by between 24% and 54%.

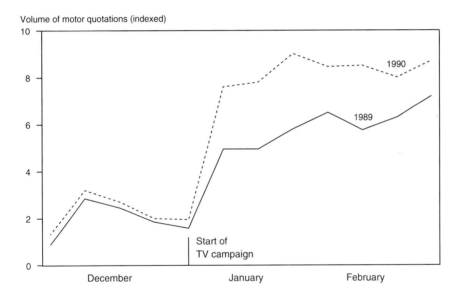

Figure 1: *Total increase in telephone inquiries (3 months ending February 1989 vs 3 months ending February 1990)*
Source: Direct Line statistics

Figure 2 shows the difference in business levels between the areas which carried the TV campaign and those that did not. Not only does this again demonstrate the pulling power of the TV campaign, it also shows how the move from national press into TV began to introduce stronger regional biases in the patterns of response – the risk of acute regionalisation was later diminished as Direct Line progressively rolled out across other TV regions in the course of 1990.

NB: There is some effect of TV in the 'non-TV' regions; this is largely because of the overlap between regional TV areas, but there is also a minor effect from the very small amount of advertising (113 TVRs) on national TV-am.

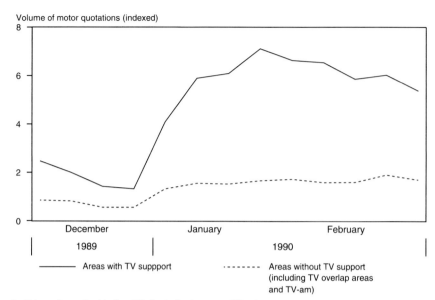

Figure 2: *Volume of motor inquiries from TV advertised regions vs non-TV regions*
Source: Direct Line statistics

Figure 3 shows the huge growth in the number of insurance quotations given to people who cited 'TV advertising' in answer to the question 'How did you hear about us?' Not surprisingly, the increase is much greater in the areas where the TV campaign rolled out, but again there is some effect in the 'non-TV areas' because of overlap and TV-am.

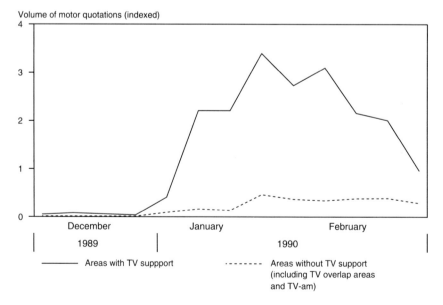

Figure 3: *Quotations to consumers citing TV advertising as source of awareness*
Source: Direct Line statistics

Although this is an imperfect measure of 'source of awareness' (which is notoriously difficult to quantify for any brand in more than one medium), it does demonstrate that consumers themselves attributed their awareness of Direct Line to the TV campaign.

(Meanwhile, response to press advertising continued to be slow, as it had been before the TV campaign.)

The Effect on Awareness and Imagery

Again, the charts showing positive shifts in Direct Line's awareness and imagery are very clear.

The percentage of people claiming to have heard of Direct Line (Figure 4) nearly doubled – from 24% to 42% – in these three months: not only is this an impressive figure in its own right, it also provides strong evidence that the commercials were well-branded.

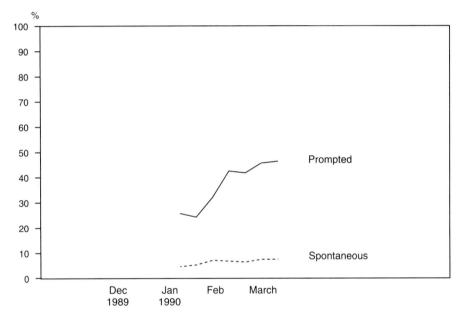

Figure 4: *Increases in awareness of Direct Line Insurance (region: London)*
Source: Millward Brown

Figure 5 shows how this increased awareness of Direct Line was effectively beginning to pull them up 'out of the pack' of minor brands, and up towards the very well-entrenched major players at the top.

Figure 6 shows how the image scores of Direct Line improved fairly rapidly over the first three months of the campaign.

Not only were consumers able to identify and acknowledge the product benefits, they were also increasingly seeing Direct Line as a sympathetic and popular brand.

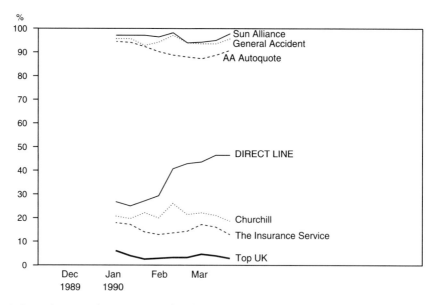

Figure 5: *Prompted awareness of Direct Line compared to other brands (region: London)*
Source: Millward Brown

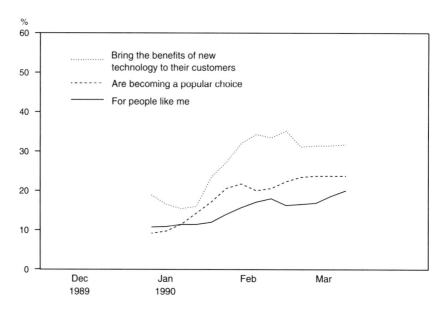

Figure 6: *Changes in imagery of Direct Line – % of consumers agreeing with description of Direct Line (region: London)*
Source: Millward Brown

THE CONTRIBUTION OF ADVERTISING

Direct Line's motor business levels had increased very substantially, its imagery had undergone significant positive change in consumers' minds and awareness of the brand was growing fast. How far can we be sure that all this was really the contribution of the TV advertising?

We feel absolutely confident that the TV campaign was the cause of these changes, for the following reasons:

1. There was no consumer public relations activity in the TV launch period.
2. The ongoing programme of direct mail was continuing at the same level, and could not therefore explain the upturn in business.
3. The decline in inquiries from press continued at the same rate, regardless of the TV support.
4. The 'shape' of the upward changes in business levels and consumer awareness closely match the shape of the TV campaign – they went up when the TV ads came on, and began to fall back when the initial burst ended.
5. There was a huge increase in the number of customers who cited TV advertising as their source of awareness of Direct Line.

CONCLUSIONS

In 1989, Direct Line faced two challenges; on the one hand, the need to pull the brand away from the growing number of 'lookalike' direct motor insurers, and on the other, the need to generate significantly increased levels of consumer response.

A brand building television advertising campaign seemed a natural solution to the first problem, by changing consumers' perceptions of Direct Line.

But could television generate sufficient levels of direct response for a relatively little-known company whose product offering – direct insurance – consumers did not readily understand?

We hope that this paper has made it absolutely clear that television successfully met both challenges; not only did it transform the brand imagery and consumer awareness of Direct Line, it also proved to be an effective and immediate direct response business-builder.

We hope it is also clear that television, although unproven when we began, was not a 'leap in the dark': at every stage of the process the emphasis was on accountability – changes in response levels and consumer perceptions were constantly measured, and that measurement continues today.

The benefit to Direct Line is that they can judge the effectiveness – and cost-effectiveness – of their advertising at any stage: one of the results of this is that their expenditure split between TV and press has changed from 61:39 (during our first campaign) to 99:1 in the year to December 1991.

Naturally we cannot reveal the level of return to Direct Line in financial terms, but their business has gone from strength to strength – they have become the ninth largest motor insurer in the UK, and are now well on course for the top five.

There are numerous advertisers today who, we would suggest, are in a similar situation to that confronting Direct Line in 1989 – advertising in the proven direct response medium of press, but unable to definitively pull away from their competitors in that medium, and unsure of whether a move into television could generate response as well as build the brand.

Naturally, circumstances vary for different product fields and different brands, but to anyone faced with this situation we would say:

'Direct response *and* brand-building *is* possible!'

POSTSCRIPT – DECEMBER 1992

It could not be more satisfying to write a postscript to this case study. Since that first TV campaign Direct Line's success, both as a brand and as a business, has been nothing short of spectacular.

In that time Direct Line has trebled its number of motor policy holders. Today, with over 750,000 motor customers, Direct Line is the UK's fifth largest insurer of comprehensively covered private cars.

And what the *Daily Express* recently called 'that infuriating little red telephone' is becoming a household name – as witness the *Punch* cartoon by Martin Ross, below.

'Sorry mate, the phone rolled out in front of me'

Section Seven

Marketing *Award for Innovation*

21

Skip Lunch. Save a Life
Advertising Success on a Plate

INTRODUCTION

Every year, for a single week in April, Save the Children Fund appeals to the British public to help it with its work. On average, it manages to generate £600k. In April 1991, its voluntary income for the week increased tenfold.

Its annual appeal succeeded in raising £5.5 million in the midst of a biting consumer recession, in the wake of a number of emergency public appeals and for a cause which strikes a depressingly familiar note – the threat of famine in Africa. All this with a total fund-raising budget set at £225k, of which £140k was allocated for media expenditure.

It was a sensitivity to the budget, and a knowledge of the powers and limitations of advertising, which lay at the heart of this campaign's success.

What this paper will serve to demonstrate is that limited resources often require a new definition of advertising's role. It demonstrates an acceptance that sometimes advertising cannot in itself provide the whole solution; but it proves that advertising *can* directly enlist the help of other 'voices' to succeed; it can act as a catalyst both for media attention and public donation; it can sow the seed of an idea which will take root, flourish and which will reap rich rewards. It can do all these things, and in the case of Ogilvy and Mather's 'Skip lunch, Save a life' idea, it did.

BACKGROUND

By October 1990, it had become clear to relief workers in several countries in Africa that there was a threat of famine on a par with the famous 1984 disaster. Some 27 million people were facing starvation. Save the Children Fund committed its annual fund-raising week to the subject of famine in Africa, and set a target figure of £2.5m to help with emergency relief. It acknowledged that this was an ambitious target – the ceiling on previous Save the Children Fund weeks stood at £600k.

Neither were external factors working in its favour;

1. *Expanding competition*
    The charity market had burgeoned during the 1980s. At the time of the planned appeal, over 170,000 charities (registered with the Charity Commission) were competing for a share of the public's generosity.

2. *Tightening purse strings*

There was clear evidence both in real and perceptual terms that the British public was undergoing what Bob Geldof called 'compassion fatigue'.

Charitable donations had shown no real growth since 1986, with voluntary income for 1989/90 growing by only 1% in real terms. The typical size of donations had fallen from £1.97 per person in 1988/89 to £1.28 in 1989/90. (Source: Charities Aid Foundation.)

The forecast for the whole charity market looked bleak. All the indications were that the UK would see a trough in discretionary spending for the period 1990–1991.

Naturally, charitable donations come from an individual's personal disposable income. As most donations, particularly those in response to fund-raising activities, are a 'knee-jerk' reaction, at any one time the charity itself is in competition with anything from a telephone bill to a chocolate bar in its demand on the individual purse.

With personal disposable income on the decline in the first quarter of 1991, not surprisingly charities had slipped in people's hierarchy of concerns.

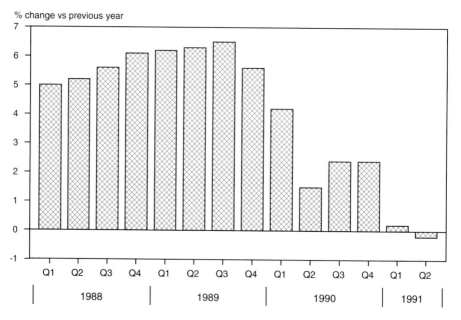

Figure 1. *Real personal disposable income 1988-91*
Source: CSO

3. *A well-worn subject*

Famine and Africa are two words which have become virtually inseparable since Bob Geldof put the spotlight on Ethiopia in 1984. Since then, there has been at least one appeal for Africa every year.

The sheer volume of appeals and apparent insolubility of the African problem had served to dent both public and media commitment to the issue:

Media

Though the situation in Africa had remained severe, the subject had lost much of its 'newsworthiness' as far as the media were concerned. This was especially true in the first few months of 1991 given the following demands for media attention:

— The Gulf War, which had been occupying the headlines for much of 1990 and 1991.

— The Kurdish refugees, who had suffered in the aftermath of the war.

— The flood victims of Bangladesh, an emergency which hit the news on the same day as the press launch for the Save the Children Fund appeal.

Consumer

The indications were that up until 1991 international aid was suffering in the proportion of voluntary income it received. Figure 2 illustrates the sharp decline in voluntary donations to international aid agencies since 1984, the year of Live Aid.

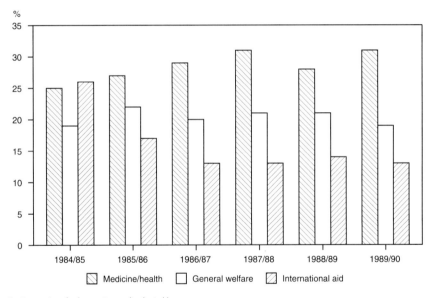

Figure 2. *Proportion of voluntary income by charitable sector*
Source: Charities Aid Foundation

Furthermore, qualitative research conducted in the autumn of 1990 indicated that the public were becoming weary of Third World problems. Their weariness was evident on two levels: fatigue about the subject (Africa) and fatigue about the way the subject is presented to them when soliciting their money (pictures of starving children).

The inertia and the compassion fatigue of the UK public are encapsulated with brutal honesty in the words of one respondent;

'I'm sure it's all very worthy, but it's all so familiar. I just think, aye aye, another attempt to bail out the African nations and I've seen it all before. We've become immune.' Source: Ogilvy and Mather qualitative research October 1990

Ironically, research hinted that Live Aid itself was counterproductive in its phenomenal success. The scale of income generated in 1984 'promised' a solution as far as consumers were concerned. The absence of that solution was interpreted as being proof of a 'bottomless pit' of need; their donation would be a mere 'drop in the ocean' as they saw it.

It was against this background that the advertising had to perform.

DEVELOPMENT OF ADVERTISING

Our sensitivity to the external barriers to the likely success of the appeal did more than merely help us to avoid pitfalls; it pointed the way both to defining the advertising brief and to the ultimate creative solution.

The options with a small budget were limited. A traditional approach to the problem would have resulted in;

Targeting: traditionally 'responsive' readers of broadsheet newspapers.
Creative: a problem-focused approach – the threat of human death if you do not give.
Media: purchasing of 'distress' media space.

The advertising strategy and creative work flouted all three 'rules' in its bid to maximise revenue for the appeal.

THE ROLE FOR ADVERTISING

£140k was a prohibitively small media budget. Advertising clearly had to provoke a response, but previous direct response advertising campaigns run for Save the Children Fund had provided an average return of £3 for every £1 spent. We could therefore expect to generate no more than £420k from a £140k media spend advertising campaign, but this would fall some £2.08m short of Save the Children Fund's target figure.

We therefore defined our advertising task less in terms of its direct role than in terms of its marketable potential. *Advertising's role was therefore to 'buy' media attention.* Advertising which has a spin-off in PR and publicity is not new; the agency's own Winalot Prime commercial achieved a level of editorial and PR attention considered to be worth half a share point (commented on in *Advertising Works 5*). Nevertheless, to make such media attention the *primary* focus of the advertising was unusual. We aimed to find an advertising idea that could be *merchandised* to maximum effect, that could act as the seedcorn for the whole campaign.

TARGET AUDIENCE

Implicit in our definition of the role for advertising was the need to make those in the media the target audience. Nevertheless, we felt that an overt message directly targeted at them would both marginalise the public's involvement and dictate an inappropriate sentiment for the advertising.

Despite a loyal donor base, the target figure of £2.5m militated against targeting Save the Children Fund donors. This appeal, if it was to succeed, would have to engage huge numbers of people; it had to solicit the support of the 'big hearted' Sun/Mirror reader.

In short, we had identified the need for a populist message which would capture the hearts of the British nation and would enlist the support of the nation's media.

THE FOCUS

As mentioned before, qualitative research conducted in 1990 had shown that consumers had become inured to shock imagery; furthermore it contravened Save the Children Fund's strict code of practice;

'Text and images should not be selected solely for "shock value" nor should they trivialise, distort or misrepresent the work of Save the Children in order to evoke concern and stimulate interest and action.' (Save the Children Fund, August 1990)

There were thus two key requirements of any advertising message: **Identification**, and identification which could be translated into **action**.

Identification:	The Third World is remote; 'over there'; we needed a message which would bring it closer to home, make it meaningful/relevant.
Action:	Empathy and understanding were not enough. At the end of the day, this was a *fund-raising* exercise. We had to ensure that this identification was channelled into a positive response; giving money.

Interestingly, the creative solution was found by having recourse to the appeal's *competition*. As we mentioned earlier, the *barriers* to donation were many fold – an act of self-indulgence like a chocolate bar, a meal you'd treated yourself with – all those things which give you pleasure but are ultimately dispensable.

What the creative team succeeded in establishing was an inspirational and simple 'rate of exchange' between life in the UK and life in Africa, setting up a direct link between the two. This immediately gave the public a yardstick for their own involvement; the sentiment was purely that a small sacrifice can make a huge difference.

The beauty of the 'rate of exchange' was that it worked as a shorthand for a web of complex issues. How could anyone resist the appeal to:

Skip Lunch. Save a Life

— No-one can claim they can't afford to forego one lunch, if that lunch holds the key to someone's survival.
— Giving up your lunch helps you understand in some small way what the people in Africa are suffering.
— You are not being asked to dig deeper into your pockets – you are merely being asked to re-channel your expenditure.
— The charity is *accountable*: your meal buys food for one family for a week, quelling the nagging doubts about where your money might be going.

THE ADVERTISING

Client:	SAVE THE CHILDREN	Ref:	GREASY BACON
Length:	30 SECONDS	Date:	19th April 1991
Title:	GREASY BACON		

Open on a fat-spattered hot plate. The type most often found in transport cafes.

Fat is dolloped on and begins to fizzle.
Two eggs are cracked into the fat.
Three sausages are dropped on and they begin to sizzle.

VO: THIS COULD FEED SOMEONE FOR A MONTH.

Bacon rashers add to the spitting.

VO: BUT ONLY IF **YOU** DON'T EAT IT.

Followed by black puddings.

VO: IN AFRICA THE PRICE OF THIS LUNCH COULD BUY SOMEONE FOOD FOR A MONTH. OR, PAY THEIR MEDICAL COSTS FOR A YEAR.

VO: 27 MILLION PEOPLE ARE FACING FAMINE (A SITUATION WORSE THAN THE DISASTER OF 1984).

Cut to food on the plate.

VO: IF EVERY ADULT SKIPS JUST ONE LUNCH THIS WEEK, WE COULD SAVE MILLIONS OF LIVES.

Mix to an empty plate with SKIP LUNCH. SAVE A LIFE. (Plate device).

SUPER: FOR CREDIT CARD DONATIONS AND INFORMATION PACK PHONE: 0898 448844. SAVE THE CHILDREN.

(Calls charged at 34p per minute cheap rate and 45p at all other times, including VAT.)

VO: SKIP LUNCH. SAVE A LIFE.

Client:	SAVE THE CHILDREN	Ref:	BREAKFAST
Length:	40 SECONDS	Date:	17th April 1991
Title:	BREAKFAST		

SFX: Breakfast noises. Sizzling bacon etc.

DAD: WHAT'S THIS?

MUM: YOUR BREAKFAST.

DAD: BUT I DON'T WANT A COOKED BREAKFAST.

MUM: YOU DO TODAY.

DAD: WHY?

MUM: BECAUSE YOU'RE NOT HAVING ANY LUNCH.

DAD: WHY?

MUM: BECAUSE YOU'RE GIVING THE MONEY TO SAVE THE CHILDREN INSTEAD.

Fade under

VO: IN AFRICA, 27 MILLION PEOPLE ARE FACING FAMINE.

  IF EVERY ADULT SKIPS JUST **ONE** LUNCH, WE COULD SAVE MILLIONS OF LIVES.

  FOR CREDIT CARD DONATIONS AND INFORMATION PACK, PHONE SAVE THE CHILDREN ON 0898 448844. 0898 448844.

  SKIP LUNCH. SAVE A LIFE.

SFX: Cutlery noise.

DOG: WOOF!

MUM: AND YOU'D BETTER EAT UP AS WELL.

VO: (CALLS CHARGED AT 34P PER MINUTE CHEAP RATE & 45P AT ALL OTHER TIMES.)

Client:	SAVE THE CHILDREN	Ref:	LUNCH
Length:	40 SECONDS	Date:	17th April 1991
Title:	LUNCH		

SFX: Typewriters (Fade under).

WENDY: I'M FEELING A BIT PECKISH, WHAT SHALL WE DO FOR LUNCH?

         HAVE SOMETHING IN THE CANTEEN?

JULIE: NAH.

WENDY: OR A PIZZA?

JULIE: NAH.

WENDY: NIP DOWN THE WINE BAR?

JULIE: ...NAH.

WENDY: HOW ABOUT A SANDWICH?

JULIE: ERR... NAH.

WENDY: HELP MILLIONS OF PEOPLE FACING FAMINE IN AFRICA?

JULIE: NOW YOU'RE TALKING!

Fade under

VO: IN AFRICA, 27 MILLION PEOPLE ARE FACING FAMINE. IF EVERY ADULT SKIPS JUST **ONE** LUNCH, WE COULD SAVE MILLIONS OF LIVES.

         FOR CREDIT CARD DONATIONS AND INFORMATION, PHONE SAVE THE CHILDREN ON 0898 448844. 0898 448844.

         SKIP LUNCH. SAVE A LIFE.

VO: (CALLS CHARGED AT 34P A MINUTE CHEAP RATE & 45P AT ALL OTHER TIMES).

IF PEOPLE IN AFRICA ARE GOING WITHOUT FOOD FOR WEEKS, YOU CAN SKIP LUNCH TODAY.

Could you miss lunch for a day? Of course you could. But for a week? Not so easy.

Particularly if you have to watch your family going hungry too.

In Africa, 27 million people are facing famine. Some have been forced to eat the seed corn that was their only chance of growing a crop this year.

Others have nothing, except the prospect of a slow death.

But you could help change the situation, this lunchtime.

Simply send the money you would have spent on lunch to Save the Children.

A mere cheese roll (50p) provides a child with vital food and vitamins for one day.

A pizza and a glass of wine for two (£10) would feed one adult for three months. We're standing by now to get the aid to wherever it is needed.

You can easily go without lunch for a day. Millions in Africa can't.

I've skipped lunch and I'd like to donate what it would have cost. £20 ☐ £10 ☐ £5 ☐ Other £

Please send me a free fund raising pack. ☐

Name Mr/Mrs/Ms/Miss: _____ (BLOCK CAPITALS PLEASE)

Address: _____

_____ Postcode: _____

I enclose my:
Giro No. 5173000 ☐ Cash ☐ Postal Order ☐ Cheque ☐

Or charge my:
American Express ☐ Access ☐ Visa ☐ Diners Club ☐

Account No. ☐☐☐☐☐☐☐☐☐☐☐☐☐☐

Signature: _____ (Credit Cards only)

Return to: Dept.1860049, Save the Children, PO Box 100, Swadlincote, Derbyshire DE12 7DR. Registered Charity No. 213880.

Save the Children

IT WON'T KILL YOU TO GO WITHOUT LUNCH FOR A DAY.

(BUT IT COULD SAVE A LIFE IN AFRICA.)

If you were to skip lunch today, it's a safe bet you'd make it to tea time.

The survival of 27 million people in Africa though, is less certain.

They are facing a famine worse than the disaster of 1984.

But you can help. This lunchtime.

By sending the money you usually spend on lunch, you could save a life.

Go without a cheeseburger (£1) and we can supply one person with food for more than a week.

Give up a ploughman's and a pint (£3) and a family of six can have clean water for three days.

It's encouraging to see how little you need to give, to make a big difference?

Save the Children is standing by now to get aid to wherever it is needed.

You can easily go without lunch for a day. Millions in Africa can't.

I've skipped lunch and I'd like to donate what it would have cost. £20 ☐ £10 ☐ £5 ☐ Other £ ☐

Please send me a free fund raising pack. ☐

Name Mr/Mrs/Ms/Miss: _____
(BLOCK CAPITALS PLEASE)

Address: _____

_____ Postcode: _____

I enclose my:
Giro No. 5173000 ☐ Cash ☐ Postal Order ☐ Cheque ☐

Or charge my:
American Express ☐ Access ☐ Visa ☐ Diners Club ☐

Account No. ☐☐☐☐☐☐☐☐☐☐☐☐☐☐

Signature: _____ (Credit Cards only)

Return to: Dept.1860046, Save the Children, PO Box 100, Swadlincote, Derbyshire DE12 7DR. Registered Charity No. 213880

Save the Children

MEDIA STRATEGY

As mentioned before, a traditional strategy for fund-raising is to maximise revenue through the purchase of 'distress' media space.

In this case, the strategy adopted was to generate an illusion of advertising 'noise', by using multiple media, with the aim of attracting the attention of those very media. Hence, posters, press (both national and regional), radio and even television were included within the media plan.

Press was the bedrock of the campaign, taking the majority of the media budget. Nevertheless, the rationale for investing in television was interesting; the execution was used as a vehicle for getting coverage on the national news programmes. This is a similar strategy to the 'Politician's Poster' ruse during elections, where the media are invited for the unveiling of a poster and the nation witnesses a 'snowball' effect with reprinted versions of the poster.

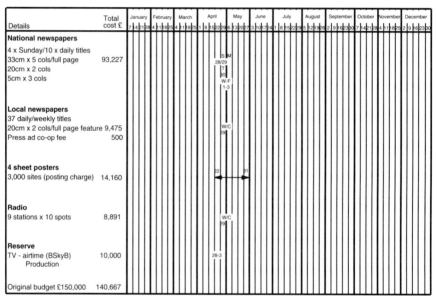

Figure 3. *Media Plan*
Note: All costs are net of agency commission and correct as at 29 April 1991

SKIP LUNCH WEEK

Monday 27th April commenced with the press launch for Skip Lunch Week hosted by the Princess Royal. This ended at 11.30am. By 12.00 the appeal was featured on all the major news programmes.

The following are examples drawn from the large amount of press coverage generated during the week.

EVALUATION

The main focus for the evaluation of the 'Skip Lunch' appeal rests on the amount of media attention generated subsequent to the launch. For this, we have no sophisticated measures at our disposal – all the available budget was channelled into maximising revenue for the appeal.

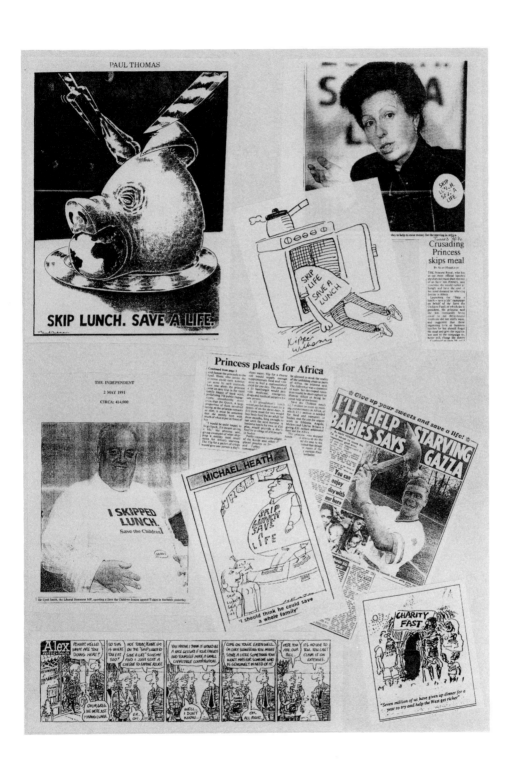

Above and beyond the media response, other factors which demonstrate the significant contribution of the advertising idea have been included. These are divided into short-term and long-term effects. By short-term is meant the effectiveness of the idea *within* the week of the appeal, and longer term, the enhancement effect of 'Skip Lunch' on other Save the Children Fund activity.

The paper concludes by aiming to answer some of the nagging doubts that may remain.

SHORT-TERM PERFORMANCE

Advertising

One robust measure of the success of the 'Skip Lunch' idea was the level of direct response to the advertising. As mentioned before, total advertising budget stood at £140k; this was split by medium as follows:

Press	£106k
TV	£10k
Radio	£10k
Posters	£14k

The press campaign for 'Skip Lunch' brought in £1.1m of the appeal's £5.5m total, achieving £10 for every £1 spent. As mentioned earlier, across the year, Save the Children Fund would expect to achieve an average level of return of £3 for every £1 spent. This achievement is all the more significant given that the primary objective of the advertising was to publicise an idea, providing the public with a *mechanism for giving*.

MEDIA COVERAGE

The launch of the appeal was a media success story. Following the conference on April 27th, both BBC and ITN news, and the national newspapers broadcast the simple message to 'Skip Lunch and Save a Life in Africa'.

Our calculated risk of £18k investment in television (media and production) reaped dividends. The TV ad was featured on BBC (1pm/6pm/9pm), ITV (12.30 pm/5.40pm/10pm), Sky News, Breakfast Time and *Wogan*. By Wednesday the TV ad had received free airtime worth a remarkable £480k at station average prices.

Interestingly, and significantly for this paper, the weighting of media attention was in favour of the appeal's *theme* over and above its cause.

In press alone, hundreds of articles both in national and regional press were written to cover the appeal. Naturally, the idea for 'Skip Lunch' is inextricably linked to the cause of famine in Africa. Nevertheless, we have tried to demonstrate here how 'Skip Lunch' acted as a prompt for increased media attention on Africa.

For this a crude measure of media coverage pre and post campaign launch is illustrated in Figure 4. It operates simply on a total count of press articles.

Not only did the campaign restimulate interest in Africa, but also in 74% of the articles, the advertising copy was used as a means of expressing the issue.

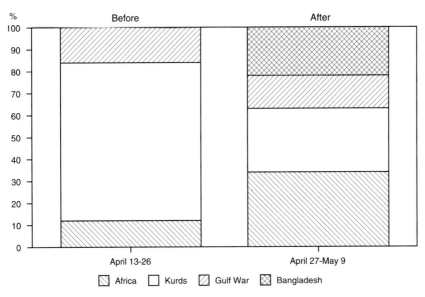

Figure 4. *Effect of skip lunch on media coverage of Africa*
Source: Textline/O&M

Attendant media activity supplementary to a mere reporting of the launch was also significant. Within a week of the appeal, the British public were witness to;

Personality endorsement:	*News of the World* 'Gazza' appeal, Cyril Smith, England Football squad photo calls.
Cartoon features:	Alex, Heath etc.
TV features:	Princess Royal on *Wogan, Newsround*.

Examples of these are featured earlier in this paper.

Significantly again, the appeal particularly fired the imagination of the populist press, historically a more difficult medium for Save the Children Fund. The success of the appeal in diverting attention from the Gulf and onto the plight in Africa should not be underestimated.

For the week following the launch, 'Skip Lunch' had clearly become part of the vernacular, as demonstrated by the numerous unsolicited cartoons.

Branches

In previous years, the branch contribution to annual Save the Children Fund week had stood static at £600k. In 1991, with the same number of branches and a similar number of volunteers, branch activity contributed some £1.5m to the cause.

The only variable in this instance was 'Skip Lunch'.

LONG-TERM PERFORMANCE

The benefits to Save the Children Fund of the 'Skip Lunch' idea went beyond the direct appeal of famine in Africa. These are worth noting, and form part of this paper's claim to the strength of the idea.

Awareness

In an annual survey conducted by *Marketing* magazine each October, advertising awareness for the charities sector is measured. The table for 1991 is shown below, with Save the Children Fund at the head.

TABLE 1: SECTOR SURVEY: CHARITIES
Q: Which of the following charities have you seen or heard any advertising for recently?

	Account	Agency	%	%Oct 90
1	Save the Children Fund	O&M	48	(–)
2	World Wildlife Fund	Young & Rubicam	48	(56)
3	The Samaritans	Saatchis	42	(43)
4	National Trust	Lowe Howard-Spink	35	(44)
5	Poppy Day Appeal	DFSDB	29	(–)
6	Christian Aid	BDDH	26	(–)
7	British Paralympic Society	Still Price: Lintas	25	(–)
8	British Red Cross Gulf War Appeal	JWT	21	(–)
9	Cerebral Palsy Charity	JWT	13	(–)
10	Variety Club Golden Heart Appeal	In-house	12	(–)
11	Sick Kids Appeal	Faulds	10	(–)
12	World Vision	Ayer	7	(–)

Source: *Marketing*, October 1991

From a position of no consumer awareness, Save the Children Fund has topped the league, overtaking amongst others, the National Trust, the UK's biggest charity.

As *Marketing* itself comments, 'fund-raising drives, including the "Skip Lunch, Save a Life" campaign last April, have no doubt increased Save the Children Fund's popularity.'

Subsequent Appeals

Save the Children Fund soon discovered in separate direct mailing exercises subsequent to the 'Skip Lunch' appeal that they were achieving above average returns. A mailing that was sent out twice, once in December 1990 and again in June 1991 had a greater level of response following 'Skip Lunch'.

How was this to be explained?

—   The same lists were used in December 1990 and June 1991
—   Christmas is traditionally a more profitable time for fund-raising than June.

Yet June returns were 14.5%, compared to 7.5% for December 1990. The only conclusion must be that 'Skip Lunch' had an enhancement effect on donor response.

Figure 5 also serves to show the impact of the 'Skip Lunch' appeal on Save the Children Fund's direct response advertising activity, and as the charity's Head of Appeals, John Lister comments;

'These results seem to prove what we suspected, namely that the awareness & image enhancement benefits from "Skip Lunch" crossed over to other fund-raising themes.'

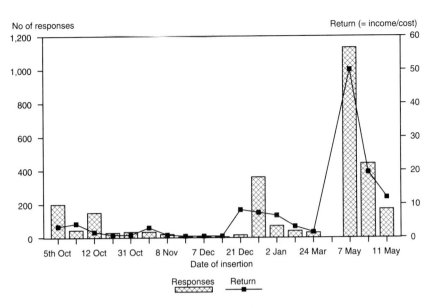

Figure 5. *The incremental effects of 'Skip Lunch': return on Save The Children direct response advertising*
Source: SCF/O&MD

Total Income

The only authoritative source of data on the charity sector is *Charity Trends*, published annually by the Charity Aids Foundation. Unfortunately, data for 1991 will not be available until October 1992. Nevertheless, the indications of a healthy performance for Save the Children Fund are clear.

The first six months of 1991 marked a historic performance for Save the Children Fund. A quote from the 20th December, 1991 issue of *The Observer* summarises the achievement;

'In the first six months of 1991 Save the Children Fund received more money than in any other half year in its (72) year life.'

The most significant event for Save the Children Fund within this six month period was 'Skip Lunch'. The appeal was launched in the last week of April. *The Observer* article continues;

'In May, when it seemed that one international catastrophe was following another every week, Save the Children Fund was besieged with letters, calls, offers of help.'

ELIMINATING OTHER VARIABLES

This section is more than usually difficult in the context of 'Skip Lunch' as our advertising strategy was designed to galvanise PR and media activity. They have been used as measures of the advertising's effectiveness rather than external variables, which could be said to 'take away' some of its glory.

There are two issues that could cast doubt over the effectiveness of the 'Skip Lunch' campaign. One, that the scale of the cause itself may have been the sole reason for generating public reaction, has been addressed in the main paper (see Figure 4). The second, that the Princess Royal as spokesperson was the sole catalyst for public response, will be addressed here.

Power of the Messenger Rather Than the Message?

HRH the Princess Royal, official patron of Save the Children Fund, launched the 'Skip Lunch' appeal on April 29th. Her influence was significant – a joke about 'auctioning Gazza' prompted the *News of the World*'s participation. Subsequent to the launch, she;

— Rejected a Council lunch and hit the headlines

— Appeared on *Wogan* to discuss the appeal

Her contribution undoubtedly boosted income for the appeal. For example, after her *Wogan* appearance SCF collectors reported real public interest in supporting the appeal.

Our argument however, stands on the belief that *what* she said was what prompted the level of media and public response, not purely *who* she was. Her status added credibility to the appeal, as it has done on numerous other occasions when she is called upon at the inception of a new appeal. To a degree, she herself is a constant, it is her *message* which is the determining variable. In the case of 'Skip Lunch', her message (an encapsulation of the advertising idea) determined phenomenal success.

An emergency appeal highlighting the growing refugee crisis, which mirrored the formula for 'Skip Lunch' was launched by Save the Children in October 1991, even to the extent of being launched by the Princess Royal. Sadly, the Children on the Move campaign, which was as pressing a need as Africa, had an overall response rate of £1.80 per £1 spent. This compares with the 10:1 response ratio for the 'Skip Lunch' press campaign. The missing element from the October Children on the Move appeal was a creative concept, suggesting that it was this, rather than the personality of the Princess Royal that created the media interest for the 'Skip Lunch' appeal.

SUMMARY

A single week of advertising activity in April 1991 generated a revenue of £5.5m.

It did so by making a campaign budget of £140k work like a budget worth twelve times as much.

It did so by avoiding the numerous pitfalls of a huge and complex issue and by providing a simple 'rate of exchange' mechanism which encouraged participation.

It did so by linking two worlds which are apparently poles apart via a common concern – *food*.

It captured the imagination of the media and the hearts (and stomachs) of the public, engaging them in a collective effort to combat famine.

But the case study would be incomplete if the true value of advertising's effectiveness were not measured. The £5.5m from 'Skip Lunch' on behalf of Save the Children Fund bought time for millions of African families. It bought emergency food aid, transportation, seed distribution, health services, education and family reunification to the 27 million adults and children living in Angola, Ethiopia, Liberia, Mozambique, Somalia and Sudan, all of whom had been at risk from famine.

POSTSCRIPT

At the time of writing this paper Save the Children's financial results for the year ending March 1992 had not been published. Accordingly, we lacked hard, concrete evidence to demonstrate the effectiveness of the campaign.

The Annual Report was published in October 1992 and showed that Save the Children's income for the period incorporating 'Skip Lunch' had reached a staggering £99,603,000. To put this figure into perspective, Save the Children's income in 1979 was £6 million rising to an all time high in 1991 of £54 million. In the course of one year its income had been doubled putting it for the first time at the top of the Charity League Tables: above the RNLI and above the National Trust. The only credible explanation for this huge growth was 'Skip Lunch' as this was the only event in the year that broke the norms and differed from their historical fund-raising activity.

Following the success of 'Skip Lunch', Save the Children ran the campaign again in 1992. As with all events of this nature it did not have the same effect the second time round. For the media it was 'yesterday's story' and we were unable to command the levels of publicity and public donation that we had had in 1991.

Index